BRANDO

BRANDO

Songs My Mother Taught Me

WITH ROBERT LINDSEY

RANDOM HOUSE OF CANADA

TORONTO

PLAYBILL ® covers printed by permission of PLAYBILL Incorporated.
PLAYBILL ® is a registered trademark of PLAYBILL Incorporated,
New York, N.Y.

Canadian Cataloguing in Publication Data
Brando, Marlon
Brando : songs my mother taught me
Includes index.
ISBN 0-394-22425-6
1. Brando, Marlon.   2. Actors—United States—Biography.
I. Lindsey, Robert.   II. Title.
PN2287.B683A3   1994
791.43'028'092   C94-931272-X

Endpaper photograph © Phil Stern Photo
Book design by Victoria Wong
Photo-insert design by Matthew Waldman

Manufactured in the United States of America on acid-free paper
2 4 6 8 9 7 5 3
First Edition

To my sisters, Tiddy and Frannie;
to G. L. Harrington, Clyde Warrior,
and Bobby Hutton;
and to my children, who brought me up.

MARLON
BRANDO

Family Album: My Early Years

The shingled house on Mason
Street, Omaha, Nebraska, where
we lived until I was seven. The
house is no longer standing.

I was born one hour before midnight on
April 3, 1924. I inherited my instinctual
traits from my mother, and my endurance
from my father, a tough monkey.
Here I am, nine months old.

Age three, in the garden with my sister
Frannie, five. A time of magical events.

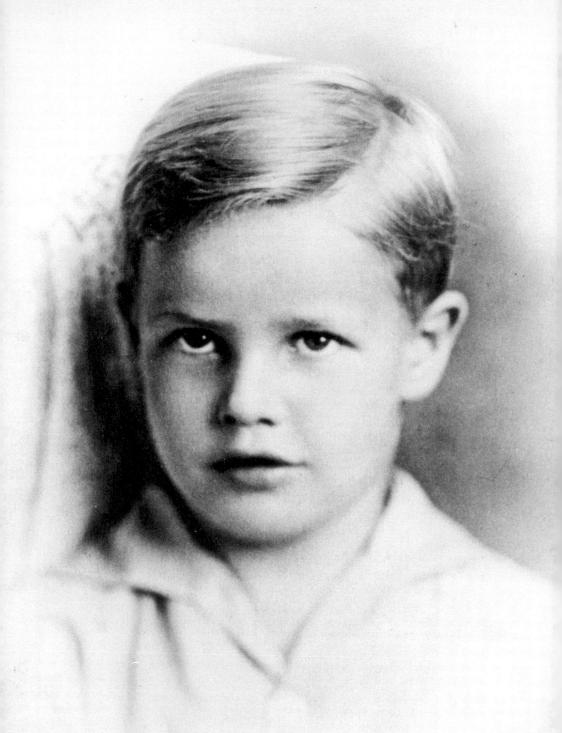

Love: I was three or four when Ermi came
to live with us. She was my governess, eighteen years of age, with fine, silky dark hair.
I worshiped her, and then she deserted me.
I am six years old in this picture.

Rebellion at age nine: with Ermi gone,
I became a vandal. I trashed houses, shot
birds and burned insects.

Like father

like son

The Fightin' Brandos

Above: In Libertyville, "The Fightin' Brandos," as
my sister dubbed this page from her album. Right:
The genesis of *One-Eyed Jacks*...With my BB gun
I accidentally shot a chauffeur in Evanston.

Age eight, in Evanston, with my mother: she was vivacious, funny and unconventional. She was seldom home when I was growing up, but she gave me a love of nature and animals and the night sky. She knew every song ever written. To this day I remember thousands of songs she taught me.

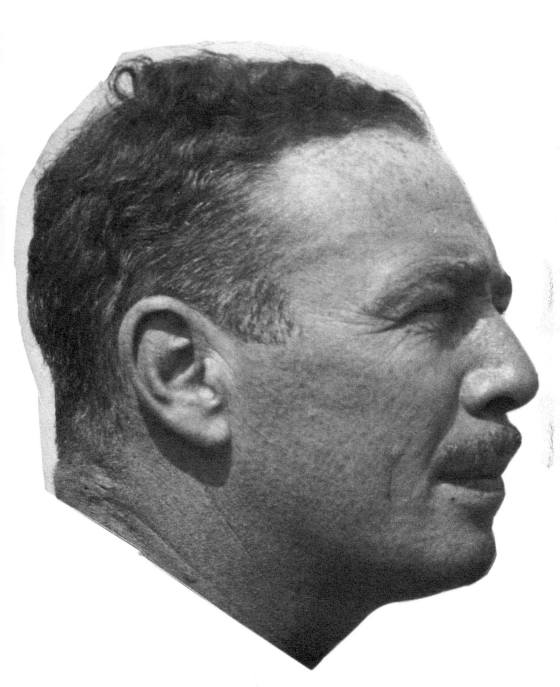

"When Poppa wasn't beset by his inner irrational fears," Frannie once wrote me, "he could be sweet and loving and considerate, amusing and amused, charming and sensitive, and then all this could be blotted out by black moods, thunderous silences, and anger that could burst out furiously."
Evanston, 1930 (left), 1935 (right).

On vacation at the beach in Balboa, California, when I was eleven. I had stopped shooting birds and had become the protector of weaker things. My parents were embarrassed when I brought home a woman I found lying on the ground; she turned out to be a drunk.

At about this time, one of my sisters scrawled on the back of a family-album picture: "Bud—and is he a grand boy! Sweet and funny, *idealistic* and oh, so young." With Frannie (left) and Jocelyn (center).

Frannie and I seem to have a spat
brewing. . . . By this time we were
without my father. My parents had
separated, and my mother, my sisters
and I went to live in Orange County,
California, with my grandmother
Bess. (In these shots, I'm thirteen.)

At sixteen, I was one of the bad boys of
Libertyville High. I was anathema to
many of my teachers and the parents of
many of my friends, some of whom
treated me as if I were poison.

Jocelyn—Tiddy, as I call her—once told me:
"You were constantly bringing home starving
animals, sick birds, people you thought were in
some distress, and if you had a choice you'd
pick the girl who was cross-eyed or the fattest
one because nobody paid any attention to her
and you wanted her to feel good." At age eighteen, by St. Mary's Road in Libertyville.

Coffee with Jocelyn in
her cold-water flat on
Sixty-eighth Street, 1948.
We were both performing
on Broadway, and this photo
was taken for a *Life* article.
She was in *Mister Roberts*
and I was Stanley Kowalski
in *A Streetcar Named Desire*.

To My Old Man from Me:
I still have the happy-days
album, bound in leather and
embossed in gold leaf, that I
gave my father on April 1,
1955. But I only have this picture of the Oscar for *On the
Waterfront* (bottom right);
somehow the award itself
ended up in a London auction
house. All these pictures were
shot during a *Person to Person*
interview; Edward R. Murrow
has his back to the camera
(below left).

At sixteen I was a cadet at Shattuck Military Academy, where my father had been before me. After all these years, I can now come forward to solve the great mystery of the bell tower that suddenly went silent....This picture is from Shattuck's 1940 yearbook.

INTRODUCTION

IN 1988, I received a telephone call from an old friend, the wife of a Hollywood actor and a gifted writer and actress. She asked me if she could give my private telephone number to one of her friends, but didn't explain who it was or why. A few moments later, my telephone rang again and I heard a familiar voice say slowly: "This is Marlon Brando."

It really wasn't necessary for him to identify himself. Like millions of people who had spent a sizable portion of their lives in a darkened motion picture theater, I recognized his voice. Like millions of other people during the past forty years, I had grown up with it.

He said he wanted me to write a book about a passage in his life during which he believed someone had terribly wronged someone he loved.

A few days later I arrived at a locked gate beside Mulholland Drive in Beverly Hills. The gate swung open, and I followed a winding road lined with pepper trees, uncertain where I was going. Then something almost ghostly happened: it seemed that a part of the forest of bamboo next to me began to move. A gap appeared in this leafy tangle as an electric gate, camouflaged with dense foliage, suddenly swung open. It might have been a wall of granite peeling open in an Arabian Nights fantasy.

The gap in the forest widened, inviting me not only to Marlon Brando's home at the top of a mountain, but into his life. After my first visit, I returned many times to the house on Mulholland Drive and he and I became close friends. We are an odd couple: I am a journalist with an ordinary past who has been married to the same woman for over thirty years and who, while reporting from Los Angeles as a correspondent for *The New York Times,* acquired a passionate disdain for the shallow and self-centered egotism and puerility that afflicts most movie actors I had encountered; he is an unconventional and reclusive actor who, after nearly fifty years of public life, despises the press, has had hundreds of women in his life and told me that he hadn't "spent more than two minutes" with any one of them.

Within twenty minutes of our first meeting, he had my shoes off, my belt loosened and my fingers wired to an instrument that measured my galvanic skin response, all the while explaining that it was a technique he sometimes used to get a personality profile of people by asking questions and observing the reaction of the meter. I was more puzzled than jittery. At our first meeting, I discovered that he was the most curious man I had ever met and that he felt uncomfortable, possibly even embarrassed, to be thought of as a movie star. The movies, he said, were the least important aspect of his life, a thought that he would repeat over and over. As a writer, I was accustomed to asking people questions, but he turned it around and bombarded me with endless questions about my family, my childhood, my marriage, my ideas. I felt as if I were being debriefed by a CIA interrogator. He was inquisitive about everything and informed about many topics—physics, Shakespeare, philosophy, chess, religion, music, chemistry, genetics, scatology, psychology, shoe making, or whatever else he might suggest we discuss.

To my surprise, I learned that we had much in common, and

our friendship deepened. The one thing that he didn't like to talk about was show business. He never touched on the subject unless I brought it up. We talked for hours at a time—sometimes late into the night via long-distance telephone, other times sitting across from each other in the living room of his home overlooking the wide swath of the San Fernando Valley. Some of the conversations lasted until dawn and ended in his heated swimming pool or with the two of us amicably arguing about something in his superheated sauna.

I never wrote the book that was the topic of our first conversation. He began to change, and told me that he was beginning to see things in less polarized dimensions and that he no longer felt the need he once had to exact revenge on his enemies.

As curious as he was about me, he was remarkably candid about his own intimate thoughts, experiences and vulnerabilities, which initially made me suspicious, but I learned during the course of our friendship that it was genuine. At first he told me he intended never to write his autobiography: to make available his private musings to satisfy what he regarded as the public's prurient curiosity about a movie star, he said, would be crass and degrading. But over time, as he changed in other ways, his attitude about recounting the story of his life shifted as well. He had persuaded himself, he told me, that there were "useful aspects in setting down the facts of my life," and he set about to write his autobiography for Random House. But after almost two years and little progress, he told me that he didn't have the emotional reserve to write a full-blown autobiography and asked me to help him. At first I declined. I said it was unwise for a journalist to deal professionally with a friend because it is impossible under such circumstances to maintain objectivity. But he promised to hide nothing, to be completely honest with me and to answer any questions I asked him about any topic I wanted except his marriages and his children—a promise he kept. I agreed to help him and began to make notes of our conversations, then to tape-record them. Our hours of talks stretched into days, then weeks. Inevitably, I told him, it would be necessary for him to talk about his experiences in films if he were going to tell the story of his life; he agreed, but with a reluctance that has never changed. He never relented, however, in his determination to say nothing about his children or his former wives, and he insisted that none of the other women in his life be identified in the book by their real names, except for a handful who are now dead. To do otherwise, he said, would be in bad taste.

Our conversations are the basis of this book, along with some of Marlon's own writings and meanderings he has committed to paper. I've taken the stories he told me, his writings, thoughts, reflections and experiences, and attempted to create from them a concise and accurate account of his life. Inevitably, in deciding on the structure of the book and selecting the words, events, metaphors and anecdotes in it, I have filtered the story of Marlon's life through the prism of my own perceptions, experiences and interests. When the preliminary draft of the manuscript was finished, he edited and revised it to confirm its accuracy and then added additional recollections, observations and insights. He also decided what would remain in the manuscript and what would be omitted.

ROBERT LINDSEY

BRANDO

1

AS I STUMBLE BACK across the years of my life trying to recall what it was about, I find that nothing is really clear. I suppose the first memory I have was when I was too young to remember how young I was. I opened my eyes, looked around in the mouse-colored light and realized that Ermi was still asleep, so I dressed myself as best I could and went down the stairs, left foot first on each step. I had to scuff my way to the porch because I couldn't buckle my sandals. I sat on the one step in the sun at the dead end of Thirty-second Street and waited. It must have been spring because the big tree in front of the house was shedding pods with two wings like a dragonfly. On days when there wasn't any wind, they would spin around in the air as they drifted softly to the ground.

I watched them float all the way down, sitting with my neck craned back until my mouth opened and holding out my hand just in case, but they never landed on it. When one hit the ground I'd look up again, my eyes darting, waiting for the next magical event, the sun warming the yellow hairs on my head.

Waiting like that for the next magic was as good a moment as any other that I can remember in the last sixty-five years.

. . .

As I sit at home now, winnowing the remembrances, they often come across my mind as unrelated images and feelings with smoky edges. I remember the sweet aroma of fresh-cut hay, the fragrance of burning leaves and the redolence of leaf dust as I scuffed through them. I remember the fragrance of the lilies of the valley in the garden where I often slept on the hot afternoons in Omaha, and I suppose the fragrance will always be with me. I don't think I'll ever forget the smell of lilacs or wild roses or the almost chic appearance of the trees in our neighborhood dressed in the silver lamé of a spring ice storm. Or the unforgettable sound that grates on me even today, the squeak of midwestern snow beneath my boots when the temperature was fifteen below. Nor can I forget the smoky fragrance of toast and burning bacon with grits and eggs that drifted up the stairwell of our house on Sunday mornings.

We had an old-fashioned cast-iron wood-burning stove that always embarrassed me. It was a wonderful stove, but in those days I was ashamed of it because it made me feel that we were poor. If I ever invited friends over and we passed through the kitchen, I tried to engage them and lock their eyes on me so they wouldn't notice the stove.

When my mother drank, her breath had a sweetness that I lack the vocabulary to describe. It was a strange marriage, the sweetness of her breath and my hatred of her drinking. She was always sipping surreptitiously from her bottle of Empirin, which she called "my change-of-life medicine." It was usually filled with gin. As I got older, occasionally I would find myself with a woman whose breath had that sweetness that still defies description. I was always sexually aroused by the smell. As much as I hated it, it had an undeniable allure for me.

As her drinking increased, it became more and more difficult for my mother to disguise the fact that she was simply an off-the-shelf drunk. The anguish that her drinking produced was that she preferred getting drunk to caring for us.

My mother was always unconventional. Sometimes when it

rained, she wore a shopping bag over her head with a little visor she had torn at the corners; it looked absurd, but she thought it was funny. I was embarrassed by it, though if she did it today, I'd be gasping with laughter.

The memories of those times drift in and out of my mind like the hoboes who used to come and go near the railroad tracks not far from our house. It is surprising that those remembrances visit my mind and that most of the time, pain and shame are mercifully absent.

I have been told that I was born one hour before midnight, April 3, 1924, in the Omaha Maternity Hospital. It was a breech birth, but otherwise unremarkable. My family had lived for generations in Nebraska and was mostly of Irish ancestry. My mother, Dorothy Pennebaker Brando, was twenty-seven; my father, Marlon Brando, Sr., was twenty-nine. I rounded out the family and made it complete: my older sister, Jocelyn, was almost five when I was born, my sister Frances almost two. Each of us had nicknames: my mother's was Dodie, my father's, Bowie, although he was Pop to me and Poppa to my sisters, Jocelyn was Tiddy, Frances was Frannie and I was Bud.

Until I was seven, we lived in a big wood-shingled house on a broad street in Omaha lined on both sides with houses much like our own, and with leafy elm trees that at the time seemed taller than anything that a young boy could imagine. Some of my memories of those days are pleasant. At first I was unaware of my mother's nipping from the bottle or the unhappiness of my father, who was also an alcoholic, which probably was the cause of his vanishing so often, getting drunk himself and looking for hookers.

When I was very small, I remember carrying a tiny pillow around everywhere, a talisman of childhood. Hugging it, I went to sleep at odd times and odd places, and as I grew older, I even carried it when I started climbing trees and laying claim to empty lots in our neighborhood as my own private kingdom.

It's hard—probably impossible—to sort out the extent to

I am six, Frannie is eight and Jocelyn (center) is eleven. (Personal collection of Marlon Brando)

which our experiences as children shape our outlook, behavior and personalities as adults, as opposed to the extent to which genetics are responsible. One has to be a genius to give a simple or absolute answer to anything in this world, and I don't know any tougher question than this one, although I suspect it's a subtle mixture of both. From my mother, I imagine I inherited my instinctual traits, which are fairly highly developed, as well as an affection for music. From my father, I probably acquired my strength of endurance, for he was truly a tough monkey. In later years, he reminded me of a British officer in the Bengal Lancers, perhaps a Victor McLaglen with more refinement. He was a traveling salesman who spent most of his time on the road selling calcium carbonate products—materials from the fossilized remains of ancient marine animals used in building, manufacturing and farming. It was an era when a traveling salesman slipped $5 to a bellboy, who would return with a pint of whiskey and a hooker. Then the house detective got a dollar so that the woman could stay in his room. My pop was such a man.

Most of my childhood memories of my father are of being ignored. I was his namesake, but nothing I did ever pleased or even interested him. He enjoyed telling me I couldn't do anything right. He had a habit of telling me I would never amount to anything. He was far more emotionally destructive than he realized. I was never rewarded by him with a comment, a look or a hug. He was a card-carrying prick whose mother deserted him when he was four years old—just disappeared, ran off someplace—and he was shunted from one spinster aunt to another. I think he deeply resented women because of that experience. I loved him and hated him at the same time. He was a frightening, silent, brooding, angry, hard-drinking, rude man, a bully who loved to give orders and issue ultimatums—and he was just as tough as he talked. Perhaps that's why I've had a lifelong aversion to authority. He had reddish, sandy hair, was tall and handsome and had an overwhelming masculine presence. His blood consisted of compounds of alcohol, testosterone, adrenaline and anger. On the other hand, he could make any room fill with laughter. Women found him fetching, strong and handsome. And surprisingly, he had an extraordinary sense of the absurd.

But my father could also slip quickly into the role of a bar fighter. I imagine him as the fellow at the bar who, when you look over at him, says, "Who the fuck do you think you're looking at?" I remember a story—I don't remember who told it to me—that once he got drunk in San Francisco in a bar, and Sunday-punched his fighting partner out of the door and onto the trolley tracks, where they continued to exchange knuckle sandwiches until a streetcar nearly ran them over. I never actually saw him fight, but I remember him coming home with a shiner. He was a man whose emotional disorders took the form of pathological stinginess: he wouldn't spend a nickel if he didn't have to, and he socked away his cash like a miser. He insisted on controlling people, which—who knows?—may have something to do with why I've spent much of my life trying to control other people. Once I remember his putting his arm around my shoulder and playing with my earlobes at a movie, and there was always a perfunctory kiss when he returned from one of his trips, but such moments were exceptional. Perhaps he didn't know how, or was too proud or too frightened to do it. I don't remember him being affectionate with anybody except maybe our dogs.

After his mother disappeared, my father was brought up by his aunts, who were very Victorian in their outlook, and by my equally Victorian grandfather, whom we called Pa, an imposing man in celluloid collars who was stiff, frugal and cautious.

My father fell in love with my mother when they were in high school, I think because she was vivacious, funny and unconventional and enjoyed a good laugh like he did. He was a man who had known great pain and had never forgiven his mother for her desertion, and the residue of that anger had to be absorbed by my mother, by us three children and by whoever tried to stare him down at a bar.

Recently, Frannie sent me a letter in which she said that growing up in our family was "in a way like having four parents, or six, or eight. When Poppa wasn't beset by his inner irrational fears, he could be sweet and loving and considerate, amusing and amused, charming and sensitive, and then all this could be blotted out by black moods, thunderous silences, and anger that could burst out furiously over what seemed to us to be minor infractions. It was a lonely, friendless household. I don't think Poppa wanted to be such an abusive person, but he had no means to escape the consequences of the abuse and abandonment that he had suffered."

What was absent most conspicuously in our family was forgiveness. "I don't remember forgiveness," Frannie wrote. "No forgiveness! In our home, there was blame, shame, and punishment that very often had no relationship to the 'crime,' and I think the sense of burning injustice it left with all of us marked us deeply."

My mother was a delicate, funny woman who loved music and learning, but was not much more affectionate than my father. To this day, I don't understand the psychodynamics and pathology of her disorder or the forces that made her an alcoholic. Perhaps it was genetic, or perhaps alcohol was the anesthesia she required to numb the disappointments in her life. I always wondered about the reasons, but never learned the answer. She was seldom home when I was growing up, although I have a few good memories of lying in bed with her, with her light brown curls strewn over the pillows, while she read a book to me and we shared a bowl of crackers and milk. And occasionally we all stood around the piano and sang while she played, one of the few times I remember any sort of family activity.

My mother knew every song that was ever written, and for

reasons that are unclear to me—perhaps because I wanted to please her—I memorized as many as I could. To this day, I remember the music and lyrics to thousands of songs my mother taught me. I have never been able to remember the number of my driver's license, and there have been times when I couldn't even remember my own telephone number, but when I hear a song, sometimes only once, I never forget the melody or the lyric. I am forever humming tunes in my head. I know African songs, Chinese songs, Tahitian songs, French songs, German songs and, of course, the songs my mother taught me. There is hardly a culture whose music I am not familiar with. Surprisingly, I can't remember a single song that was written after the seventies.

2

SOME OF MY EARLIEST and best memories of childhood
are of Ermi and of moonlight cascading through the window of
my bedroom late at night. I was three or four when Ermi came
to live with us in Omaha as my governess, and I see her as viv-
idly now as I did then; she was eighteen years old, slightly cross-
eyed and had fine, silky dark hair. She was Danish, but a touch
of Indonesian blood gave her skin a slightly dusky, smoky pa-
tina. Her laugh I will always remember. When she entered a
room, I knew it without seeing or hearing her because she had a
fragrant breath that was extraordinary. I don't know its chemical composition but her breath was sweet, like crushed and
slightly fermented fruit. During the day, we played constantly.
At night, we slept together. She was nude, and so was I, and it
was a lovely experience. She was a deep sleeper, and I can visu-
alize her now lying in our bed while the moonlight burst
through my window and illuminated her skin with a soft, magical amber glow. I sat there looking at her body and fondling
her breasts, and arranged myself on her and crawled over her.
She was all mine; she belonged to me and to me alone. Had she
known of my blinding worship of her, we would have married
on the pinnacle of Magellan's cloud and then, bejeweled in our

love, I would have taken her in my chariot made of flawless diamonds beyond the stars, beyond time, and farther than light to eternity.

Ermi had a boyfriend named Wally. When I was seven, I was playing by myself near a stream when I saw them kissing in a car. I was mystified, but had no idea of the disaster that this event foreshadowed. When Ermi left me not long after that to get married—not to Wally, but to a boy named Eric—I was devastated. She never told me she was going to leave or to be married. She merely said one day that she was leaving on a trip and would return soon. (In fact, she did return—twenty years later.)

The night I realized Ermi was gone forever, I looked up and saw a buttermilk sky. There was a full moon behind the clouds and as it seemed to skip overhead across the saffron universe, I felt my dreams die. It had been weeks since she had gone. I'd waited and waited for her. But I finally knew that she wasn't coming back. I felt abandoned. My mother had long ago deserted me for her bottle; now Ermi was gone, too. That's why in life I would always find women who were going to desert me; I had to repeat the process. From that day forward, I became estranged from this world.

When I was six years old, we moved from Omaha to Evanston, Illinois, near Chicago, where my father established his own company, the Calcium Carbonate Corporation. I think I was probably ready for a change.

At Field Elementary School in Omaha, I'd been the only one in my class to flunk kindergarten; I don't remember why. Perhaps it was because I was starting to resist authority. All I remember about kindergarten was that I was the bad boy of the class and had to sit under the teacher's desk, where my primary activity was staring up her dress. I must have had dyslexia, although there wasn't a name for it then. Even now I often have to work carefully with words and numbers, one at a time, one

In Evanston with Frannie. (Personal collection of Marlon Brando)

sentence at a time, especially if I feel under stress, and I still can't dial a telephone correctly if I look at the numbers; I have to dial without looking at the keyboard as if I were touch-typing.

My mother's drinking got worse in Evanston. Sometimes alcohol sent her into a crying jag, but initially it usually made her happy, giddy and full of mirth, and she might sit down at the piano and sing to herself, and we often joined in. But she was seldom home. With Ermi gone, I was alone a lot, and it was shortly after this that I found myself behaving in odd ways. I was failing in school, I was truant, I became a vandal and trashed houses that were being renovated; I shot birds, burned insects, slashed tires and stole money. At the same time I began finding myself not wanting to go home, and spent most of my time at the house of Jimmy Ferguson, a classmate and longtime friend, or at the house of a Greek family who lived up the block and across the alley.

I also began to stammer, so noticeably that I was taken to Northwestern University for speech therapy, where I was treated unsuccessfully. With my BB gun, I accidentally shot a chauffeur, and I also shot the big bay window in our house and cracked it, which brought a ferocious reaction from my father. In one of the lighter moments that I remember, we had a woman helping us who was from Martinique, and in an effort to please my father, she emptied a carafe of water and filled it with gin. The next morning he sat down to breakfast, took several large gulps of it and went to the office half snockered.

Like all recollections, my memories of those times are colored by later events and distorted by the blurred prism through which my mind now chooses to examine my life. I have learned that it is easy to convince yourself that an event occurred a certain way when it did not—to think you know exactly what hap-

Days at the beach: wrestling with Frannie at Balboa Beach, California.
(Personal collection of Marlon Brando)

With my father near Lake Michigan. (Personal collection of Marlon Brando)

pened until someone tells you, "No, that never happened. You weren't even there." We all invent things in our minds and can be astounded to learn they really didn't happen the way that they are recalled. So as I reflect on my life in these pages, I advise the reader of my limitations and the fallibility of my brain.

I've often thought I would have been much better off if I had grown up in an orphanage. My parents seldom fought in front of us, but there was a constant, grinding, unseen miasma of anger. After we moved to Evanston, the tension and unspoken hostility became more acute. Why, I don't know, but I suspect my mother was growing more disillusioned and angry with my father's philandering, and he was growing more unhappy with her drinking.

3

CAROL HICKOCK HAD A curious malady that made her
fall asleep suddenly. One moment she was awake, the next she
was sound asleep even if she was standing up; then a minute or
two later, her eyes blinked open slowly, she woke up and didn't
realize she'd been asleep. When one of our teachers at Lincoln
School told the class about her problem and asked us to look
out for her, I relished the assignment. I wanted to care for her.
Then I decided I was going to marry her. I occasionally walked
her home from school, and soon I asked her for a date. I felt
very sporty inviting her to Coolie's Restaurant for lunch, and
then we went to see Boris Karloff in *The Mummy*. When the
scary part of the movie came on, I told her that I had to go to
the bathroom and left. The truth was, I was scared stiff. Instead
of going to the bathroom, I went to the lobby and waited until
the scary part was over, then returned to my seat. When the
next scary scene came on, I disappeared again, then a third
time. I don't know what Carol thought of my bathroom habits.

One afternoon I was visiting Carol and we were sitting on the
sofa when she suddenly lost consciousness. I leaned over and
kissed her—my first kiss. After she came to a minute later, I
said, "How are you?" But I never mentioned my thievery.

Maybe she was the girl I should have married. I don't know whatever happened to her.

There were only two black kids in Lincoln School, and they were both my friends, especially Asa Lee. I was at his house one day when he and his cousin and I decided to form a club. When it was time to elect the president, vice president and secretary, we had difficulty in deciding who was going to be president, and I said, "Well, that's simple: 'Eeny, meeny, miney, moe. Catch a nigger by the toe. If he hollers, let him go—eeny, meeny, miney, moe . . .' " At that moment I felt a hand on my shoulder. It was Asa's mother. She bent down and said, "Dahlin', we don't use that word in this house." I looked up with some surprise and I said, "What word?" She answered, "Nigger." I said, "Oh." I had no idea what the word meant, but I could tell from Asa's expression that it was significant. Then she put a sweet gum ball in my mouth, patted my head affectionately and said, "You're a sweet thing." That was my first experience with a sense of race.

During my four years at Lincoln School, a few teachers liked me, but because I would not conform and was often rebellious, most had no hope for me. Among them was Miss Miles, whose name was appropriate because she was about six feet three inches tall and had the personality of a large granite obelisk.

After noticing that Asa and I spent a lot of time together, Miss Miles called us out of class into the hallway one day and said, "All right, you two, tell me what's going on here."

I had no idea what she was talking about. I said, "Nothing is going on."

"Don't tell me that," she said. "How come you two are hanging around together?"

When I said we were in the same club, she asked, "What kind of club is it?"

When neither of us said anything, she grabbed me by one arm and shook me violently. I began crying and maybe Asa did, too.

"Now, you tell me the truth," she said. "What kind of club do you have?"

"It's our *club*," I said. "He's the president, and I'm the vice president."

I didn't mention that we had only one other member in the club, Asa's cousin.

Miss Miles said, "You better watch yourselves."

When I returned to the class, I slumped to my desk, still crying. I felt humiliated and didn't know what was going on. I remember crying, then becoming aware that mucus was hanging from my nose when it landed on my desk. I pretended it was funny, causing the other kids to howl, but I felt humiliated and hid it as best I could.

In our family picture album, there is a photograph of me with a few words scrawled on the back by one of my sisters: "Bud— and is he a grand boy! Sweet and funny, *idealistic* and oh, so young." Once Tiddy told me, "By the time you were seven or eight you were constantly bringing home starving animals, sick birds, people you thought were in some kind of distress, and if you had a choice, you'd pick the girl who was cross-eyed or the fattest one because nobody paid attention to her and you wanted her to feel good."

I suppose it was true. I fashioned myself into the protector of weaker beings. I stopped shooting birds and became their guardians. I scolded friends who stepped on ants, telling them the ants had as much right to live as they did. While I was riding my bike near the beach in Evanston one day, I passed a woman who was lying on the ground; it turned out she was falling-down drunk, but I thought she was just sick. I rode her home on my bicycle and told my parents, who were outside on the porch, that we should help her because she was sick. They were embarrassed and uncomfortable, but they knew I was sincere and so they helped her. The memory of this incident suggests, I realized later, that early on I felt an obligation to help

In Evanston when I was about eight.
Above: Doing my homework is an
improvement on Omaha, where I
flunked kindergarten. (Personal collection
of Marlon Brando)

people who were less fortunate than me, or didn't have friends. But it wasn't only people to whom I felt an obligation. Curiously, after I moved to New York, whenever I saw a piece of paper on a sidewalk, I thought, If I don't pick it up, who will? So, I would bend over and put it in a trash basket.

When I was eleven, my parents separated, and my mother, my sisters and I went to live with my grandmother—the matriarch of the family, whom we called Bess or Nana—in California.

She was buxom and sharp-featured, with white hair, an aristocratic bearing and the look of a Gibson girl. Like my mother, she was also very much an individual and a renegade who refused to accept unblinkingly Victorian standards of behavior. Being Irish, she was witty and amusing. Humor, I suppose, is probably the hallmark of my family; if anything kept us sane, it was humor. We never knew what would come out of my grandmother's mouth. She had an enormous laugh and a sense of absurdity about human behavior, but there was also a serious side to her. She was a Christian Scientist practitioner, and a good one, I was told.

I attended the seventh and eighth grades at Julius C. Lathrop Junior High School in Santa Ana, a farming community in Orange County, south of Los Angeles. It was a period when my mother drank more than ever; she'd promise to stop, then disappear on another bender for four or five days—trying to love us, I suppose, when she was home, but rarely paying much attention to us. I probably didn't realize yet what an alcoholic was, but, like my sisters, I had to live with the effects of her disorder. My mother would get drunk on the sly, then try to hide it in classic alcoholic fashion. For a time in Santa Ana, I had a fantasy that the important people in my life were all dead and were only pretending to be alive. I lay in bed for hours, sweating and looking up at the ceiling, convinced I was the only one in the world who was still alive. For a twelve-year-old—for anyone—it was frightening.

At home I was always on skinny rations when it came to praise. I never received accolades or adulation, not even encouragement. Nobody ever thought I was good for anything except a few kindly teachers. One was my shop teacher at Julius C. Lathrop Junior High, a man whose name I've forgotten but whose words of encouragement affect me to this day. Once he gave me a piece of metal with the assignment to make something with it. I pounded it on a forge into the shape of a screwdriver, put it in a box of wet sand to make a mold, melted some aluminum and poured it into the mold. I had made a screwdriver, and he praised me for it. For the first time in my life, I had done something of which I was proud.

I also discovered at Lathrop that I wasn't bad at sports; I won the school decathlon championship and set a record by doing a thousand push-ups without stopping. I was still going when the coach stopped me. He said I had to stop because if I didn't, I might damage my heart.

Even now, I still get a thrill savoring these small successes so long ago.

After almost two years, my mother decided to reconcile with my father, and we moved to Libertyville, Illinois, a small town north of Chicago near Lake Michigan. Once again, we all looked forward to a fresh start.

Almost sixty years later, I can still feel the rhythm of the train that returned us to Illinois. While it rocked and swayed, I walked to a vestibule between two cars and felt the energy of the wheels rattling across the steel joints in the tracks. Spontaneously, I started banging on the doors and walls with my hands, grooving to the beat of the train as if it were a jazz quartet. After that, I was a changed boy: I wanted to be a drummer. Never again did I ride a train without getting the urge to pound my hands and fingers against something in accompaniment to the melody of the rails, and whenever I heard a train whistle in the middle of the night, I'd rise up on my elbows in bed and listen for the clack of wheels against rails and look out the window for a trail of steam. Long before I knew anything about the Doppler effect, I tried to figure out where a train was headed and how fast it was traveling by listening to the fading sound of its whistle and the steely song of its wheels. I really miss those old trains.

4

WES MICKLER WAS BALANCED in his chair, leaning against the barn by the tack-room door when I rode up. I was riding Peavine Frenzy. She was lathered a bit and flaring her nostrils.

"Was you *runnin'* that horse, Bud?"

"Maybe a little."

"If you do that again I swear I'll knock a fart outta ya."

My face jerked while I tried to suppress my laughter.

"Can't you see that old horse is goin' lame?" Wes asked.

"I didn't notice it, Wes."

"Wut the hell's amatter wichu?"

The way Wes said almost anything made me laugh.

He was part owner of a farm on Bradley Road, where my family rented a house five miles outside Libertyville. It wasn't a full-time farm anymore; it was more a horse ranch where people could keep their horses or rent them for a day. Wes's partner, Bill Booth, was the horse trader, always making deals and trucking horses to one place or another.

Wes loved horses, and even though my family owned Peavine, he made me feel she was his.

I pretended to adjust the stirrup on Peavine's far side so Wes couldn't see my face wrestling with a smile. He almost always broke me up. He said things he didn't intend to be funny, and the more serious he got, the more my throat tightened, fighting to suppress a laugh. I realize now it probably didn't mean a damn to him whether I laughed or not, but at the time I thought it might make him angry, so I coughed and spit a lot trying to mask my laughter.

When I was cleaning the stall of a new boarding pony one day, Wes stood outside looking through the bars as the pony watched me. The pony didn't move, but he was flexing his nostrils and his ears were bent back. I reached out slowly to touch his nose and Wes said, "You better grab your nuts, kid. That damn dink can kick you frontways just as good as back."

I lost air like a ripped gas bag and sank gently to the warm manure. Wes didn't say anything, just stared at me, and the more he did and the more he remained silent, the more I had to thrash around trying to gulp some air into my body as I laughed.

Wes finally walked away, but when the pony looked at me with its big eyes that seemed to be saying, "What in the world is the matter with you?" I went into a life-threatening seizure. Finally I was able to manage a few hoots and crawled around the stable looking for my hat.

Wes was in the terminal stages of tuberculosis. Pretty soon his back was a hump and he was carrying his elbows a little higher, so that when he walked they pointed back like arrows. He was always coughing, hacking and spitting out thick wads of mucus that sometimes was so lumpy it caught on his front teeth when he tried to spit. He almost never smiled, but when he did his mouth looked like a golden cemetery. You could see his skull showing through his face, and his smoky blue eyes seemed to be falling out of his head whenever he bent over to spit.

But when Wes was on a horse, he had a smile, golden cemetery or not, that made you feel that he knew something you didn't. He always glittered when he was up there, looking like he grew out of the horse's back. And he always talked softly to any horse under him—like it was a woman. He was sure of himself on a horse; he was home. But after a while, he couldn't mount up anymore. Mostly he just sat in the chair outside the tack room and waited for death. I thought he would spit away his whole body, and one day he did.

Wes Mickler, born someplace, died on Bradley Road. He never said what happened in between.

Sometimes when my mother got bent out of shape, an acquaintance from a bar or a stranger brought her home; other times we'd have to go looking for her or the phone would ring and I'd hear a police sergeant say: *"We have a Dorothy Pennebaker Brando here. Could you come down to the station and get her?"*

Jocelyn usually ran the show at home. Even though she was only a few years older than Frannie and me, she had to assume the responsibility for bringing us up, for which I owe her a debt of gratitude that is unpayable. Although I may have argued more with Frannie than I did with Jocelyn, we were close, too. After all, we shared the same bunk in purgatory. But it was Tiddy who kept the family together. When my mother was missing, I always looked to her for instructions about what to do. She made sure I had something to eat and clean clothes to wear. She was as magnificent, as strong a person as I've ever known, but everybody reaches their breaking point sooner or later, and in time both she and Frannie did.

The three of us, and sometimes my father, spent a lot of time looking for my mother. I'd tramp door-to-door through Chicago's skid row on a sunny afternoon, push open the door of each bar in succession, peer into a dark cavern and try to spot her on one of the stools.

When I was about fourteen, my father brought her home

once and took her upstairs. I was downstairs in the living room. I heard her fall, then the sounds of slapping and hitting, and I ran upstairs. She was lying on the bed crying and he was standing over her. I became insane with rage and set my teeth in an attack mode; filled with Goliath strength, through a clenched mouth nine inches away from his nose, I said in a low, clear voice, "If you ever hit her again, I'll kill you."

He looked in my eyes and froze. He knew he was staring at more adrenaline than he had ever seen in his life. My father was afraid of nothing and we probably would have fought to the death had it not been for the fact that perhaps he felt guilty. It was probably the only time in his life that he backed off from a physical challenge. He just walked out of the bedroom, leaving my mother on the bed.

The country road we lived on was named for Old Man Bradley, who presided over a pretty forty-acre farm about a mile down the road. He had two sons, Dutch and Indian. He had blackheads on his nose so big that you could have scooped them out with a soupspoon. I could never remember anything he said because I couldn't keep my eyes off the wondrousness of those blackheads. He was missing most of his front teeth, and he must have been eighty years old, but almost every day he walked down that gravel road past our farm, paused and, if she was around, said hello to my cow, Violet. Our family always had animals, but they became more important to me as the years passed because they helped me deal with the absence of love. I used to come home from school and nobody would be home. There would be dirty dishes in the sink and piles of cat turds under the piano. The beds weren't made, and the whole house would be unkempt and empty. My sisters were either still at school or with friends, my mother was out drinking and my father was out whoring. As a result, I sought—as I still do—affection, loyalty and friendship from animals.

One was a huge, black Great Dane named Dutchy. Every

In Libertyville: I sought affection from animals. Dutchy, our Great Dane, had a touch of Nureyev. Below: Aboard Peavine Frenzy. (Personal collection of Marlon Brando)

spring the meadow in front of the house became an ocean of canary-colored mustard blossoms, and when a wind came up, it was like watching a sea of rippling golden waves rising and falling with the breeze like breakers just before they pound into a reef. There was a trail through the field that led to the other side of town, and we often rode our horses along the trail three miles to the Des Plaines River. Dutchy liked to chase rabbits through the mustard field, which was nearly five feet high by late spring. She'd lose one and suddenly stop. A moment or two would pass, and then she'd leap about six feet in the air, a big, pitch-black dog silhouetted against the yellow mustard, looking to see if the mustard was vibrating in any direction. Like Nureyev, she seemed to be able to stay elevated for an extraordinary length of time. Then the chase would be on again. The sight of Dutchy seemingly frozen in midair is one of those memories imprinted on my brain that will last forever and a day. I don't think she ever caught a rabbit, but she never stopped trying.

Besides Dutchy, I was attached to Violet, our Jersey cow. It was my job to milk her twice a day, and on some winter mornings, it was so cold she would be steaming. I'd get out of bed, put on my coveralls and galoshes and walk to the barn, where I could barely see her shrouded behind the mists of her own body heat. Usually there was a bantam rooster and a couple of hens roosting between her horns, which, when she turned her head and looked at me, made Violet look as if she were wearing an elegant flowered hat from Paris. She'd look up at me, twist her head, watch me as I came through the door and utter a friendly good morning moo.

I've always found animals easy to love because their love is unconditional. They are trusting, loyal and undemanding except in wanting love in return. In the summer I'd open the gate, climb on Violet and ride into the pasture. She never complained. I'd put my arms around her, kiss her and feel her return my affection. Cows have very sweet breath because of the hay that they eat, and I felt the warmth from it. In the summer there were usually a dozen or two barn cats around the farm, welcome if uninvited squatters, and they knew exactly when I milked Violet. Every morning when I went to the barn, they were waiting for me, lined up fifteen or twenty feet away. As soon as I started milking her, they got on their haunches, in a queue, and stuck their front paws out, waiting for me to squirt some milk into their faces, which I did. I don't remember a time when they didn't make me laugh. Sometimes when I was milking her, Violet would suddenly lift her leg and stick it in my bucket, fouling it with bits of manure, hay and dirt from the floor of the stable. Since I didn't want to waste the milk or the time I'd spent getting it, I kept a piece of cheesecloth handy, and every time she did this, I poured the milk through the cheesecloth to remove the hay and manure before taking the milk inside. Everybody drank it, and I never told anyone about using my makeshift sieve or that manure had been in their milk.

Every time I milked Violet, fed the chickens and cleaned the stable, manure affixed itself to my galoshes, which caused me a lot of embarrassment. I washed and scrubbed the galoshes as hard as I could, but never truly got rid of the smell. It was especially discomfiting because it branded me as a farm kid. There was a kind of snobbery at Libertyville Township High that ranked kids who lived in town as superior to those who lived on farms or—even worse—in a place called Roundout, a railroad switching center where a lot of poor kids lived. Our farm wasn't far from Roundout, so as a result a kind of double stigma rubbed off on my sisters and me, and we didn't rank high in Libertyville's adolescent pecking order. Every morning before school, I scrubbed my shoes and galoshes trying to clean off the manure, and when I got to school I waited until everybody else was in the classroom before walking in at the last moment, hoping no one would smell it. If I took a girl to a basketball game, I always sniffed the air while trying not to let her know I was doing so, embarrassed that she might smell the cow manure in the car.

I have many pleasant memories of my childhood, however. The school was in town, so I either hitched a ride with a neighbor or took a trolley on the branch line connecting Libertyville with Chicago via Lake Forest and Waukegan. If the weather was good, I sometimes walked the five miles home and threw rocks at the glass insulators on telephone poles along the way; it was a triumph to break one, or better yet, to knock one of the wires off the crossbar. And sometimes friends and I took a detour to Roundout and chatted with the gandy dancers who walked the tracks searching for loose spikes. Or we'd hijack a handcar from a siding and ride several miles, watching for trains in both directions. In winter the rails became slippery and caked with ice, and we'd go to Roundout and watch the steam locomotives labor to get going, with their wheels sliding and slipping; in summer we sat beside the rails, stuck a penny on the tracks with a wad of gum and waited for a train to flatten it, then made necklaces and belts out of the flattened coins.

When we heard a train approaching, everybody started yelling, "Come on, come on, come on . . . the train is coming!" We stood as close to the tracks as we dared and as soon as the train was a few yards away, we all turned our backs to avoid being splattered in the face by the hail of pebbles and rocks that were whipped up by the train and stung like hornets.

At fourteen or fifteen, I decided to earn my living when I grew up playing drums made from wooden beer kegs and leading a group called Keg Brando and His Kegliners. We organized a little band, but it didn't last long and didn't make any money. Instead I became an usher at a local movie theater to earn some spending money. On Saturdays most of the farmers brought their families into town to see a movie, no matter what was playing. I enjoyed directing customers to a row of seats that was already filled. To see a line of a dozen people file down a row of seats in the dark, sitting on other people, stepping on feet and causing a general ruckus, then coming out the other side, was a hoot. I had to wear a stiff, formal uniform I never liked, especially during hot weather. To cool off, I started taking off my shirt, but I sewed a pair of cuffs to my jacket to make it look like I was wearing one. I figured no one would know about it because I was wearing a dickey under the jacket. After one of the other ushers squealed on me and I was fired for being out of uniform, I chopped up some rotting broccoli—few things smell worse than broccoli that's been out in the sun two or three weeks—mixed it with Limburger cheese I had ripened until it was pure bacteria, and stuffed it into the intake pipe of the air-conditioning system, flooding the theater with an odor that sent the audience out to the street. It was a great act of revenge. The guy who fired me never figured out who did it.

At Libertyville High, I was a bad student, chronic truant and all-round incorrigible. I was forever being sent to the principal's office to be disciplined. Mr. Underbrink didn't like me much, and seated behind his big wooden desk, with a stern, worn look on his face, he gave me one lecture after another. My homeroom teacher, Mr. Russell, was just as enraged by my contempt for authority, and his response was to belittle me; once he lost his temper and shook me as hard as he could, and announced to the class that I had an IQ of ninety and that I had better pay attention if I wanted to keep up with the rest of the class. I didn't try hard because I was bored and irritated.

The situation didn't improve during my second year. I failed or dropped out of so many classes that by the end of the term I was informed that I had to repeat my sophomore year.

I was one of the bad boys of the school. I always had friends, boys as well as girls, but I was anathema to many of my teachers and the parents of many of my friends, some of whom treated me as if I were poison. Though I didn't realize it then, I was beginning to discover one of the realities of life: members of almost every group in human society try hard to convince themselves that they are superior to the other groups, whether they are religions, nations, neighboring tribes in the rain forest or members of rival suburban country clubs who claim that membership in their club proves they have a higher social standing than those in others. The caste system may be more highly developed in countries like India or England, but every tier of society in almost every culture tries to dominate a group it perceives as beneath it. In Libertyville I was in the caste right near the bottom.

My father's solution to my difficulties at Libertyville High was to send me to the same school he had once attended, Shattuck Military Academy in Faribault, Minnesota. He thought the discipline would benefit me greatly.

My tenure at Shattuck was probably fated from the beginning to be short. By then I was rebelling against any authority and against conformity in general with every ounce of energy in my body.

5

THE CAMPUS OF Shattuck Military Academy was attractive in the way of a sedate English country boarding school. From a distance it almost looked like one, with symmetrical rows of Gothic limestone buildings and a tall, square bell tower cloaked in ivy. The tower overlooked the parade grounds, where I was soon marching two or three times a day. Beyond the buildings were a football field and hiking trails for extended-order drills. Reveille was at six-thirty, when we shined our shoes and put on our uniforms for the first inspection of the day; after calisthenics there was a formation, morning drill and breakfast. Following five or six hours in a classroom, afternoons were devoted to sports.

I was sixteen when I arrived at Shattuck. Since I had to repeat my sophomore year, I was a year behind other cadets my age. Shattuck had been producing soldiers for the United States Army since shortly after the Civil War. From the first day, we were indoctrinated with its traditions and the exploits of alumni who had demonstrated the values that our teachers said they were going to teach us: discipline, order, honor, obedience, courage, loyalty, patriotism.

As it did for many military academies then, the federal gov-

Shattuck Military Academy, in Faribault, Minnesota, where I followed my father. My letters home to my family have survived and reveal much. (© Robert LaRose)

ernment subsidized Shattuck by providing rifles and cannons for us to drill with. Every year several graduates went on to West Point. Our teachers were called "masters," and their task was to educate and mold us into proper citizens, instilling in us the kind of acquiescence to authority that generals have sought to impose on their troops from the beginning of time. The military mind has one aim, and that is to make soldiers react as mechanically as possible. They want the same predictability in a man as they do in a telephone or a machine gun, and they train their soldiers to act as a unit, not as individuals. That's the only way you can run an army. It is only through order, submission to discipline and the exorcising of individuality that you make a good soldier. Many people really enjoy it. I witnessed it at Shattuck, and I've seen it in a hundred different ways since then. But I hated it. To regiment people—to make them march in step, all in uniform, marching in a unit—was nauseating to me.

I missed my parents, who rarely visited or wrote, but I had a lot of fun at Shattuck along with much anguish and sometimes loneliness. I did my best to tear the school apart and not get caught at it. I wanted to destroy the place. I hated authority and did everything I could to defeat it by resisting it, subverting it, tricking it and outmaneuvering it. I would do anything to avoid being treated like a cipher, which is what they aim for when they put you in a military uniform and demand conformity and discipline.

Not long ago, I ran across a pile of letters that I'd sent home from Shattuck and that my sister Frannie saved. In my first letter a few weeks after I got there, I told my parents: "The school work is terribly hard to start with, plus my not knowing how to concentrate and my rotten foundation in English, French and Algebra makes things awfully tough. I'm learning, though, not fast maybe, but learning about everything. I hope I will be able to carry all my subjects. I'm working hard and I think I can . . .

I'm rooming with an awful nice kid from Portland named John Adams (good guy). . . ." The food served by the Shattuck mess, I observed, was "grand and you can have all you can hold. I have gained ten pounds and now weigh 157 with clothes on and about 150 without. I feel swell except for my back, which I messed up in football. It's coming along, though, and I've found I can get plenty tough if I want to in football. People think you have to be a big bruiser to play football. That's bunk. All it takes is a little callousing of the constitution. . . . You don't have time to blow your nose here. On the run all the time. The seniors are plenty tough on you. Some are swell fellows just having a bit of fun. Others get nasty sometimes. I don't like that, but I've found that it's best to just let things slide. . . ." I went to a dance at a local girls' school, but apparently it was disappointing: "The girls are grand, but all but bored to tears, and all they can offer you is a roaring game of Chinese checkers or sitting in the middle of the front lawn. . . . Sometimes I get very lonely and wish I could be home, of course. Mother, please write me. *I've gone away to school, you know. Address to Shattuck School, Faribault, Minn.*"

In other letters saved by my sister, I reported on the ups and downs of my first year:

September, 1941

Dear Folks:

Well, the routine has been unleashed in all its fury. I'm going like hell every second. I would have written sooner but honest to my dear God, I just haven't had time.

So you don't think I can play football? I am now first-team first-string right half. Am I sore! My lord above couldn't know how sore I am. It's all I can do to lace my shoes. . . . We have had two tests and in both I think I have done quite well.

I like John very much and think—as a matter of fact I know—we will get along fine. . . . This work has sapped all my strength. I can't write another line.

Your loving son, Bud

———

September, 1941

Dear Folks:

I am settled materially but not spiritually. The staff is tough and the reward is usually a good, sweet, but firm kick in the ass. I'm playing first-string football but the studies are pretty rigid so I think I'll have to drop it. All I went out for was to see whether or not I could take it. I've found I can get hit hard and like it. There will be plenty of time for fight and glory next year. I want to really accomplish something in the academic aspect. I like geometry and Latin American history, much to my surprise. . . . I'm kinda homesick and want my mother, but I guess I will get over that. I've received exactly one letter since I've been here. Fine support for the baby of the family. You guys have no idea how much a few words of cheer and goodwill are appreciated here.

Wistfully, Bud

———

October, 1941

Dear Folks:

I am not as good a football player as I thought, but I'm still trying. I've learned an awful lot about the game I didn't know before. I've gotten to play a few times, but I was so scared I couldn't do anything. Regardless of what anyone says, I am trying to better myself in every way. I don't smoke or swear or do anything my sisters or mother wouldn't approve of. . . . I had to read *Wuthering Heights* for English and I never enjoyed a book in all my life as much as that one. . . .

John is getting in a lot of trouble. He goes out at night in spite of the fact that it is a serious offense and he has been caught at it once before. He spits on the floor. He has an automatic that he fires at the drop of a hat out the window or any place he feels like it. He got a date at 2 A.M. this morning with some disreputable little number in Faribault. You can't tell him a thing. He is always nice and pleasant though. . . . I've much to say to you when you come, so hurry up.

Love ya, Bud

P.S. Please hurry.

———

October, 1941

Dear Frannie:

This is just a prelude to a manuscript I shall write you in a little while. I was awfully glad to get your letter of goodwill. A letter is very appreciated nowadays. I'm sorry I haven't written sooner, but I haven't had time to go to the "John." That, sister, is a fact! I was actually constipated for almost four days because I couldn't get to the "John."

School is unbelievably tough and I'm having a lot of trouble making myself study conscientiously, but I'll manage somehow. I was playing first-string football but I have a back injury and now am able to have no athletics at all. I'm in the drum and bugle corps, the orchestra and dance band. Jesus, I can't wait to see you and tell you some of the Godawful funny things that happen here. . . .

Love, Bud

———

November, 1941

Dear Folks:

This has been quite an eventful day. . . . I was asked by all the influential senior officers at a special meeting to pledge their fraternity (which is by far the best in school). It is quite an honor to be a member as only the very best-liked fellas get in, and me "a new boy"! My, my. There are few members but very influential as far as they go. I won't have very much trouble getting on the Crack Squad next year . . . we are reading *The Three Musketeers* and not ever having read it before, I find it very interesting.

I love you both very much.

Bud

————

November, 1941

Dear Folks:

You are the most patient, swellest folks a guy could have. I will be glad to get home and talk and just be home. School is fine but bewildering. Life is so gad dammed bewildering. I am learning a whole lot and am really becoming a man, a young man, perhaps, but a man. Many things I used to think of as important aren't at all now. . . .

Love to all, Bud

————

December, 1941

Dear Folks:

You've probably gotten my grades and they don't look like much. I don't care what the masters have written in the comments. I am trying. I am being more systematic and orderly about my work and everything concerned. PLEASE have faith in me. I will get through, I know it. Things should be breaking any minute. They are in so many small ways. I have improved since John left, and with Christmas vacation coming up and everything, I'll have an excellent chance to review while every other fella will be out on a toot. I certainly look forward to coming home. I'll leave about the twentieth. . . . These last

days are grueling. They are piling on work so fast that it dazes
you. I guess they have to because three weeks is a long time in
which to forget things. I've had an awful cold and I've been in
the hospital for a couple of days.

P.S. Please don't mention my grades to me. I am working and
I won't let you down.

Bud

6

IT WAS ONE of the cadets' responsibilities to write home once a week, and I did my duty. As I look at these letters from Shattuck that Frannie saved, I am struck by the innocence, naïveté and dishonesty expressed by their author. I see an eager, lonely child who never had much of a childhood, who needed affection and assurance and lied to his parents in the hope that something he might say would make them want to love him. He was a boy with little faith in himself, a child who hungered for their approval and would do anything to get it. He told them constantly how much he loved them, hoping his words would persuade them to tell him that *they* loved *him,* and he always wrote that everything was okay when of course it wasn't. But these were not conscious feelings; at the time I had no idea why I was troubled. Now I realize that by then any hope I'd ever had of receiving love or support from my parents was probably moribund. But I was in denial. I tried not to think about it while sending home letters in which a part of me was still trying to make them think I was worthy of their love. In being a loving son, I suppose I was trying to become a loved son. What my letters failed to say was that in those days I blamed myself for all my insecurities and other problems. I didn't understand yet about the lethal weapons that parents employ in their words and actions when they deal with their children, or the obligation of parents to give their children self-esteem instead of shame.

I don't want to give the wrong impression: my youth was not an unremitting stretch of sadness and unhappiness; it wasn't like that. I had a lot of fun and a lot of laughs. But my life was largely a series of acts of hostility designed to subvert authority. I had no sense of emotional security. I didn't know until much later why I felt valueless, or that I was responding to a sense of worthlessness with hostility. In summary, my time at Shattuck was a mixed experience; sometimes I felt lonely and bereft of love and affection, and other times I had a great deal of satisfaction in being able to challenge authority successfully and get away with it by clever wiles and lies.

When I entered Shattuck, I had a hair-trigger temper. I had—and still have—an intense hatred of loud, sudden noises and of being startled, and these could cause me to explode. At home I once knocked down one of my sisters after she came into my bedroom while I was asleep, shook me and told me dinner was ready. I was so startled that I got up, walked across the room and punched her, and was bewildered and contrite afterward. Even today when I'm startled I instinctively put my hands up and pull back my right fist ready to strike. I don't hit people anymore, but I still automatically assume the posture. I've never understood why. One incident at Shattuck suggests that I've been that way a long time. I was always the last person in formation. I couldn't bear the loud ruckus, and the intensity of the noise in the gym, especially early in the morning when we were summoned to formation and somebody was shouting orders, so I was always tardy. I usually got there just as the bugle blew or someone said, "Battalion, attention." On one occasion, I shuffled my way reluctantly into the gym in wintertime and a friend of mine came up behind me, slapped me on the shoulder and said, "Good morning, Banjo" (one of my nicknames). I turned around and without a conscious thought decked him. Then I stood over him and said, "If you ever do that to me again, you son of a bitch, I'll kill you." I saw his anger rise, but when he saw the intensity he was dealing with, he backed off. Then I immediately apologized.

About three months after I arrived at Shattuck, the chief administrator at the school—his name was Dr. Nuba Fletcher but we called him "Nuba the Tuba"—convened a formation to announce to the battalion that we were at war with Japan. I was in the front row, and he looked at me and told me I was sitting in the very same seat where my father had been sitting when the battalion was informed of America's entry into the First World War. Since my father had gone on from Shattuck to become a lieutenant in the artillery, I suspect the Tuba expected and certainly hoped I'd receive a commission. Occasionally he or one of the masters would say something like, "Marlon, if you ever stop being a smart-ass, you might make a good officer." But I wouldn't have lasted a nanosecond in a uniform. All my life I have questioned why I should do something. My first response always is, Why should I? Reasonable arguments can change my mind, but I won't do something if I don't agree. I have never been able to snap to and salute, and that's what they ordered you to do at Shattuck.

Still, I have wonderful, warm memories of breaking the rules—of pranks, high jinks, teasing the masters and assorted silliness that almost made being there worth it.

Once the war started, many of the younger masters went into the army, and we had to deal with whatever faculty the management of the school could scrape together. As a group they were mostly tired older men who were no match for the cadets. By nature, adolescent boys, especially when they organize as a group, can be a diabolical force, testing adults to the limit and pushing those limits to the extreme, and that's what we did.

I had discovered that a hair tonic called Vitalis contained alcohol and that if you touched a match to it, it glowed spectacularly for a few seconds in a stunning electric blue flame.

After this discovery, in the middle of the night I'd take a bottle of Vitalis down two flights of stairs, squirting it on the floor and walls until I came to the doorway of one of the boys I didn't like, then return to the safety of my room and set the Vitalis afire. The flame raced down the stairs, leaving behind a glorious fiery ribbon.

Another time, a bunch of us got together and poured Vitalis over the transom of a master who was terrified by this wild, savage group of boys who would never relent once they saw a grain of weakness in a master. We scared him nearly to death, and we could hear him beating the flames out with his clothes. It didn't cause any damage, merely an eerie blue flame.

I was also responsible for one of the great unsolved mysteries in the history of Shattuck. Besides being easily startled, I have, again, never been able to stand loud noises, although admittedly it is selective: I can listen for hours to music played so loud that other people have to leave the room. But most loud noises—especially sounds associated with authority—annoy me. The bell in the tower at Shattuck constantly bonged every fifteen minutes—on the hour, quarter hour, half hour, three-quarter hour—ordering us to go to class, eat, sleep, get in formation or report for a drill. It was the voice of authority and I hated it. At some point I decided I simply couldn't bear it any longer and climbed into the tower late one night—an act that alone made me subject to immediate dismissal—intending to sabotage the mechanism that made the bell ring. But I discovered that the only way I could silence the bell was to steal the clapper; it must have weighed 150 pounds, but I decided to take it. I waited until the bell tolled at the quarter hour, nearly deafening myself, leaned over, unhooked the clapper, hoisted it on my shoulders and made my way down the stairs to the ground. It was spring,

I can finally solve the mystery of the bell tower at Shattuck. (© Robert LaRose)

the night was flooded with moonlight and I felt glorious. I lugged the clapper a couple of hundred yards and buried it, where it is to this day. Anybody with a metal detector could find it. As I covered the clapper in the grave I'd dug for it, I smirked and chuckled in a way that only an adolescent could smirk and chuckle. The next morning the school was wonderfully quiet. The masters gathered outside the tower, looked up, shook their heads and tried to figure out what had happened. I could hardly contain my laughter at everyone's bewilderment. It was wartime, and every ounce of metal was needed for tanks, guns and airplanes, which meant they couldn't replace the clapper—good news for me, but a crisis for the staff, because the masters had always relied on the bell to order cadets to their classes and other events. Perplexed, they found a cadet who played the trumpet and ordered him to toot his horn every hour. But they couldn't agree what he should play, so he had to keep trying different songs; he could have played "Annie Laurie" and it would have served the purpose, but they kept telling him to learn another new tune, and he was constantly missing notes, which was comical, and his poor playing almost hospitalized me with laughter. I'll never forget that poor benighted cadet with his horn at his lips trying new bugle calls and constantly hitting wrong notes.

When they realized the clapper was gone, the faculty decided that a cadet must have been responsible for its disappearance, so they summoned all the cadets to a formation and ordered the culprit to identify himself. When no one came forward, the battalion was put "on bounds," which meant we couldn't go into town, normal privileges were suspended and we were confined to the study hall during our free time. The masters were sure that the offender would have bragged about his larceny, and that by punishing the entire battalion one of the other cadets would rat on him.

I promptly announced I was forming an ad hoc committee of

cadets to conduct its own investigation of the crime, which I called a sacrilegious assault on one of the most hallowed traditions of Shattuck. Of course the staff loved me for this. Then I named all my enemies—cadets I didn't like—as probable conspirators in the theft. Even today I find myself laughing at this elaborate hoax and the style with which I carried it off.

No one has ever discovered the truth. Eventually the faculty had to surrender; they restored our privileges and everything returned to normal. Meanwhile, I had looked like a knight, the one cadet at Shattuck who'd had the courage, honor and sense of its venerable traditions to demand that the perpetrator be held accountable for his deed. The secret of being a successful vandal in military school is not taking on a partner. If you are the only one who knows a secret, and you keep it and are deft and careful, you will never be apprehended.

7

AFTER TWO SEMESTERS at Shattuck, I went on the bum for a summer, riding the rails, living in hobo camps and hanging out with tramps. My traveling companions were drifters from all over America—professional full-time hoboes—and I learned that they had a social system of rules, customs and traditions as rigid and well defined as those of any culture I ever encountered later. The first thing I learned was never to ask a stranger about his previous life. Many were on the run from a wife, the police or a life they no longer wanted, and when you asked what they did, more often than not, they'd answer, "Just wasting time." I learned their lingo, jargon and secret codes: a certain sign marked with chalk in an alley meant that a vicious dog lived nearby; a different symbol indicated that residents of the nearest house were generous. Around noon, everyone who lived in the camps had to contribute something to the mulligan stew. We returned to the camp with our respective contribution and dumped it into a common pot, then ate together—from a tin plate if we had one or right out of the pot if we didn't. The camps were democratic, with a prescribed pecking order like most cultures: younger, greener hoboes like me were expected to pay a certain respect to those with more miles under their belt; often an unelected senior hobo was regarded as a kind of de facto headman who could arbitrate disputes, although it wasn't unusual for disagreements to be settled with fists. A fire blazed in the camp all day, usually with a charred, steaming pot of coffee perched on a rusty steel grate. The hoboes simply dumped the coffee grounds straight into the pot. Everyone drank the coffee black because that was the way they did it—no sugar, no cream.

A small Jewish man named Hasso befriended me. He was an itinerant scissor sharpener who went door-to-door selling needles and offering to fix things in exchange for a meal, and he taught me a lot: who to trust and who to avoid, how to get supper for a little sweat, how to avoid the railroad dicks who prowled the railroad yards with oak clubs that they smashed on your head if they caught you on a freight. Hasso told me to jump off the train a mile or so before the train arrived at a freight yard, walk a mile or so past it, then hop aboard another train after it had left the yard. He taught me to avoid empty boxcars whenever I could because they bounced up and down at least eight inches, and rattled so much that you couldn't sleep. Find a loaded boxcar, he said, and make your bed on a stack of cardboard boxes if you can. If you can't, ride the rods—the steel bars stretching beneath the boxcars a foot or two above the tracks. The safest way to do it, he said, was to place a piece of wood across the rods and stretch out on it. It was safe enough to ride that way, he said, but you had to be wary of gravel bouncing up from the track bed when the train moved at high speed. When it got cold, Hasso taught me, wood was a poor insulator, but newspapers could keep you warm. Three or four sheets of newsprint on damp ground, he said, kept you dry and, stuffed under your shirt, they kept you warm in a high wind. I remembered this trick later when I started riding motorcycles.

If I didn't spend the night in a hobo camp, I'd stay with a

stranger or friend I had met along the way. There was usually a note on each freight car instructing the switching crews where to direct it. At one point I traveled across Wisconsin with the intention of going to harvest time in Minnesota. I got sick and didn't make it and wound up at Jimmy Ferguson's—my dear friend—in Rice Lake, Wisconsin.

In those days people were generous, and if they had it to spare, they'd give you a meal in exchange for a little work. There wasn't much crime, and my only real worry was the yard dicks. At one farmer's house, I knocked on the door and offered, as usual, to work for my supper.

"Well, what can you do to earn it?" the man asked.

"Anything."

When he asked me if I knew anything about farming, I said that I lived on a farm, so he took me out to his barn and I milked the cows and fed the pigs. Then I went into the kitchen and sat down with his family for supper. After dinner he sent me upstairs to sleep in his daughter's bedroom. It was the old traveling salesman's dream come true. She was very pretty, and after the lights went out, I had a few urges to get into her bed, but then I thought to myself, After they've been so nice to me, how could I do it?

I've never repeated that stupidity.

When I returned to Shattuck that fall, the freedom I'd enjoyed all summer quickly evaporated. It was uniforms, formations, close-order drills, inspections and rigidly enforced conformity again, and I resumed my old tricks.

I didn't like studying or attending classes at Shattuck any more than I had at other schools. Whether it had something to do with my dyslexia or for other reasons, I'll never know, but I never did well in school and was constantly searching for ways to avoid it. Like the other cadets, I began each semester with five classes, but it wasn't long before I'd fail one and drop it, then another and another, so that by the end of the semester I usually had only one or two classes left.

Sometimes I faked an illness to get out of going to class. One nurse at Shattuck named Mahalia (we called her Mahoola) was a kind woman, although years of looking after rowdy adolescents had left her looking exhausted. When I told her I was sick, she always felt my forehead and said, "Well, you don't *feel* hot. Let's take your temperature." Then she would stick a thermometer in my mouth and leave to go look after someone else; then I would take it out, vigorously rub it on my pants and put it back. When she returned to check, the thermometer indicated that my temperature was 103 or 104. Mahoola always gave me a compassionate look and said, "That's *high*. You don't feel that hot, but you'd better go to bed right now." Then I would say, "Do I have to?" For three or four days I didn't have to go to class, and a couple of weeks later I'd do it again.

Some mornings when I didn't feel like studying, I got up early, stuck a paper clip in the lock on the classroom door and worked it back and forth till it broke off. By the time the locksmith would be summoned from town, everybody would be locked out, and there would be no class that day. I ruined lots of locks that way. Then I found out it was just as easy to lock the masters into their apartments so they couldn't get to class. They lived across from each other along a hallway, and I discovered that by tying a rope to the door knobs of two opposing apartments the occupants of neither of them could open their doors, which swung inside. Since they usually lived on the second floor, they couldn't get out a window, so they would be prisoners in their own rooms and there would be no class that day.

Because I flunked or dropped out of so many classes, I ended up spending a lot of time in study hall, which is where you were sent if you were kicked out of a class. I made a list of 125 or so of the songs my mother had taught me, and every time I went to study hall, I'd pull out the list, pick a song and whistle it softly into my cupped hands.

One of the few classes I liked was English, which was taught by Earle Wagner, a master known to everyone as Duke. Through him, I discovered Shakespeare, whose marvelous use of language transported me into a new universe. In the study hall, I had many hours to read Shakespeare, memorizing lines that I remember to this day. I also liked to riffle through the pages of the *National Geographic*, where I made another wonderful discovery, Tahiti. I was entranced by the beauty of its beaches and the customs of the Tahitians, but most of all by the expressions on their faces. They were happy, *unmanaged* faces. No manicured expressions, just kind, open maps of contentment. To a captive on what seemed like Devil's Island, Tahiti appeared to me at least a sanctuary, and at best nirvana.

8

DUKE WAGNER WORE an old battered hat at an improbable angle and thought of himself as a debonair, rakish figure, although I think he was too frightened of the world ever really to be a rake. He had a slanted smile and a devil-may-care mustache, and walked around the campus with his dog, an English bulldog, a few steps behind him, his trench coat worn off the shoulders, dashing and capelike. He was cavalier and regal in his bearing and theatrical in his style—a duke, I suppose, in his own mind.

Besides heading the English department, Duke was in charge of the Dramatic Association of Shattuck School. He invited me to try out for a part in *A Message from Khufu*, a one-act play inspired by the King Tut legend. I got the part of a character named Ben. When my friends said that I had done well and Duke did too, I felt good. Except for sports, it was the first time since my shop teacher at Julius C. Lathrop Junior High in Santa Ana had said he liked my work that anyone had ever told me I did anything well. When tryouts for other plays came up, I went after them, too. "I am learning lots of new words and am studying *Hamlet* in English class," I wrote Frannie. "The way Wagner teaches things you are smart when it's over." In a letter to my parents, I said, "English is very hard but very interesting because we are studying plays. We are doing Shakespeare. *What a man Duke!*"

In my second year at Shattuck, I made the drill team, which was called the Crack Squad. It was considered one of the best in the country and was a prestigious assignment. In parades and competitions with other schools, we marched in close-order formation, threw our rifles into the air and did complicated drills with everything synchronized and coordinated. We were never defeated in competition, but it was hard work; for every minute of our performance, we probably spent ten hours practicing.

In my letters home that year, I kept appealing to my parents to visit or write. "Which one of you died and which one of you has broken your right arm?" I asked in one letter. In another that autumn, I told my father:

We had our last football practice Thursday and the team is going to play the last game of the season at Culver on Saturday. We've got about a four-to-one chance of winning, although it should be a good game with all the rivalry and what not. The coach gave me consolation in saying that I would have been first-string material had I not been hurt and lost those three weeks of important practice. Next year though. I got my dress uniform and am the "king dude." Boy, will I wow 'em. It's tailored perfectly and really looks very military and snappy. . . .

I never realized how much I didn't know about things until I came up here. It's astounding. I certainly hope you get here soon. I've surely missed you and Mom. My God, but she's a sweet woman. When you come you will find yourself at very gala activities. First of all, it is Thanksgiving; secondly, we are having plays (one of which I am in). Then we have a big dance. About girls, I find myself entirely indifferent. I don't give one damn if I never see one again. I'm glad I've passed the "girlie" stage of this adolescence stuff at least. And would you believe it, I'd rather not go to any dances?

Love, Bud

———

Dear Folks:

Time is moving too slowly. It seems as though I've been up here for eight months. Everybody hates the coach. So do I. The Crack Squad deal is shaping up good for me. The captain said that I would make it . . . the campus is just ablaze with autumn colors. It is a knockout. Duke becomes in my estimation smarter and smarter every day. What a guy. English is very hard for me now because we are doing grammar, but I'm at it.

Love you both *very much*
Bud

Every Sunday we had to go to the chapel for a service, where most of the cadets fell asleep, and Duke, who was very religious, and the other masters peered down the pews trying to catch us snoozing. Like everyone else, I was bored by it all. There was always a lot of elbowing in the ribs to break the boredom, and occasionally a farting contest would develop. As adolescents, we were capable of high-compression expulsions, which bounced off the boards of the wooden pews and produced loud, satisfying reports. Once a cadet released his bomb, the trick was for him to stare accusingly at his neighbor. If his neighbor laughed, it was all the better because it could be construed as an admission of guilt, and once guilt was established, everyone looked at the culprit with disgust. Then it was someone else's turn to try to fart louder.

One Sunday, after several cadets approached the altar to receive communion, my curiosity got the better of me and I decided to find out what they were experiencing. I had been told they were being given something to eat and maybe even wine, so I went up and knelt. When it was my turn, the priest put a wafer in my mouth, but instead of swallowing it, I stuck it in my cheek and rolled it around with my tongue to investigate it. When he offered wine, I gulped and held onto the cup so tightly that he had to put his foot on the railing to gain enough leverage to take it away from me. Back at my seat, I pulled the communion bread out of my mouth and studied it carefully. Peripherally I spotted Duke looking down at me darkly from the opposite end of the pew, and after the service he called me to his chambers and said, "My boy, you were toying with the most profound power in the universe. God help you. You must never insult the Lord again as you did today. *Never again.*"

"What did I do?"

"I saw you playing with the Holy Sacrament. You have to treat it with the greatest respect because if you don't, you are tempting the Devil."

I felt awful for having offended Duke. This man who was so dear to me seemed frightened by what I'd done. I told him I was sorry, but that I had no idea what the ceremony meant.

"It's the body of Christ," he said, "and the blood of Christ."

My first thought was, "That sounds cannibalistic," but I didn't say it because I didn't want to hurt Duke.

Despite my failures in the classroom, some of the masters still thought they could make an officer out of me. As a stimulant, or perhaps as a way of inspiring me to agree with them that I had a talent for leadership, they gave me a stripe of Private First Class and put me in charge of a floor. I immediately used my authority to blackmail cadets for food and candy; I said I would not put them on report after the Sunday inspection if they gave me just a taste of what they had; it was a variation of the gang-ster's protection racket, but I only picked on the kids I knew to be my enemies and who were squealers. I was soon relieved of my command, needless to say.

Periodically the army sent inspection teams to Shattuck, as it did to other military schools subsidized by the government, to review how we were doing. They were looking for military talent, and could offer Shattuck graduates a lieutenant's or captain's commission. A few days before each inspection, the cadet corps was summoned to a formation, and we would be informed about how important the inspection would be, not only for Shattuck but for our futures as army officers. It was vital, we were told, to pay deference and respect to the inspectors while doing our utmost to show them how much we had learned about such things as map reading, tactics and general military discipline.

That second year, a tough-as-nails colonel got the assignment to come to Shattuck, and one of the masters told him about me. He said I'd been something of a troublemaker, but I must have some of the qualities of a leader because I always managed to get other cadets involved in my mischief, and also, when the bell tower clapper disappeared, I'd been the only cadet with enough sense of honor and duty to demand punishment of the perpetrators.

We were ordered into the woods on extended-order drill with rifles and other paraphernalia. I was the officer in charge of the blue team, which was supposed to outmaneuver the red team. The colonel came up to me and said, "Soldier, your battalion leader has been killed. What do you do?"

"Sir," I said, "I'd ask the company commander."

"He's been killed, too. What would you do then?"

"Well, I'd ask the squad leader," I said.

"He's been killed, too," the colonel answered. "What would you do then?"

"Sir," I answered, "I guess I'd run like hell."

It was not the answer he expected, and it was viewed as

insubordination. I was put on probation and confined to my room, which delighted me because it meant I wouldn't have to take part in the extended close-order drill scheduled later in the day. But after an hour or so of being alone in my room, I got bored and decided to go into town. Unfortunately, my unauthorized absence was quickly discovered, and since I was on probation I was expelled.

"Marlon, this school is not meant for a person like you," Nuba the Tuba told me when he broke the news. "We can't put up with you anymore."

Sadly I went from room to room saying good-bye to all my friends. When I got to Duke, he surprised me by saying, "Don't worry, Marlon, everything will be all right. I know the world is going to hear from you."

I'll never forget his words.

My eyes suddenly filled with tears as he embraced me. I put my head on his shoulder and couldn't stop sobbing. I hadn't realized that I had been holding back a desire to be loved and reaffirmed. I guess I didn't even realize it then. It was the only time anyone had ever been so loving and so directly encouraging and concerned about me. I looked into Duke's eyes and saw that he really meant it. Even now, as I recall that moment, I am moved and touched by how much he meant to me.

When I got home, I looked at the faces of my mother and my father and sensed their hopelessness and disappointment. But I was used to it by then.

About two weeks later a letter arrived from Shattuck: "Dear Cadet Brando," it said. "The Student Body and all the officers in the entire battalion have been on strike because we feel you were unfairly treated. We declared we will not go back to class until and unless you are reinstated. . . ." After describing the strike, the letter concluded: "We are happy to inform you that we have succeeded in winning your reinstatement. The administration have agreed to let you return to Shattuck and make up the time you lost in summer school." The letter was signed by every cadet in the battalion.

My mother was moved to tears by this, and I was proud. I was unconcerned about how my father reacted and I don't recall his response.

After thinking it over a day or so, I responded with the adolescent reply that I would always remember what the cadets had done and would forever be grateful to them for supporting me, but that I had decided not to return to Shattuck; I had reached a fork in the road and was going to take a different path.

I got a job paying $35 a week with a small construction company digging trenches, laying pipe, setting tile and helping to build houses. For the first time in my life, I had money in my jeans that I had earned myself. I can still taste that first beer I bought with my own paycheck.

There were only three of us at home now because both my sisters had moved to New York. Tiddy, who had done some acting in high school, was taking classes at the American Academy of Dramatic Arts, and Frannie was studying painting at the Art Students League and starting a career as an artist in Greenwich Village.

Despite the bravado of my letter to the cadets, I didn't know what that path I was going to take was or where I wanted it to lead me, but I suspected it wouldn't be long before I was in uniform again. Most of the boys my age in Libertyville were being drafted, and others were volunteering. The army was snapping up students with military-school backgrounds and commissioning them as officers, so I decided to sign up.

At the induction center, a doctor asked me if I had any physical problems.

"Sometimes my knee bothers me a little," I said.

I'd injured it in a football scrimmage at Shattuck when someone tackled me from behind and snapped the semilunar cartilage, which had been removed. The doctor grabbed my leg and pulled it sideways, causing my knee to spin a little like a ball in a socket.

"Sorry, son, you've got a trick knee," he said. "You're 4-F."

My parents bravely sat me down and asked me what I was going to do now. "I don't know," I said, but I had a few ideas. The previous Christmas I'd visited my sisters in New York, and afterward I wrote Frannie: "I like N.Y. and I am going to live there when I start living. . . . God, I wish I were there. It is the most fascinating town in the world. . . ."

My mother said it was important for me to decide what I wanted to do with my life, and my father offered to pay for my education to learn a trade. Since the only thing I had ever done except sports that anyone had praised me for was acting, I told them, "Why don't I go to New York and try to be an actor?"

9

AS I GOT OUT OF the cab delivering me from Pennsylvania Station to my sister's apartment in Greenwich Village in the spring of 1943, I was sporting a bright red fedora that I thought was going to knock everybody dead.

I cherish my memories of those first few days of freedom in New York, especially my sense of liberation from not having to submit to any authority, and knowing that I could go anyplace and do anything at any time. No more uniforms, no more formations, no more bugles, no more extended-order drills, no more parades, curfews or masters. I had hated school, and now I was free.

One night I went to Washington Square and got drunk for the first time. I fell asleep on the sidewalk and nobody bothered me. When I had to piss, I got up and relieved myself behind a bush. No one said I couldn't. It was ecstasy sleeping on the sidewalk of Washington Square, realizing I had no commitments to anything or anyone. If I didn't feel like going to bed, I didn't. In those first weeks I formed the sleeping patterns of a lifetime: stay up till past midnight, sleep till ten or eleven the next morning.

Once I stayed up all night at a party in Brooklyn and looked out the window at a gray dawn at about six A.M. and watched the streets glow with the headlights of buses, cars and taxis. Then the sidewalks began to fill up with people carrying brief-cases and scurrying to their offices. I thought, God, wouldn't it be awful if I had to get up and go to work like that every day?

Frannie, who lived in an apartment near Patchin Place in the Village, invited me to move in with her. I got a job as an elevator operator at Best & Company department store, then worked as a waiter, a short-order cook, a sandwich man, and at other jobs that I don't remember now.

One afternoon I went to a cafeteria on Fourth Street and Seventh Avenue and sat down beside two men. When we started talking, one man spoke with a thick Texas accent, so I asked him where he was from.

"New York," he said.

"How did you get that Texas accent?" I asked.

"I was in the army."

"But why would you get a Texas accent in the army?" I'm sure I had a look of puzzlement on my face.

"It was protective coloration," he said, "because if you were a Jew in the army, they called you all kinds of names, teased you and made it hard on you. So I pretended to be a Texan." He said he had been out of the army for about eight months, but still hadn't broken the habit. Then we introduced ourselves. He told me his name was Norman Mailer and the other man said he was Jimmy Baldwin.

Although Mailer, who was as yet unpublished, and I never became good friends, Jimmy Baldwin and I became close after that meeting in Hector's Cafeteria. It was a special relationship, and one of its hallmarks was an absence of any sense of racial differences between us, something I have seldom experienced with other black friends. Neither of us ever felt we had to speak about race. Our relationship was simply that of two human beings with no barriers between us, and we could tell each other

In Frannie's apartment in New York City, 1944. (Personal collection of Marlon Brando)

anything about ourselves with frankness. I was working at a
dull job and so was he; he hadn't written much yet and I didn't
know what I was doing or where I was going.

Unfortunately, Jimmy became one of the many friends I've
loved since I left Libertyville who had much to offer but died
senselessly and tragically long before they should have. He
never told me he was dying, and I didn't learn about his cancer
until after he was dead.

In the apartment next to my sister's lived a woman named
Estrelita Rosa Maria Consuelo Cruz. I called her Luke. She was
Colombian and ten or fifteen years older than me; she was
olive-skinned, fetching, extremely artistic and a great cook. Her
husband was overseas with the marines, and one night she
invited me for dinner; there was a fireplace, candlelight and
wine, and I lost my virginity.

Luke was extremely passionate and sexually unconventional.
She never wore underpants, and we'd often walk down a street
in New York, duck in an alley and have at it. At the ballet one
night, she put her hand on my prick and I put my hand up her
dress. We both came, and she yipped and tittered so loudly that
others in the audience must have wondered about her. After her
husband came back from overseas, he learned about our affair
and divorced her. Our friendship lasted for many years. She was
very important to me then, but after her there were many other
women in my life.

10

THE BEST BANDS in the world were constantly coming in and out of Manhattan and making wonderful music in Harlem and behind the neon lights and red awnings of jazz clubs along West Fifty-second Street. I thrived on this feast. In Libertyville my idols in the jazz world had been Gene Krupa and Buddy Rich, but one night I went to the Palladium, a ballroom on Broadway, to dance and almost lost my mind with excitement when I discovered Afro-Cuban music. Every Wednesday night there was a mambo contest, and it seemed as if every Puerto Rican in New York got out on the dance floor and released a week of frustration after working as a waiter or pushing a cart in the garment district. People moved their bodies in ways that were unimaginable; it was the most beautiful dancing I'd ever seen and I was mesmerized by it. Every Wednesday night was a festival, and I looked forward to it each week. The place exploded with joy, excitement and enthusiasm. Tito Puente and Tito Rodriguez, the very best of the Afro-Cuban bands, played there, and when one finished a set, another took over. I had always been stimulated by rhythm, even by the ticking of a clock, and the rhythms they played were irresistible. Each band usually had two or three conga drummers, and I couldn't sit still because of their extraordinary, complicated syncopations. I had been a pretty good stick drummer—I'd taken lessons—but had never played the congas. After going to the Palladium, I gave up stick drumming, bought my own conga drums and signed up for a class with Katherine Dunham, a wonderful black dancer, and for a while thought of trying to make my living as a modern dancer. She had been all over the world learning what was then called "primitive dancing," and I was hypnotized by it, although in class whenever I was given the choice of either playing the drums or dancing, I much preferred to play.

There were only two white people in my class at Dunham's; the rest were black, including a nurse from Jamaica named Floretta who had a very distinctive look in her eyes. Her eyelids fell deep over her eyes, which make them look almost closed. For some reason, I found this very sensual. After we made love, I realized that she had never been with a white man and that I had never slept with a black woman before, so we shared the kind of curiosity that people of different races have for each other. I don't know why it surprised me, but I found it interesting that there was no difference in making love to a woman of color than to a woman who was white. The *only* difference was her color, a symphony in sepia. When I pressed my thumb on her skin, it became luminous around the edges; it was like skin I had never touched before. We had great times together, but eventually we went our separate ways. She left school for some reason, and I never heard from her again.

One night, after someone told me about a good band in Harlem, I took the subway to a small, dark club on 132nd Street with a bar out front and a small dance floor in the back where the band was playing. I had a pleasant buzz on, and after listening awhile I walked up to the bandstand and asked the musician who was playing conga drums if I could play a set. I pulled a $5 bill out of my pocket and offered it to him, but he wouldn't look at me. A guy next to him with a big scowl on his face wouldn't look at me either. Then a huge guy with eyes like ball bearings came out of nowhere and said, "I'll take your money, boy. Do you want to play the drums? Gimme your money. I'll see that you play the drums."

"Well, I think I'll just listen now," I said, "and play later."

Suddenly the place was silent. That's strange, I thought. Then it registered on me that the big man was the only person in the club who had made eye contact with me, and I realized that I was the only white person in the room.

As I sat down again, I noticed that several women were sitting at a table behind mine. The band started up again, and I sat back and listened, still happy to be there. Then I heard a voice: "You want to dance?"

I looked up and saw a very pretty woman. "Dance? Yeah, sure."

We started dancing and I asked what her name was.

"Ruby."

"My name's Buddy."

"Buddy. *Buddy?*"

"That's right," I said, and suddenly a slanted smile stole across her face, a charming smile illuminated by a bright gold tooth. We danced, and when the music stopped, we sat down and started to chat. While I was talking, I noticed her look behind me, and suddenly she said, "My name's still Sugar."

I turned around and looked into the faces of five or six women, then saw a man sitting directly behind me, a black icebox with eyes like two .45s. I realized I'd looked into the wrong face; I had crossed an infuriated cement tank. I got out of my chair, swallowed hard, looked down at the floor, then at my feet, while trying to think of something to say. Finally I turned and walked over to him, my stomach fluttering like the hands of a jazz pianist. I stood beside him with all the girls staring dead-eyed at me, but he didn't look back, just kept staring straight ahead. Trying to appear nonchalant, I said, "Hey, man, I'm just in from out of town."

He interrupted me and very slowly said, "My name is Leroy, L-E-R-O-Y." Those letters are burned into my brain to this day.

"Well, actually, Mr. Leroy," I said, "I was just looking for a good time and trying to dig the music . . ."

I didn't know much black jargon, but I had heard the word "dig," so I used it as often as I could. "My name's Bud. I'm from out of town," I said. "I just came in from Chicago. I don't mean to be stepping on anybody's toes or anything like that."

"That's cool," Leroy said. "That's *cool*."

It took him about five seconds to draw out the one syllable of "cool"; in fact, he may have turned it into four syllables. "That's *cool*, my man," he repeated.

I said, "Thank you very much. Are you sure it's all right?"

He looked at me and said "Mmmm, hmmmm." It was a long "Mmmmm hmmmmm." He never once looked at me.

I went back to my seat mentally reciting my catechism, sat down and started talking to the girl again while trying to do something about the tortured smile on my face. "Is that your boyfriend?" I asked.

"Well," she said, moving her head slightly and smiling again, *"kind of."*

"Listen," I said, "why don't we go downtown? I know some nice places there where we could have some fun and dance. Would you like to go downtown?"

"Sure," she said. "Why not, baby? Let's make it."

I put some money down to pay the bill and went to the checkroom, which was near the bar in the front, to get my coat. As I was putting it on, I turned around and looked back toward the doorway and saw a body flying horizontally past me directly into a pile of chairs and tables that had been piled on top of each other. It was Ruby/Sugar. Without stopping to evaluate the situation, I pivoted on my right foot, opened the door and ran like a nine-year-old girl who had just seen her first snake. Behind me, I heard feet scuffling out of the jazz club, so I ran faster, passing several guys in a doorway who said, "Where you goin', white boy?" I had so much adrenaline in my bloodstream that I could have outrun Jesse Owens on his best day. At an intersection two blocks away, a car was stopped at a red light; I vaulted over its hood like a high hurdler, then ran toward the subway at 110th Street and down the stairs to the platform four steps at a time. At the end of the platform, I peeked from behind a post searching for my pursuers. After several eternities, a train arrived, and as it did, several guys piled down the stairs. Well, that's it, I thought, I'm going to die in a pool of blood on a subway train underneath Central Park, and I'm only nineteen. I knew that the train wouldn't stop at another station until Fifty-ninth Street, and the trip seemed to last a thousand years. I waited for those guys to come polish me off, sweating from the back of my knees to between my toes, everywhere I had a sweat gland. At Fifty-ninth Street, I rushed off the train and looked around, but nobody else got off. Then I realized that *nobody* had been chasing me; it was all in my head.

11

FOR ALL THE FREEDOM I savored in New York, a letter I wrote home that fall suggests that I was a confused young man:

> School starts tomorrow and I'm very glad because I've been plenty antsy for a long time, what with bitter busdrivers, pacifists, philosophers, kooks, funny people, New York and myself.
>
> Oh, God! Round and round I go looking for an answer of some kind. No answer. No nothing. I've tried relaxing, but it's still the same. I've gone nuts thinking about truth and its aspects. I don't get anything. Nothing adds up. There is so damn much bitterness and fear and hate and untruths all around me. I want to do something about it. It makes me mad when I get scared of sticking my neck out. If you try to be good and thoughtful and kind and truthful, people call you a liar and suspect you and resent you and hate you. I try my damnedest to understand and forgive, but if I were to put into words and actions what I sometimes feel, it would cost me my life almost. Society won't let you be decent because they're so God-damned afraid all the time. I've tried to be smart and stay on the line but it makes me feel as though I weren't living

up to my own ideas and principles. . . . I'm going to miss the fall at home and the apples and leaves and smells and stuff. I've got a lump in my throat now just thinking about it. . . .

Love, Bud.

I attended the New School for Social Research for only a year, but what a year it was. The school and New York itself had become a sanctuary for hundreds of extraordinary European Jews who had fled Germany and other countries before and during World War II, and they were enriching the city's intellectual life with an intensity that has probably never been equaled anywhere during a comparable period of time. I was raised largely by these Jews. I lived in a world of Jews. They were my teachers; they were my employers. They were my friends. They introduced me to a world of books and ideas that I didn't know existed. I stayed up all night with them—asking questions, arguing, probing, discovering how little I knew, learning how inarticulate I was and how abysmal my education was. I hadn't even finished high school, and many of them had advanced degrees from the finest institutes in Europe. I felt dumb and ashamed, but they gave me an appetite to learn everything. They made me hungry for information. I believed that if I had more knowledge I'd be smarter, which I now realize isn't true. I read Kant, Rousseau, Nietzsche, Locke, Melville, Tolstoy, Faulkner, Dostoyevsky and books by dozens of other authors, many of which I never understood.

The New School was a way station for some of the finest Jewish intellectuals from Europe, a temporary haven before they left to join the faculties at universities like Princeton, Yale and Harvard. They were the cream of Europe's academicians, and as teachers they were extraordinary.

One of the great mysteries that has always puzzled me is how Jews, who account for such a tiny fraction of the world's population, have been able to achieve so much and excel in so many different fields—science, music, medicine, literature, arts, business and more. If you listed the most influential people of the last hundred years, three at the top of the list would be Einstein, Freud and Marx; all were Jews. Many more belong on the list, yet Jews comprise at most less than 3 percent of the United States population. They are an amazing people. Imagine the persecution they endured over the centuries: pogroms, temple burnings, Cossack raids, uprootings of families, their dispersal to the winds and the Holocaust. After the Diaspora, they could not own land or worship in much of the world; they were prohibited from voting and were told where to live. Yet their culture survived and Jews became by far the most accomplished people per capita that the world has ever produced.

For a while I thought that the brilliance and success of Jews was the cumulative yield of an extraordinarily rich pool of genes in the Middle East produced over eons by evolution. But then I realized that my theory didn't hold up because following the Diaspora, Ashkenazic Jews evolved into a group physically much different from Sephardic Jews. Spanish Jews had nothing in common with Russian Jews; in fact they could not even speak to them. Russian Jews were isolated from German Jews, who thought of themselves as separate and superior, and Eastern European Jews had nothing to do with the Sephardic Jews. Besides, there had been so much intermarriage over the centuries that genetics alone couldn't explain the phenomenon.

After talking to many Jews and reading about Jewish history and culture, I finally came to the conclusion that in the end being Jewish was a cultural phenomenon rather than a genetic one. It is a state of mind. There's a Yiddish word, *seychel,* that provides a key to explaining the most profound aspects of Jewish culture. It means to pursue knowledge and to leave the world a better place than when you entered it. Jews revere education and hard work, and they pass these values on from one generation to the next. As far as I am aware, this dynamic and emphasis on excellence is paralleled only in certain Asian cultures. It must be this cultural tradition that accounts for their amazing success, along with Judaism, the one constant that survived while the Jews were dispersed around the world.

Traditions passed on via the Torah and Talmud have somehow helped Jews to fulfill the destiny they have claimed, a kind of "chosen people," if spectacular success in so many, many fields is proof of that. Whatever the reasons for their brilliance and success, I was never educated until I was exposed to them. They introduced me to a sense of culture that has lasted me a lifetime.

As well as academics and scholars from Eastern Europe, Jewish girls, most of whom were more educated, sophisticated and experienced in the ways of the world than I was, were my teachers during those early days in New York. It was common in those days for girls from wealthy New York Jewish families to rent an apartment in the city and have a little fling before striking out on a career or marriage after they had graduated from college. With my inept, simple ways, I must have seemed to them like an alien from a galaxy beyond the Milky Way. I was a gentile in a Jewish world who had hardly been to school; I rode a motorcycle; I was young, reasonably attractive, full of vim, vigor and sexuality, an exotic specimen if for no other reason than I was different from the boys these girls had grown up with. I didn't follow any of their rules and they didn't follow any of mine. They were fascinated by me and I by them. Many were more experienced sexually than I was, and I was a willing and happy pupil. I remember especially Caroline Burke, a beautiful woman who was about ten years older than I was, in whom I always regretted not making a more permanent investment. She was not only physically attractive and well educated, but bursting with elegance, charm, taste and appreciation for beautiful things. She lived in an apartment filled with antiques and always wore delicious perfume. To her, I suppose I was a kind of bumpkin—a nineteen-year-old farm boy who still worried secretly that he had manure on his shoes, but she taught me a great deal.

I was walking down Fifty-seventh Street with Caroline one day and innocently asked, "Isn't it funny how you see so many women with blond hair and a mink coat?" There was a woman in front of us with blond hair wearing a mink coat and we were talking about her, when Caroline said, "She's Jewish." I asked, "How do you know?" She answered, "Well, it's because . . . I don't know, she's just Jewish." I said, "You mean to say, just because she has blond hair and a mink—" She interrupted, "Look, I'm a Jew, and I know what Jews are like from the front, back, side or top." "Well, how can you tell a Jew from a non-Jew?" She replied, "Well, you have to be Jewish to know that." I was stunned, and I thought Caroline had remarkable powers of perception.

After several months in New York, I was still interested in becoming a modern dancer, but then I took an acting class at the New School's Dramatic Workshop and everything changed. During that fall of 1943, I kept my parents informed of my progress in letters that seem to have been written by a person I barely recognize, a naïve kid trying hard to understand the galaxy he had stumbled into and looking for a place in it as well as a purpose in life:

Dear Folks:

I am fine, depimpled and healthy. I haven't found a room as yet but I think by the end of this week I will have gotten one that I've had my eye on . . . last week, we did "Tonight We Improvise" by Pirandello and it was good. Piscator liked me in it. It was lots of fun. I have met an interesting girl whose name is Renata (beautiful name). She plays the piano for her work and she speaks German, Italian, French and English. Very charming. She was born in Germany. . . .

I am learning that you just can't have a completely frank and sincere relationship with any girl. All most of them do is bore me, truly. . . . I have been reading the Bible. It is full of beautiful thoughts but they don't mean much to me. Nana, why do they tell you to fear God? I can't understand . . . I am writing this on the subway and putting my thoughts down as they come . . . Joy Thompson (summer theater girl) fell on her head and went to the hospital—fractured skull and concussion. She has gone back to Canada. . . .

How goes it at home? Pop, many things you have said are beginning to take shape and content. Ma, how is your cold? I don't understand life, but I am living like mad anyhow. You are all good people and much comfort to me.

All my love
Bud

———

Dear Folks:

I want to thank you for being so nice about my not writing. Have I forgotten any birthdays? I have been tearing like mad of late. . . . School is fine. We are doing Moliere in "The Imaginary Invalid" in which I am a young lover of the 18th cent. It's a good part. I am studying the part of the Templar in "Nathan the Wise," which is a very good part for me. My philosophy class is real good and Dr. Kaplan in his lectures confirms all I have professed (not openly) about ecclesiastical power and aspects of religion. It is wonderful. I have much to say. I am washing my stuff now in my wash stand.

I don't like my landlady. She gives the young lad too much advice. Much too much.

I am beginning to know how to act—learning to act and developing a sense of direction of action and feeling. It is hard work just as anything else but a source of enjoyment for me because I like it.

Fran is working like hell and having manifestly wondrous results. She is fine. . . . I am systematizing my budget.

Love to you all
Bud

12

THE DIRECTOR of the New School's Dramatic Workshop was Erwin Piscator, a man of great repute in the German theater, but to me Stella Adler was its soul. During the early thirties, she went to Europe and studied under Konstantin Stanislavsky of the Moscow Art Theater, then brought home his disciplines and techniques and taught them to other members of the Group Theatre, a company of actors, writers and directors who for a decade, starting in 1931, tried to mount an alternative to the commercial Broadway theater, staging productions they felt were the cutting edge of social change.

When I met her, Stella was about forty-one, quite tall and very beautiful, with blue eyes, stunning blond hair and a leonine presence, but a woman much disappointed by what life had dealt her. She was a marvelous actress who unfortunately never got a chance to become a great star, and I think this embittered her. A member of one of the great theatrical families of America, she appeared in almost two hundred plays over a span of thirty years, and wanted very much to be a famous performer. But like many Jewish actors of her era, she faced a cruel and insidious form of anti-Semitism; producers in New York and especially in Hollywood wouldn't hire actors if they "looked Jewish," no matter how good they were.

Hollywood was always a Jewish community; it was started by Jews and to this day is run largely by Jews. But for a long time it was venomously anti-Semitic in a perverse way, especially before the war, when Jewish performers had to disguise their Jewishness if they wanted a job. These actors were frightened, and understandably so. When I was breaking into acting, I constantly heard about agents submitting an actor or actress for a part, taking them to the theater for a reading and afterward hearing the producer say, "Terrific. Thank you very much. We'll call you."

After the actor was gone, the agent would ask, "Well, Al, what did you think?"

"Great," the producer would say, "He was terrific, *but he's too Jewish*."

If you "looked Jewish," you didn't get a part and couldn't make a living. You had to look like Kirk Douglas, Tony Curtis, Paul Muni or Paulette Goddard and change your name. They were Jews, but didn't "look Jewish" and employed the camouflage of non-Jewish names. Hence Julius Garfinkle became John Garfield, Marion Levy became Paulette Goddard, Emmanuel Goldenberg became Edward G. Robinson and Muni Weisenfreund became Paul Muni. Later this changed when people like Barbra Streisand said, "I'll be damned if I'm going to change my name. I'm a Jew and I'm proud of it." Now Jews don't have to get their noses operated on to get a job, but Stella was part of a different era. She went to Hollywood, made three movies and changed her last name to "Ardler," hoping it would help, but she had a sharp, aquiline nose that gave her the "Jewish look." She had it operated on and the result made her look more like a shiksa; but producers still said she looked too Jewish to offer her the kind of jobs her talent deserved and that would have made her a star.

But while Stella never fulfilled her dream, she left an astounding legacy. Virtually all acting in motion pictures today stems from her, and she had an extraordinary effect on the culture of

Stella Adler: an astounding legacy. (Personal collection of Marlon Brando)

her time. I don't think audiences realize how much we are in debt to her, to other Jews and to the Russian theater for most performances we see now. The techniques she brought back to this country and taught others changed acting enormously. First she passed them on to the other members of the Group Theatre, and then to actors like me who became her students. We plied our trade according to the manner and style she taught us, and since American movies dominate the world market, Stella's teachings have influenced actors throughout the world.

Stella always said no one could teach acting, but *she* could. She had a knack for teaching people about themselves, enabling them to use their emotions and bring out their hidden sensitivity. She also had a gift for communicating her knowledge; she could tell you not only *when* you were wrong, but *why*. Her instincts were unerring and extraordinary. If I hit a sour note in a scene, she knew it immediately and said, "No, wait, wait, wait . . . that's wrong!" and then dug into her large reserve of intuitive intelligence to explain why my character would behave in a certain way based on the author's vision.

"Method acting" was a term popularized, bastardized and misused by Lee Strasberg, a man for whom I had little respect, and therefore I hesitate to use it. What Stella taught her students was how to discover the nature of their own emotional mechanics and therefore those of others. She taught me to be real and not to try to act out an emotion I didn't personally experience during a performance.

Because of Stella, acting changed completely during the fifties and sixties. Until the generation she inspired came along, most actors were what I have always thought of as "personality" actors, like Sarah Bernhardt, Katharine Cornell or Ruth Gordon. George Bernard Shaw once said, "A character actor is one who cannot act and therefore makes an elaborate study of disguise and stage tricks by which acting can be grotesquely simulated." A lot of actors believed that by growing a beard, checking out a robe from the wardrobe department and carrying a staff they could become Moses, but they were seldom anything other than themselves playing the same role time after time. To indicate torment or confusion, they put their hands on their foreheads and sighed loudly. They acted externally rather than internally.

There were a few good natural actors from the past. I once saw a clip from a 1916 movie, *Cenere,* starring Eleonora Duse, a fine actress whose career was unfortunately overshadowed by her rival, the more flamboyant Bernhardt. Her acting was understated, simple, without theatrical artifice and enormously effective. Other natural actors whose instincts showed in their work were Paul Muni and Jimmy Cagney, but I believe they were exceptions. Until Stella came along, stage acting was mostly declaiming, superficial gestures, exaggerated expression, loud voices, theatrical elocution and unfelt emotion. Most actors did nothing to *experience* a character's feelings and emotions.

Acting is the least mysterious of all crafts. *Everybody* acts, whether it's a toddler who quickly learns how to behave to get its mother's attention, or a husband and wife in the daily rituals of a marriage, with all the artifices and role-playing that occur in a conjugal relationship. Politicians are among our most flashy and worst actors. It's hard to imagine anyone surviving in our world without acting. It is a necessary social device: we use it to protect our interests and to gain advantage in every aspect of our lives, and it is instinctive, a skill built into all of us. Whenever we want something from somebody or when we want to hide something or pretend, we're acting. Most people do it all day long. When we don't feel the emotions someone expects of us and want to please them, we act out the emotion we think they expect of us; we're enthusiastic about their project even though it bores us. Someone says something that hurts our feelings but we hide our hurt. The difference is that most people act unconsciously and automatically, while stage and movie actors do it to tell a story. In fact, most actors give their best performances after the camera stops rolling.

A lot of the old movie stars couldn't act their way out of a box of wet tissue paper, but they were successful because they had distinctive personalities. They were predictable brands of breakfast cereal: on Wednesdays we had Quaker Oats and Gary Cooper; on Fridays we had Wheaties and Clark Gable. They were off-the-shelf products you expected always to be the same, actors and actresses with likable personalities who played themselves in more or less the same role the same way every time out. Clark Gable was Clark Gable in every role; Humphrey Bogart always played himself; Claudette Colbert was always Claudette Colbert. Loretta Young was virtually the same character in every part, and as she got older, cinematographers kept putting more layers of silky gauze between her and their lenses to keep her that way and convince audiences she was still Loretta Young. Nowadays movie grips call the devices they use to conceal the physical evidence of aging "Loretta Young silks."

I was lucky because I became an actor at the beginning of an era when the craft was becoming more interesting, thanks to Stella. Once she told a reporter that she thought one of the assets I brought to acting was a high degree of curiosity about people. It's true that I have always had an unwavering curiosity about people—what they feel, what they think, how they're motivated—and I have always made it my business to find out. If I can't figure somebody out, I'll follow him like a weasel with persistence until I find out what his nature is and how he functions, not for any reasons of advantage—although I admit that when I was young I sometimes did it to gain an advantage—but because I'm curious not only about others, but about myself. I am endlessly absorbed by human motivations. How is it that we behave the way we do? What are those compulsions within us that drive us one way or another?

It is my lifelong preoccupation. I used to hang around the

coffeehouses on Washington Square just watching people. If I was out with a woman, I tried to figure out why she decided to cross her legs or light a cigarette at a certain moment, or what it meant if she chose at a certain point in our conversation to clear her throat or brush back a lock of hair from her forehead. I used to sit in the phone booth of the Optima Cigar Store at Broadway and Forty-second Street looking out the window at people walking by. I saw them for perhaps two or three seconds before they disappeared; if they were close to the phone booth, they might even disappear in a second. In that flick of time I studied their faces, the way they carried their heads and swung their arms; I tried to absorb who they were—their history, their job, whether they were married, troubled or in love. The face is an extraordinarily subtle instrument; I believe it has 155 muscles in it. The interaction of those muscles can hide a great deal, and people are always concealing emotions. Some people have very nonexpressive faces. They carry a neutral expression around all the time, and it is often difficult to read their faces, especially Orientals and the Indians of North and South America. In such cases I try to read their body posture, the increase in the blink rate of their eyes, their aimless yawning or a failure to complete a yawn—anything that denotes emotions they don't want to display.

These are matters I have been interested in since I was a child. I was determined to know, to guess and to assess quirks that people did not know about themselves. I have tried to push and probe until I learned their potential for loving, for hating, for anger, for self-interest, for their taste in the things they wanted in life and how much they wanted them, to discover their perimeters and limits and find out how they were truly constituted. I have always been equally curious about my own potential and limits, and tested myself to learn how much I could stand of one thing or another—how honest I could be, how false, how materialistic or otherwordly, how frightened, to what extent I could take a risk and what terrified me most.

. . .

After I had some success, Lee Strasberg tried to take credit for teaching me how to act. He never taught me anything. He would have claimed credit for the sun and the moon if he believed he could get away with it. He was an ambitious, selfish man who exploited the people who attended the Actors Studio, and he tried to project himself as an acting oracle and guru. Some people worshiped him, but I never knew why. To me he was a tasteless and untalented person whom I didn't like very much. I sometimes went to the Actors Studio on Saturday mornings because Elia Kazan was teaching, and there were usually a lot of good-looking girls. But Strasberg never taught me acting. Stella did—and later Kazan.

13

MY MOTHER followed Frannie, Tiddy and me to New York a few months after I got there; my parents had split up again. She got an apartment on West End Avenue, and the three of us moved in with her, along with Tiddy's year-old son, Gahan. She promised to stay sober, but she couldn't manage it, and before long it was like Libertyville and Evanston all over again. She hid bottles under her bed and in the kitchen cabinets and started disappearing again. We tried to get her to stop, and sometimes she did for a few weeks, but then she would go on another bender. For us it was an emotional seesaw.

During my year at the New School, I was a conscientious student, if unschooled in many aspects of life. Once, during rehearsals for a play, another member of the Dramatic Workshop came over to me and said he wanted to help me. Since I was eager to do my best, I listened intently to him. He said I should play my part with dignity.

"Yes," I agreed, "I'm trying to."

"But you should stand up a little straighter," he said. "Put your shoulders back, your chest out, lower your shoulders."

I tried to do all that.

New York family reunion, 1944. My mother (right) had split again with my father. Jocelyn's son, Gahan, is one year old. (Personal collection of Marlon Brando)

Then he patted my crotch. "Pull this in a little."

I was horrified and stood motionless in stunned silence. When he did it again, I was almost paralyzed. Then he said, "What do you like? Men, women or children?"

Planting my foot for leverage against a scenery board nailed to the floor, I unleashed a punch that sent him sailing across the room and to a hospital with a smashed face. When I was chastised for this by Erwin Piscator, I told him that the man had made sexual advances to me. He replied that hitting people wasn't the way people in the theater dealt with such matters.

At the end of the school year, Piscator took our group to Sayville, Long Island, to reprise several productions in summer stock, including *Twelfth Night,* in which I played Sebastian. A lot of unbridled fornication occurred during that summer of 1944, and I was in the thick of it. One day Piscator lifted up the trapdoor to the loft where I was sleeping above a garage, found me with a girl and said I had to leave because I'd broken the "Rules of Summer Stock." I was disappointed because I was enjoying myself, but in those days I was like a newspaper blowing down the street in a strong wind: I went this way or that way depending on the gale. As luck would have it, because I was expelled I got my first acting job about three weeks later in *I Remember Mama.* I simply stepped off one lily pad onto another. It has been that way most of my life. I've had lots of problems, but also lots of luck; in many ways I have led a charmed life. Subsequently I learned that one of the ladies in our company had been servicing Piscator all that summer. This tickled me; what an act of hypocrisy it was to send me home!

It was an agent, Maynard Morris, who suggested me for *I Remember Mama,* a play by John Van Druten and the first nonmusical produced by Richard Rodgers and Oscar Hammerstein II. I was twenty, but he thought I could play Nels, the son of two Norwegian immigrants, who was fourteen during most of the play. He sent me over for an audition at the office of Rodgers and Hammerstein. When I got there, Richard Rodgers looked up at me skeptically with dark, hooded eyes, shirtsleeves rolled up and a nasty expression. It was my first interview for an acting job, and I didn't know what to say or how to behave.

Rodgers looked at me impatiently and asked, "What's your name?"

"Marlon Brando."

"What have you done?"

"Well, I was in summer stock and played in *Twelfth Night* and I—"

"*C'mon, what have you done?*" he said, raising his voice unpleasantly.

I said, "Besides that, nothing."

After I read for the part, Rodgers told Hammerstein that he hated my audition and didn't want to use me, but John Van Druten liked me; he prevailed and I got the part.

I Remember Mama opened October 19, 1944, at the Music Box Theatre and I got a few fair reviews, but nothing special. The play was a hit and ran for two years. I remember it mostly for my fun offstage. On a questionnaire for my biography for *Playbill,* I made up stories about myself, including my birthplace: Calcutta, India. Later on I told *Playbill* I'd been born in other places—Bangkok, Thailand, and Mukden, China. I have always enjoyed making up bizarre stories to see if people would believe them. Generally they do.

Oscar Homolka, who played my father in the play, was a brusque, unpleasant, pompous man, which made him enjoyable to irritate. In one scene, as he got into a car that was pulled across the stage by a wire, he was supposed to blow the horn to summon the rest of the family. As he honked the horn, a prop man was supposed to blow a trumpetlike horn offstage loud enough to be heard in the back of the house. But every so often

WHO'S WHO IN THE CAST

MARLON BRANDO (Nels) makes his first professional appearance in "I Remember Mama," having served his apprenticeship at the New School for Social Research, where he studied dramatics under Erwin Piscator and Stella and Luther Adler. Born in Calcutta, India, where his father was engaged in geological research, he came to this country when he was six months old.

MARLON BRANDO (Sage McRae), who is playing his second role in the theatre, was born in Bangkok, while his father was engaged in zoological research. His first appearance on the professional stage was as Nels in "I Remember Mama," which he left for his current role.

MARLON BRANDO (Stanley Kowalski) made his first appearance on Broadway three seasons ago as Nels in "I Remember Mama." He went from that to a leading role in Maxwell Anderson's "Truckline Cafe" when he was first singled out by the critics for his performance in the role of Sage. Also impressed was Guthrie McClintic, who chose him to play Marchbanks in Katharine Cornell's revival of "Candida." He next appeared in Ben Hecht's "A Flag Is Born." Born in Omaha, Neb., Brando spent his school years in Evanston, Ill., California and Minnesota. The choice of the stage as a career had never entered his mind until after he had come to New York and spent several months engaged in such odd jobs as running an elevator and operating a switchboard. When he did decide to go on the stage he spent a year studying with Stella Adler and followed that with a summer season of stock at Sayville, L. I. It was there that a New York actors' agent saw him and helped him get his first acting job with "I Remember Mama."

Misdirection: my *Playbill*® bios for *I Remember Mama* (top left), *Truckline Cafe* (bottom left) and *A Streetcar Named Desire* (right).

Homolka honked his horn and the prop man missed his cue and was several seconds late. This made Homolka furious; sometimes he would turn around and shout into the wings at the poor old cricket of a stagehand so loudly that the audience could hear him, and matters became very tense between them. The prop man kept promising to get it right, but one day when he wasn't looking, I stuffed his horn with Kleenex, and the next time Homolka honked his horn onstage and the prop man, with perfect timing, blew his, there was complete silence. He blew harder and harder. Still no sound. Homolka got red in the face and started bellowing at him from the stage while the prop man reached deeper and deeper into his lungs and blew with all his heart—so hard that he blew his false teeth out of his mouth. It was uproarious to see him fighting to get a grip on his choppers with his lips while still trying to blow the horn, and I almost had apoplexy.

In another scene Mama's sister had to say, "You certainly make a wonderful cup of coffee. It's so delicious I think I'll have another cup." On one occasion I poured salt and some Tabasco sauce into the coffee, and she had to drink a cup of this witches' brew, keep a straight face and ask for another cup.

Shortly after the play opened, I started stammering again. When I was supposed to say words like "the," "that," "there" or "those," my tongue got stuck on "th" and I couldn't finish the word. It was sporadic. Some nights I was fine; on others I suddenly started stammering midway through the play. Finally I taught myself how to deal with it: before a word in the play starting with "th" came up, I put my tongue in place so that it was ready. Keeping my tongue in the right place wasn't as easy as it sounds. It took a lot of concentration to do it without letting the audience know, and sometimes it stayed, sometimes it didn't.

I kept a bookcase at the theater, and when I wasn't onstage, I sat in a corner under a lamp set up by the prop man and stud-

With Mady Christians, my mother in *I Remember Mama*. (© Bradley Smith)

ied. One night Richard Rodgers came to the theater, saw me reading in my corner in the short pants I wore onstage, and came over to say hello.

"Boy, you've got a lot of books there," he said.

"Hello, Mr. Rodgers," I said.

"What are you reading?"

He leaned over and peered at the book in my hands. It was the *Discourses of Epictetus;* then he scanned the other titles in the bookcase—Kant's *Critique of Pure Reason* and books by Thoreau, Gibbon and Rousseau. Then he looked at me with a perplexed expression and walked away without saying another word. He never knew how to say hello to me again.

Edith Van Cleve, of the New York office of the Music Corporation of America (later MCA, Inc.), was now my agent. After I had been in *I Remember Mama* about a year, she said that Alfred Lunt and Lynn Fontanne were about to produce a new play and she arranged for me to read for it. When I arrived at the theater, I discovered it was a cattle call. Dozens of young actors were waiting to compete for the same part. Every few minutes the stage manager called one to the stage where he recited a few lines and was then dismissed. When it was my turn, I walked onstage and an invisible voice said, "What is your name?"

"Marlon Brando."

"Have you been in a play recently?"

"Yes."

The lights were on me. It was pitch dark on the other side of the footlights.

"What play, Mr. Brindel?" the disembodied voice asked.

"I'm in *I Remember Mama.*"

There was a long pause in which I didn't say anything.

"Would you mind saying something?"

I thought the situation utterly stupid and absurd. After a lengthy pause, I said: "Hickory, dickory, dock, the mouse ran up the clock. The clock struck one, the mouse ran down, hickory, dickory, dumb." I accentuated the word *dumb*.

There was another long pause, then a lot of muttering in the dark, and finally someone said, "Well, thank you, Mr. er-ah, Brindle, we'll be in touch with you."

That was my career with the Lunts.

During those early years in New York, I made friendships that would last a lifetime: Janice Mars, William Redfield, Sam Gilman, Maureen Stapleton, Philip and Marie Rhodes, Carlo Fiore and others. Janice, who was from Lincoln, Nebraska, and had the same sense of humor I did, was an extraordinary singer, the host and main performer at a place called the Back Room, and in her view, we were like a family of waifs. "Flouting all the conventions, we were like orphans in rebellion against everything," she recalled in a letter to me recently. "None of us had emotionally secure family backgrounds, but we gravitated to each other and created a family among ourselves. I've never gotten over the feeling of family we had, even if it was all in my imagination. I'm nostalgic for it—that feeling—youth, our mutual support system, uncritical acceptance of each other—foibles, faults and all. Orphans of the storm clinging together."

Janice said I preferred women who were older than me, like Estrelita: "You were always looking for a substitute mother. You used to go to her when you got sick. Sometimes she'd come looking for you as if you were a bad boy. You hid from her in our closet. . . . You also had a perverse need to humiliate, to see just how far a female would go to indulge you. For you, sex had as much significance as eating a Mars bar or taking a pill . . . your attitude toward women was very ambivalent. I felt your power as a palpable aura, a magnetism you knew how to use manipulatively but also protectively. There was a seductive comfort in your touch. Nobody could hold you, then or now. . . ."

. . .

In a lifetime of making friends, none was ever closer or more important to me than Wally Cox. We had been playmates in Evanston at seven or eight, and we both moved to New York about the same time. He was making a living as a silversmith and craftsman of fine jewelry, but would entertain us with hilarious monologues. We resumed our friendship and it lasted until he died in 1973.

I'm not sure I will ever forgive Wally for dying. He was more than a friend; he was my brother, closer to me than any human being in my life except my sisters. We were born in the same part of the country, came from the same culture, shared the same values and had the same sense of humor. He was extremely funny and found me amusing, and we had wonderful times. The character he invented, "Mr. Peepers," was no more like him than he was like Nancy Reagan. Wally probably came closer than anyone I've ever known to being a genius. He spoke four or five languages and could talk knowledgeably about botany, history, physics, chemistry, electronics and many more topics. If he had chosen to, he could have been an outstanding scientist. We liked to hike in the woods together and never returned without an interesting rock, a delicate leaf, a gnarled branch or a face full of poison oak. He was as absorbed as I was by human foibles, and was one of my greatest teachers. At twenty, I was untutored and uncertain in my use of language. Almost as if he were leading me by the hand, Wally taught me how to speak and to see in words the melodies of life. When he died, I felt mystified and could not accept it. I took some things that belonged to him, including the pajamas in which he died, and saved them. Even now I have conversations with him; I curse him—"You son of a bitch"—and chastise him for dying. I also laugh at things when I'm alone because I imagine that he is there, laughing with me.

Not a day goes by when I don't think of Wally. Sometimes I

wander around my house, pick up one of the chestnut walking sticks we brought home from a woodland long ago, think of something funny he said, and laugh. Then I swear at him, because he was an alcoholic who didn't take care of himself and died from a massive heart attack.

14

WHILE I WAS IN *I Remember Mama,* my mother returned to Libertyville and reconciled with my father. Not long after she left, I had a kind of nervous breakdown that came on gradually, then was severe for several months. I stopped eating, lost ten pounds and felt depressed and vulnerable, but didn't know why. I still acted every night, but I was in emotional disarray. I never missed a performance, but life made less and less sense to me. I moved into a one-room apartment at Fifty-eighth Street and Sixth Avenue, and despite bringing a new girl to my bed almost every night, I was often lonely. I couldn't stand to hear people argue. If I heard anyone quarreling, I felt as if I were being consumed by insects and had to leave. I couldn't stand loud voices or loud noises. Even the slamming of a door sent me into a panic. Something was frightening me, but I didn't know what. I couldn't sleep well, was nervous, and I sometimes thought I was losing my mind. If I was offended in the slightest, I wanted to punch somebody. Nothing I did made sense or made me feel better. I didn't know what to do. I wandered around the city or went into a Christian Science reading room, sat alone and read for hours. I had never had much religion in my life—neither of my parents were believers—though a few times my mother had encouraged me to look for solace in the faith of my grandmother and Mary Baker Eddy. So I did, searching for anything that could help me understand what was wrong with me and make me feel better. It was the beginning of a difficult period of my life.

I spent more and more time with Stella Adler's family, who virtually adopted me after my mother left, and they may have saved my sanity. Stella was the daughter of Sarah and Jacob P. Adler, a great star of the Yiddish stage, and her husband, Harold Clurman, was a prominent and respected writer, producer and critic. Having dinner with them was like spending an evening with the Marx Brothers. In Libertyville I'd only met one or two Jews and never experienced Jewish humor, which is subtle, powerful and hilarious. The Adlers were so funny that I was convulsed every time I went there; jokes flew around the dinner table like bullets, half in Yiddish and half in English, and I laughed so hard that I nearly got a hernia.

Like all of us, Stella was an imperfect person, and her imperfections sometimes offended others. To some people, she was downright nasty. She would excoriate them in front of others, tear them apart and criticize them in the most vicious way, but she had great integrity as a teacher. During that troubled time of my life, she taught me not only acting, but about life itself. For reasons that I cannot understand, she was very fond of me and I am eternally grateful to her for it. I always sat next to her at dinner, and she was forever holding my hand. Sometimes I went into her bedroom before she went out to dinner and watched her while she was getting dressed. She would be sitting in front of the mirror in her panties and bra and would cover herself as I came in and say, "Oh, Marlon. Please, darling. I'm getting dressed."

"That's why I'm here," I said, "in order to see that you're dressed *properly.*"

A couple of times I grabbed her breasts in my palms and she would say with a half smile, "Marlon, don't do that or I'll slap you."

I would look at her and say, "You know you don't want to do that to me."

We had a lot of flirtatious exchanges, and I suppose that somewhere not far beyond the horizon there was the possibility of a real encounter, but it never materialized.

There were three important teachers in my life. Like Duke Wagner and my shop teacher in Santa Ana, Stella gave me emotional strength at a time when I needed it by making me feel I was capable of something. When I was suffering, disjointed and disoriented, experiencing shock and feeling physically and emotionally disordered, she offered me not only her skill and talent as a teacher, but her home, her family, the largess of her personality and her love. She introduced me to her daughter Ellen, who, like Stella, was a beautiful, intelligent woman with a great deal of charm and presence, but who was almost always shorn of individuality by the presence of her mother. She was very photogenic and could have been a great screen personality, but because of conflicts with her mother, she never pursued the acting career that she should have had. After I met Ellen, one thing led to another, and I began a relationship with her that continued, off and on, for many years.

While I was being given a home and an education by the Jews who befriended me in New York, World War II was ending. The war had been remote from my vantage point of the Adlers' dinner table and the stage of the Music Box Theatre. No one had any real sense yet of what was happening to the Jews of Europe, and my knowledge of the war came mostly from the Translux Theatre on Forty-seventh Street and Broadway, where I went between shows to watch the pyrotechnics of mortal combat. While others were suffering and dying, to me the war had only meant not always getting the kind of cigarettes or candy I liked, crowded trains, a lot of people in New York wearing uniforms and the USO shows in which we performed. I had a sense that though the world had gone through a cataclysm, little had changed: in Harlem black people were still being treated as less than human, there was still rampant poverty and anti-Semitism and there seemed to be as much injustice as before. I was beginning to hear a voice in my head that said I had a responsibility to do something about it and that acting was not an important vocation in life when the world was still facing so many problems.

I was offered the chance to go on the road with *I Remember Mama,* but I was sick of it and turned it down. It had taken me only one role to realize how much I hated playing the same part eight times a week—six evenings and two matinees—in a long-running production. Luckily, before I ran out of money I was offered a part in a new Maxwell Anderson play, *Truckline Cafe,* which was to be produced by Elia Kazan, Harold Clurman and other members of the Group Theatre, including Stella, Cheryl Crawford and Lee Strasberg. In a letter I sent home telling my parents I had gotten the part, I told them:

What is with the U.S. mail system? I fully realize that a carrier pigeon is fairly dependable, but in recent years Mr. Farley has made great strides in the field of postal communication, believe me! So why are you not writing? What about a letter?

I am signed, sealed and delivered (the latter almost) into a show which was written by Max Anderson, to be produced by Harold Clurman and Elia Kazan and directed by H. Clurman. The play is called *Truckline Cafe*—a play that deals with returning vets. I have a good part, however comparatively small (for which I am glad), but they liked me so much they are willing to pay two hundred a week, of which I shall net, what with agency fees and tax, about $154. This will enable me to save and at the same time allow me to cover any additional expenses I might have. It's a good break!

Rehearsals start in two weeks. I leave "Mama" Feb. 6th. Got a nice long letter from Nana. She and you, Mom, are the greatest women in the world. I love you both dearly. It won't be long until I can give you the *world*.

Pop, you ain't 'rit' for years. I'm a little mad.

Love, all of it
Bud

P.S. Happy Birthday Pappy! I couldn't send a telegram because of the strike! The years to come will bring joy and contentment, Pop, if you let 'em, as Nana says.

Love and a kiss, old man
Me.

I was given the part in *Truckline Cafe* largely because of Stella. Harold had seen me in *I Remember Mama,* but was dubious until she persuaded him to take a chance on me; then he gave me a volcanic part, the role of a psychopathic soldier named Sage McRae who returns home from the war and discovers that his wife, played by Ann Shepherd, has been unfaithful to him while he was at war. At first he refuses to believe it, then confirms his suspicions and kills her. There is an explosive, incandescent moment in the play when Sage admits shooting his wife and then breaks down, and it electrified audiences.

On the eve of leaving New York for out-of-town tryouts, I sent a letter to my parents that seemed to express my optimism and idealism at the time:

Dear Folks:

Well, I leave for Schenectady on Wednesday 13th and open on the 16th, then to Baltimore for a week and on to Newark for a week, then to New York tentatively in the first week of March.

The show looks good. It's hard to tell at this stage of rehearsal just how good. My part is a sensational role that takes plenty of sweat. It's coming along all right, however. People that see it tell me I'm going to be very good, so I guess things will be O.K. I'm working like a truck and I hope to God the show is successful because I'd love a little rest and some time and money for piano and dancing lessons and a week or two in the country. On the other hand, it's well to keep busy and accomplishing every day. We've been on the go day and night for about a week and a half. All this plus doing my show (which I left last Thursday) and I am sufficiently enervated for any occasion . . .

You know, the more I hear the lines of the play, the more I am concerned that it is vitally urgent that every one of us do our utmost to arrange our lives in a rigidly self-disciplined pattern with precise direction and foresight in order to exist as a guide for others who are utterly confused and misdirected. Hysteria is as infectious as flu or dysentery. Half of the world is running crazily and fearfully toward the other half of the world with a lust for security, and it has no other choice than to meet the other half, which is rushing just as fast and just as scared, with a ripping smash that leaves the whole in the blue funks of blue funks. As Max Anderson says in the play, "You've got to take the lives in your two hands and change them—twist them and change them *till you make a way to live!*" If I see somebody who can take care of himself and live and work and be happy, then I can do the same. This is such a necessary play. *I hope to God it runs.*

Well, my sweet ones, good night for now.

Love, Bud

• • •

The play opened on February 17, 1946, at the Belasco Theatre. I got good reviews and so did Ann and Karl Malden, who became my lifelong friends, but the critics didn't like it and it closed after less than two weeks. Still, short-lived though it was, *Truckline Cafe* changed my life. Nothing, I learned, attracts women more than fame, money and success.

I was out of work only a few weeks. After *Truckline Cafe*, other job offers came in, including one from Guthrie McClintic, a producer, director and the husband of Katharine Cornell, who, with Helen Hayes and Lynn Fontanne, was one of the reigning queens of Broadway. Guthrie had seen *Truckline Cafe* and offered me the part opposite his wife, of Eugene March-banks, a young poet who falls in love with an older woman in George Bernard Shaw's *Candida*. Guthrie was an entertaining, emphatic man with a bizarre sense of humor and a hernia that kept popping out when he laughed; when it did, he punched himself in the groin and pushed it back, which made him laugh even harder. Katharine Cornell was proper, quite empty-headed and very beautiful. She had the kind of stage presence that made her a star without having to be good, and there was a nebulous quality to her acting that I found difficult to relate to onstage; performing with her was like trying to bite down on a tomato seed. She acted and spoke lines in ways that were some-times inconsistent with the character she was playing, but I tried to keep up with her. It was like two people dancing to a different beat, one of them constantly struggling to get in step with the other. Still, I enjoyed the play, which opened on my twenty-second birthday. Sir Cedric Hardwicke was in the cast, along with Wesley Addy and Mildred Natwick, whom I adored. Hardwicke was a Johnny One Note actor who had a single expression throughout the play and his career. He never blinked or flinched. Once he stood offstage watching me act, muttering and shaking his head in disapproval, and one of my friends heard him say, "Must be sex appeal." He was probably right because I was hopelessly miscast in the role.

After *Truckline Cafe* and *Candida,* more offers came in, including some from television and Hollywood. I was in one television show called *Come Out Fighting* in which I played a boxer, but which required the talents of a sprinter. Because the show was live, I had to make a twenty-five-yard dash every few minutes from one set to another without missing a beat. In the script, after supposedly losing a boxing match, I had to take a shower and create the impression that I was depressed. I stood in my shorts waiting for the water to hit me, but the prop man missed his cue and forgot to turn it on. The camera kept rolling, but no water came out of the spigot. I didn't know what to do, so I thought, "Well, I'll look up forlornly and regretfully at the showerhead and think about how awful it was to lose the fight." Meanwhile I tried to will water to flow out of the shower. Then suddenly a deluge of water hit my face and my body that was so cold that the prop man must have gotten it out of the freezing compartment of a refrigerator. The shock took my breath away and I wasn't sure I could live through it. But the camera was on me and I had to keep going. I yelled, "Jesus Christ," completely dropping out of character. Afterward, someone complimented me for a fine job of acting in the shower scene. This was my last experience with live television.

In those days the Hollywood studios all had scouts in New York who kept an eye out for new faces on Broadway. It was the twilight of the old system when the studios all kept large stables of actors, directors, writers and producers under contract. I got feelers from several that wanted me to sign a standard seven-year contract, but I said I wasn't interested; if a good story came along, I said, I might sign for a single picture.

One of the talent scouts got word to Joe Schenck, a Twentieth Century–Fox executive who was one of the pioneers in the movie business, that there was a young actor he might be interested in. I went over for an interview, and Schenck, a frail near-octogenarian who had all but been put out to pasture by the studio, looked at this young kid in front of him and said, "What have you done, son?"

"I've done a couple of plays—"

"Why don't you get your nose fixed?" he asked.

"Why should I get my nose fixed?"

"Because you'll look better," he said. Then he turned around and looked at a huge picture of Tyrone Power covering the entire wall behind him. "Well, we'll talk some other time," he said, and that was the end of my interview.

Broadway producer Edward Dowling told me that the American Theatre Wing was going to produce a new play by Eugene O'Neill and asked me to try out for it. Although I had read several of O'Neill's plays, including *Desire Under the Elms,* I'd always thought he was dour, negative and too dark, and I couldn't understand the philosophical import of what he was trying to say. But I told Mr. Dowling I'd come over for an audition. The night before, he sent me a copy of the script, which was about an inch and a half thick. I started reading it, but couldn't get through it because I thought the speeches were too long and boring. After reading about a tenth of it, I fell asleep. The next day I went to the theater and argued with Mr. Dowling and Margaret Webster, the coproducer, for about half an hour about why I thought the play was ineptly written, poorly constructed and would never be a success. "What did *you* think of it?" I finally asked. "Tell me its virtues."

I had to ask the question because even though I was spouting off with self-assurance, I hardly knew anything about it, since I hadn't even read all of the first act.

Patiently, Eddie told me why he thought it was a good play and what he thought O'Neill was trying to say. I continued bluffing, still not having any idea of what the story was about, and finally told him that I didn't want to do it.

Of course when it opened *The Iceman Cometh* was called O'Neill's masterpiece.

15

INSTEAD OF *The Iceman Cometh,* I acted in a play directed by Stella's brother Luther, *A Flag Is Born.* It was a powerful, well-written pageant by Ben Hecht with music by Kurt Weill, although it was essentially a piece of political propaganda advocating the creation of the state of Israel and indirectly condemning the British for stopping the Jewish refugees en route from Europe to colonize Palestine. At that time, September 1946, the New York Jewish community and Jews throughout the world were fixated on the future of Palestine and Zionism. I wanted to act in the play because of what we were beginning to learn about the true nature of the killing of the Jews and because of the empathy I felt for the Adlers and the other Jews who had become my friends and teachers and who told me of their dreams for a Jewish state. In hindsight, I think it was also because I was starting what would become a journey to try to understand the human impulse that makes it not only possible but easy for one group of people to single out another and try to destroy it. It was the beginning of a lifelong interest in the dark side of human behavior.

Everyone in *A Flag Is Born* was Jewish except me. Paul

Muni, the star, gave an astonishing performance, the best acting I have ever seen. I was onstage with him and he gave *me* goosebumps. His performance was magical and affected me deeply. He was the only actor who ever moved me to leave my dressing room to watch him from the wings. He never failed to chill me with one particular speech. I played a young Jewish firebrand named David struggling to find his way to Palestine; in a graveyard he meets the wounded and dying Tevya, a prophetlike man, played by Muni, who tries to help him but dies. David covers him with a Jewish flag, then exits, presumably to carry on the fight to make a homeland in Palestine. At the beginning of the second act I had a speech during which a sharp light came down from above and two other lights hit me from the side. It was a fiery, accusatory speech that began with a pause. I waited a long time after the curtain went up, then quietly said, "Where were you?" I paused again and said, "Where were you, Jews?" Another long pause, and then I started to yell at the top of my lungs, "Where were you Jews when six million Jews were being burned to death in the ovens? Where were you?" It sent chills through the audience, which was almost always all-Jewish, because at the time there was a great deal of soul-searching within the Jewish community over whether they had done enough to stop the slaughter of their people—some argued that they should have applied pressure on President Roosevelt to bomb Auschwitz, for example—so the speech touched a sensitive nerve. At some performances, Jewish girls got out of their seats and screamed and cried from the aisles in sadness, and at one, when I asked, "Where were *you* when six million Jews were being burned to death in the ovens of Auschwitz?" a woman was so overcome with anger and guilt that she rose and shouted back at me, "Where were *you*?"

At the time, I was outraged along with most people, Jews and gentiles alike, that the British were stopping ships from carrying the half-starved survivors of Hitler's death camps to a new life—people with little food, nothing to go on except a few dried-up handfuls of hope, including children still suffering from typhus and bleeding internally. That people fresh out of Bergen-Belsen, Dachau and Auschwitz should be stopped on the open sea by British warships and interned again behind barbed wire on Cyprus was enraging. I did not know then that Jewish terrorists were indiscriminately killing Arabs and making refugees out of them in order to take their land; nor did I understand that the British had taken it upon themselves to authorize the forced removal of millions of Arabs who had lived on that land as long as the biblical Jews had.

The play, as well as my friendship with the Adlers, helped make me a zealous advocate for Israel and later a kind of traveling salesman for it. I explained my plans in this letter to my parents shortly after the play closed:

Dear Folks:

I am now an active and integral part of a political organization, i.e., *The American League for a Free Palestine*. My job is to travel about the country and lecture to sympathetic groups in order to solicit money and to organize groups that will in turn get money and support us. The work will be approximately for two months. I don't know just exactly when I'm to be sent to Chicago.

The facts concerning the Palestine conflict are little known but nonetheless shocking. You wouldn't believe the injustices and cruelties that the British Colonial Office are capable of. I'm not being rash. We have had an intensive training period—three weeks—at the end of which there is no viewpoint that has not been presented fairly and unbiased. I am sending you some literature on the subject. We will be leaving in about a week's time.

I am not slighting my career nor am I slacking on my job. The work that we'll be doing won't be easy by any matter of means. It is a tougher and vastly more responsible job than anything the theater could offer. I'm going to do my best to add my little bit. I'm really stimulated more than I've ever been. I must rush away now. I will write in detail later.

After volunteering to raise money, I realized that the American Jewish community was divided over the issue of just how militant Jews should be in pursuing their aspirations for a homeland. Some supported David Ben-Gurion, who while publicly seeming to acquiesce to Britain's insistence that Jewish refugees be interned on Cyprus and other places, was secretly smuggling boatloads of them into Palestine. Others were more impatient and supported Jewish underground groups such as the Stern Gang and the Irgun Zvai Leumi, whose leaders believed that terrorism and military action were necessary to wear down British resistance and lead to the early creation of Israel. I sided with the militants, as did a lot of my Jewish friends. Seeing the films made during the liberation of the Nazi death camps had been a searing experience for me, and I thought that Jews, who had suffered so much, had to do whatever was necessary to acquire a safe place where they could not be punished further by the world. I contributed as much money as I could to the Irgun and helped raise money to buy food for the internment camps, then became a member of one of about twenty two-man teams that traveled around the country soliciting support for the League for a Free Palestine, which in fact was a front for the Irgun. In Jewish schools, synagogues and other places, we described how European Jews who had been lucky enough to survive Hitler's death camps were being imprisoned in displaced-person camps nearly as inhumane as those the Nazis operated. And we argued that the British had to be pushed out of Palestine. There was always a lot of yelling at the temples we visited between the Jews who favored Ben-Gurion's approach and those favoring the terrorists whom I supported and who at the time were called "Freedom Fighters." Now I understand much more about the complexity of the situation than I did then.

16

IN A LETTER written to my parents from Washington while I was helping the Irgun, I told them: "Washington is strongly anti-Negro and I'm getting awfully mad, so I hope we leave soon. Saw in the newsreel that the Ku Klux Klan is beginning to function en masse again. . . . It makes you gape in awe to think about it. When I get to Chicago, I'm going out to Libertyville to speak on the food drive. I send almost all my salary over to Europe, but I can't feel that it's enough. . . . No definite plans for the summer yet, but a thousand possibilities, maybe a play with Tallulah Bankhead . . ."

Edie Van Cleve wanted me to try out for a production of Jean Cocteau's *The Eagle Has Two Heads,* starring Tallulah, who was a close friend of Edie's. I would have done just about anything Edie asked me to because she was kind, extremely generous and helpful to me during those formative years. Besides, I needed the money.

Before Edie sent me to up to Tallulah's home in Westchester County for an audition, a friend told me that she was gay, but I quickly discovered otherwise. Tallulah was an example of a performer who wasn't much of an actress but who became a star because of a distinctive and unusual personality. She had an engaging deep voice, smelled of Russian Leather perfume and smoked English cigarettes, which she pulled out of a red box, pressed into a long silver holder, and lit slowly and deliberately, as if she were doing it onstage. She had a sharp nose and chin and a slash mouth—perfect casting for the Wicked Witch in *The Wizard of Oz*. With her low, alcohol-fouled voice, Tallulah could be very entertaining. She was intelligent and witty and told funny stories. She informed me she'd recently been involved with a man with a huge nose that was covered with warts; he was truly a monument to ugliness, she said, and after she spent a weekend with him, she told a friend she had performed fellatio on him.

Her friend, who knew how ugly the man was, said she was astonished. "How could you possibly have done that?"

"Darling," Tallulah said, "anything to get away from that face."

As soon as I finished the reading, Tallulah asked me to be in the play, but I think she was more interested in me for sex than for the part of Stanislas. After rehearsals started I discovered that she usually got sloshed early in the day and spent the remaining hours getting drunker. She began inventing reasons for me to visit her at the Elysee Hotel, supposedly to go over the script, and I dreaded it, but she was the star of the show and I needed the money. She would spend the early part of these evenings with her eyes at half-mast, her lips lurking around the fracture of a smile, and then begin the arabesque of seduction. She was forty-three, I was twenty-two, and apparently she liked young men. I have more compassion for her now than I did then. I've since met other actresses whose beauty and attractiveness was the core of their sense of self-esteem and have had difficulty accepting the loss of it as they grew older; like Tallulah, some of them have turned to younger men to restore what they think they've lost. Tallulah was like that, although I didn't understand it then.

I wrote Frannie about Tallulah after my first encounter with her: "My mind feels like ten octopi in a space the size of a matchbox, each trying to manicure just its own toenails." Frannie also saved a letter to my father:

Dear Pop:

I've been rehearsing day and night for about a week now. . . . Bankhead is O.K. to work with but she's quite despicable on social terms. I absolutely detest decadence, self-indulgence and her uncomplimentary familiarity with people. Her political views are gnarled and distorted. It's going to be a tough tour trying tactfully to avoid having her make altogether too many personal demands.

I'm going to act the part of a fresh young puritan and inspire her conscience to revise her mode of living . . .

Gee, I enjoyed having Mom here. She looks so wonderful. . . . I do hope she will have the time soon to do a little sitting on ass and doing what comes naturally. If she writes a play, I'll get it produced. She said wonderful things about you, Pop, which made me very happy and content. Do you think there is much chance of your coming to the opening, which will be sometime in Feb? I am enclosing a schedule of our run which will let you know where I am. And Pop, I want to thank you very much for sending me the money plan and the income tax dope. The reason I didn't want to take you up on the contract was because I felt very strongly that I must learn to handle money myself or suffer the consequences. . . . I'm having my salary made out in deposit-check form which will be mailed to my own bank on 57th Street each week. I'm opening a savings and checking account and am really and earnestly going to make my money work for me. My gratitude is much, Pop. You're damn swell to always offer your dummy son help when he thinks he does or doesn't need it . . . write soon.

My love to you, Pop
Bud

The play opened in New England with me playing Tallulah's young lover. I don't think I was very good. Among other things, I didn't have the accent right; I hadn't studied accents yet. Worse, whenever I was onstage with her and the moment approached when I was supposed to kiss her, I couldn't bear it. For some reason, she had a cool mouth and her tongue was especially cold. Onstage, she was forever plunging it into my mouth without so much as a how-do-you-do. It was like an eel trying to slide backward into a hole. At first I was as casual as I could be under the circumstances and tried to avoid her tongue without offending her, thinking, How am I going to keep the part? Her tongue would explore every cranny in my mouth before forcing itself down my throat. I tried to back away coyly, pretending my character was bashful, then I began kissing her on the neck, trying to look appropriately romantic as the male ingenue. But she didn't like neck kisses and lowered her head and pursued my mouth with her lips. I tried eating a lot of garlic, but that didn't stop her, so I asked a stagehand to buy me a bottle of mouthwash, and after each time I had to kiss her I went offstage and took a swig, but that didn't work either, so I bought a very strong astringent lotion and began gargling with it in the wings after every kiss.

Tallulah had experienced a lot of suffering and unhappiness in her life and liked to talk about it. I couldn't help feeling sympathy for her; she'd had it tough. I've always thought that if she hadn't been so banged up emotionally, she could have been a great actress and an extraordinarily attractive person, but I think she really cared more about fucking and alcohol than about performing. Unfortunately, a spy informed her that I was gargling after kissing her, and she was offended by this along with my refusal to visit her room anymore. She told the producers I wasn't right for the part, and after about six weeks of out-of-town tryouts I was fired, my virtue still intact. I would rather have been dragged over broken pottery than make love to Tallulah.

I was through with acting, I decided. After being fired, I wrote this letter to my parents from New Haven:

Dear Folks:

I leave 'Eagle Rampant' with this prayer: the next time T. Bankhead goes swimming I hope that whales shit on her. God preserve the lizards and let Tallulah die! It is almost over and so is my life. Horrors of horror . . . I'm going to school when I get back and take a course in piano and harmony and Katherine Dunham dance. I'm looking forward to it very much. I bought a flute and I am *great* on it. I'm soon going to have an upper lip not unlike a camel's or Pop's.

I met a little man on the train whose wife is fast becoming a drunk. I told him about A.A. and told him I would send him a book on A.A. What else should I do? When he talks to her about drinking, she gets mad and belligerent. What to do?

Love
Bud

The day I was fired, I had a bad cold and remember feeling vaguely depressed and relieved at the same time. On the train ride from Boston to New York that night, I fell asleep and somebody stole my wallet and about eight hundred dollars, all the money I had earned on the play. I arrived in New York with no money, holes in my socks and holes in my mind, not sure what I'd do next, but knowing I needed a job.

Then once again good luck came my way. A few weeks later I told my father about it:

Dear Pop:

Well, I'm all set. I start rehearsals Oct. 4th for a "Streetcar Named Desire." I'm getting $550 [a week] and second billing.

Elia Kazan is directing. The female lead—Jessica Tandy. Karl Malden plays supporting role. It's a strong, violent, sincere play—emotional rather than intellectual impact. Mom will write and tell you of my part.

Pop, I want the money I make to help in a large part to take the load you've been handling. I'm not counting my eggs, but I want it known that I would like to have my money be of use. We'll talk more of it when you come.

Bud

17

A COUPLE OF WEEKS before I sent that letter, Edie Van Cleve had informed me that Elia Kazan was planning to direct a new play by Tennessee Williams. Originally called *The Poker Night,* it had been renamed *A Streetcar Named Desire.* Jessica Tandy had already been chosen for the female lead of Blanche DuBois, but they were having trouble casting an actor to play the male lead, Stanley Kowalski.

John Garfield was originally set for it, but he wasn't able to come to terms with the producer, Irene Selznick, the daughter of Louis B. Mayer, the head of MGM, and the wife (though separated) of movie producer David O. Selznick. Next they offered it to Burt Lancaster, but he couldn't get out of a studio contract in Hollywood. Harold Clurman suggested me for the part to Kazan, but Gadg (Kazan's nickname) and Irene both said I was probably too young, and she was especially unenthusiastic about me. In the end they decided to leave it up to Tennessee Williams. Gadg suggested that I visit him on Cape Cod, where he had a vacation house, and loaned me $20 to buy a train ticket. But I was broke and spent most of it before leaving New York, so I had to hitchhike to Provincetown. It took longer than I expected and I was a day or two late for the reading. When I found Tennessee's house, he apologized because the toilet was overflowing, so I volunteered to fix it. I read for the part, we talked for an hour or so and then he called Gadg and said he wanted me to have the role.

Years later the executor of Tennessee's estate, Lady Maria St. Just, gave me a copy of the letter he sent his agent, Audrey Wood, after the reading, which reveals much of his vision of the play. She gave me permission to reprint the letter:

August 29, 1947

Dear Audrey:

. . . I can't tell you what a relief it is that we have found such a God-sent Stanley in the person of Brando. It had not occurred to me before what an excellent value would come through casting a very young actor in this part. It humanizes the character of Stanley in that it becomes the brutality or callousness of youth rather than a vicious older man. I don't want to focus guilt or blame particularly on any one character but to have it a tragedy of misunderstanding and insensitivity to others. A new value came out of Brando's reading which was by far the best reading I have ever heard. He seemed to have already created a dimensional character, of the sort that the war has produced among young veterans. This is a value beyond any that Garfield could have contributed, and in addition to his gifts as an actor he has great physical appeal and sensuality, at least as much as Burt Lancaster. When Brando is signed I think we will have a really remarkable 4-star cast, as exciting as any that could possibly be assembled and worth all the trouble that we have gone through. Having him instead of a Hollywood star will create a highly favorable impression, as it will remove the Hollywood stigma that seemed to be attached to the production. Please use all your influence to oppose any move on the part of Irene's office to reconsider or delay signing the boy, in case she doesn't take to him. I hope he will be signed before she shows in New York.

We have a full house this week, Joanna, Margo [Jones, a producer] and Marlon in addition to Pancho [Tennessee's companion] and I. Things were so badly arranged that Margo and Brando had to sleep in the same room—on twin cots. I believe they behaved themselves—the fools! We had fixed a double-decker bunk for Margo and Joanna to occupy but when Margo climbed into her upper bunk several of the slats refused to support her. Also the plumbing went bad, so we had to go out in the bushes.

I had a violent quarrel with the plumber over the phone so he would not come out. Also the electric wiring broke down and "plunged us into everlasting darkness" like the Wingfields at supper. All this at once! Oh, and the kitchen was flooded! Marlon arrived in the middle of this domestic cataclysm and set everything straight. That, however, is not what determined me to give him the part. It was all too much for Pancho. He packed up and said he was going back to Eagle Pass. However, he changed his mind, as usual. I am hoping that he will go home, at least to New Orleans, while the play is in rehearsal, until December. He is not a calm person. In spite of his temperamental difficulties, he is very lovable and I have grown to depend on his affection and companionship, but he is too capricious and excitable for New York, especially when I have a play in rehearsal. I hope it can be worked out to keep him in the South for that period or at least occupied with a job. That would make things easier for me . . .

With love,
Tennessee

After his success with *Streetcar,* Tennessee wrote other plays, but this play was the pinnacle of his career, and afterward he sort of wrote in circles, as if he didn't know where to go. He was locked in somehow. But at the height of his powers, he was an extraordinary writer as well as a lovely man, extremely modest and soft-spoken. Kazan accurately described him as a man with no skin: he was skinless, defenseless, vulnerable to everything and everybody, cruelly honest, a poet with a pristine soul who suffered from a deep-seated neurosis, a sensitive, gentle man destined to destroy himself. He never lied, never said anything nasty about anybody, and was always witty, but he led a wounded life. If we had a culture that gave adequate support and assistance to a man of Tennessee's delicacy, perhaps he could have survived. He was a homosexual, but not effeminate or outwardly aggressive about it, and he never made a pass at the actors in his plays. You wouldn't have known he was gay if he didn't tell you. But there was something eating at his insides that ultimately propelled him to his death.

A Streetcar Named Desire opened at the Ethel Barrymore Theatre in New York on December 3, 1947, after tryouts in New Haven, Boston and Philadelphia. My sister still has the telegram I sent to my father from Boston: NEED MONEY BY TONIGHT SHOW SPLENDID LETTER TO FOLLOW MARLON. After the opening night in New York, we went to the Russian Tea Room and read the reviews, starting with *The New York Times*. Before long, all the reviews were in and everyone relaxed; we had a hit.

A few writers have suggested that in portraying the insensitive, brutish Stanley Kowalski, I was really playing myself; in other words, the performance succeeded because *I* was Stanley Kowalski. I've run into a few Stanley Kowalskis in my life—muscled, inarticulate, aggressive animals who go through life responding to nothing but their urges and never doubting themselves, men brawny in body and manner of speech who act only on instinct, with little awareness of themselves. But they weren't me. I was the antithesis of Stanley Kowalski. I was sensitive by nature and he was coarse, a man with unerring animal instincts and intuition. Later in my acting career, I did a lot of research before playing a part, but I didn't do any on him. He was a compendium of my imagination, based on the lines of the play. I created him from Tennessee's words.

A lot of roles, I've since learned, have to be made up by the actor, especially in the movies. If you don't have a well-written story, the performer has to invent the character to make him believable. But when an actor has as good a play under him as *Streetcar,* he doesn't have to do much. His job is to get out of the way and let the part play itself. Improvisation doesn't work in a play by Tennessee Williams, just as it doesn't work in a play by Shakespeare. They give actors such good lines that the words carry them along.

Admittedly it is impossible for anyone to judge themselves objectively, but I have never believed that I played the part of Stanley successfully. I think the best review of the play was written by a critic who said I was miscast. Kim Hunter was terrific and well cast as Stella, and so was Karl Malden—a fine actor who, despite enormous success, has always remained one of the most decent men I've ever known. But I think Jessica and I were both miscast, and between us we threw the play out of balance. Jessica is a very good actress, but I never thought she was believable as Blanche. I didn't think she had the finesse or cultivated femininity that the part required, nor the fragility that Tennessee envisioned. In his view, there was something pure about Blanche DuBois; she was a shattered butterfly, soft and delicate, while Stanley represented the dark side of the human condition. When Blanche says to Stella, "Don't hang back with the beasts," she was talking about the animalistic side of human beings. It's true that Blanche was a liar and a hypocrite, but she was lying for her life—lying to keep her illusions alive. When she said, "I don't tell truth, I tell what ought to be true" and "I didn't lie in my heart," Tennessee meant those words. He told Kazan he wanted the audience to feel pity for Blanche. "Blanche," he said, "must finally have the understanding and

With Jessica Tandy in *A Streetcar Named Desire*. Laughs in the wrong places. (© Eileen Darby)

compassion of the audience . . . without creating a black-dyed villain in Stanley."

I think Jessica could have made Blanche a truly pathetic person, but she was too shrill to elicit the sympathy and pity that the woman deserved. This threw the play out of balance because the audience was not able to realize the potential of her character, and as a result my character got a more sympathetic reaction than Tennessee intended. Because it was out of balance, people laughed at me at several points in the play, turning Blanche into a foolish character, which was never Tennessee's intention. I didn't try to make Stanley funny. People simply laughed, and Jessica was furious because of this, so angry that she asked Gadg to fix it somehow, which he never did. I saw a flash of resentment in her every time the audience laughed at me. She really disliked me for it, although I've always suspected that in her heart she must have known it wasn't my fault. I was simply doing what the script called on me to do; the laughter surprised me, too.

But we had a wonderful play under us and it was a big success. An actor can never act his way out of a bad play; no matter how well he performs, if he doesn't have real drama beneath him he can act his best all day and it won't work. He could have the twelve disciples in the cast and Jesus Christ playing the lead and still get bad reviews if the play is poorly written. An actor can help a play, but he can't make it a success. In *A Streetcar Named Desire,* we had under us one of the best-written plays ever produced, and we couldn't miss.

18

THE INTERVALS of anxiety and depression that began when my mother left New York City continued off and on through the run of *A Streetcar Named Desire* and for long afterward. It would take years for me to escape my acceptance of what I had been taught as a child—that I was worthless. Of course, I had no idea then that I even had such feelings about myself. Something was chewing on me and I didn't know what it was, but I had to hide my emotions and appear strong. It has been this way most of my life; I have always had to pretend that I was strong when I wasn't. Nonetheless, sometime after the play opened I realized I needed help, and Gadg referred me to his psychiatrist, a well-known Freudian analyst in New York named Bela Mittelman, the coldest man I've ever known. I saw him for several years, seeking empathy, insight and guidance, but all I got was ice. He had absolutely no warmth. Even the furnishings in his office were frigid; I almost shivered every time I walked into it. Maybe he was following the rules of his particular school of psychiatry, but to me he had no insight into human behavior and never gave me any help. I was still on my own, trying to deal alone with emotions I didn't yet understand.

Why these feelings surfaced when they did, I don't know, although I suppose they had something to do with my mother going away. In New York I'd had another chance to offer her my love, which I did, but it hadn't been enough for her.

I didn't begin to understand the reason for any of these things until I was in my forties. Until then, I usually responded to emotions that I didn't understand with anger.

I've always thought that one benefit of acting is that it gives actors a chance to express feelings that they are normally unable to vent in real life. Intense emotions buried inside you can come smoking out the back of your head, and I suppose in terms of psychodrama this can be helpful. In hindsight, I guess my emotional insecurity as a child—the frustrations of not being allowed to be who I was, of wanting love and not being able to get it, of realizing that I was of no value—may have helped me as an actor, at least in a small way. It probably gave me a certain intensity I could call upon that most people don't have. It also gave me a capacity to mimic, because when you are a child who is unwanted or unwelcome, and the essence of what you are seems to be unacceptable, you look for an identity that *will* be acceptable. Usually this identity is found in faces you are talking to. You make a habit of studying people, finding out the way they talk, the answers that they give and their points of view; then, in a form of self-defense, you reflect what's on their faces and how they act because most people like to see reflections of themselves. So when I became an actor, I had a wide variety of performances inside me to produce reactions in other people, and I think this served me as well as my intensity.

I was always very close to my sisters because we were all scorched, though perhaps in different ways, by the experience of growing up in the furnace that was our family. We each went our own way, but there has always been the love and intimacy that can be shared only by those trying to escape in the same lifeboat. Tiddy probably knows me better than anyone else.

Not long ago, she wrote me a letter about my early years in New York:

"You were a twenty-three-year-old when all the 'Streetcar' stuff hit the fan—a kid—and you were just trying to get along. In the beginning, you really didn't have much control of your craft. You could only follow your instincts—good ones as it turned out—but how were you to know if the choices you were making were the right ones? Can anyone remember how insecure [it is to be] twenty-three and be suddenly saddled with all the kudos and the notoriety you received? It was embarrassing. You couldn't think it was deserved. You couldn't believe you were actually responsible, and Poppa had always said you'd never amount to a tinker's damn. What the hell was going on? Sure, it's nice to know you're doing something right for once, but can it rate all that? You became an actor because acting seemed to be the only thing you had any aptitude for, the only place you'd found where people said, 'You're pretty good at that.' And it was fun and a good place to hide. Most actors hide behind the characters they play. It's a way of exploring life from a lot of other folks' point of view. It is exciting to get to 'be' all those other people without the responsibility for their actions. The trouble is that the public identifies the actor with the characters he plays, and that creates a schism right there. . . . Certainly the perks and the money aren't bad. They can grease the skids, but everyone should know that money and perks can't buy the important things."

Was Jocelyn right when she said that rapid success and, more important, other people's reactions to it, were hard to handle for an uncertain kid from Illinois? It's difficult for me to remember exactly what I felt so long ago. What I remember most about *A Streetcar Named Desire* was the emotional grind of acting in it six nights and two afternoons a week. Try to imagine what it was like walking on a stage at 8:30 every night having to yell, scream, cry, break dishes, kick the furniture, punch the walls and *experience* the same intense, wrenching emotions night after night, trying each time to evoke in audiences the same emotions I felt. It was exhausting. Then imagine what it was like to walk off the stage after pulling these emotions out of yourself and waking up in a few hours knowing you had to do it all over again a few hours later. In sports I was always a very competitive person, and there was a fundamental part of me that was determined not to fail as Stanley Kowalski, to excel and be the best, so I applied pressure on myself to act the part well every time. But it was emotionally draining, wearisome, mentally oppressive, and after a few weeks I wanted out of it. I couldn't quit, however, because I had a run-of-the-play contract.

What I hated most was matinee days, when I'd wake up, look at the clock, discover I was late, and have to run across town to get to the theater on time. Several times I ran all the way from my apartment at Fifty-second Street and Fifth Avenue to Forty-second Street and Broadway for a matinee only to discover that it was the wrong day: it wasn't Wednesday or Saturday, and I could have slept longer. Most days, I got up about two in the afternoon after an adventure or two the night before, then fell asleep about an hour before I was supposed to be at the theater; when I woke up, I had to dash across town in a sweat. I was due there no later than eight-fifteen to put on makeup, but I liked to arrive a little earlier to lift some weights and work up a sweat to give Stanley the appearance I wanted for him. I usually showed up as late as I possibly could and sometimes got there late. I hated going to work.

Of course there were advantages to success in a Broadway play, and not merely the $550-a-week paycheck, which I suppose was equivalent to about $5,000 now. Although I'd told my

father when I was rehearsing for *The Eagle Has Two Heads*
that I wanted to look after my own financial affairs, he persuaded me that I was not only too busy, but too inexperienced
with money to handle it properly, so I turned my check over to
him; he paid my rent, gave me pocket change and invested the
rest. The money that came with *A Streetcar Named Desire* was
less important to me, however, than something else: every night
after the performance, there would be seven or eight girls waiting in my dressing room. I looked them over and chose one for
the night. For a twenty-four-year-old who was eager to follow
his penis wherever it could go, it was wonderful. It was more
than that; to be able to get just about any woman I wanted into
bed was intoxicating. I loved parties, danced, played the congas, and I loved to fuck women—any woman, anybody's wife.
Sometimes I did insane things. When I lived on the eleventh
floor of an apartment building on Seventy-second Street, I gave
a party one night where just about everyone, including me, was
smashed or close to it, and I went over to a window, opened it
and shouted to my guests: "I'm sick of this world and everything in it. I can't stand you people, I'm sick of this life." I
stepped out the window and disappeared. I stood on a ledge
about six inches wide beneath the window, ducked and lay flat
against the wall, and clung to the windowsill with my hands.
Then I held onto a cement balustrade on the side of the building
with one hand and let go of the windowsill. My guests
screamed. They thought I'd become a blotter on Seventy-second
Street. I hid under the window giggling, then looked down, saw
the street and gulped. Everyone was still screaming, and one girl
finally ran over to the window and looked up and down
Seventy-second Street, searching for my body before spotting
me. Then she said, "Go ahead, drop. See if I care." I crawled
back up, laughing. Everybody was red in the face. Their veins
were popping out of their foreheads, and everyone shook their
fists at me. It was nuts; I was fearless after two or three drinks.

We did a lot of crazy things in that apartment. Sometimes my friends and I took boxes of old-fashioned kitchen matches and emptied them out the window. When they hit the street, they would all ignite at once and create a spectacular show. Several times we tore the New York City telephone book to shreds and threw it out the window, or we'd rip *The New York Times* apart and fling the pieces out the window. I had many adventures when I lived in that apartment. One night a friend called and said, "I've got a couple of great groovy broads. They're driving around in a black Cadillac, they're well-heeled and lookin' good. You can have either one you want, but I think they've both 'got eyes.' " (In those days that was jargon for accommodating women.) The girls picked us up and I agreed with my friend Freddie that he was right. They were black, very attractive and wore sweet-smelling perfume that almost made me dizzy.

"Where should we go?" one of the girls asked, and I answered, "I don't know. I'm happy as a pig where I am." I was already starting to fool around with the girl in the backseat.

"How about going to our pad?" she said, and I said, "That's cool. Where is it?"

"Harlem."

A red light went off somewhere in my head, but I said, "Let's go, what the hell."

Her apartment was a third-floor walk-up. After we finished what we'd come there to do, I started playing cards with one of the girls in the kitchen while my friend and her friend returned to the bedroom. Suddenly I heard something outside that sounded like the footsteps of a raging dinosaur. I thought it was my imagination, but the dinosaur got closer and louder, then stopped in front of the door and started pounding, making me wonder fleetingly if dinosaurs had fists. The attractive woman sitting opposite me in her underwear suddenly looked at me with enormous eyes, her mouth forming a huge O. We heard louder and louder pounding on the door, and each time it caved in another inch.

"Who's that?" I asked, trying to seem calm.

"That's my *daddy*," she answered.

I said, "Your father?"

"Baby, that's my *daddy*."

I had never heard the phrase; I didn't know that some women referred to their boyfriends as their "daddies" or "my old man," but I got the drift. I looked at her as calmly as I could and said, "Do you have a fire escape in this building?"

She glanced in the direction of the bedroom, and I grabbed my clothes and shoes, shook Freddie and said, "I'm going out the fire escape because her *daddy*'s at the door. I'll meet you down the block if you're not coming right now."

But Freddie also got the drift and broke off what he was doing, and we ran down the fire escape as fast as we could. When we reached the bottom and the ladder lowered us to the sidewalk, we looked up three stories and saw a head shouting, "Hey, motherfuckers, you wait right there! Don't you be running!"

We ran like hell, but it had been well worth it. They were very attractive girls.

My pal that night was a friend I'd met in an acting class at the New School, Carlo Fiore, although he had changed his name to Freddie Stevens because he thought it would make it easier for him to get acting jobs. He was one of my first friends in New York, and we shared a lot of girls; he'd get one and I'd try to move in on him, or I'd get one and he'd try to get her in his bed.

Freddie had a huge Roman nose, spoke from the bowels of Brooklyn and didn't have much acting talent, all of which conspired to work against his becoming a star. He had his nose operated on two or three times, the last time by a surgeon who must have used a can opener instead of a scalpel, but it didn't help. He fancied himself an intellectual and budding member of the New York literati, and was so full of himself that one of our friends, paraphrasing Shakespeare, described the stories he told as "tales told by an idiot full of sound and Fiore, signifying nothing." Later I tried to get Freddie jobs, but never had much luck unless I could give him one myself. He was charming and funny but troubled; I don't know whether his lack of success as an actor contributed or not, but he became a junkie and tried hard to get me to take heroin—a "skin pop," as he called it. When I refused, he always said, "You don't know how to live." I watched him fall deeper and deeper into the abyss of addiction while doing whatever I could to make him stop. I was with him once when he tried to go cold turkey, and it was awful. He shook, shivered and threw up, and finally said he had to go home to his Italian neighborhood in Brooklyn and ask his family to help him. A couple of hours later he called me from home and told me frantically that he needed some Seconal. I bought some and went to his house, where I saw something very touching. He had once told me that his mother was mentally deranged, and when I arrived I could see in his face that he was ashamed of her, but he stood next to her lovingly and put his arms around her because he didn't want to reject her.

After I'd had some success as an actor, things began to sour between Freddie and me. He became envious then resentful of me, a problem I was starting to have with other friends, a lot of whom were actors or writers, especially if their careers weren't going well. It was hurtful to experience this because I was too young to understand it. Many years later, Janice Mars told me she thought Freddie in some ways was a victim of his friendship with me. "Poor Carlo just couldn't survive being your sidekick, and he never carved out a life for himself. . . . The attraction of your fame and money was too much for him. To be too close to you could be fatal. You were quicksand for anyone without the strength to pull out. It wasn't your fault. You wanted to help people, but at the same time their availability to you took priority over their own best interests. They lost themselves. Carlo ended up being expendable, involved in drugs, a hostage to failure."

Freddie finally got off dope, but then he became an alcoholic and wrote a book about me, probably all that he had left to sell. He continued on his path of self-destruction until he died.

19

IT STILL PLEASES ME to be awake during the dark, early
hours before morning when everyone else is still asleep. I've
been that way since I first moved to New York. I do my best
thinking and writing then. During those early years in New
York, I often got on my motorcycle in the middle of the night
and went for a ride—anyplace. There wasn't much crime in the
city then, and if you owned a motorcycle, you parked it outside
your apartment and in the morning it was still there. It was
wonderful on summer nights to cruise around the city at one,
two or three A.M. wearing jeans and a T-shirt with a girl on the
seat behind me. If I didn't start out with one, I'd find one. There
was a lovely Jewish girl named Edna whose father was very
rich. She was bright, well educated and beautiful, with lovely
brown hair and skin that was almost Oriental in color, and she
lived with her father in a deluxe apartment on Park Avenue. For
some reason, what I remember best about it were the drapes:
the windows were covered with two layers of gossamer white
curtains, first a lush tier of pleated satin, then floor-length folds
of feathery white silk with the texture of a bridal veil. About
two o'clock one morning, when I pulled up to her building on
my motorcycle, the doorman looked at me as if I were a long-

shoreman who'd taken a wrong turn on his way to the docks. I climbed off the motorcycle and asked him to call Edna on the house telephone and tell her that Mr. Brando wanted to see her.

"Do you know what time it is?" he asked.

I told him Edna was expecting me, which was not true, and said she would be very put out if she were informed later that I had called and not been allowed to come up.

With a doubtful look, the doorman dialed her apartment and woke her up. Over the phone, pressed to his ear, I heard a frail, sleepy voice say, "*Who?*"

"Mr. Brando."

I couldn't hear the next exchange, but the man hung up the phone and said, "Take the elevator to the left."

"I know it well," I said and turned my back on him to express how annoyed I was at the delay.

Edna's father was asleep in his bedroom and we went into hers. There was a soft breeze, and the silk and satin curtains billowed behind her like the canopy of a silken parachute. She was wearing a very attractive soft satin nightgown. I pulled the sheets back and was almost paralyzed by the fragrance of her warm body.

Edna didn't say anything while I got undressed. I got into bed and she put a soft, lovely arm around me. After we made love, she asked, "Would you like something to eat?" It was about four A.M. and still dark outside, although a narrow shaft of yellow moonlight pierced the curtains, casting a glow across the room. When I nodded, she went into the kitchen and fixed a tray set with Irish linen, English silver, French crystal, orange juice, eggs and perfectly done toast, all wonderfully arranged. I remember eating that breakfast with her beside me, the silver and crystal in front of me, thinking, This is the life, boy. If this ain't it, you're never gonna find it.

I had many romantic experiences like this, but I'll always remember that particular one. I don't know where Edna is now.

It's been years since I've spoken to her, but I've often wondered what became of her.

After the opening of *A Streetcar Named Desire,* Shattuck Military Academy began sending me letters inviting me to return. The commandant said that I was the most famous Shattuck man ever. "Please come back," he said, "we're really proud of you."

I always thought it was unstylish of them to do this after they had kicked me out, and I ignored the letters. I've never gone back to Shattuck and never intend to.

20

FOR A LONG TIME I had the adolescent notion that I was a tough guy. I liked to box because of a silly idea that it would make me more of a man. I wanted to be tough like my father, who was not only a good boxer but a mean barroom fighter. I'm not saying I consciously wanted to be *like* my father—that was the last thing I wanted because I hated him—but I probably absorbed some of his characteristics inadvertently. He was a strong man; I may have believed that being strong meant being worthy, and, in my twenties, I considered myself a pretty decent boxer. During the run of *Streetcar,* I often persuaded a member of the crew to spar with me between acts. I bought some gloves and we threw a few punches at each other in a room underneath the stage. It helped to pass the time and to relieve the boredom when I wasn't onstage. One night during the intermission between the second and third acts, I had about forty minutes before going on, but none of my regular partners wanted to box. I asked a stagehand I'd never sparred with if he'd join me, but he refused.

"C'mon," I said, "we're not going to *fight,* we're just gonna box a little."

He was a big guy in his early twenties with a thick mop of

wavy black hair, about six foot four and 220 pounds. "I don't feel like it," he said.

"You need some exercise, and so do I," I said.

"No."

I kept it up, but he kept refusing until finally I talked him into it, probably because he'd decided I wouldn't stop pestering him until he did. We went downstairs, put on the gloves and started sparring, but he was lethargic, so I said, "Come on, give me something I can work with. I'm trying to work on defense. *Hit me*. I'm not going to hurt you, for Chrissake."

But he kept up his little patter of soft thrusts against my gloves until I said, "*Come on, would you please throw a real punch? I'm not going to hurt—*"

I don't remember exactly what happened next, but I felt his fist smash into my nose like a sledgehammer, and the next instant blood poured out of it in a crimson deluge. Until then I'd never been hurt while boxing, but now I was really in pain. I went upstairs to my dressing room, looked in the mirror and saw my face covered with blood. As I tried to wipe it away I took a drag on a cigarette and saw something startling: the smoke from my cigarette was billowing out of my forehead in a big, white cloud.

It struck me that something was drastically wrong. I looked again in the mirror and saw that my nose was split across the bridge and that the smoke was taking the path of least resistance.

How did I get into this mess? I asked myself. In less than a minute, I had to go out onstage. According to the script, I was coming home after having gotten drunk celebrating the birth of my child, and after arguing with Jessica I was going to pick her up and carry her off to bed. With not much choice, I wiped my face and walked onstage.

Jessica, who had always disapproved of my boxing between acts, looked up at me from behind the desk where she was sitting and ad-libbed, "*You bloody fool.*"

We finished the scene and the third act as if nothing had happened, though when I picked her up and laid her down on the bed, I felt so nauseous for a moment from swallowing blood that I nearly passed out on top of her. But apparently no one in the audience knew the difference; they probably assumed I'd gotten into a bar fight or other mischief while I was offstage celebrating fatherhood, and that my blood was makeup.

When we took our curtain call, blood was still cascading out of my nose and falling on my shoes, shirt, pants and onto the stage. Then I went to the hospital, where I was treated by a butcher and sadist. He began by trying to put my nose back together by squeezing the bones in his fingers without giving me any anesthesia. I have a high threshold of pain, but he quickly surpassed it: he kept squeezing and pressing until I was barely conscious. Finally he got the nose stabilized, put a piece of tape over it and that was that. For a long time, I wanted to break the nose of that son of a bitch, even though he did me a favor by ordering me to spend a week in the hospital so my bones could heal. I was delighted to have a vacation. Jack Palance took over the part and I had a lot of fun taking the nurses up to the roof. I didn't have to go to work, but still got paid for it.

After several days, the discoloration around my eyes started to fade and my swollen nose got smaller. When I began looking fit enough to go back to work, the doctor said, "Mr. Brando, I have some good news for you: I think you should be getting out of here in a day or two."

I didn't want to leave yet. I was enjoying it too much. Then I heard that Irene Selznick was coming to the hospital to see me. I asked a friend to go a theatrical supply store and buy some makeup. He brought back a rainbow of colors—yellow, green, purple, red and blue—and I made up my eyes until they looked like I'd just had a run-in with a bus on Fifth Avenue. Then I wrapped a big padded bandage over my nose, making it look as swollen as a melon.

When Irene walked into my room, I sank into my bed with

the covers up to my chin, my eyes half closed, and asked wearily, "Irene, when are they going to let me out of here?"

From the frightened look on her face, I knew she was stunned. She looked down at me and said, "My God, Marlon. You can't go back to work. You stay right where you are; we'll get by without you until you're better. Get some rest. We'll tell you when it's time for you to get out."

"*Please,*" I said. "Irene, I'm dying in here, I've got to get out."

"You stay right where you are," she ordered.

So I got another week in the hospital.

21

WHEN *A Streetcar Named Desire* closed in 1949, after a run of two years, I spent three months in Europe, mostly in Paris, picking up a little French and having a wonderful time. I was one of the wild boys of Paris. I did everything, slept with a lot of women, had no sense of time and slept until two P.M. every day. Anything that was imaginable, I did in Paris. When I returned to New York, most of my clothes and almost everything else I owned were gone. I'd always been generous with my friends and had given away a lot of the money I made, but if I didn't give it, sometimes they stole it. One night I awoke and looked up at the face of one of my closest friends. There was a table between us; on it was a box where I kept my money and his hands were in it. When I opened my eyes, he withdrew his hands, put them on his hips, said "Hi," and gave me the look of a jackal. He wasn't the only friend who took advantage of the fact that I didn't pay much attention to material things, and when I was in Paris some of these friends came to my apartment, fought over my clothes and stole everything in sight.

The success of *Streetcar* meant I'd found a way to support myself in a fashion I liked, but it also skewed and shaped my life in ways that saddened me. Fame cuts two ways, I learned: it has at least as many disadvantages as it does advantages. It gives you certain comforts and power, and if you want to do a favor for a friend, your calls are answered. If you want to focus attention on a problem that bothers you, you may be listened to—something, incidentally, that I find ludicrous because why is a movie star's opinion valued more than that of any other citizen? I've had interviewers ask me questions about quantum physics and the sex life of fruit flies as if I knew what I was talking about—*and I've answered the questions!* It doesn't matter what the question is; people listen to you. A lot of reporters have come to see me after having already written their articles in their heads; they expect Marlon Brando to be eccentric, and so they say to themselves, I'll ask him a silly question and he'll answer it.

The power and influence of a movie star is curious: I didn't ask for it or take it; people *gave* it to me. Simply because you're a movie star, people empower you with special rights and privileges. Fame and its effects on people are a fairly new phenomenon; until a couple of centuries ago, unless they were royalty or a religious prophet whose image was polished by their court or disciples who produced Scripture and Holy Writ, people were seldom famous beyond their own villages. Most people couldn't read, and what knowledge they had was passed on via word of mouth. Then along came better schools, newspapers, magazines, the dime novel, radio, movies and television, and fame became an instant global commodity. It took 1,500 years for Buddhism to travel up the Silk Road and establish itself in China; it took only two weeks for the Twist to go from the Peppermint Lounge to Tahiti. A century and a half ago, many Americans didn't know who they had elected president until weeks after an election because it took that long for news to reach the hinterlands. Now when something happens in Bombay, people from Green Bay to Greenland know it instantly; a face is recognized around the world and people who have never accomplished anything become professional celebrities.

A lot of people who don't have it lust after fame and find it impossible to imagine that someone else wouldn't be interested in being famous; they can't envisage anyone turning his back on fame and all its appurtenances. But fame has been the bane of my life, and I would have gladly given it up. Once I was famous, I was never able to be Bud Brando of Libertyville, Illinois, again. One of my consistent objections to my way of making a living has been that I have been forced to live a false life, and all the people I know, with the exception of a handful, have been affected by my fame. To one degree or another everybody is affected by it, consciously or unconsciously. People don't relate to you as the person you are, but to a myth they believe you are, and the myth is always wrong. You are scorned or loved for mythic reasons that, once given a life, like zombies that stalk you from the grave—or newspaper-morgue files—live forever. Even today I meet people who think of me automatically as a tough, insensitive, coarse guy named Stanley Kowalski. They can't help it, but it is troubling. We are all voyeurs to one degree or another, including me, but with fame comes the predatory prowl of a carrion press that has an insatiable appetite for salaciousness and abhors being denied access to anyone, from pimps to presidents (a journey that becomes shorter every year), and, confused and resentful because it can't get what it wants, resorts to inventing stories about you because it is part of a culture whose most pressing moral imperative is that anything is acceptable if it makes money.

I'm not an innocent: I do things for money, too. I've made stupid movies because I wanted the money. I'm writing this book for money because Harry Evans of Random House offered it to me. He said that if his company published a book about a movie star, the profits would enable him to publish books by talented unpublished authors that might not make money. At least he was honest, although I thought it was odd for him to admit that he published trashy books so that he could issue those that had real value. In his own way, Harry is a hooker just like me, looking for a way to make money any way he can. I'm only a hooker who has been working the other side of the street. A little self-hatred? I think not, but I admit to perhaps a touch of vanity in being able to see it clearly and confess it.

Alice Marchak, my secretary for over thirty years, once said she thought I had a kind of split personality: one side of me enjoys the recognition and power of being a movie star while the other side hates the part of me that enjoys it. I doubt this, but it's impossible to understand oneself. There are yogis and swamis who have lived close to their unconscious, who have a sense of their own character and know themselves deeply, but most people cannot allow themselves to see what they actually are because everybody has a mythological sense of himself. The person Alice sees is not the person somebody else would see. Wally Cox, who was like my brother, would not see me that way. Everyone we know in our lives views us through a slightly different prism. These are Alice's impressions, and they are right in respect to the lens through which she looks at me. Everything is perception. There is no such thing as being able to judge anything objectively. It is a pose that scientists have foisted upon the world.

Other than the money, have I enjoyed being a movie star? I don't think so, regardless of Alice's opinion. I have always examined myself with precision and determination. Ever since I was young, I have attempted to find out what was unbalanced about myself. I've had to take hard looks at my vanities and sullied ambitions in order to find solutions to a pattern of behavior that seems difficult to change. But I don't see anything in my career, or in the manner in which I pursue life, that indicates I have ever been in love with the accolades of fame.

No, I don't think I have ever liked being a movie star. I think of myself as one of a race apart from other actors. Not that I condemn them or what they have done; I simply don't want to be considered among them. When I was thirty, I tried to express some of my feelings in a letter to a young woman who'd sent me an adoring letter about *The Wild One:* "Dear Cleola . . . thanks for your kind letter. It really was very flattering. You shouldn't make such a fuss about me, though, because I am simply a human being just like you. I am happy and sad, quiet and gay—in short, nothing more or less than one of some four billion human animals on the earth. Don't make something out of me that I am not."

But I've learned that no matter what I say or do, people mythologize me. The greatest change that success has brought me has nothing to do with my concept of myself or my reaction to fame, but of *other* people's reactions to it. I haven't changed. I have never forgotten my life in Libertyville when I felt unwanted, and my formative years when I didn't have the advantages I do now. I have always been suspicious of success, its pitfalls and how it can undo you.

All in all, I think it would have been better not to have been famous because my entire adult life's experience, my view of life, and the lives and outlook of my friends and family, have been colored and distorted by it. If Janice Mars was right in believing that intimacy with a famous friend can victimize those around him, there is also a flip side: people without fame try to attach themselves to it, making it difficult to trust anyone. Ever since I became famous, it's been difficult for me to judge if a potential friend was attracted to me or to my fame and to the myths about me. It is the first thing I notice. And even though they may say it doesn't, my fame affects them. I've given jobs to friends, then discovered they were using me, or worse, stealing from me. I have also been disappointed when former friends like Carlo Fiore, having led empty lives and with nothing else to sell, have chosen to publish intimate, private accounts about our friendship. But I suppose they were simply trying to pay their bills and survive.

Once you are famous, everything and everybody changes. Even my father. After *A Streetcar Named Desire,* he started doing something that really annoyed me: he began calling me Marlon. Until then he'd always called me Bud or Buddy like everyone else in the family. Ever since then, it has annoyed me deeply whenever somebody who once called me Bud begins calling me Marlon or somebody who called me Marlon begins calling me Bud.

The worst thing that can happen when someone becomes famous is for him to believe the myths about himself—and that, I have the conceit to say, I have never done. Still, I am stung by the realization that I am covered with the same muck as some of the people I have criticized because fame thrives in the manure of the success of which I allowed myself to become a part. Though I am not directly responsible, I could have chosen a less putrid trail to walk, but without a high school education, and with no sense that becoming famous would put me next to a sewage plant, I was obliged to develop indifference to the consequences.

I never planned or aspired or had any ambition to become a movie star. It just happened. I never felt a passion to act for any other reason than to supply myself with the needs of life. When it happened, I was grateful to find something at which I could make a living. I didn't have anything better to do, acting didn't grate on me, and after a while I could do it without expending a lot of effort. Later, when it became less enjoyable, it was still the best way I knew to make a lot of money in a short time. To me, acting has always been only a means to an end, a source of money for which I didn't have to work very hard. The hours are short, the pay good, and when you're done, you're as free as a bird. Acting is like playing house. I don't look down on it, but I have always been much more interested in other aspects of life. Sometimes the themes of plays and movies I have been in have been interesting, but the acting itself doesn't really absorb me. It has advantages over some jobs. I wouldn't have wanted to spend my life as a real estate salesman or lawyer. Any nine-to-five job I don't think I could bear. I don't do well under circumstances in which I have to be highly disciplined and responsible to other people. But if a studio offered to pay me as much to sweep the floor as it did to act, I'd sweep the floor. Better yet, I would just as soon someone drove up to my house once a week, handed me some money and said, "Good morning, Marlon, how you doing?"

"Just fine, thank you. See you next week when you bring more money."

After I returned from Paris, there were a lot of proposals for new plays and movies, and I accepted one of them—a one-picture deal, not a seven-year studio contract. It was *The Men*, a story about a group of paraplegic and quadriplegic soldiers in a California Veterans Hospital after World War II. The producer was Stanley Kramer, and the director was Fred Zinnemann. The script by Carl Foreman was a good one. I played a young army lieutenant, Ken Wilocek, whose spine had been smashed by a German sniper's bullet in the closing days of the war. I had no idea what it was like to be confined to a wheelchair or to spend the rest of my life in one, so I asked to be admitted to the Birmingham Veterans Hospital in southern California as a paralyzed veteran with a background similar to Ken Wilocek's. A few patients and members of the staff were informed, but most of the patients didn't know I was an actor, and because it was my first movie, no one recognized me. For three weeks I tried to do everything the patients did and learn what their lives were like. The first thing I discovered was that they hated pity. Once

I was a crippled army lieutenant in my first movie, *The
Men,* with Teresa Wright (top)
and Jack Webb (bottom).
(United Artists Corporation)

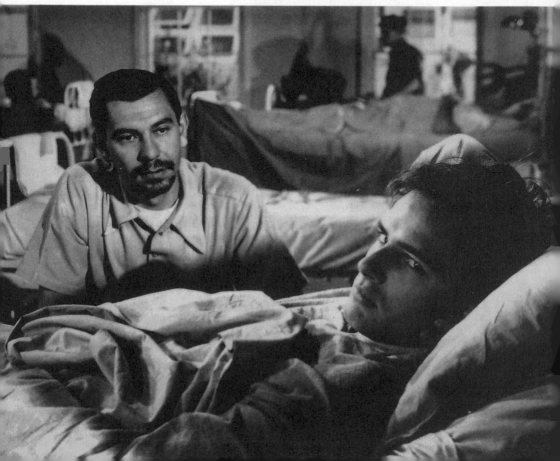

we went out for dinner to an Italian restaurant on Ventura Boulevard, all of us in our wheelchairs, and a woman came over and said to us, "I'm so proud of you, boys. I know what you've done for your country."

She kept repeating herself, going on and on while the guys became increasingly uncomfortable. They didn't want her pity. They weren't interested in what she had to say; the only thing they wanted to do was enjoy their night out.

"I know you boys will be able to walk someday. You just have to work hard and you'll do it. I have faith in God that he will help you and you'll be all right. You've got to believe because you are with the Lord and the Lord is with you and will help you."

They were really getting sick of her, so I said, "You know, ma'am, I believe you. I believe in the Lord."

"Well," she said, "I *want* you to believe. You should believe it, soldier, because I know that with the Lord's work you can recover."

I said, "I *do* believe! I *do* believe! I feel the Lord has come right into this room and into my body. The Lord is in my body! I feel it . . ."

I got up and started tap dancing, then ran around the restaurant and sprinted out the door shouting, *"Hallelujah!"*

The guys in their wheelchairs cracked up. Unfortunately they didn't get many laughs. They were young, virile men—some of them seventeen- or eighteen-year-old boys with good brains who were trapped in inoperative bodies and would never be able to move their arms or legs or make love. Many fought like tigers to make the most of their broken bodies; some put paintbrushes in their teeth and created beautiful paintings. But it was excruciatingly difficult; many were upbeat and determined to get on with their lives, while others gave up. Perhaps the saddest aspect of these men was that they believed they had let their wives down; in most cases, they had lost their capacity for sexual performance, and it ate at them. Some told me that the emotional pain of knowing that their wives did not want to be dishonest and disloyal, yet realizing that eventually they would succumb to temptation, was worse. Some of the friends I made at Birmingham killed themselves, unable to take it anymore.

I don't know whether making *The Men* had anything to do with it, but when the army tried to draft me for the Korean War, I wasn't interested. During World War II I'd been ready, but by 1950 I was more savvy about the world—or so I thought. I had read enough to become more skeptical about what my government did in my name.

Notified that my draft status had been changed from 4-F to 1-A, I went to the induction center in New York. I'd had an operation on the knee I injured at Shattuck, and was no longer lame enough to be excluded from the draft. I was given a questionnaire and instructed to fill it out.

Race?

"Human," I wrote.

Color?

"Seasonal—oyster white to beige."

When an army doctor asked me if I knew of any reasons why I shouldn't be inducted into the armed services, I answered, "I'm psychoneurotic."

He referred me to a psychiatrist, who asked, "Why do you think you are psychoneurotic and unsuitable for military service?"

"I had a very bad history in military school," I answered. "I don't respond well to authority and I got kicked out. Besides, I have emotional problems."

Skeptically the doctor asked if I was being treated for any psychological problems, and I told him that I was seeing Dr. Bela Mittelman.

He gave me a funny look and said, "Who?"

"Bela Mittelman."

"Bela Mittelman! For Chrissake, where is he?"

I said he had an office down the street about two blocks away.

"I'll be goddamned," he said. They were old friends. Then he scribbled on my induction papers: "Not suited for military service."

We chatted a few more minutes, and then as I was going out the door, he gave me his card and said, "Tell Bela to call me."

I answered, "He's in the book, but I'll tell him . . ."

And that was why I didn't go to Korea.

22

MY SECOND MOTION picture was *A Streetcar Named Desire*. Although Hollywood censors sapped Tennessee's story of some of its sting, I thought it was better than the play. Vivien Leigh, who had played Blanche in the London stage production, was brought over from England for the movie, and I've always thought it was perfect casting. In many ways she *was* Blanche. She was memorably beautiful, one of the great beauties of the screen, but she was also vulnerable, and her own life had been very much like that of Tennessee's wounded butterfly. It had paralleled Blanche's in several ways, especially when her mind began to wobble and her sense of self became vague. Like Blanche, she slept with almost everybody and was beginning to dissolve mentally and to fray at the ends physically. I might have given her a tumble if it hadn't been for Larry Olivier. I'm sure he knew she was playing around, but like a lot of husbands I've known, he pretended not to see it, and I liked him too much to invade his chicken coop.

Making the movie reinforced my decision not to take on another Broadway play. I've heard it said that I sold out to Hollywood. In a way it's true, but I knew exactly what I was doing. I've never had any respect for Hollywood. It stands for

The screen version of *A Streetcar Named Desire,* with Vivien Leigh. (Warner Bros./Courtesy Kobal Collection)

With Elia Kazan, a very rare kind of director. (Warner Bros.)

avarice, phoniness, greed, crassness and bad taste, but when you act in a movie, you only have to work three months a year, then you can do as you please for the rest.

Although I decided not to make another long-term commitment to the stage, I was glad to get back to New York after the filming of *Streetcar*. I lived in an apartment at Sixth Avenue and Fifty-seventh Street near Carnegie Hall and dropped in from time to time at the Actors Studio to meet girls. One of them was Marilyn Monroe, who was being exploited by Lee Strasberg. I had first met her briefly shortly after the war and bumped into her again—literally—at a party in New York. While the other people at the party drank and danced, she sat by herself almost unnoticed in a corner, playing the piano. I was talking to someone with a drink in my hand, having a good time, when someone tapped me on the shoulder; I spun around quickly and hit her with a sharp elbow to the head. It was a solid knock and I knew it must have hurt.

"Oh, my God," I said, "I'm sorry. I'm really sorry. It was an accident."

Marilyn looked me in the face and said, "There are no accidents."

She meant it to be funny and I laughed. I sat down beside her and said, "Let me show you how to play a piano. You can't play worth a damn."

I did my best for a few bars; then we chatted, and thereafter I called her from time to time. Finally one night I phoned her and said, "I want to come over and see you right now, and if you can't give me a good reason why I shouldn't—maybe you just don't want me to—tell me now."

She invited me over, and it wasn't long before every soldier's dream came true.

Marilyn was a sensitive, misunderstood person, much more perceptive than was generally assumed. She had been beaten down, but had a strong emotional intelligence—a keen intuition for the feelings of others, the most refined type of intelligence. After that first visit, we had an affair and saw each other intermittently until she died in 1962. She often called me and we would talk for hours, sometimes about how she was beginning to realize that Strasberg and other people were trying to use her. She was becoming a much healthier person emotionally. The last time we spoke was two or three days before she died. She called from her home in Los Angeles and invited me to come over for dinner that night. I said I had already made plans for the evening and couldn't, but I promised to call the following week to set a date for dinner. She said, "Fine," and that was it. It's been speculated that she had a secret rendezvous with Robert Kennedy that week and was distraught because he wanted to end an affair between them. But she didn't seem depressed to me, and I don't think that if she was sleeping with him at the time she would have invited me over for dinner.

I'm pretty good at reading people's moods and perceiving their feelings, and with Marilyn I didn't sense any depression or clue of impending self-destruction during her call. That's why I'm sure she didn't commit suicide. If someone is terminally depressed, no matter how clever they may be or how expertly they try to conceal it, they will always give themselves away. I've always had an unquenchable curiosity about people, and I believe I would have sensed something was wrong if thoughts of suicide were anywhere near the surface of Marilyn's mind. I would have known it. Maybe she died because of an accidental drug overdose, but I have always believed that she was murdered.

Another friend from that era who died sadly and prematurely was Montgomery Clift. We were both from Omaha and broke into acting about the same time. We had the same agent, Edie Van Cleve, and, although he was four years older than me, we were sometimes described as rivals for the same parts. There may have been a rivalry between us—in those days I was a competitive young man determined to be the best and he was a very good actor—but I don't remember ever feeling that way about him. In my memory he was simply a friend with a tragic destiny.

We met while I was in *Truckline Cafe*. By then Monty had been in several plays, and I was curious about how good he was and went to see him in *The Searching Wind*. He *was* good, and after the play I introduced myself and we went out for dinner. Since we shared a lot of similar experiences, there was a lot to talk about and we became friends, though not close ones. There was a quality about Monty that was very endearing; besides a great deal of charm, he had a powerful emotional intensity, and, like me, he was troubled, something I empathized with. But what troubled him wasn't evident. Later on, I went out with a girl he had dated, and she said she thought he might be a bisexual or a homosexual, but I found it hard to believe. I never asked him and never suspected it, but if he was a homosexual, I imagine he was torn asunder by it. Whatever the reason, he was a tortured man, and to deaden his pain he began drinking chloral hydrate and then became an alcoholic.

At the time I didn't understand what was happening or why Monty wanted to destroy himself, but it was tragic to watch. By 1957, when I was in *The Young Lions*, nobody wanted to hire him, but I encouraged the producers to give him a job. It had been hard for him to find work after being injured in a bad car wreck not far from my house, and his upper lip was paralyzed. He'd had plastic surgery, but the doctors hadn't been able to repair the damage completely. He could smile with his eyes, but his upper lip wouldn't move, giving him a twisted, confused look. He had always taken great pride in his looks, and he was self-conscious about the injury.

When Monty showed up in Paris for *The Young Lions*, he was consuming more chloral hydrate and alcohol than ever. His face was gray and gaunt, and he had lost a lot of weight. I saw he was on the trajectory to personal destruction and talked to him frankly, opening myself completely to him; I told him about my mother's drinking and my experiences with therapy and said, "Monty, there's awful anguish ahead for you if you don't get hold of yourself. You've got to get some help. You can't take refuge in chemicals, because that's a wall you can't ever climb. You can't get around it, you can't drive through it. You're just gonna die sitting up huddled in front of that wall."

I gave him the name of a therapist I thought might be able to help him, encouraged him to join Alcoholics Anonymous and talked to him for hours trying to persuade him to stop taking dope and alcohol. But when we shot the picture, he often slurred his lines. I tried to shore him up and did the best I could to get him through the picture, but afterward his descent continued until he died in 1966 at the age of forty-six.

I do not know for a fact that Monty was a homosexual. Afterward, some people told me he was, but I have heard so many lies told about myself that I no longer believe what people say about others. I do know he carried around a heavy emotional burden and never learned how to bear it.

23

WHEN I LIVED in the apartment at Fifty-seventh Street and Sixth Avenue, someone began making anonymous telephone calls to me that always followed the same pattern: the phone would ring, I would pick it up and say "Hello," there would be silence and then the caller would hang up. Then a few minutes later, the phone would ring again and the caller would listen silently while I kept repeating, "Who is this? Why don't you say something? Look, I think it would be advisable for you to see a psychiatrist at your earliest convenience."

After about three months, the caller, a woman, spoke for the first time in frightened, tremulous low tones. I asked her who she was and why she kept calling me, and finally wheedled some answers out of her; she said she had been fixated on me for years, ever since *A Streetcar Named Desire* was on Broadway. I asked her what she did for a living and she said that she was a hold-up artist—that is, she masterminded robberies, mostly of liquor stores; she planned the "jobs," as she put it, while a deaf-and-dumb friend who drove a motorcycle did the dirty work. After a three-hour conversation, she revealed that for months she and this friend had been making plans to kidnap me and take me to Long Island, where she was going to imprison and cannibalize me.

I didn't know if she was crazy or serious, but realized that whether it was fact or fantasy, I was dealing with a very disturbed mind. I finally decided that she was deadly serious; she explained in great detail how she was going to kidnap me, and she clearly had an intimate knowledge of my life and routine. She said that she had made her deaf-and-dumb friend tear down a billboard of *A Streetcar Named Desire,* and had papered her entire bedroom with it—walls, ceiling and floor. Sometimes she locked herself in her room without food or water and spent days just looking at the pictures, she said; she also kept a picture of me beneath her pillow and talked to it. After she captured me, she said she was going to eat me because she loved me.

I decided to meet this woman face-to-face. I was interested to find out why anyone could develop such a fixation, the depth of her disorder and the seriousness of her imbalance. I invited her to my apartment, and when she arrived I opened the door, with the chain still in place, and looked past her to see if her deaf friend was hiding behind her. I told her to stick her hands through the opening, held them with one hand, and reached out and frisked her with the other to make sure she didn't have a gun. She didn't, but when I unbolted the chain I half-expected her friend to appear out of nowhere and grab me.

After she entered the room, she sat on a small ottoman and her first words to me were, "I bet you could beat up anybody."

"Nobody can beat up *anybody,*" I said. "There's always somebody who can beat you up, and he's probably just around the corner at the next tavern."

She argued with me. "Oh, no, no, no. You can beat anybody up. Don't say you can't, because I know you can."

"Well, all right," I said, "I can beat anybody up. Now what?"

"Do you need any money?"

"No," I said.

"Because if you do, I have lots." She pulled a wad of hun-

dred-dollar bills out of her purse that would have choked a
rhino—at least the top bills were hundreds—and offered them
to me.

"I really don't need any money."

As she sat there, I tried to size her up. She was in her early
twenties and wearing a jacket with a fringe on it; she was possibly Italian, big-busted and attractive. She said her name was
Maria, and I asked her more questions.

She answered a few, then interrupted me. "I want to ask *you*
a question. You won't be mad at me if I ask you something, will
you?"

"No, of course not."

"Are you sure you won't be mad?"

I said: "I promise you I won't be mad."

She said: "Can I do something?"

"Well, what is it?"

"May I wash your feet?"

I did about a twelve count after the question, then said, "You
want to wash my feet?"

"Yes."

"Why?"

"It's just something I want to do. I don't know why."

I found myself saying, "Yes."

She went into the kitchen, filled a big basin with warm water
and then began washing my feet. I was surprised, a little frightened and unfortunately a little excited, but curious at the same
time. I wanted to see how far she'd go. There is nothing more
seductive than understanding the dynamics of the human mind
and its odd ways.

Maria washed my feet slowly, deliberately, reverentially, and
then dried them lovingly with her hair. Unfortunately it felt
wonderful. Of course I understood what was going on; she was
fantasizing that I was Jesus and that she was Mary Magdalene.
As I looked down at her, the carnal aspect of my personality

began to take over, and when she sat on my bed, it over-whelmed anything that was reasonable, rational, moral or decent in me. Without anticipating it, I put my hands on her breasts. I realized I was going over the falls in a barrel. The first thing I knew I was groping with her on the bed, and she was terrified because she was very passionate, and in the grip of her delusion must have thought she was being seduced by Jesus Christ.

When it passes a certain point, the penis has its own agenda that has nothing to do with you, especially in those days when I was young, uncontrolled, passionate and determined. One is led around by one's lust and a lot of one's decisions are not made by one's brain. When I penetrated Maria, she said, "I'm dying, I'm dying . . ."

"No, you're not," I said. "You're living. This is the first time you've ever come to life." I realized she was having an orgasm, and I reassured her that it was all right. She was, I had discovered, a virgin.

Afterward I felt remorse and asked myself how I could have done this; I had just seduced a girl who thought I was Jesus and who wanted to eat my body. I told her, "I think you need help."

I suggested the name of a psychiatrist, and after a lot of sales-manship persuaded her to go see him. A week or two later, I called him because I knew I was involved in something that could be very dangerous.

"There's nothing I can do for her," he said. "She's fixated on you, and the only reason she came to see me was because you instructed her to. She doesn't want help. She wants you." He went on to say that her disturbances were of such a character that he couldn't treat her. I asked him if he thought she was seri-ous about kidnapping me or was potentially dangerous in other ways. He said he couldn't be sure, but that in her obsessive state of mind anything was possible, so I should be careful. I decided never to see her again, but was fascinated by her, though no longer in a sexual way, because she was wounded and likable and I felt compassion for her. Still, I realized I had to break the tie between us and I tried hard. For months she called, saying she wanted to see me, and I refused, trying to be evasive and kind at the same time. Then she began sending food and expensive presents to my apartment and imploring me to go to bed with her again. She would come to the apartment and pound on the door and I wouldn't answer.

Six months later I decided to employ a new tactic. "Listen," I told her gruffly when Maria called the next time, "I don't want you ever to call me ever again. You're making a mess out of your own life and you're boring the hell out of me. I don't want you in my life. I'll never want you. I never want to see your face again."

I felt bad saying this. She cried, screamed and pleaded with me: "Don't say that, please don't say that . . ."

She was calling from a telephone booth at a drugstore not far from my apartment. This I learned because one of my friends, who knew the story and had seen her before, happened to be in the store, heard her screaming at me and saw her smash her fists into the glass of the booth, breaking it and cutting her wrists until blood was dripping all over her. Then she went out into the fifteen-degree night and vanished. When he called to tell me what he'd seen, I had already called her home and spoken to her brother, who said her family knew all about her fixation on me but hadn't been able to help her. He said Maria had seven locks on her bedroom door, had been spending more and more time in her room staring at my pictures without eating, and that other members of the family were intimidated by her.

Four hours later I called the house again, and her brother told me Maria had come home.

"How is she?" I asked.

He said she had arrived with her clothes covered with blood, and that she had smashed everything in the living room—pictures, the television set, chairs, glassware; then she had gone to her room, taken down all her *Streetcar* posters and set fire to them.

"What's she doing now?" I asked.

"She's down on the street staring at the ashes of the billboard."

"Is she still bleeding?"

"Yeah."

I was afraid she might have cut the arteries in her wrist, but he said he had bandaged her wounds and that she would be all right.

"Okay," I said, "treat her as best as you can and let me know what happens."

I didn't see or hear from Maria for several months until I was walking down the street one day on my way home with a woman who had been staying with me. Maria came up to us and I realized she had been waiting for me outside my apartment. This was long before celebrities entertained thoughts that they might be shot by a stalker—it wasn't in fashion yet—so I wasn't worried when I saw her. She matched our stride step by step, then turned to me and said, "That bitch can't take care of you. I'm the only person who knows how to . . ."

I said, "Maria, you'll have to go away. Don't come around here anymore. *I mean it.*"

Her step slowed then and she faded behind us as we walked into the apartment building. That was the last I saw of Maria, though she sent me a card wishing me well after I moved to Los Angeles.

When I was twenty-six, I had a casual affair with Lisa, a designer, who was half Filipino and half Swedish and lived around the corner from my apartment above Carnegie Hall. After I moved to California, she came by my old apartment occasionally and asked the elevator operator—a man from Barbados named Susho—if he ever saw me.

Susho, who had designs on Lisa, said, "Yes, but very infrequently. You know, it's very sad about Mr. Brando."

"What do you mean?"

Susho told her that I had cancer and now came to New York only for my treatments.

Lisa said she was horrified and asked him what kind of treatment I was receiving.

"It's experimental cancer therapy," he said, "in which he is injected with live sperm. But they're having trouble because live sperm is so hard to get."

The next time Lisa saw Susho, she asked him about me again and he said I was scheduled to come to New York shortly for a treatment, but that my doctors didn't know where they would find the live sperm they needed. "I was wondering," he said, "if you would like to help me make a contribution to Marlon."

For months Susho took her into the supply room at Carnegie Hall apartments and had intercourse with Lisa while holding a plastic bag under her to capture his semen. Then he'd thank her and said he had to rush it to my doctor. She thought she was helping me by doing it.

This story seems staggeringly implausible, but it is absolutely true. After it had been going on awhile, Lisa said, Susho told her that he had seen me and that I looked wonderful, but that the treatments were so expensive that I was going broke, so she started giving him money and jewelry for me.

Though I didn't see Lisa again for ten years, she became convinced that I was communicating with her after an anonymous caller started phoning her and breathing heavily. She decided it must be me and began talking about our relationship, the sex we had shared, my cancer and so forth. The other person never spoke, but using a code suggested by Lisa, communicated by making kissing sounds with his lips: one kiss meant "Yes," two meant "No," three meant "I love you."

I don't know who was on the other end of the line, but Lisa

was convinced that it was me, and this went on for years. She said that she had a spirit on her shoulder who told her that it was me and what she should say. Lisa was exceptionally intelligent and the only person I've ever known who could multiply three numbers by three numbers in her head instantaneously, and yet was not an idiot savant.

Because I was living in California, I didn't know about Susho's cancer "treatments" or the phone calls. But several years later, I was in New York, walking down Fifty-seventh Street at about 1:30 A.M., when I thought about Lisa and wondered if she still lived in the same apartment. I asked the man at the desk and he said she did.

I went upstairs and rang the bell. Lisa was in shock when she saw me. She opened the door hesitantly, then started talking fast about my cancer and how happy she was to have helped save my life. Then she talked about the love affair she thought we had carried on via the telephone for almost ten years.

"Lisa," I said finally, "none of this ever happened. I never had cancer, and I never called you on the phone."

She didn't believe me. "Yes, it was you. I *know* it was you."

"Why would I call you on the phone," I said, "and not speak? I'm the biggest blabbermouth in town. This is too weird for words."

I asked how much money she had given Susho and she said, "About seven thousand dollars."

I called Susho and told him I wanted to see him the next day. He denied everything, but I said that I believed Lisa, that the New York police commissioner was a friend of mine and that I was going to tell the commissioner everything. Then Susho admitted it. "You're going to have to make payments to Lisa every week," I said, "and we'll alert the U.S. government and the government in Barbados, so don't try to run because we'll find you."

Unfortunately, Lisa decided she didn't want to put Susho

through this, wouldn't demand her money back and wouldn't testify against him. I've always wished she had.

When I was living above Carnegie Hall, I woke up one night and was startled by a woman standing over me beside my bed. It was a small apartment with only one room, a kitchenette and bathroom, and she was only inches away from me. I jumped and put up my arms. This must have looked amusing to her because I was still flat on my back in bed. I was so startled that I almost pinched her, thinking that she was an apparition.

"Who are you?" I asked.

"Why have you brought me here?" she answered.

"I didn't bring you here."

"I'm confused. You told me you wanted me here, so I came . . ."

"You're mistaken. Where are you from?"

"Philadelphia."

"What brought you here?"

"You called me," she said, "you told me to come."

"No, I didn't. How did you get in?"

"Through the transom above the door."

She was a prim-looking, plain girl with dark hair close-cropped in twenties style. I couldn't see her figure because she was wearing a winter coat. "Are you religious?" I asked her because something about her suggested that she was.

"Yes."

"Do you have a priest?"

"Yes."

"Why don't you go home and tell this to the priest? Tell him what you've done and what happened."

I must have been convincing, because she went out the door without another word. I watched her walk down the hall and disappear into the elevator. Two years later, when I was living in Hollywood, a woman, wearing a tam-o'-shanter topped by a fuzzy white ball, approached me as I was walking up the side-walk toward my house. I ignored her and started to open the front door, but she followed me right up the steps and stood next to me. I still hadn't recognized her.

"What do you want?" I asked. Then I realized it was the woman who had climbed over the transom of my apartment. "Why have you come here?"

"I have a message for you," she answered.

"Who is it from?"

"From God."

I was quick with an excuse about needing a root canal and said, "I have to go now. Just tell God I was too busy to listen to his message. Thank him but tell him I had to go to the dentist."

I went out to the garage as if to leave in order to get rid of her. But when I got into my car she followed me. "You'll have to go," I said.

"But what about the message from God?"

"All right," I said. "What is the message?"

She stuck her finger an inch from my crotch and said, "This."

"That's the message from God?"

"Yes."

"Well," I said, "tell God I'm very glad that he gave me the message, and I'll certainly take care of it." I said good-bye, drove away and never saw her again.

Another time, three teenage girls knocked at my door and asked for a photograph of me. I asked, "How did you find out where I live?" After they gave a garbled explanation, I was polite to them, but I didn't have any photographs of myself to give them, and they left. But then—I guess they were sixteen or seventeen—they began appearing in my life wherever I went, either in California or New York. I don't know how they were able to afford it, but they followed me from coast to coast and appeared at restaurants, hotels and other places I visited. "Please, girls," I told them, "don't follow me. I can't go through this anymore. I don't want to see you." On one occasion I was at the Plaza Hotel in New York and heard a knock at the door. When I opened it, there they were. I said, "I'm going to have the manager of the hotel send up a detective and have you arrested." In unison, they pleaded: "*Please,* Marlon, please," but I'd had enough and called the desk. The house detective came up to my room and said he had searched the floor but hadn't been able to find any girls. Five minutes later, they pounded on my door again; they had been hiding under some sheets in a linen closet.

This went on for another year and a half or so. Years later I got a letter from one of them with an apology for pestering me; they hadn't been able to help themselves, she said. She asked to be forgiven and I wrote her a letter saying as kindly as I could that I was glad they'd come to their senses. But not long after that, I opened my door, and one of the other girls was standing there. She too apologized and said that all three of them were seeing psychiatrists. I praised her for tackling her problem and then she left.

24

WHILE WE WERE MAKING the movie of *Streetcar*, Elia Kazan directed a love scene between Karl Malden and Vivien Leigh from a rolling camera dolly. While they acted in front of the camera, he sat on the moving dolly and unconsciously acted their parts with them, moving his hands with theirs, raising his feet, sticking his knees together, mouthing Karl's lines, then Vivien's, taking on the expressions and gestures of their characters, raising his eyebrows, pursing his lips, shaking his head. Finally he got so wrought up that he started chewing on his hat.

I've never seen a director who became as deeply and emotionally involved in a scene as Gadg. The amazing thing about him was that after such a scene was over, he'd realize the flaws in the scene and have them do it over.

Gadg never shaved completely. He used an electric razor, and for some reason he always had patches of stubble somewhere on his jaw. On *Streetcar*—first the play, then the movie—I discovered he was that rarest of directors, one with the wisdom to know when to leave actors alone. He understood intuitively what they could bring to a performance and he gave them freedom. Then he manicured the scene, pushed it around and shaped it until it was satisfactory.

I have worked with many movie directors—some good, some fair, some terrible. Kazan was the best actors' director by far of any I've worked for. Gadg, who got his nickname because of an affection for gadgets, was the only one who ever really stimulated me, got into a part with me and virtually acted it with me. Before being a director, he had been an actor in the Group Theatre, and I think this gave him great insight. Creating emotions in an actor is a delicate proposition. Most of the time you have to bring your part fully rehearsed in your back pocket and appear on the set, having done your rehearsal off camera. Gadg knew when to intervene after a few takes and say something that would provoke a strong emotion in you, and most of the time he would get the result he was looking for. He was an arch-manipulator of actors' feelings, and he was extraordinarily talented; perhaps we will never see his like again.

Performances evolve. On film it may take several or even many attempts to get it right; you may not hit your pace until the third or fourth take. Gadg knew this; he nursed you along and shaped a better performance with each take. Some directors don't want you to improvise; they're either too insecure or too inflexible to see the possibilities. They cannot bear improvisations trapped in unstable egos, or, like Bernardo Bertolucci, who has the highest degree of sensitivity and is delicately attuned to the actor, they encourage you to improvise but add nothing to the performance, relying on you to offer your craft to them.

Gadg was different: he chose good actors, encouraged them to improvise and then improved on the improvisation. He understood that every performer has to bring his own inspiration and characterization to a part; he gave his cast freedom and would be pleased and excited when he got something good. He was always emotionally involved in the process and his instincts were perfect. Sometimes they were conveyed in just a brief sentence at exactly the right moment, or sometimes he inspired me simply by being there because I trusted his judgment.

When we had a scene coming up, he often said, "Listen, go work on it, then bring it to me and show me what you've got." So another actor and I would go off by ourselves, rehearse a scene in various ways, try something we thought was real and then show Gadg what we had come up with. Then he'd say, "That's good, that's good," or "No, don't do that, move it over here . . ." He almost demanded that you argue with him, but it was never a question of whose ego was in charge. We often had very creative fights over how a scene should be played. He had strong convictions and stuck with them unless you showed him he was wrong. I could stand toe-to-toe with him and tell him he was wrong and he never held it against me. He had the sense to remove his ego from the conversation, and if you convinced him you were right, he'd let you do what you wanted. If you proved you were right, he was the happier for it. "For Chrissake," I'd say, "you can't do that; it's not going to work, people won't believe it. *It's no good.* Nobody behaves that way, but okay, I'll try it your way." Then I'd do it as best I could, but when I was finished I'd say, "Now let's do it my way," and then it would be decided in the cutting room.

After *A Streetcar Named Desire,* Gadge asked me to be in *Viva Zapata!,* a film that he wanted to direct, written by John Steinbeck and based on the life of the Mexican revolutionary Emiliano Zapata, whom I played. It was a pretty good picture, but I think Kazan made a mistake in not requiring everyone in the cast to speak with a Mexican accent. I affected a slight one, but it wasn't well done, and most of the other actors spoke standard English, which made it seem artificial.

Tony Quinn, whom I admired professionally and liked personally, played my brother, but he was extremely cold to me while we shot the picture. During our scenes together, I sensed a bitterness toward me, and if I suggested a drink after work, he either turned me down or else was sullen and said little. Only years later did I learn why.

The film was produced by Twentieth Century–Fox, and until it was a hit, Darryl F. Zanuck, who ran the studio, was lukewarm about it. An absurd-looking man, Zanuck bore a striking resemblance to Bugs Bunny; when he entered a room, his front teeth preceded him by about three seconds. He also had a tremendously inflated opinion of himself; he considered himself larger than life, was totally self-absorbed, was cruel to many of the people who worked for him and always had a new bimbo in tow. When we made *Viva Zapata!,* he complained constantly to Gadg about the color of Jean Peters's skin. He was a bigot of the old Hollywood school, when studios often cast whites as blacks or Asians, and he kept warning Gadg that Jean looked too dark in the rushes and that no one would buy a ticket to see a movie whose leading lady didn't look white. Time after time he made her change her makeup, and he kept ordering Gadg to reshoot scenes with different lighting so that she wouldn't "look so dark."

Jean was seeing Howard Hughes at the time, and he had sent a woman with her to Mexico to accompany her twenty-four hours a day as a kind of security guard, chaperone and lady-in-waiting. Since nothing ever energized my libido more than a well-guarded target, I was determined to have her. We did a little casual flirting, but her chaperone was always in watchful attendance, so I didn't get anywhere. Deciding to bring the matter to a head, one night about two A.M., I climbed up on the roof of the house she was living in, intending to implement my plan of seduction. But just as I was about to lower myself on a rope to Jean's window, the chaperone woke up and saw me, so I had to make a quick exit. Undaunted, I tried other ways to effect my plan, but was never able to get past Howard Hughes's security.

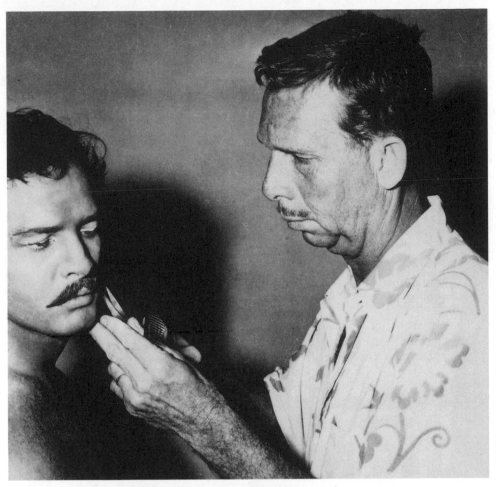

Viva Zapata!: with a
makeup man; and with
Jean Peters. (Twentieth
Century–Fox)

• • •

After being a Mexican revolutionary, I played Mark Antony in *Julius Caesar*. Joseph L. Mankiewicz, the director, assembled a good cast, including Louis Calhern, James Mason, Greer Garson, Deborah Kerr, Edmond O'Brien and John Gielgud, who played Cassius. Though English actors generally are far superior to American actors in their style, speech and familiarity with Shakespeare, many British actors, like Maurice Evans, are no better than we are in his plays. It takes someone of Gielgud's stature to perform with authority because he has played most of the important Shakespeare roles. But for me to walk onto a movie set and play Mark Antony without more experience was asinine.

25

THE WILD ONE, my fifth picture, was based on a real incident, a motorcycle gang's terrorizing of a small California farm town. I had fun making it, but never expected it to have the impact it did. I was as surprised as anyone when T-shirts, jeans and leather jackets suddenly became symbols of rebellion. In the film there was a scene in which somebody asked my character, Johnny, what I was rebelling against, and I answered, *"Whaddya got?"* But none of us involved in the picture ever imagined that it would instigate or encourage youthful rebellion. Stanley Kramer, the producer, Laslo Benedek, the director, and John Paxton, who wrote the script, may have thought it would illustrate how groups of men—in this case the bikers and townspeople—can be transformed spontaneously into predatory bands by a kind of fraternal herd instinct that enables them to cast aside whatever moral principles they have, the same instinct that led American soldiers to massacre unarmed Vietnamese civilians at My Lai. But I think they were really interested only in telling an entertaining story. If anything, the reaction to the picture said more about the audience than it did about the film. A few nuts even claimed that *The Wild One* was part of a Hollywood campaign to loosen our morals and incite young people to rebel against their elders. Sales of leather jackets soared, reminding me of *It Happened One Night,* when Clark Gable took his shirt off and revealed that he wasn't wearing an undershirt, which created a disaster for the garment industry.

In this film we were accused of glamorizing motorcycle gangs, whose members were considered inherently evil, with no redeeming qualities. Judeo-Christian values categorize people as good or evil, and society then punishes the evil. But this is absurd. Most people who commit crimes do so because they have been deprived socially, emotionally and economically. To cure this problem, society in its wisdom punishes them, and when they commit other crimes, it is inspired with the brilliant idea of putting three-time losers away forever. All we need to do is build more prisons and the problem is solved!

As I've grown older I've realized that no people are inherently bad, including the bullies portrayed in *The Wild One*. In this regard I agree with the words Tennessee Williams wrote to Elia Kazan (which Gadg quoted in his autobiography) about the characters in *A Streetcar Named Desire*: "There are no 'good' or 'bad' people," Tennessee wrote. "Some are a little better or a little worse, but all are activated more by misunderstanding than malice. A blindness to what is going on in each other's hearts . . . nobody sees anybody truly but all through the flaws of their own egos. That is the way we all see each other in life. Vanity, fear, desire, competition—all such distortions within our own egos—condition our vision of those in relation to us. Add to those distortions in our *own* egos the corresponding distortions in the egos of *others,* and you see how cloudy the glass must become through which we look at each other. That's how it is in all living relationships except when there is that rare case of two people who love intensely enough to burn through all those layers of opacity and see each other's naked hearts. Such cases seem purely theoretical to me. . . ."

As Johnny on the set of *The Wild One:* "Whaddya got?" (© Phil Stern Photo)

. . .

The public's reaction to *The Wild One* was, I believe, a product of its time and circumstances. It was only seventy-nine minutes long, short by modern standards, and it looks dated and corny now; I don't think it has aged well. But it became a kind of cult film, and it certainly helped my career, though once again it was a matter of luck. I've always been amazed at how lucky I've been, and that picture is a good example. For one thing, the part was actor-proof. Also, I never knew that there were sleeping desires and feelings in our society whose buttons would be hit so uncannily in that film. In hindsight, I think people responded to the movie because of the budding social and cultural currents that a few years later exploded volcanically on college campuses and the streets of America. Right or wrong, we were at the beginning of a new era after several years of transition following World War II; young people were beginning to doubt and question their elders and to challenge their values, morals and the established institutions of authority. There was a wisp of steam just beneath the surface when we made that picture. Young people were looking for a reason— any reason—to rebel. I simply happened to be at the right place at the right time in the right part—and I also had the appropriate state of mind for the role.

More than most parts I've played in the movies or onstage, I related to Johnny, and because of this, I believe I played him as more sensitive and sympathetic than the script envisioned. There's a line in the picture where he snarls, "Nobody tells *me* what to do." That's exactly how I've felt all my life. Like Johnny, I have always resented authority. I have been constantly discomfited by people telling me what to do, and have always thought that Johnny took refuge in his lifestyle because he was wounded—that he'd had little love as a kid and was trying to survive the emotional insecurity that his childhood had forced him to carry into adulthood. Because of the emotional pain of feeling like a nobody, he became arrogant and adopted a pose of indifference to criticism. He did everything to appear strong when inside he was soft and vulnerable and fought hard to conceal it. He had lost faith in the fabric of society and had made his own world. He was a rebel, but a strong part of him was sensitive and tender. At the time I told a reporter that "I wanted to show that gentleness and tolerance is the only way to dissipate the forces of social destruction" because I viewed Johnny as a man torn by an inner struggle beyond his capacity to express it. He had been so disappointed in life that it was difficult for him to express love, but beneath his hostility lay a desperate yearning and desire to feel love because he'd had so little of it. I could have just as easily been describing myself. It seemed perfectly natural for me to play this role.

After *The Wild One* was finished, I couldn't look at it for weeks; when I did, I didn't like it because I thought it was too violent. I couldn't wait to get back to New York, but wasn't anxious to return to work. Instead, I wanted to return to my friends—Billy Redfield, Maureen Stapleton, Janice Mars, Sam Gilman, Wally Cox and others—so I organized a summer stock company and took a George Bernard Shaw play, *Arms and the Man,* on a tour of small towns in New England.

In her recent letter to me, Janice has these memories of the tour: "It was a wild summer. You and Billy cut a swath through the waitresses and apprentices all along the route. I sat pained, feeling outcast, in backseats of cars while you and Billy cuddled your pickups in the front seat. I thought you were good in your part, although you enlarged the image to the size of a blown-up cartoon. You seemed really disturbed when you showed me a review that was . . . unfair and mean, and which said, 'Marlon Brando opened last night in "Arms and the Man" and made a fool of himself. . . .' But you were marvelous when you blew your lines; you would improvise double talk that was com-

Still from *The Wild One*. I don't think the movie has aged well. (Courtesy of Columbia Pictures)

pletely convincing and exit with a flourish. Once there was a terrific commotion outside the theater—the sound of ambulances or police cars honking—and the dialogue was totally drowned out. You filled in our dumb show by walking around me, directing attention to my rear end, as if to locate the source of the honking. At other times, to entertain yourself and dispel boredom, you invented games for us to play—games with your own rules. When I objected and asked what right you had to change rules to suit yourself, you laughed and said in self-mockery, 'Because I'm a star.' "

As the following passages from a letter I wrote my parents indicate, we apparently did have some fun—but these lines also tell me that I was still lying to them about the state of my mental health.

July 28, 1953

Dear Ma and Pop:

At long, long last. I am sitting on the edge of a lovely lake with a card table and a typewriter and a thousand twittering little creatures. I am bound and determined to build up our correspondence to some sensible proportion. Time slips away so fast that we are certainly years ahead of ourselves in our plans. . . .

I have the following plans: to go to Europe and to be in a film by around fall, either here or in Europe. A report is out that I have been offered $200,000 for a film in Italy. Jay [Kantor, my agent then] read "The Egyptian" and wasn't too enthusiastic. I am reading same. Will be in New York by late winter, if not sooner.

"Arms and the Man" has been received as the most embarrassing fiasco since Agamemnon goosed Agrippa, or the most exciting . . . bit of creative buffoonery since Aunt Betty played

Santa Claus. I am having a good time and so are most of the people in the cast. It's a lovely vacation, and I am neither seriously ruffled by my dissenters nor . . . titillated by my supporters. I am much more interested in laughing and swimming. The audience seems to enjoy itself, and that is the measure of importance most worth considering. . . .

When are you going to Mexico? I want you to go right away and I want you to go to the place where the girls put fireflies in their hair at night [so that you can] do some reconnoitering for me.

I think I am happier than I have been since I was a little boy. I have found the world a much nicer place in the last year than I have in a long time. I have felt more at home with my thoughts and conceptions in spite of the sharp and painful backlash of events. . . . I hope and believe that this will be my last year in analysis. Mittelman corroborates my feeling. . . .

Mother, it is your duty as a mother to write more frequently than you do. My correspondence has admittedly been lacking, but so has yours. This is about the longest letter I ever wrote. I wish you could see New England. Boy, oh boy! Its grace and tranquility are quiet and refreshing. It must be marvelous in the fall. We are staying in a place where George Washington passed water. The way these snobbish yokels glom on to the slightest . . . historic incidentals would make you laugh. That sentence is as stupid as I can make it. Let's see—what have I left unsaid? Nothing, I guess—except to say I love you both.

Your little boy,
Bud

26

ONE DAY about this time my mother gave me a raccoon, which she named Russell. For as long as I can remember, the Brando family had pets. At different times throughout my life, I've had horses, cows, rabbits, uncountable cats, dogs and a goose named Mr. Levy that my mother once dressed up as Santa Claus, perhaps to distract from the skimpy presents that were under the tree. I've also had monkeys, white doves that had the freedom to fly around the house, snakes, rats, gerbils, an anteater named Chuck, margays and even three electric eels. Someday I am looking forward to getting a four-hundred-pound Yorkshire pig. Pig intelligence has been widely overlooked. They can be housebroken, and they're clean animals by nature. I've always had the sense that animals are not fundamentally different from humans, and have treated them accordingly. It's been my feeling that they have greater intelligence in some ways—as, of course, we are superior to them in other ways. The lines between intelligence get fuzzier every day with new claims about dolphins, whales and apes who can speak through computers or in sign language. Genetically there is less than 1 percent difference between ourselves and chimpanzees, and only a 2 percent difference that distinguishes us from mice.

When I was making *The Wild One,* in between camera setups one afternoon I was lying on the grass outside the sound stage when I noticed a man nearby, sitting with a chimpanzee.

"What's its name?" I asked.

"Peggy."

"How old is she?"

"Six."

"Is it all right if I touch her?"

"Sure," her keeper said, "she likes people."

I sat down in front of Peggy and put my face a few inches from hers. I was close enough to kiss her. She didn't move, except for her eyes, which roamed over my face. She stared back at me in the same way I was staring at her; I imagined that she was thinking, Who is this nut? What does he want? We sat this way for perhaps four minutes before she gently took hold of my motorcycle jacket and pulled me toward her. She inspected me thoroughly, then hooked one finger inside my T-shirt and took a gander at my chest. Next she looked into my eyes, and ever so gently reached up with one finger and removed some sleep crystals that were in the corner of one eye. She studied her find curiously for a moment or two, then put her nail in her mouth, licked the sandman's gifts off her nail and chewed them up with her front teeth. I chuckled at this. Next Peggy unzipped my jacket and started going through the pockets, occasionally glancing up at me to see if I objected. I wondered how strong she was, so I took her wrists and held them apart. At first she let her hands hang limply, but then she began to pull them together; she had decided that enough was enough and did it with ease, as if I didn't exist. She was ten times stronger than me. When I touched her nose and tickled her neck, she pulled her neck close to her chest and started to laugh: *cac cac cac.* It was startlingly human, but when she'd had enough she reached up with one foot and grabbed my wrist. I used all my strength to keep on tickling her, but to no avail.

Clearly, inside Peggy there was someone very much like me. Those moments I shared with her were awesome, and they will stay fresh in my mind till they close the lid.

After this experience I decided to buy a chimp, but before I did, my mother gave me Russell, the young raccoon. My mother had a great imagination that went along with her marvelous sense of humor. To make a pet out of a raccoon, you have to start when they are young; as with most animals, it is best to feed a raccoon by hand and handle it until it becomes trusting and familiar with your touch. Raccoons don't see well, but they have a keen sense of smell and unquenchable curiosity, and their tactile sense is unequaled in the world of animals. When Russell was awake, he never stopped moving, feeling and exploring every crack he could find; once he completely took apart a wristwatch, springs and all. Sometimes he slept down by my feet in my bed, and when he woke up he would stick his paws between my toes and tickle me. He was a sleep wrecker, so I didn't let him get in bed with me often. We would chase each other around the apartment and play fight and tickle, which he loved.

Russell also loved water and played for hours in the bathtub, which I would fill with stones and any objects that it would be fun to feel. He also enjoyed sitting on my bathroom windowsill and looking at the street five floors below. He was a hit at parties and liked to sit on my shoulders and watch the guests. He would play with my hair or stick his fingers in my ears, then reach around and try to get his paw into my nose or mouth. He was always unpredictable.

It is generally believed that raccoons wash their food, but that's a misinterpretation; they do this simply because they love water. During their waking hours, they move ceaselessly, putting their paws into cracks and recesses looking for grubs, crayfish or worms.

When I had people over to the apartment or had to leave it, I usually put him in the bathroom. He also slept there because he would tear any other room apart. In the winter the bathroom was cold; I remember going in there one morning, and because I was still sleepy I sat down to piss. Russell was wide awake. He came over and stood on his hind feet and put his freezing cold front paws on the edge of the toilet seat. Then he went around to the back of the john. I had my elbows on my knees and my chin in my hands, trying to stay as close to sleep as possible. The next instant, I found myself shrieking and two feet off the floor. Russell had found the space between my ass and the toilet seat and had put the coldest paw in North America under my behind, giving me the goose of a lifetime, right on target.

Russell spent a great deal of time sitting on the ledge of the bathroom window. During lunch hour more than once he stopped traffic on Fifty-seventh Street and Sixth Avenue. Crowds would gather below the apartment and wonder what they were looking at; to collect a crowd in New York, all you have to do is look up and point. One day I was reading, and the doorbell rang. Usually I never answer the door if I don't know who it is; my friends always use code knocks. But this time someone was thumping on the door with his fist, so I opened the door. I found myself staring at a belt buckle; then, as my eyes floated upward, I saw a badge and a face. It was one of New York's finest bulls, and he asked me, "Do you own a wild animal?" I answered, "I, ahh . . . well, he's an animal, but he's not wild." The cop said, "Do you know where he is?" I said, "He's in the bathroom." "No, he isn't. He's in your *neighbor's* bathroom." I replied, "What? What's he doing in there?" "I don't know, buddy, but you'll have to get him out of there. Does he bite?" "Oh, my goodness, no, he wouldn't even bite a cookie," I replied, lying as fast as my brain would work. (Russell nipped almost everybody who didn't know how to handle him on the back of their necks.)

I went over to my neighbor's apartment. The woman was

Russell, the pet raccoon given to me by my mother, had a mind of his own. Here he is (above right), heading for my neighbor's apartment on Fifty-seventh Street. (Personal collection of Marlon Brando)

standing with her hands between her breasts, her mouth open, and she looked at me with Eddie Cantor eyes; she was stunned. "Where is he?" I asked, but she couldn't speak; she raised her entire arm and pointed toward her bathroom. I went in, and there was Russell playing in the toilet. When I called him and his head popped up, I said, "What the hell are you doing?" and he twittered some raccoon reply. He was soaking wet. I gave him my palm, he put his paws in it and I gripped him. I always carried him around this way. As I left the woman's apartment, I said, "I'm terribly sorry about this. I don't know how it could have happened." While I was apologizing, Russell's tail was dripping toilet water all over her beige rug. She was still aghast, bewildered and silent. As I passed the giant policeman, I said, "I'm awfully sorry, officer, it will never happen again." I entered my apartment still mumbling apologies, closed the door and waited for that ham-fisted policeman to knock on it with a ticket, but nothing happened. To this day, I cannot understand how Russell got into Mrs. Goldman's bathroom because both bathroom window ledges were only two inches wide and were separated by a one-foot gap five stories up.

One of the fondest memories I have of Russell was when my mother was showing him off to a couple of snooty ladies. He was sitting on her shoulder, playing with her beads and sticking a paw in each ear, which provoked a titter from the ladies, as well as a proud "Ain't he cute" smirk from my mother. Then he reached around and was feeling the crevice of her smile when she made the fatal error of opening her mouth slightly to say, "No, dear." That's all he needed. He shot his paw into her mouth and out came her false teeth. She grabbed them and tried to put them back in her mouth, but Russell was sure he had a good thing and wanted to keep them out of her mouth just as much as she wanted to keep them in. Her hat went one way and her dignity went the other. Finally she was able to outwrestle him and recovered her dentures, if not her poise. I had a seizure and had to hold on to the kitchen door to remain erect. It was one of the silliest scenes I have ever witnessed.

Eventually as Russell matured, he became uncontrollable. He had thrown all the books out of the bookcase, had peed on every record I owned, and the apartment looked as though it had been through a drug raid. It was time to let Russell go. I took him back to the family farm in Illinois in early winter, when his semihibernating instincts would take over. I carried him out to the barn, made him a nest of some hay and left some food there for him. Every couple of hours I would tiptoe through the snow and peek through a crack in the wall to see him all curled up in a ball. I wanted so much to play with him, but I knew I couldn't. I had a lump in my throat when I turned away.

When spring came and the sap began to run in the trees, Russell had left the security of the barn for whatever destiny promises a raccoon. He returned every once in a while in hopes of finding a treat in his bowl, but later in the spring his sap was running, too. He must have found some irresistible lady raccoon and begun to raise his family, and I never saw him again. I miss him.

27

UNBEKNOWNST TO ME I had been snookered into making a two-picture deal with Darryl Zanuck that would include *Viva Zapata!* and one other. In those days I never read a contract. I remember that my agent and friend Jay Kantor chased me for quite a while to get me to renew the agency contract. He finally cornered me and told me he was going to lose his job if I didn't sign it. "Please do this as a favor to me," he said. So I went into my bedroom, got my special pen and affixed my moniker. I have never seen a man so relieved as Jay when he walked out the door with the contract under his arm. What he didn't know was that I had signed it with disappearing ink so that when he arrived back at the agency, it would be discovered that there was no signature on it. Finally he called and asked me if I had kept the signed copy. His brain was in a whirl. I said, "Don't you remember? You took it with you."

I suppose the reasons I was averse to signing contracts was because I didn't want to feel hemmed in. In those days it was even hard for me to make a commitment for the next day. Even now I still put things off, although I'm much better than I used to be. But I still play practical jokes, and when they are played on me, I always laugh the hardest.

Above: With Jay Kantor, my friend, agent and "victim" (Personal collection of Marlon Brando); left: rehearsing a dance sequence for *Desirée* with Jean Simmons (Twentieth Century–Fox).

• • •

When Zanuck insisted that I do *The Egyptian*, I simply went back to New York and waited for the hit teams from my agency. He had sued me for two million dollars. Sure enough, the designated hitters showed up, Jerry Gershwin and Jay Kantor. At the time my father was telling me that I had run out of money, but I didn't care. I said, "Let them sue." The hitters said, "Come on, Marlon, pay the two dollars," and I said, "Hell, no."

Finally Zanuck backed off and came back with the counter-proposal that I play the role of Napoleon in a movie called *Desirée*. It was half a victory. So I accepted the arrangement. The film was directed by Henry Koster. I did all my homework and did the best I could. A kind and pleasant man, Koster was a lightweight who was much more interested in uniforms than in the impact of Napoleon on European history. I had a chance to work with Jean Simmons, who was cast in the role of Josephine. She was winning, charming, beautiful and experienced, and we had fun together. Unfortunately, she was married to Stewart Granger, the great white hunter. By my lights, *Desirée* was superficial and dismal, and I was astonished when told that it had been a success. H. L. Mencken's words came to mind; he said, "No one ever lost money underestimating the taste of the American public." In this case it seemed to have been borne out.

28

DURING THE THIRTIES, several members of the Group Theatre, including Gadg, joined the Communist party—largely, I suppose, because of an idealistic belief that it offered a progressive approach to ending the Depression and the increasing economic inequity in the country, confronted racial injustice and stood up to fascism. Many, including Gadg, soon became disenchanted with the party, but they were appealing targets during the hysteria of the McCarthy era.

The House Un-American Activities Committee was headed by J. Parnell Thomas, a righteous pillar of our political community who later was sent to jail for fraud. The other members of the committee were much more concerned with exploiting the public's fascination with Hollywood and with generating publicity for themselves than with anything else. They subpoenaed Gadg, and his testimony has wounded him to this day. Not only did he admit that he had been a Communist, but he identified all the other members of the Group Theatre who had also been Communists. Many of his oldest friends were furious, called the testimony an act of betrayal and refused to speak to him or work with him again.

Until then, Gadg had collaborated with Arthur Miller, for

whom he had directed *All My Sons*. After that, he presented me with a movie script about life on the New York waterfront. When Miller backed out of the project, Gadg called Budd Schulberg, the novelist, who like himself had named names before the House Un-American Activities Committee. Schulberg had been working on a script about corruption on the docks that was based on a prize-winning newspaper series describing how the Mafia took a bite out of every piece of cargo moving in and out of the ports of New York and New Jersey. Gadg and Schulberg merged their subjects, and for months tried to find a studio that would finance it. Darryl F. Zanuck tentatively agreed to do so, then backed out, saying he thought it a poor story to tell on the wide Technicolor screen of CinemaScope, which he thought of as Hollywood's salvation from television. Finally Sam Spiegel, an independent producer and the last of the great schnorrers, who had made *The African Queen,* agreed to produce it, and Harry Cohn at Columbia agreed to finance the picture that eventually would be called *On the Waterfront.*

The part I would play was that of Terry Malloy, an ex–pro boxer whose character was based on a real longshoreman who, despite threats against his life, testified against the "Goodfellas" who ran the Jersey waterfront. I was reluctant to take the part because I was conflicted about what Gadg had done and knew some of the people who had been deeply hurt. It was especially stupid because most of the people named were no longer Communists. Innocent people were also blacklisted, including me, although I never had a political affiliation of any kind. It was simply because I had signed a petition to protest the lynching of a black man in the South. My sister Jocelyn, who'd appeared in *Mister Roberts* on Broadway and became a very successful actress, was also blacklisted because her married name was Asinof and there was another J. Asinof. In those days, stepping off the sidewalk with your left foot first was grounds for suspicion that you were a member of the

Communist party. To this day I believe that we missed the establishment of fascism in this country by a hair.

Gadg had to justify what he had done and gave the appearance of sincerely believing that there was a global conspiracy to take over the world, and that communism was a serious threat to America's freedoms. Like his friends, he told me, he had experimented with communism because at the time it seemed to promise a better world, but he abandoned it when he learned better. To speak up before the committee truthfully and in defiance of his former friends who had not abandoned the cause was a hugely difficult decision, he said, but though he was ostracized by former friends, he had no regrets for what he'd done.

I finally decided to do the film, but what I didn't realize then was that *On the Waterfront* was really a metaphorical argument by Gadg and Budd Schulberg: they made the film to justify finking on their friends. Evidently, as Terry Malloy I represented the spirit of the brave, courageous man who defied evil. Neither Gadg nor Budd Schulberg ever had second thoughts about testifying before that committee.

At that time, Gadg was the director on the cutting edge of changing the way movies were made. He had been influenced by Stella Adler and what she had brought back from Europe, and he always tried to create spontaneity and the illusion of reality. He hired longshoremen as extras. He shot most of the picture in the most rundown section of the New Jersey waterfront. He was pleased because the weather was really cold. The chill added reality, and he was delighted with the fact that our breath showed on the screen. The irony of all this was that he had to get permission from the Mafia to shoot there. When they invited him to lunch, he dragged me along, and I didn't know until afterward that the gentleman we had lunch with was in fact the head of the Jersey waterfront. Although Gadg turned his friends in to the House committee over communism, he

On the Waterfront: on the docks with John Hamilton and Pat Henning (above); and with Karl Malden and Eva Marie Saint (below). (Columbia Pictures/Courtesy of the Academy of Motion Picture Arts and Sciences)

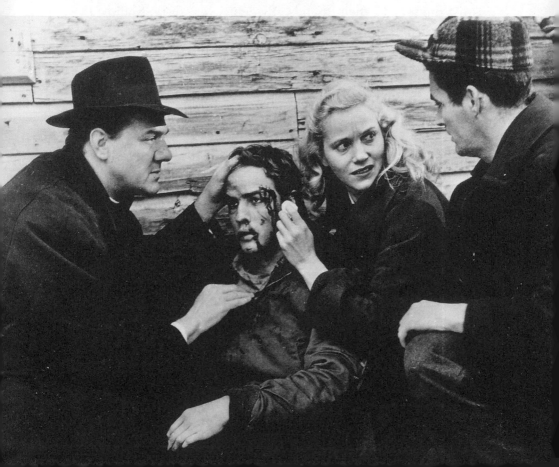

didn't even blink at having to cooperate with the Costa Nostra. By his own standards, it would seem that this was an act of remarkable hypocrisy, but when Gadg wanted to make a picture and had to move some furniture around to do so, he was perfectly willing. Actually, I met a number of people from the Costa Nostra at that time, and I would prefer them any day to some of the politicians we have.

The cast included my longtime friend Karl Malden, Eva Marie Saint, Lee J. Cobb and Rod Steiger. One of the reasons Gadg was an effective actors' director was because he was able to manipulate people's emotions. He tried to find out everything about his actors and participated emotionally in all the scenes. He would come up between takes and tell you something to excite feelings in you that fit the scene. Still, he did create mischief with his technique. In *Viva Zapata!* I played Tony Quinn's brother, and Gadg told Tony some lies about what I had supposedly said behind his back. This intensified Tony's emotional state and was very good for the picture because it brought out the conflict between the brothers; unfortunately, Gadg never bothered to tell Tony afterward that he had made up those remarks. I didn't learn about it until fifteen years later on a talk show, where Tony expressed himself on the subject. I called him up and told him that I never said those things, and that Gadg was just manipulating him. It was a relief to be able to clear up this fifteen-year deceit. From then on, Tony and I started speaking again.

Gadg was wonderful in inspiring actors to give a performance, but you had to pay the price.

People have often commented to me about the scene in *On the Waterfront* that takes place in the backseat of a taxi. It illustrates how Kazan worked.

I played Rod Steiger's unsuccessful ne'er-do-well brother, and he played a corrupt union leader who was trying to improve my position with the Mafia. He had been told in so many words to set me up for a hit because I was going to testify before the Waterfront Commission about the misdeeds that I was aware of. In the script Steiger was supposed to pull a gun in the taxi, point it at me and say, "Make up your mind before we get to 437 River Street," which was where I was going to be killed.

I told Kazan, "I can't believe he would say that to his brother, and the audience is certainly not going to believe that this guy who's been close to his brother all his life, and who's looked after him for thirty years, would suddenly stick a gun in his ribs and threaten to kill him. It's just not believable."

This was typical of the creative fights we had. "I can't do it that way," I said, and Gadg answered, "Yes, you can; it will work."

"It's ridiculous," I replied. "No one would speak to his brother that way."

We did the scene his way several times, but I kept saying, "It just doesn't work, Gadg, it really doesn't work." Finally he said, "All right, wing one." So Rod and I improvised the scene and ended up changing it completely. Gadg was convinced and printed it.

In our improvisation, when my brother flashed the gun in the cab, I looked at it, then up at him in disbelief. I didn't believe for a second that he would ever pull the trigger. I felt sorry for him. Then Rod started talking about my boxing career. If I'd had a better manager, he said, things would have gone better for me in the ring. "He brought you along too fast."

"That wasn't *him,* Charlie," I said, "it was *you.* Remember that night at the Garden you came down to my dressing room and said, 'Kid, this isn't your night. We're going for the price on Wilson'? Remember that? 'This ain't your night.' *My night!* I could have taken Wilson apart. So what happened? He gets the shot at the title outdoors at a ballpark and what do I get? A one-way ticket to Palookaville. You was my brother, Charlie, you should have looked out for me a little bit. You should have taken care of me better so I didn't have to take the dives for the short-end money . . . I could have had class. I could have been a contender. I could have been *somebody* instead of a bum, which is what I am, let's face it. It was *you*, Charlie . . ."

When the movie came out, a lot of people credited me with a marvelous job of acting and called the scene moving. But it was actor-proof, a scene that demonstrated how audiences often do much of the acting themselves in an effectively told story. It couldn't miss because almost everyone believes he could have been a contender, that he could have been somebody if he'd been dealt different cards by fate, so when people saw this in the film, they identified with it. That's the magic of theater; everybody in the audience became Terry Malloy, a man who'd had the guts not only to stand up to the Mob, but to say, "I'm a bum. Let's face it; that's what I am. . . ."

On the day Gadg showed me the completed picture, I was so depressed by my performance I got up and left the screening room. I thought I was a huge failure, and walked out without a word to him. I was simply embarrassed for myself.

None of us are perfect, and I think Gadg has done great injury to others, but mostly to himself. I am indebted to him for all that I learned. He was a wonderful teacher.

I had a great conflict about going to the Academy Awards and accepting an Oscar. I never believed that the accomplishment was more important than the effort. I remember being driven to the Awards still wondering whether I should have put on my tuxedo. I finally thought, what the hell; people want to express their thanks, and if it is a big deal for them, why not go? I have since altered my opinion about awards in general, and will never again accept one of any kind. This doesn't mean that what other people believe has any less validity; many people I know and care about believe that awards are valuable and

My *Waterfront* taxi scene with Rod Steiger. (Columbia Pictures/Courtesy Kobal Collection)

involve themselves in the process of the Academy Awards and others. I don't look down upon them for doing so, and I hope that they do not look down upon me.

If I regretted anything, it may have been that Duke Wagner wasn't around for that evening. By that time he was dead.

I don't know what happened to the Oscar they gave me for *On the Waterfront*. Somewhere in the passage of time it disappeared. I didn't think about it until a year or so ago, when my lawyer called and told me that an auction house in London was planning to sell it. When I wrote a letter to them saying that they had no right to do so, they replied that they would abide by my wishes, but that the person who had put it up for sale wouldn't relinquish it because supposedly I had given it to him or her. This is simply untrue.

29

WHEN I MUMBLED my lines in some parts, it puzzled the-ater critics. I played many roles in which I didn't mumble a sin-gle syllable, but in others I did it because it is the way people speak in ordinary life. I wasn't the first actor to do it. Dame May Whitty, who, like Eleonora Duse, was a fine actress who deviated from the traditional acting school's techniques of declaiming, superficial gesture and stilted dialogue, was famous for muttering and mumbling. In her day it was unheard of for actors to mumble or slur their words and speak like ordinary people, but she got away with it.

If everyone spoke according to the rules of the old school of acting, we'd never pause to search for words, never slur a word, never say something like, "Uh . . ." or "What did you say?"

In ordinary life people seldom know exactly what they're going to say when they open their mouths and start to express a thought. They're still thinking, and the fact that they are look-ing for words shows on their faces. They pause for an instant to find the right word, search their minds to compose a sentence, then express it.

Until Stella Adler came along, few actors understood this; they recited speeches given to them by a writer in the style of an elocution school, and if audiences didn't instantly understand them or had to work a little to do so, the performers were criticized. The audience was conditioned to expect actors to speak in a way seldom heard outside a theater. Today actors are expected to speak, think and search for words to give the impression that they are actually living in that moment. Most actors in America now strive for this effect. However, there are other affectations that have crept in. For example, many actors rely on cigarettes to convey naturalness. When smoking was in vogue, Stella criticized some actors' behavior and would refer to it as cigarette-acting. Generally actors don't realize how deeply affected the technique of acting was by the fact that Stella went to Russia and studied with Stanislavsky. This school of acting served the American theater and motion pictures well, but it was restricting. The American theater had never been able to present Shakespeare or classical drama of any kind satisfactorily. We simply do not have the style, the regard for language or the cultural disposition that fosters a tradition of presenting Shakespeare or any other classical drama. You cannot mumble in Shakespeare. You cannot improvise, and you are required to adhere strictly to the text. The English theater has a sense of language that we do not recognize and a capacity for understanding Shakespeare that we do not. In the United States the English language has developed almost into a patois. Not long ago, perhaps only fifty years or so ago, there was a style of classical acting in England in which Shakespeare was declaimed with an ample distribution of spittle. Even today there are English actors and directors who, to their artistic peril, choose to ignore the precise instructions that Shakespeare gave them in his speech to the players in *Hamlet*. This not only pertains to acting but to all forms of art. I quote it here:

Speak the speech, I pray you, as I pronounc'd it to you, trippingly on the tongue; but if you mouth it, as many of your players do, I had as lief the town-crier spoke my lines. Nor do not saw the air too much with your hand, thus, but use all gently; for in the very torrent, tempest, and, as I may say, the whirlwind of passion, you must acquire and beget a temperance that may give it smoothness. Oh, it offends me to the soul to see a robustious periwig-pated fellow tear a passion to tatters, to very rags, to split the ears of the groundlings, who for the most part are capable of nothing but inexplicable dumb-shows and noise. I would have such a fellow whipp'd for o'erdoing Termagant. It out-herods Herod. Pray you, avoid it.

What follows is excellent advice for every actor:

Be not too tame, neither, but let your own discretion be your tutor. Suit the action to the word, the word to the action; with this special observance, that you o'erstep not the modesty of nature. For anything so overdone is from the purpose of playing, whose end, both at the first and now, was and is, to hold, as 'twere, the mirror up to nature; to show virtue her own feature, scorn her own image, and the very age and body of the time his form and pressure. Now this overdone, or come tardy off, though it make the unskillful laugh, cannot but make the judicious grieve . . .

The evolution of English theater came to full flower in Kenneth Branagh's production of *Henry V*. He did not injure the language; he showed a reverence for it, and followed Shakespeare's instructions precisely. It was an extraordinary accomplishment of melding the realities of human behavior with the poetry of language. I can't imagine Shakespeare being performed with more refinement. In America we are unable to approach such refinements, and of course we have no taste for it. If given the choice between Branagh's production of *Henry V* or Arnold Schwarzenegger's *The Terminator*, there's hardly a question of where most television dials would be turned. If the expenditure of money for entertainment in America is any indication of taste, clearly the majority of us are addicted to trash.

The theatrical experience is a little-understood phenomenon. I'm not sure that *I* understand it. It seems mysterious to me that people will spend hard-earned cash to go to a building that contains a large darkened room where people sit and look at two-dimensional figures reflected on a screen and invest the entire spectrum of their emotions in what appears to be an approximation of reality. They'll be moved to tears, laughter, empathy, or experience truly deep fear, sometimes becoming frightened for days, perhaps years, by the memory of what they saw. It is even harder to understand that audiences in Japan can be so deeply moved by the Noh theater, in which actors wear masks and classical clothing, and where movement and voice are restricted and highly stylized. On the other hand, humans are able to see images in clouds, in cracks in the ceiling and in Rorschach tests. They are also able to look at drawings and make up stories suggested to them by their unconscious. These kinds of tests are often used to establish psychological profiles, so what seems apparent in this peculiar ability is that we don't see what we behold in front of us. As Shakespeare wisely pointed out, we hold a mirror up to our "nature." We are forever reading emotions into people's comments or facial expressions—emotions that are not intended. It seems clear that this peculiarity of the human mind determines to a large extent the composition of our psyche. All of us are looking through the lens of our own perspective, and this applies even to such subjects as a particular interpretation of quantum physics.

These strange characteristics can be witnessed in an actor's performance. Often actors choose to underplay a moment in the drama. If he shows little or no reaction, the audience will try to imagine what he is feeling. Sometimes actors are superb in their underplaying, but others can't wait to hit their head on the top of their part. The great Jewish actor Jacob P. Adler, Stella's father, advised his company of actors, "If you come to the theater and feel a hundred percent, show them eighty percent. If you feel sixty percent, show them forty percent, but if you only *feel* forty percent, put the understudy onstage."

Never hit your head on the top of your part, Stella said. There are some roles in which less is more, and you should underplay them. Jimmy Cagney had both great acting talent and a terrific presence. He had a distinctive look, a very strong, clear personality, and was a self-made actor. He never went to acting school. But unlike most actors of his generation, he tried to take on the subtle aspects of his characters. He believed he was the character and made audiences believe it.

One of the most difficult lessons an actor has to learn is not to leave the fight in the gym. In other words, you must learn to keep your emotion simmering all day long, but never boiling over. If you give everything you've got in the long shot, you will have less in the medium shot and, where you need it most, in the close shots. You must learn to pace yourself so that you don't dry up when the close shot comes. Even smart performance directors—and God knows there are few of them—misuse the actor unless they are experienced.

As an example, in my first movie, *The Men,* I had an emotional scene in which I had to admit to myself that I would never be able to walk again or to make love. It was a scene in which it was proper to cry. I got to the studio at 7:30 A.M. and went to my dressing room loaded with mood music, poetry and anything else that would elicit an emotional response. I played the scene over and over in my mind, rehearsed it quietly and was moved. But by 9:30 A.M., when I had to play the scene, I had nothing left. I had left the fight in the gym. I have remembered that moment ever since.

Unless you're fully experienced, some directors can destroy you with their insensitivity. An actor's motivation often depends on focusing sharply on small details. If a director doesn't prepare the crew and the other actors, he can destroy the mood of a scene. Directors don't realize how hard it is to create a fragile emotional impression, and how easy it is to break the spell. The most fatiguing aspect about acting is turning your emotions on and off. It's not like pushing a light switch and saying, "I'm going to be angry and kick the walls now," and then becoming yourself again. If you have an intense scene involving sadness or anger, you may have to hover in the same emotional territory for hours, and this can be extremely taxing. Some directors don't understand this because they were never actors, or else were bad ones.

An actor can profit greatly from a good director, but often directors who have a sense of inadequacy try to conceal this by being authoritative and issuing commands and ultimatums. With such directors, who mistake you for a draft horse pulling a beer wagon, you're obliged to fight back. A surprising number of directors think they know everything. Not only do they have little insight into or understanding of what it is to be an actor or what the acting process is, but they have no notion of how one develops a characterization. They hand you a script and tell you to report for work on Monday; it's left to you to create your role. If you're working with a director who doesn't have good taste, or who is dangerous because he lacks sound instincts, you have to take over and make sure a scene works right; in effect, you must direct it yourself. If the director has misconceived a part and continues to insist that you play it his way, you have to outmaneuver him by giving such a poor performance that you know he won't be able to use it—though in the process you may ruin your reputation. In a close-up or a shot taken over the shoulder—anything close—give him nine bad takes, blow your lines, give a weak performance and wear him down. Then, finally, when you know he's tired and frustrated, you give him the one take in which you do it the way it should be done. By then he's so pleased and grateful to get the scene out of the way that he'll print it. You don't give him a choice. You have to play such games with untalented directors.

If someone decided to produce a play the way people make movies in Hollywood, he'd be laughed off the stage. Before putting a play on Broadway, the actors and director sit around for five to six weeks, talk about motivation, discuss the script and the characters, go through the story, walk around the stage, try different approaches and eventually put the show on its feet. Then they take the play to Schenectady or New Haven, test it before audiences, fine-tune it and after eight weeks return to New York to hold previews. Eventually, after everything has been edited, reedited and refined, there is an opening night. In Hollywood you usually have a meeting to make a deal where the talk is all about money, "points" and "profit participation." Then you're given a script, told to come to the set with your part in your pocket, and from then on are mostly on your own. Motion-picture directors rarely give you the vaguest hint of how to realize your character. If it's any good, most acting in pictures is improvisational because the cast receives such little help from its director. Sometimes when you improvise you advance the story and the drama, but not always. If you're playing Tennessee Williams, you should stick to the script, but most scripts are not written in stone, so you can change them in a way that makes you feel more comfortable. Every once in a while you run into a script that is not very good, with a director who thinks that it is. Such a situation is to be avoided at all costs from the beginning.

In my experience one of the few directors who prepared a movie sensibly was Elia Kazan, who was not only an actor but had directed stage plays. What if Broadway producers hired an actor for a part, met with him once or twice, then told him to report to work that evening for opening night? It would be considered irresponsible, and no one in the theater would do it, but in motion pictures, those are normal operating procedures.

On the stage you can change the emphasis of a scene, set the tempo and determine from the response of the out-of-town audience the key emotional points in a play. But in the movies the director says, "Cut" and "Print," and that's it. In the cutting room they can make chicken feed out of the scene if they want to. The actor has no control unless he has enough experience to know how to play the game, take charge and give only the performance he wants to give.

The moral is, never give a stupid, egotistical, insensitive or inept director an even break.

30

OFTEN WE HEAR SOMEONE coming out of a movie theater say, "My God, what a picture! What a job of acting! I was so *moved* that I cried my heart out!" while his or her companion says, "I was bored to death." For the latter there was no emotional resonance to the particular story or character. The reason for this is that we all bring to the theater varying experiences and attitudes that affect how we respond to a story. The same thing happens to people who hear a political speech and have diametrically opposite reactions about it.

Not long ago I saw *Runaway Train*, a film, directed by Andrei Konchalovsky, about the flight of two escaped prisoners, with wonderful performances by Jon Voight, Eric Roberts, Rebecca DeMornay and Kyle T. Heffner. The picture was only moderately successful at the box office, but I was overwhelmed by it, largely because of what I brought to the characters. As mentioned previously, throughout my life I have always had a strong need to feel free, so in the escaped convict (played by Jon Voight), who stood atop the runaway train in temperatures twenty degrees below zero determined never to return to prison, even knowing that he was likely to die, I saw myself and *experienced his feelings*. The emotional reverberation made the picture an extraordinary experience for me. Other people, who don't want that freedom, would see it differently; for them the natural desirable state is to submit to authority.

I recall watching the Nazi propaganda films made by Hitler's filmmaker, Leni Riefenstahl, in which thousands of people gathered in a stadium, and as the Führer arrived they raised their hands in the Nazi salute, transfixed and mesmerized by the experience. In such moments as this the German people invented Hitler, just as Americans invented some of their myths about FDR when they listened to his Fireside Chats, wanting to believe that he had a solution to their problems in the depth of the Depression.

The Germans in the stadium at Nuremberg didn't know that Hitler was an unstable, maniacal personality, and that the people around him were thugs, liars and murderers. They were creating myths about him in the theater of their minds. They cheered, marched and saluted on automatic pilot, no longer masters of themselves because they imbued Hitler with their dreams of wanting to be led and to feel proud of Germany again. There is theater in everything we see or do during the day. As Hitler demonstrated, one of the basic characteristics of the human psyche is that it is easily swayed by suggestion. Our susceptibility to it is phenomenal, and it is the job of the actor to manipulate this suggestibility.

As in *On the Waterfront* (or, for me, *Runaway Train*), the most effective performances are those in which audiences identify with the characters and the situations they face, then become the characters in their own minds. If the story is well written and the actor doesn't get in the way, it's a natural process.

Ultimately, I suppose that what makes people willing to part with their hard-earned cash and enter a theater is that it allows them to savor a variety of human experiences without having to pay the normal price for them. Maybe it's equivalent to the emotion people feel when they jump off a bridge with a bungee cord tied to their ankles: they fall two hundred feet and experience the sensation of being at the edge of death, then bounce back safely, just as we do when we walk out of a theater unscathed after undergoing a harrowing experience.

It is no accident that plays are performed in the dark, for this allows audiences to exclude others and be alone with the characters; in the dark other people cease to exist. There is something peculiar about the process, which started long before Greek drama. It probably began when men first left their caves to hunt, and the women, children and old men left behind danced and acted out stories to counteract their boredom.

Acting, not prostitution, is the oldest profession in the world. Even apes act. If you want to invite trouble from one, lock your eyes on his and stare. It's enough of an assault to make the animal rise, pound his chest and feign a charge; he is acting, hoping that his gestures will make you avert your eyes.

Storytelling is a basic part of every human culture—people have always had a need to participate emotionally in stories—and so the actor has probably played an important part in every society. But he should never forget that it is the audience that really does the work and is a pivotal part of the process: every theatrical event, from those taking place in Stone Age caves to Punch-and-Judy shows and Broadway plays, can produce an emotional participation from the audience, who become the actors in the drama.

A lot of actors are credited with great performances that really weren't extraordinary because the audience simply was moved by a well-written story and the situation facing a character. As I've already said, Terry Malloy in *On the Waterfront* is a good example of this. I was moved by *The Elephant Man,* in which John Hurt portrayed a man in Victorian England who was afflicted by a horrible, disfiguring disease and was heckled and ridiculed by strangers. But as the story evolved, his humanity was revealed and he became every member of the audience who ever maintained dignity in the face of hardship or abuse. When I saw the picture, I cried because I was touched. John Hurt is a very good actor, and has proved it in several parts, including Caligula in the television production of *I, Claudius,* in which he was brilliant. But his role in *The Elephant Man* was one of those actor-proof parts and he just couldn't miss.

Still, the reverse is often true: sometimes actors are given a nearly impossible challenge because a story is poorly written or not realistic, and when they do a good job, they don't get the credit they deserve. I've seen many great performances go unrecognized because audiences don't realize how difficult they were.

Of course, different actors apply different techniques to attain their goals. Laurence Olivier is an example. After the sun set on the British Empire, England began to lose touch with Shakespeare and the great traditions of the British theater that were the legacy of the greatest writer the world has ever known. But almost single-handedly Olivier revived the classical British theater and helped to stabilize English culture. His contributions were unequaled, though of course he had the help of the wonderful repertory actors at the Old Vic. While I believe that Larry did his best acting toward the end of his life, when I think of him as an actor, I perceive him mostly as an architect. He designed his parts beautifully, but they were like sketches engraved with an etching tool on a sheet of copper. He said every line the same way every time. He hated the thought of improvising and said, "I'm an 'outside-in' actor, not an 'inside-out actor.' " Everything he did had to be structured in advance, and he always stuck to the blueprint. He was uncomfortable with me and other actors influenced by Stella Adler and the Russian school of acting, and probably felt a much deeper kinship with performers whose roots were more traditional. This kind of acting can be effective on the stage because audiences are far away, but it becomes absurd in movies, in which audiences can see actors' expressions magnified hundreds of times in close-ups.

Larry shared one characteristic with other British actors I've known who wouldn't "play down." In *The Entertainer*, for example, he played a decrepit Cockney vaudeville song-and-dance man, Archie Rice, but he refused to talk in a Cockney accent, even though the part called for it. He wouldn't use an accent beneath his own station in life; he simply spoke in perfect English.

I've heard it said that I should have devoted my life to the classical theater as Olivier did. If I had wanted to be a great actor, I agree that I should have played Hamlet, but I never had that goal or interest. For the reader who has gotten this far in the book, I hope that by now it is apparent that I have never had the actor's bug. I took acting seriously because it was my job; I almost always worked hard at it, but it was simply a way to make a living.

Still, even if I had chosen to go on the classical stage, it would have been a mistake. I revere Shakespeare, the English language and English theater, but American culture is simply not structured for them. Theatrical ventures ambitious enough to accomplish something truly worthwhile seldom survive. The British are the last English-speaking people on the planet who love and cherish their language. They preserve it and care about it, but Americans do not have the style, finesse, refinement or sense of language to make a success out of Shakespeare. Our audiences would make a pauper of any actor who dedicated his career to Shakespeare. Ours is a television and movie culture.

31

IN 1955, I took the part of Sky Masterson, the gambler who falls in love with a Salvation Army sergeant played by Jean Simmons, in *Guys and Dolls*. When the director, Joe Mankiewicz, asked me to be in the picture, I told him I couldn't sing and had never been in a musical, but he said he'd never directed one before, and that we'd be learning together. Frank Loesser, who wrote the music for the Broadway show on which it was based, recruited an Italian singing coach to teach me to sing, and after a couple of weeks with him I went to a recording studio with Frank to record my songs, which were to be synchronized later with shots of me mouthing the words on film. I couldn't hit a note in the dubbing room with a baseball bat; some notes I missed by extraordinary margins. But the engineers kept telling me to do them over again, and they would stitch together a word here, a note there, until they had a recording that sounded like I'd sung the bars consecutively. They sewed my words together on one song so tightly that when I mouthed it in front of the camera, I nearly asphyxiated myself because I couldn't breathe while trying to synchronize my lips. The audience never realized that when I sang a song, it was a product of many, many attempts.

Joe Mankiewicz, the director, said we would be learning together when I agreed to sing in the musical *Guys and Dolls* (© Phil Stern Photo); below: with Frank Sinatra (MGM/Courtesy of the Academy of Motion Picture Arts and Sciences).

When the picture was finished, Sam Goldwyn conned me into attending the picture's premiere in New York by giving me a car. I had always refused to go to one, but when he offered me the car I felt obligated to go. I didn't realize that such gifts didn't cost him a cent because he could charge them to the picture's budget.

Jean Simmons and I were picked up at the Plaza Hotel by a limousine and driven to Times Square, which was aglow with searchlights and floodlights and jammed with people and police who were trying to restrain them behind wooden barricades. As we approached the theater, the crowd suddenly surged forward, broke through the barricades and attacked the limousine like a horde of Mongol warriors. Screaming hysterically, they engulfed the car, flattening their noses and cheeks against the windows until they looked like putty that had been softened in a warm oven. One girl was pushed so hard by the people that her head broke a window in the car, panicking the driver, and he stepped on the gas and almost ran over a bunch of other teenagers. Finally several policemen on horseback pushed through the melee to clear a path, but there were still so many people that we had to stop across the street from the theater.

Measuring the distance, I figured we were at least fifty yards from the goal line and wondered how we were going to make it the rest of the way. Then six big cops came up to the car, opened the door, grabbed Jean, lifted her in the air and carried her into the theater. Then it was my turn: six other cops grabbed me, lifted me up and began steamrolling toward the theater. There was so much screaming I couldn't hear anything. One cop lifted me by one arm and another got under my other shoulder, and others lifted my feet off the ground. We inched through the crowd and pretty soon hands from all sides were pinching me and grabbing my groin. Then someone got my tie and held it, but the cops didn't know this and kept forging ahead like a team of draft horses on extra rations. I became dizzier and dizzier. I couldn't scream because I was being strangled; but even if I had, there was so much noise the cops wouldn't have heard me.

Finally the cops won the tug-of-war and the tie puller had to let go. They carried me into the lobby, where I sat on a flight of stairs, shaking and muttering to myself, "Jesus Christ, what the hell am I doing here?"

As I wiped my brow I saw there was a piece of paper in my hand. I unfolded it and saw that it was a summons with my name on it, a subpoena to appear to testify in a lawsuit involving Sam Spiegel, who was being sued by someone who claimed he was owed money from *On the Waterfront*. That process server is a man I'd like to meet. How he got that subpoena in my hand, I'll never know.

I've always been amazed by the qualities in human nature that can turn crowds into mobs. Those people with hungry, glazed eyes looking at us through those car windows were in a trance. They were like helpless robots swaying to a magic flute. Much the same sort of thing happened when Frank Sinatra bewitched bobby-soxers at the same theater a few years earlier, and ten years later the Beatles would similarly mesmerize a different generation. For some reason celebrities of a certain kind are treated as messiahs whether they like it or not; people encapsulate them in myths that touch their deepest yearnings and needs. It seems to me hilarious that our government put the face of Elvis Presley on a postage stamp after he died from an overdose of drugs. His fans don't mention that because they don't want to give up their myths. They ignore the fact that he was a drug addict and claim he invented rock 'n' roll when in fact he took it from black culture; they had been singing that way for years before he came along, copied them and became a star.

Of course mythologizing isn't limited to celebrities or political leaders. We all create myths about our friends as well as our enemies. We can't help it. Whether it's Michael Jackson or Richard Nixon, we run instinctively to their defense because we don't want our myths demolished. When the news broke about Watergate, many Americans who worshiped Nixon refused to believe what they had heard. Years later, some began to admit that he had orchestrated a coverup, but said he wasn't so bad. "Sure, people stumble in their lives," they rationalized, "but taken all and all, he was a great president." They refused to acknowledge the lies and deceit that were so much a part of the character of a man who called himself a law-and-order president. Some people who have heard his recorded voice on the Oval Office tapes proving that he abused the presidency and the trust of the people who elected him justify him by arguing that presidents are under great pressure and what he did was perfectly understandable. By the time he died in 1994, it seemed history had been totally rewritten by the mythmakers. As one newspaper columnist put it during the days of mourning for Nixon, it was if he had suddenly been canonized.

We make up any excuse to preserve myths about people we love, but the reverse is also true; if we dislike an individual we adamantly resist changing our opinion, even when somebody offers proof of his decency, because it's vital to have myths about both the gods and the devils in our lives.

32

I WAS GETTING READY to sing in *Guys and Dolls* when Elia Kazan invited me to visit him on the set of a new movie he was filming called *East of Eden*. Several months earlier he had asked me to be in the movie, John Steinbeck's retelling of the Cain and Abel story set in California's Salinas Valley, playing opposite Montgomery Clift as my brother. But I was busy and I think Monty was, too. Instead, Gadg cast as one of the brothers a new actor named James Dean, who, he said, wanted to meet me. Before introducing us, Gadg told me that his new star was constantly asking about me and seemed bent on patterning his acting technique and life after me—or at least on the person he thought I was after seeing *The Wild One*.

Jimmy was then about twenty, seven years younger than me, and had a simplicity that I found endearing. When we met, I sensed some of the same aspects of the midwestern farm boy who had suddenly been transplanted to the big city that I'd had when I went to New York—as well as some of the same anxieties I'd felt after being thrust into the status of celebrity at a young age. He was nervous when we met and made it clear that he was not only mimicking my acting but also what he believed was my lifestyle. He said he was learning to play the conga drums and had taken up motorcycling, and he obviously wanted my approval of his work.

As I've observed before, acting talent alone doesn't make an actor a *star*. It takes a combination of qualities: looks, personality, presence, ability. Like Tallulah Bankhead, Greta Garbo wasn't much of an actress, but she had presence. She probably played the same character in every film she ever made, but she was beautiful and had an unusual personality. Mickey Rooney, on the other hand, is an unsung hero of the actors' world. He never became a leading man—he was too short, his teeth weren't straight and he didn't have sex appeal—but like Jimmy Cagney he could do almost anything. Charlie Chaplin was also one of the best. But a lot of people became movie stars simply by playing themselves. Their looks and personalities were so interesting, attractive or intriguing that audiences were satisfied by these qualities alone.

Jimmy Dean, who made only three pictures, *East of Eden, Rebel Without a Cause* and *Giant,* had everything going for him. He was not only on his way to becoming a good actor, but he had a personality and presence that made audiences curious about him, as well as looks and a vulnerability that women found especially appealing. They wanted to take care of him. He was sensitive, and there were elements of surprise in his personality. He wasn't volcanic or dynamic, but he had a subtle energy and an intangible injured quality that had a tremendous impact on audiences.

Like me, he became a symbol of social change during the 1950s by happenstance. *Rebel Without a Cause* was a story about a new lost generation of young people, and the reaction to it, like that to *The Wild One,* was a sign of the tremors that were beginning to quake beneath the surface of our culture. I always think of the years leading up to that period as the Brylcreem Era, when people wore pompadours and society's smug attitudes and values were as rigidly set in place as the coiffure of a ladies' man. Rock 'n' roll, the Beatles, Woodstock, the civil rights movement, rioting in the streets because of racial injustice and the Vietnam War were just around the corner. A sense of alienation was rising among different generations and different layers of society, but it hadn't openly manifested itself yet. Old traditions and venerated institutions were distrusted and the social fabric was being replaced by something new, for better or worse.

Because we were around when it happened, Jimmy Dean and I were sometimes cast as symbols of this transformation—and in some cases as instigators of alienation. But the sea change in society had nothing to do with us; it would have occurred with or without us. Our movies didn't precipitate the new attitudes, but the response to them mirrored the changes bubbling to the surface. Some people looked in this mirror and saw things that weren't there. That's how myths originate. They grow up around celebrities almost by spontaneous generation, a process over which they have no control and are usually unaware of until they are trapped by them.

Laurence Olivier became a legend as Heathcliff in *Wuthering Heights;* with his beautiful face, he was perfect for the part and a very good actor. But Emily Brontë's novel about star-crossed lovers moved half the world to tears, and it was another of those actor-proof roles. Nobody knew at the time that the picture would make Olivier a larger-than-life figure and shape the world's perception of him for the rest of his life. The public retained in its collective memory the mythic image of Olivier as Heathcliff, just as they remembered Jimmy Dean drag-racing in an old Mercury coupe or me riding off on a motorcycle. Actors have no way of anticipating the myths they may create when they take on a role. Humphrey Bogart was an effective performer, but no great shakes as an actor. I doubt if he understood the subtext of *Casablanca* or gave any thought to the possibility that it would become a cult film, but his role in that movie affected the public's perception of him forever. Charlie Chaplin was one of the few actors who had the intuitive sense to consciously create a myth about himself as the Tramp, and then he exploited it.

The closer you come to the successful portrayal of a character, the more people mythologize about you in that role. Perception is everything. I didn't wear jeans as a badge of anything, they were just comfortable. But because I wore blue jeans and a T-shirt in *Streetcar* and rode a motorcycle in *The Wild One,* I was considered a rebel. It's true that I always hated conformity because it breeds mediocrity, but the real source of my reputation as a rebel was my refusal to follow some of the normal Hollywood rules. I wouldn't give interviews to Hedda Hopper or Louella Parsons because the practice seemed phony and degrading. Every actor was expected to butter up the columnists. You were supposed to put on a happy face, give them tidbits about your life, play the game because they would help sell tickets to your movies and determine the course of your career. But I didn't care if I got publicity. When I first became an actor, I had tried to be open and honest with reporters, but they put words in my mouth and focused on prurience, so after a while I refused to do it anymore. I was tired of being asked the same inane, irrelevant questions, then seeing my answers distorted. It grated on me that movie stars were elevated into icons; Hollywood was simply a place where people, including me, made money, like a mill town in New England or an oil field in Texas.

After we met on the set of *East of Eden,* Jimmy began calling me for advice or to suggest a night out. We talked on the phone and ran into each other at parties, but never became close. I think he regarded me as a kind of older brother or mentor, and I suppose I responded to him as if I was. I felt a kinship with him and was sorry for him. He was hypersensitive, and I could see in his eyes and in the way he moved and spoke that he had suffered a lot. He was tortured by insecurities, the origin of which I never determined, though he said he'd had a difficult childhood and a lot of problems with his father. I urged him to seek assistance, perhaps go into therapy. I have no idea whether he ever did, but I did know it can be hard for a troubled kid like him to have to live up to sudden fame and the ballyhoo Hollywood created around him. I saw it happen to Marilyn, and I also knew it from my own experience. In trying to copy me, I think Jimmy was only attempting to deal with these insecurities, but I told him it was a mistake. Once he showed up at a party and I saw him take off his jacket, roll it into a ball and throw it on the floor. It struck me that he was imitating something I had done and I took him aside and said, "Don't do that, Jimmy. Just hang your coat up like everybody else. You don't have to throw your coat in the corner. It's much easier to hang it up than pick it up off the floor."

Another time, I told him I thought he was foolish to try to copy me as an actor. "Jimmy, you have to be who you are, not who I am. You mustn't try to copy me. Emulate the best aspects of yourself." I said it was a dead-end street to try to be somebody else. In retrospect, I realize it's not unusual for people to borrow someone else's form until they find their own, and in time Jimmy did. He was still developing when I first met him, but by the time he made *Giant*, he was no longer trying to imitate me. He still had his insecurities, but he had become his own man. He was awfully good in that last picture, and people identified with his pain and made him a cult hero. We can only guess what kind of actor he would have become in another twenty years. I think he could have become a great one. Instead he died and was forever entombed in his myth.

33

IN A FADED BROWN ENVELOPE saved by my sisters are the remains of a long-ago romance that some readers may find as touching as one by Shakespeare. It's the story of a boy and a girl in their teens who were very much in love, told in their own words in letters to each other.

"Sweetheart," the boy writes, "if you should be taken away from me, I don't know what I'd do. Do you know that you mean everything to me? A fellow can do most anything, dear, if he has a little girl like you to back him up. With you backing me up, I feel as if I could go through the seven fires of hell and come out rather cool. . . ."

"I love you every second," the girl responded. "I love and adore you. There couldn't be anyone else in the world for us but each other . . . it was ordained from the first that we should be together. I have always known it. You will never, never know how I love you . . . you are everything in the world I hold dearest. If anything should happen to you, I think I should go insane. . . ."

"Dearest, I'm the most fortunate man in the world, and I can't see how I deserve it at all," the boy wrote after landing in France, bound for the trenches of World War I. "I am so happy in knowing that you are mine, that I seem to be walking on air. You're the only one I could ever marry and to think that you're mine is wonderful. It's us for the rest of our life that is going to be the happiest that ever was."

"You are as necessary to me as air and water," she wrote on the eve of her wedding day. "I love and adore you. . . . I have now and since the first time I saw you a feeling of absolute security whenever I think of you. I know that whatever happens, you'll always be there to help me, and you know, dearest, I would move the world for you. . . . I am absolutely yours and you are mine. I don't think the ceremony will be necessary as far as we are concerned, for we are honestly married as two people could be. It was ordained from the first that we should be. I have always known it and so has everyone who has ever known us. . . ."

There are scores of these letters, passionate and brimming with love, all written by my mother and father.

Like other things in life, what people glean from their words will vary according to their own experiences, values and prejudices. I do not find these letters moving, but I have read them searching for answers to what went wrong in their lives. I have spent almost seven decades examining every aspect of my life trying to understand the forces that made me what I am, and while I never expect to find the final answer, because I realize it is impossible to be objective about oneself, I've tried to reconcile the sweet, hopeful, passionate people in these letters with the parents I knew—one an alcoholic whom I loved but who ignored me, the other an alcoholic who tortured me emotionally and made my mother's life a misery. I mourn the sadness of their lives while looking for clues to their psyches and, by extension, my own.

My father, the letters tell me, was kicked out of the University of Nebraska for drinking, and when she was away at college in New England my mother wrote him, "I drank half a quart of whiskey with ginger ale, smoked six cigarettes, drank port wine and more whiskey. . . . I've been sick ever since. . . . I wanted to get stewed once to see what it was like. I wouldn't do it in public and I couldn't at home, and I wouldn't when I was married because if I ever thought you'd see me in the state I was in last night, I'd get under a bed and stay there for the rest of my natural life. Dearest, that's one thing we'll never, never do is get stewed. I think it's horrible."

Is there a clue to why my father behaved as he did in a letter written to them by one of his aunts on the eve of their wedding? "Marlon," she wrote, "*be the boss*. Dodie will be happier for having someone who makes her do the thing as it should be done, and don't think that giving in to her is an action of love, for it isn't. . . ."

Clues, but no answers.

After my mother left New York, she reconciled with my father, and with the help of Alcoholics Anonymous they both stopped drinking. They then had almost ten years together. I bought them a ranch in the sand hills of Nebraska, which my mother called a frozen ocean because in the winter the broad, sweeping plains were glazed with vast sheets of snow and ice. The ranch was near Broken Bow, not far from where Crazy Horse was assassinated, and she named it Penny Poke Farm as a joke. In the Midwest, a poke was where you kept your money, as in a pig in a poke.

I don't know if my dad gave up the whoremongering that brought so much sadness to my mother's life, but she loved the ranch and the two of them shared a life of sorts, though I never knew its inner dynamics. They went to AA and somehow muddled through, taking the shards of their broken lives and fitting them into a sort of mirror that reflected their togetherness and allowed them to live free of alcohol.

When my mother became seriously ill during a trip to Mexico

On the set of *On the Waterfront* with my mother. This is one of the last photographs of her; she died a few months later. (AP/Wide World Photos)

with my father in 1953, she was brought to California, and I was beside her hospital bed with her hand in mine when she died. She was only fifty-five years old. After hearing her death rattle, I took a lock of her hair, the pillow she died on, and a beautiful aquamarine ring from her finger and walked outside. It was about five A.M. on a spring morning in Pasadena, and it seemed as if everything in nature had been imbued with her spirit: the birds, the leaves, the flowers and especially the wind, all seemed to reflect it. She had given me a love of nature and animals, and the night sky, and a sense of closeness to the earth. I felt she was with me there, outside the hospital, and it helped get me through the loss. She was gone, but I felt she had been transformed into everything that was reflective of nature and was going to be all right. Suddenly I had a vision of a great bird climbing into the sky higher and higher and I heard Ferde Grofé's *Mississippi Suite*. Now I often hear the music and see her in the same way, a majestic bird floating on thermals of warm air, gliding higher and higher past a great stone cliff.

I keep my mother's ring close to me. For a long while after she died, the stone was vibrant and full of color, pigmented with deeper and deeper shades of blue, but recently I've noticed that the colors have begun to fade. With each year it fades more; now it's not blue anymore, but a misty, foggy gray. I don't know why.

34

IN THE MIDDLE YEARS of my life, I spent a lot of time searching for something to dedicate my life to and give it more meaning. Elia Kazan claimed I once told him, "Here I am, a balding middle-aged failure, and I feel like a fraud when I act. I've tried everything—fucking, drinking, work—and none of it means anything." I don't remember saying that, but I may have. With so much prejudice, racial discrimination, injustice, hatred, poverty, starvation and suffering in the world, making movies seemed increasingly silly and irrelevant, and I felt I had to do what I could to make things better.

I spent these years of my life in a philosophical quandary, thinking, If I am not my brother's keeper, who am I? Where are the lines between that which is mine, and that which is Caesar's? Where does my life end and my responsibility to others begin?

For a long time I was driven to involve myself in a war against what I perceived as social injustice and political hypocrisy. As I've grown older, I am less sure of many of the things I felt then, but it was another time. For most of my life, a black-and-white world was attractive and convenient for me; it was easier to take sides. As when I sided with Jewish terrorists without acknowledging that they were killing innocent Palestinians in their effort to create the state of Israel, I believed there was right and wrong about everything, with nothing in between, and I wanted to be sure I was always on the right side. There were good people and bad people, and the bad people were my enemies. The human mind finds it difficult to deal with gray areas. It's much more convenient to say, "These people are evil," "This is bad," or "This is good." With age, I've come to realize that nothing is wholly right or wholly wrong, and that everything human beings do is a product of their heritage, perspective, genes and experience. I think a principal fault of our concept of justice is that it is based on the Judeo-Christian beliefs that separate the world into the guilty and the innocent. No child is born evil. People may be born with a genetic disposition toward one characteristic or another—they have a certain level of intelligence, a special talent, a personality feature, a physical ability—but otherwise they are naked when they enter the world. Using the word "evil" is a convenient way to label an enemy. I used to say that Roy Cohn, who spearheaded Joe McCarthy's bloodletting, personified evil more than any other person I knew. Now I realize I don't know what forces made him do what he did. I'm more forgiving now, but it took many years to become that way. Sometimes I still have an impulse to hate and exact vengeance on an enemy, but then I realize that it is a wasted emotion and that I have better things to do with the rest of my life.

However, earlier in my life I often affixed myself to what the press called "causes." What affected me most was the suffering of children. I couldn't understand how the world could let so many children starve to death. Nor could I remain silent when I saw the strong exploit the weak. People pigeonholed me as a knee-jerk liberal and mouthed clichés like, "Brando is a defender of the underdog." I bridled at words like "militant," "radical" and "liberal" because they were so glibly used to con-fuse and mislabel complex attitudes. Still, to be fair, I can understand, given the natural human proclivity to see things in black and white, how some of the things I did during the middle of my life produced this image in some minds.

I thought about becoming a minister, not because I was a religious person, other than having an inexhaustible awe and reverence for nature, but because I thought it might give me more of a purpose in life. I flirted with the idea for a while, but in the end it never developed sufficient force to make me want to do it. Or maybe it was because I became interested in the United Nations, which for a while I saw as perhaps our last hope for peace, social justice and a more equitable sharing of the earth's resources. For the first time in history, people from different nations with diverse natures, colors, religions and philosophies were working together for the common good. I was impressed by what I read about the UN's technical-assistance program, which promised to give poor people the know-how and tools to feed themselves, and to create jobs and develop industry. I volunteered to help the United Nations International Children's Emergency Fund because it was trying to feed millions of starving children around the world, and I became a roving ambassador for the agency, preaching a different kind of religion: that above all, the world owes its children a decent life. I made television spots for UNICEF and traveled to dozens of countries, holding press conferences to spread the word about the importance of its work and putting on shows to raise money for it. I also decided to make a film about the UN, believing with foolish vanity that I could make a difference by using my movie experience to focus attention on the despair and anguish so many children were enduring. In the spring of 1955, I organized my own movie production company—named Pennebaker Productions after my mother's maiden name—with three objectives: to make films that would be a force for good in the world, to create a job for my father that would give him something to do after my mother died and to cut taxes. He complained constantly that taxes were taking 80 percent of what I earned, and that by forming a corporation we would be able to cut them substantially to put away some money for my retirement.

As I've noted, I had earned $550 a week for *A Streetcar Named Desire* and more later, and I had given almost all of it to my father to invest. Money was never important to me once I'd fed myself, had a place to sleep and had enough to take care of my family and people I loved. My father invested it, but like most misers, he was a poor businessman and lost everything, the equivalent today of about $20 million. Some of the money was spent on bad investments in cattle, but most was squandered on abandoned gold mines, where a slick salesman had convinced him a fortune was waiting to be made by extracting gold ore from the mountains of tailings left behind by earlier generations of miners. My dad was taken in grand style; after investing all of my money, he discovered that the price of gold was too low to make mining the tailings profitable, and so I lost everything. For a long time he hid this from me and wouldn't admit what he had done; when he did tell me, he blamed it on other people.

35

PARTLY TO RAISE MONEY to finance a film about the UN's technical-assistance program in Asia, I took a part in *The Teahouse of the August Moon,* based on a wonderful play by John Patrick, which in turn was based on a novel by Vern Sneider. En route to Tokyo for the filming in the spring of 1956, I made a detour to Southeast Asia to look for story ideas and visited the Philippines, Thailand, Indonesia and several other countries. From afar I'd admired the efforts by the industrialized countries to help poorer nations improve their economies, and thought that this was the way the world ought to work. But I found something quite different; even though colonialism was dying, the industrialized countries were still exploiting the economies of these former colonies. Foreign-aid grants were given mostly for self-serving political purposes, and most Westerners never bothered to learn the language of the Asian countries and lived in hermetically sealed capsules of villas, servants, bourbon, air-conditioned offices, expense-account parties and all-white country clubs. A lot of the foreign-aid officials I met seemed arrogant and condescending, with a smug sense of superiority. Apparently because the United States had more television sets and automobiles, they were convinced that our system was infallible and that they had a God-given mission to impose our way of life on others. I was still unschooled in the ways of the diplomatic world and the hypocrisy of U.S. foreign policy, but I sensed that many of the political leaders we were supporting in these countries were looking out only for themselves and their bank accounts. They lived in palaces while their people lived in huts.

The trip yielded the draft of a script for a movie about the UN assistance program called *Tiger on a Kite* that was never made, but that in time led to *The Ugly American*.

Such trips were always among the most appealing reasons for being an actor. The opportunities to meet people and to experience cultures I would never have otherwise balanced some of the negative aspects of my profession. I remember a visit to Bali on that trip with particular affection. It was before large numbers of tourists had invaded the island, so it still had a sweet innocence. I met artisans and artists who worked all day in the rice fields, then came home, took a swim in a river, and taught dancing or worked lovingly on their artwork, and they seemed to lead a marvelous life. Before tourists polluted their culture, Balinese women didn't wear anything over their breasts, although if you encountered one on a street she usually covered herself up out of courtesy, not that she thought there was anything wrong with being bare-breasted, but as a show of respect. The women had beautiful bodies, and I kept trying to persuade them to be less respectful. Sitting in a stream with my feet braced against a boulder and water splashing over my shoulders, or looking downriver at a group of naked Balinese women bathing, I thought nothing in life could be more pleasant than this. A sailor I met had jumped ship in Bali and had decided to spend the rest of his life there. I understood why. He had learned to speak a rough form of the Balinese language and lived with two beautiful cinnamon-colored girls. A ship's carpenter skilled as a woodworker, he earned his way by making instruments for the orchestras that accompanied the *legong,* a Balinese dance in which the performers moved every part of their bodies, from eyebrows to toes. What a wonderful life he had, I thought, although he said that he had one problem; he was having trouble keeping his girlfriends satisfied. He asked me to send him some testosterone when I got home, and I did.

In *The Teahouse of the August Moon,* I played an interpreter on Okinawa named Sakini, who spends most of the movie dueling with Glenn Ford, an American army officer assigned to bring democracy and free enterprise to the island. The Broadway play, in which David Wayne had been marvelous as Sakini, was a delicate, amusing comedy of manners set against the backdrop of a stormy clash of cultures. As I've said, a well-written play is nearly actor-proof, but in *Teahouse* Glenn Ford and I proved how easily actors can ruin a good play or movie when they're so absorbed with themselves and their performances that they don't act in concert. It was a horrible picture and I was miscast.

Still, I enjoyed working again with Louis Calhern, whom I had met on *Julius Caesar.* He was an imposing, hard-drinking old actor with a classic profile, and he knew every trick in the book, had played virtually every part on Broadway and was full of stories about the theater. Once, he told me, he was getting ready to open in a new play and the producers were so frightened that he would not be sober for opening night that they locked him in a room on the fourth floor of the Lambs Club, the actors' club in New York. After they had gone, Calhern looked out the window and saw a waiter from the Lambs walking down below. He hailed him, floated a twenty-dollar bill to the sidewalk and asked him to bring up a bottle of whiskey and a straw. When the man knocked on the locked door, Louis said, "Put the straw through the keyhole and the other end in the bottle."

He emptied the bottle using the straw and was soon snockered. When the producers, who had frisked him and searched
the room for liquor before locking him in, came to get him, they
couldn't believe it, and Louis said they never figured out how he
had gotten the booze. It was like one of those English mysteries
in which a dead body is found in a drawing room but all the
windows and doors are locked from the inside. Nonetheless, on
opening night Louis got wonderful reviews for his performance.
He was a merry drunk, full of laughter and fun, but underneath
an unhappy, lonely man. His wife had just left him, which was
shattering, and he was suffering because of it, which made him
drink even more. A few weeks after we got to Tokyo, he died
from a heart attack, but I think he died happy and full of
laughter.

Someone decided we should have a religious funeral for
Louis, and selected a Catholic church with wooden pews,
kneeling benches, tatami mats on the floor and no heater. It was
freezing when we filed into the place, which, comically, was
according to our billing in the movie. Glenn began the eulogies
with an actor's performance. He described effusively how much
he missed Louis, looked to the heavens with his chin quivering
and seemed to be trying to address Calhern directly as if he
were already up there. Meanwhile the priest had kept giving us
cues to stand up, sit down, kneel, rise, kneel. For non-Catholics,
it was very confusing, as we kept going up and down like a
bank of express elevators. I noticed Glenn rubbing his knees in
pain, and the next time the priest signaled for us to kneel again,
he responded with a look of disgust and a barely audible sound
of resentment. At first he wouldn't go down, then he knelt
halfway, then finally all the way, and for some reason this
struck me as very funny and I started laughing. People turned
around and looked at me, so I tried to disguise my laughter as
the choked, tearful bereavement of someone suffering a great
loss. I clamped my hands over my eyes in sorrow and tried to

I was badly miscast in *The Teahouse of the August Moon*. Above: With Glenn Ford and Eddie Albert. (MGM/Courtesy of the Academy of Motion Picture Arts and Sciences)

A moment away from the camera in *Teahouse*. (Personal collection of Marlon Brando)

stop giggling, but I was in the clutches of a sustained and serious laughing attack, the kind that can take the wind out of you and tighten the muscles around your chest so that you can barely breathe. That I was reacting this way at a funeral made me even more hysterical. Glenn looked over at me with a surprised look that said, "Jesus, he's sure feeling a lot more grief than I am," which only made me laugh more. It was a nightmare, and I could hardly wait for the Mass to end. Afterward the priest, thinking I was immobilized by grief, came over to me and said, "My son, let's go into the rectory so we can have a private communication with Louis's spirit." Everyone had to follow or it would have been disrespectful, so we prayed some more there, and I could never stop laughing. On the ride back to the hotel, everybody, even Glenn, expressed sympathy for my loss.

After Louis's death, Paul Ford, a very funny actor, was brought in to replace him, but I, director Danny Mann and Glenn ruined the movie. On the first day of filming, I discovered that Glenn thought of himself as a masterful scene-stealer. He wouldn't be photographed from the left because he thought it was his "bad side," so before every shot he came to the set early and installed himself in the position he wanted, where the camera would see him from the right side; then, after we took our marks, he backed up a step or two, so that the camera had to follow him and he wound up full-faced in the shot, and other actors had to turn and lose three quarters of their faces. Sometimes he would gesture across my face, or as I said a line he would make a quick movement to catch the audience's eye; or he would begin stuttering to draw attention to his character.

I knew what Glenn was doing, but I don't think he ever realized how transparent he was. I had occasionally run into actors who tried to hog the camera, but had never met someone of this caliber. I knew the techniques as well as anyone; they're not mysterious. A lot of actors try to do it and manipulate the audience. Olivia de Havilland had a wonderful trick of breathing deeply to make her breasts swell in and out; when she did, she made short work of the other actors in the scene because the audience—at least all the males, and probably half the females—was preoccupied with the movement of her breasts. But Ford took scene-stealing to Olympian heights, and in this fragile story, which required the two of us to act in delicate concert, he wanted to be the center of attention in every scene.

At the beginning I tried to reassure Glenn that I wasn't a threat to his status, and in several scenes turned three quarters around so that he would appear full-faced to the camera. I wanted to let him know we weren't combatants, but he kept it up. Whenever we took our places for a shot, just before the camera started rolling he took a step or two backward, which made me pull my head around to look at him as he went upstage; in the camera's eye, I went from full face to a narrow profile. But he thought I was just stupid. I finally thought, To hell with this, and I followed him across the stage the next time he did it. When he backed up, I moved forward; he backed up again and I moved another few inches; we repeated this until we were moving across the stage inches at a time like a couple of dancers doing a tango until finally the camera operator shouted, "Hold it. I can't hold the focus anymore! You're out of focus." Eventually I decided that the picture was a dead horse and that there was no way it could be saved; it was a sensitive comedy and we were wrecking it. I didn't think it was one of Danny Mann's best efforts. Quite apart from everything else, I felt inept as a comedian; David Wayne should have played the part in the movie.

But since the picture was lost anyway, I decided to have some fun with Glenn's performance. Thereafter I made sure to arrive on the set before he did and took a position that made him face the camera from his left side. I began stepping on his lines and blowing mine when he had a big scene and trying to rattle him during his speeches. When an actor has a long take, he hates to be distracted, so before one of his big speeches to a group of Okinawans, I got a flyswatter from the prop man and started following nonexistent flies around in the background, swatting one occasionally, and during his close-ups I stuck my head in and out of the camera as if searching for a fly.

Glenn looked at me as if he had been struck with an anvil. He didn't know what to think, because with all his trickery and my letting him get away with it initially, he didn't understand what I was doing. I wore him out; he thought I was too dumb to see through him, which made it even more fun to play tricks on him on and off the set. He was a miser about food, and at one of the locations we shared a dressing room in which he kept a cache of candies and desserts he had bought at an army PX and that he was tightfisted about sharing. After he brought back a box of cookies, I saw him hide it in our room and I pinched some. When Glenn discovered that some of them were missing, he stormed out the door and blamed a group of Japanese kids from the neighborhood who were hanging about and were only about two feet high. He screamed at them, "No cookies. No cookies. Do not eat cookies. No go in there."

I didn't like how he treated the kids, and I thought he should have given them the cookies in the first place because in those days there weren't many sweets to go around. Later that day, I ate a few of the remaining cookies, then threw several others on the floor and stomped on them. When he came in and saw the crumbs, he exploded. It must have been about $1.75 worth of cookies, but it sent him into a rage, and he demanded that the producers post guards outside our dressing room, which led to a lot of jokes about the "Cookie Watch."

When he discovered more cookies crushed on the floor the next day, Glenn asked me if I knew anything about it, and I told him in my most convincing manner that it was a mystery to me.

How did those kids get into the trailer past the guards? he asked.

He never found out. Again it was one of those English drawing-room mysteries—like Louis Calhern, the whiskey and the straw.

36

IF I HADN'T BEEN an actor, I've often thought I'd have become a con man and wound up in jail. Or I might have gone crazy. Acting afforded me the luxury of being able to spend thousands of dollars on psychoanalysts, most of whom did nothing but convince me that most New York and Beverly Hills psychoanalysts are a little crazy themselves, as well as highly motivated to separate patients from their money while making their emotional problems worse. I think I'd have made a good con man; I'm good at telling lies smoothly, giving an impression of things as they are not and making people think I'm sincere. A good con man can fool anybody, but the first person he fools is himself. It occurs to me that when I was thinking about becoming a preacher I believed the talents I thought would make me a good tent-show evangelist were the same ones that would have made me a good con man.

Having had the luck to be successful as an actor also afforded me the luxury of time. I only had to do a movie once a year, for three months at the most, which paid me enough so that I didn't have to work again until my business manager called and said, "We've got to pay your taxes at the end of the year, so you'd better make another movie." When that happened, I'd look around and grab something.

After *Teahouse of the August Moon,* my father, who thought of himself as my manager even though I'd only put him on the payroll so he'd have an office to go to after my mother died, started pressing me to make another picture. Pennebaker Productions, he said, was facing serious financial problems. As always, he was preoccupied with money. He complained I was spending too much on the UN picture and on a western I wanted to make, and he claimed that a friend I'd put on the Pennebaker payroll was exploiting me. He said if I didn't make another picture soon, I'd be in trouble with the IRS. He urged me to sign for a picture based on a novel by James A. Michener that Joshua Logan wanted to direct and that Warner Brothers, with producer William Goetz, had offered to finance in a joint venture with Pennebaker. I read the novel, *Sayonara,* which was set in postwar Japan, and thought it raised interesting issues about human relations, but I didn't like the script. In the script and the novel, the character Logan wanted me to play, Major Lloyd Gruver, a Korean War–era U.S. Air Force pilot, fell in love with a beautiful Japanese woman, Hana-ogi, a member of a distinguished and elite dance troupe, but their interracial romance was doomed by the tradition in both cultures of endogamy, the custom of marrying only within one's own race or caste. In accepting this principle, I thought the story endorsed indirectly a form of racism. But with a different ending, I thought it could be an example of the pictures I wanted to make, films that exerted a positive force. I told Logan I'd do the picture if the Madame Butterfly ending was replaced by one stating that there was nothing wrong with racial intermarriage, and that it was a natural outcome when people fell in love. I wanted the two lovers to marry at the end of the picture, and Logan agreed.

But once we were in Japan, I discovered that Josh was burdened with an overwhelming depression that made him unable
to function. I ended up rewriting and improvising a lot of the
picture, and we had to limp along as best we could. With Josh's
problems and a long run of rainy weather, it was a difficult picture to make, and I don't think Logan knew what was happening most of the time.

My father now called me Marlon instead of Bud, and we
were civil to each other, but the friction between us never
ended. After he began working for me, I didn't expect him
really to do anything, but he constantly wrote memos warning
me that my company was wasting money on projects that were
going nowhere, and that I was too concerned with making a
statement and not enough with making money. "To date," he
wrote me before we had received our share of the profits from
Sayonara, "Pennebaker is almost as far away from producing a
picture as it was at the beginning, and we have spent $18,000 in
hard dollars contributed by you, $25,000 by MCA, and over
$153,000 loaned by Paramount—$196,000. Pennebaker's reputation as a producer has been declining and it can be assumed
that this is not without its reflection on you." He said we'd
wasted $72,000 alone on preparations for the UN movie.
"Some of the reasons for our diversions were that Pennebaker
wanted to be a helpful force in the world. I agree heartily with
the thought, but I think there is some question as to whether
this sort of program belongs in an embryonic production company. . . ."
Regardless of what he thought, I wanted to make pictures
that were not only entertaining but had social value and gave
me a sense that I was helping to improve the condition of the
world. My father disagreed with my priorities: "The corporation" should be "operated with the prime objective of turning
out tasteful, good pictures that are commercial until such a time

During the filming of *Sayonara:*
with my father on location in Japan
(Personal collection of Marlon Brando);
and with Josh Logan and a priest at
a Buddhist temple (Warner Bros./Cour-
tesy of the Academy of Motion Picture Arts
and Sciences).

that it can afford to do something for the emotional satisfaction involved. I think we have put the cart before the horse in some respects. Our purpose, at least the purpose of the industry, is to entertain rather than try to use loaded directive thought . . . more real lasting good is probably produced by foundations, universities, colleges, medical research, hospitals and even churches, and these are all activated and made possible by the use of dollars earned in a hard commercial way. As you say, I have a money neurosis in one way. I think you have a money neurosis in another way. Someday I think we should discuss our respective tendencies. I personally don't believe there is anything wrong in having money if it is used as an instrument rather than a means . . . if money can be used properly it can become an instrument for great good. After Pennebaker has earned sufficient money any surpluses above needs can be used as you see fit."

My father also continued to complain that my friends who worked for Pennebaker were using and exploiting me. "You have great perception and knowledge," he said, "but you allow yourself to be conned into doing things emotionally. You can afford this personally, but you cannot afford this in Pennebaker. . . ."

When the press fabricated stories about me, I feigned indifference over what was said and what others thought about me. I think I was convincing in this pose of detachment, but it was a mask. Newspapers and magazines invented things that were not only untrue, but were often gratuitously salacious and they offended me greatly. I became particularly annoyed by stories in *Time* and *Life*. I engaged a research organization to dig up all the negative unassailable facts it could find about Time Inc., the parent company, spent about $8,000 for a long profile on the company's history of distorting and slanting the news, and then went on one television and radio program after another to slam

Time and *Life*. I was after their advertising. I wanted revenge. I intended to hurt them, and there wasn't anything they could do about it because I was only repeating facts of how skewed the magazines' presentation of the news was as a result of the political biases of Henry Luce. On radio and television, I said his magazines were ruining the reputation of the United States, that they were unpatriotic and injuring the stature of our country abroad, and that they insulted other countries with distorted stories for which our nation would ultimately have to pay a price. I relished doing this. That's how I was during a large part of my life; if I thought anybody had wronged me, I hit back.

Time Inc. sent a woman out to see me who was related to a friend of mine. She called on a pretext of some sort and I invited her to dinner. We had several martinis, and by the time we headed back to my house I was driving an S pattern across the highway and she was even worse off. I pulled into my driveway, but before we got out of the car, she tried valiantly to carry out her mission. In slurred tones, she said, "Marlon, what's all this about you attacking *Time*? What's behind it? What's going on here?"

"Oh, I think they're great magazines," I said, "but there's a few corrections they should make, and I've gone on several programs to set the record straight. I'm going to keep doing it because I feel it's my civic duty to correct the press when it's wrong. Actually I think they should appreciate it. They have a letters-to-the-editor column, and in a sense this is just a letter to the editor. It's a continuing letter that will go on and on until they don't feel they have the right to ruin the reputation of America . . ."

Then I lowered her into the bushes, intending to act the beast with two backs with the emissary of my enemy, but I was so awash in alcohol, so immobilized and out of ammunition that I couldn't tell the ivy from her earlobes. She returned to New York with her virtue intact. But from that day to this, *Time* has seldom mentioned my name, and if it has, it's been in a cursory way. Time Inc. is a big company, but it was the old story of David and Goliath: it takes only one well-placed stone in the middle of the forehead.

In late 1957 I went to Europe to make *The Young Lions,* a movie based on Irwin Shaw's novel about three soldiers—two Americans and a German—whose lives intersected before and during World War II. Monty Clift played the Jewish-American soldier, Noah Ackerman, and I played the German, Christian Diestl. Jay Kantor told me that Dean Martin, whose career had been in decline after his breakup with Jerry Lewis, was desperate to play Michael Whiteacre, an American entertainer reluctantly drafted into the war, to prove that he could handle a serious dramatic role, so I helped him get the part. When we met at a restaurant in Paris before the filming started, someone spilled a pot of scalding water on my crotch. The pain was excruciating and sent me to a hospital for several days, where I thought about the script and decided to exercise the right in my contract to change it.

The original script closely followed the book, in which Shaw painted all Germans as evil caricatures, especially Christian, whom he portrayed as a symbol of everything that was bad about Nazism; he was mean, nasty, vicious, a cliché of evil. Like many books and movies produced by Jews since the war, I think it was a perfectly understandable bias that, consciously or unconsciously, Jews felt would ensure that the world would never forget the Holocaust and, not coincidentally, would increase sympathy and financial support for Israel. Indirectly Shaw was saying that *all* Germans were responsible for the Holocaust, which I didn't agree with. Much to his irritation, I changed the plot entirely so that at the beginning of the story my character believed that Hitler was a positive force because he gave Germans a sense of purpose. But as the story developed, he gradually became disenchanted and struggled to turn his back on these beliefs. Like many Germans, Christian had been misled by Hitler's propaganda and believed he would bring a lasting peace to Europe by conquering it—the same rationalization that Napoleon had employed by saying he wanted to unify Europe to bring peace. I thought the story should demonstrate that there are no inherently "bad" people in the world, but that they can easily be misled.

I'm uncomfortable with generalizations about anything because they are rarely accurate. At the time, we were just coming out of the McCarthy era, when many people's lives had been ruined because so many Americans accepted the myth that every Communist—or anyone who'd ever had a drink with one—was the devil incarnate, while overlooking the malignancy of Joe McCarthy, who was a greater menace than the people he targeted.

In *The Young Lions* I wanted to show that there were positive aspects to Germans, as there are to all people. Depending on your point of view, there are positive and negative elements in everyone. Hitler propagated the myth that the Germans were a superior race and the Jews inferior, but accepting the reverse of this is equally wrong; there are bad Jews and Germans, and decent Jews and Germans. I decided to play Christian Diestl as an illustration of one element of the human character—that is, how, because of their need to keep their myths alive, people will go to enormous lengths to ignore the negative aspects of their beliefs.

It happens all the time. I've watched parents tell television interviewers how proud they were of their son who died in Vietnam because he had been fighting to defend freedom, his country and American ideals, when I am sure they must have known in their hearts what a foolish war it was and that their son's life had been squandered for nothing. Memories and myths were all they had to cling to; they couldn't admit that their son was dead because of the senseless and destructive policies of Lyndon Johnson, Robert McNamara and the rest of the "Best and the Brightest."

In Christian Diestl I also wanted to show how people like Johnson and McNamara often have such a misguided sense of righteousness and idealism that they sincerely believe that what is inherently immoral or wrong is justifiable, will commit terrible acts to achieve their goals, and then find it easy to rationalize their actions. The perpetrators of the CIA program in Vietnam called Operation Phoenix were responsible for torturing and assassinating hundreds of people. I was once told by a CIA man who was closely associated with the program that if someone's name was put into a computer identifying him as a member of the Vietcong, it was sent out to various assassination squads and the person was killed; yet a lot of these weren't really in the Vietcong, and their names were listed by mistake or because someone had a grudge against them. The CIA man said he had complained about this to a top official of the agency and was told, "Look, innocent people get killed in all wars. If we get one right out of four, it's okay. The rest just have to be sacrificed; this is a *war*." This leader was a devout Catholic who had become conditioned to do his job without any pangs of conscience, but how different was he from Heydrich or Himmler?

People can be conditioned to do anything. If you commit murder in the name of your country, it is called patriotism. Before sending them to Vietnam, the army brainwashed young men into believing that they were on the side of God. The marines sent young people to Camp Pendleton, isolated them and put them in a kind of trance through indoctrination, conditioning and training. If they were told to do something, they did it, just like the marines in World War II on Saipan who, when told to fire phosphorus bombs into caves where women and children were hiding, did it without question, remorse or guilt. They used flamethrowers to burn people alive, just as our pilots exterminated Vietnamese civilians with napalm and antipersonnel bombs that riddled their bodies with tiny barbed arrows designed to tumble inside them violently, with enhanced killing power. The soldiers who massacred the villagers at My Lai were no more inherently evil than the German soldiers who committed atrocities in World War II. They had simply been programmed into becoming murderous predators. At places like Fort Bragg and Fort Benning, our soldiers had been conditioned by much the same creed drummed into Christian Diestl: "My country right or wrong; when my country calls me, I will do my duty; I will do *anything*."

37

WES MICKLER GAVE ME one of the best lessons of an actor's life: never trust a horse, he said, because you'll never find a smart one. He used to lean back in his old spindle chair in Libertyville, give me a long, knowing look and tell me that all horses were dumb. He was right. I've never met a smart horse. I've also known a lot of dumb riders, including me. The worst place for an actor to be when he's making a western, I discovered, is on top of a charging horse with a bunch of other horses chasing you from behind. You can't see them and they can't see you. Because of the dust, visibility is about five feet, and the horses behind you will run over you if anything goes wrong. In *Julius Caesar* I was leading an army across a field when the tongue of my shoe got caught in a stirrup. I leaned over and tried to pull it out, but couldn't reach it, so I thought I'd leave it until the take was over. It was dumb. After riding quite a distance, I looked back and saw the whole field of horses racing fast toward me, bucking and kicking and leaping; some of them were rolling on the ground. I tried to get my horse to run, but because my foot was stuck, it was impossible to convey this to the horse except in a loud, nervous voice. The horse wouldn't go any faster, I couldn't get out of the way of the ones behind me and I came within a hair of falling in front of the galloping herd, still secured neatly to my stirrup. I kept my head down while the horses stampeded past me and tried to figure out what had happened. Then I learned that I'd ridden over a hornets' nest and they had taken their revenge on the riders and horses behind me.

On *Viva Zapata!* I was in a scene in which four horsemen holding me prisoner galloped up a road and suddenly found themselves facing an army of troops loyal to me. The man holding my horse, a big stallion with a huge neck, was meant to let go of the reins after realizing that he was about to be slaughtered, and I was supposed to take off down the road and escape. But as the four men turned their horses to look at the troops, they blocked the path in front of me and my horse simply ran over them. At another point a bit player on that picture was supposed to ride up to me, jump off his horse and deliver important news to me. Wes Mickler had warned me that when you walk behind a horse who doesn't know you, you should stay close enough to it so that it can't reach out and kick you. If you pass within the outer radius of his hooves, he said, the horse can fire a knockout punch at you. Unfortunately nobody had given such advice to this bit player, and when he ran around the back of the horse, he was in exactly the wrong place. The horse kicked him in the back of the head and he went down like a shot, dead.

When we were making *Viva Zapata!* I sometimes took a ride to savor the beauty of the desert. Once, a few days after I had gone riding and had encountered an extraordinary migration of butterflies, I hopped on a horse and was barely in the saddle before it started bucking and kicking wildly. In about three seconds, I was airborne. As I sprawled on the ground, checking for broken bones, one of the studio wranglers came up and said, "Marlon, you shouldn't have gotten on *that* horse; nobody's ever ridden him before." It turned out that he'd been saddled as a kind of equine extra for the first scene after lunch, but wasn't meant to be ridden.

One of the things I always did before working with a new director was to call another actor who knew him and ask, "What's the lowdown on this guy?" Before working with John Huston on *Reflections in a Golden Eye*, I called John Saxon and asked the usual question.

"He's good," John said. "He doesn't get on your back and he leaves you alone, and near the end of the picture he'll disappear. But if you have a scene with horses in it, get a double because he'll kill you if you don't."

He was right about Huston leaving actors alone. He didn't give us any direction. He hired good actors, trusted them and let them improvise, but never helped shape a characterization the way Kazan did. He sat at the edge of the set and said, "Yeah, all right, kids, that's good, that's a good start, now why don't we try it over." He was always vague and we took our own cues. John did a lot of heavy pot smoking on that picture, and before he filmed one scene he gave me some marijuana, which I smoked. Before long, I had no idea who or where I was or what I was supposed to be doing. The only thing I knew was that everything seemed okay, that the world was very funny and that John thought so, too. I could barely stand up, and if somebody asked me a question I'd say "What?" about five seconds later, but somehow I managed to get through the scene.

At the end of the picture, Huston did what I'd been told he would: he disappeared. Some days he didn't show up on the set at all, and one of the assistant directors would have to take over; on others he came to work, then walked away after an hour or so, or we might see him off in the distance by himself. For some reason he became moody and depressed when he approached the end of a picture.

Unfortunately I didn't take seriously what John Saxon had told me about Huston and horses. I had a scene in which a horse was supposed to run away with me, and when he asked me if I could do it without a double I said, "Sure." I'd spent a lot of time on Hollywood horses and wasn't afraid of them. But when I came out of my dressing room for the scene, I saw a big stallion waiting for me, and it was shaking and shuddering so much it might have been wired to an electrical plug. John had instructed a groom to heat it up, and the man had done his job; he had trotted the horse back and forth until it was awash with perspiration and trembling with eagerness to move. I looked up at him and said to myself, "You know, Marlon, that's a lot of horse." I knew stallions had minds of their own and could be aggressive, sometimes dangerous, but I got on him anyway, and as soon as I did, he took off like a jet fighter catapulted from an aircraft carrier.

Before he'd taken four or five steps, I knew I was on the wrong horse. He was so charged up with adrenaline that I expected him to run me into a barn or a fence. I took my feet out of the stirrups, lifted my right leg and jumped, landing with both heels in the mud, then said, "John, if you need me, I'll be in my dressing room. I think I need a different horse or else a double."

For the long shot in that scene, Huston used a stunt rider, and for the close-up he put me in a saddle mounted on a pickup truck and photographed me with a lot of fright on my face.

I also got to ride a horse in *One-Eyed Jacks,* my first picture after *The Young Lions.* In its first four years, Pennebaker had spent almost as much money trying to develop a good script for a western as it had on the story about the United Nations, but none of the projects, including a western based on the plot of *The Count of Monte Cristo,* worked out for various reasons. Then I heard about a novel by Charles Neider, *The Authentic Death of Hendry Jones,* which eventually became *One-Eyed Jacks,* one of my favorite pictures. It was the first and only picture I directed, although I didn't intend to. Stanley Kubrick was supposed to direct, but he didn't like the screenplay. "Marlon," he said, "I've read the script and I just can't understand what this picture is about."

"This picture is about my having to pay two hundred and fifty thousand dollars a week to Karl Malden," I said. I'd signed him for the picture, and each week of delay meant another $250,000 lost.

"Well," Stanley said, "if that's what it's about, I think I'm doing the wrong picture."

I sent the script to Sidney Lumet, then Gadg, then two or three other directors, but no one wanted to do it, so I had to direct it myself. We shot most of it at Big Sur and on the Monterey peninsula, where I slept with many pretty women and had a lot of laughs.

On the first day of shooting, I didn't know what to do, so the cameraman handed me one of those optical viewfinders that directors use to compose a scene. I looked into it, then shook my head and said, "I don't know. . . . It's hard to tell what this scene's going to look like because it's so far away. . . ."

The cameraman came over and gently turned it around. I'd been looking through the wrong end.

"If you think this is bad, wait until we get to the fifth week," I said and laughed. I wasn't embarrassed, although there were a lot of muffled titters behind me. By the fifth week, and even the fifth month, I was still trying to learn. I thought it would take three months to do the picture, but it stretched to six, and the cost doubled to more than $6 million; naturally this didn't please Paramount, which was paying for it.

I tried to figure out what to do as I went along. Several writers worked on the screenplay—Sam Peckinpah, Calder Willingham and finally Guy Trosper—and he and I constantly improvised and rewrote between shots and setups, often hour by hour, sometimes minute by minute. Some scenes I shot over and over again from different angles with different dialogue and action because I didn't know what I was doing. I was making things up by the moment, not sure where the story was going. I also did a lot of stalling for time, trying to work the story out in my mind while hoping to make the cast think I knew what I was doing.

Maybe I liked the picture so much because it left me with a lot of pleasant memories about the people in it—Ben Johnson, Slim Pickens and especially Karl Malden, who played Dad. I don't want to do it again—a director has to get up too early in the morning—but it was entertaining to try to create reality, make a story interesting and to work with actors. Sometimes I played tricks on them. In one scene Ben Johnson had an argument with one of his compatriots, then shot him. I didn't like the expression on the other man's face before he was shot because it didn't show a fear of death. I wanted him to show shock and terror, so I said, "Let's rehearse this one more time." I put him on a saddle mounted on a piece of wood and, without telling him, kept the camera rolling. I walked over to him and said, "Larry, in this scene I want you to—" Then, boom! I slapped him hard and jumped out of the scene.

He had a wonderful expression on his face, just what I wanted, but I had slapped him so hard that I knocked off his mustache, and so I couldn't use the shot. In another scene I was supposed to get drunk, come in out of the rain and rape a Chinese girl. You can't fake drunkenness in a movie. You can in a play, but not in a close-up, so I figured the scene would work better if I really got drunk. I started drinking about 4:15 in the afternoon of the day I was going to shoot the scene after telling the other actors what I wanted them to do. It has never taken much alcohol to put me over the edge, so in no time at all I was staggering around, grabbing hold of the girl. Unfortunately I was too drunk to finish the scene, so a few days later I got drunk again and reshot it. It still wasn't right, and I had to do it on a number of afternoons until it was right.

A break in the filming of *One-Eyed Jacks*, my only directorial effort, with actress Pina Pellicer, with whom I shared my thirty-fifth birthday. (Courtesy of Paramount Pictures/Academy of Motion Picture Arts and Sciences)

When we got back to Hollywood, someone said we had enough footage to make a movie six or eight hours long. I started editing it, but pretty soon got sick of it and turned the job over to someone else. When he had finished, Paramount said it didn't like my version of the story; I'd had everybody in the picture lie except Karl Malden. The studio cut the movie to pieces and made him a liar, too. By then I was bored with the whole project and walked away from it.

Several years before *One-Eyed Jacks,* Tennessee Williams had told me he had written a new play, *Orpheus Descending,* with me in mind to play opposite Anna Magnani. I told him I didn't have any interest in returning to the stage, and Cliff Robertson and Maureen Stapleton played the parts. But when Tennessee and Sidney Lumet invited me to be in the movie *The Fugitive Kind,* which was based on the play, I was divorcing my first wife and needed money. I was a guitar-playing drifter who wandered into a small town in Mississippi and got involved with an older woman, played by Anna, who had been a powerful actress in the Italian film *Open City* and later in Tennessee's movie *The Rose Tattoo.* She was a troubled woman who I thought was miscast in *The Fugitive Kind.*

In a letter to Lady Maria St. Just while we were shooting the picture, Tennessee wrote: "Magnani is obsessed with her age; she thinks that her neck is gone, and they are putting tapes on the back to pull it up and together. She regards this as a terrible insult and yet she rages whenever she sees a neck line in the rushes." Tennessee was also growing more troubled at the time, plunging frequently into fits of depression and using alcohol and pills to pull himself out. What haunted him I don't know, though he was deeply worried about the health of his mother and sister. I've always thought of Tennessee as one of the greatest American writers, but I didn't think much of this play or the movie. Like most great American writers, he turned black people into windowpanes. In *The Fugitive Kind,* they were ren-

I was warned about Anna Magnani, seen here on the set of *The Fugitive Kind*. (United Artists/Courtesy of the Academy of Motion Picture Arts and Sciences)

dered almost invisible, as if they were props. Blacks were in the story, but they were incidental figures who had nothing to do with the central themes, just as in *A Streetcar Named Desire,* and it seemed to me a subtle form of racial discrimination. I don't mean to say that Tennessee was insensitive. He was acutely sensitive, but he expressed the prevailing perspective of virtually all American authors. The black experience was all but ignored. No one, I believe, wrote well on the subject until Jim Baldwin and Toni Morrison came along. Hollywood was even worse; the black experience was a topic it never touched unless it was bigoted claptrap like *The Birth of a Nation,* with its undisguised contempt for black people.

Tennessee warned me that Anna Magnani, who was sixteen years older than me and had a reputation for enjoying the company of young men, had told him that she was in love with me, and before we left for upstate New York to film the picture she confirmed it. After we had some meetings in California, she tried several times to see me alone, and finally succeeded one afternoon at the Beverly Hills Hotel. Without any encouragement from me, she started kissing me with great passion. I tried to be responsive because I knew she was worried about growing older and losing her beauty, and as a matter of kindness I felt I had to return her kisses; to refuse her would have been a terrible insult. But once she got her arms around me, she wouldn't let go. If I started to pull away, she held on tight and bit my lip, which really hurt. With her teeth gnawing at my lower lip, the two of us locked in an embrace, I was reminded of one of those fatal mating rituals of insects that end when the female administers the coup de grâce. We rocked back and forth as she tried to lead me to the bed. My eyes were wide open, and as I looked at her eyeball-to-eyeball I saw that she was in a frenzy, Attila the Hun in full attack. Finally the pain got so intense that I grabbed her nose and squeezed it as hard as I could, as if I were squeezing a lemon, to push her away. It startled her, and I made my escape.

38

A FEW YEARS AFTER my mother died in 1953, my father remarried, and at seventy he had an affair with one of my secretaries. He changed little as he grew older; always handsome, always a miser, always a charmer, always a philanderer. He never lost the shyness that people, especially women, liked about him. It was something he came by naturally. Though he was very masculine, he also had a gentleness, humility and quietness that people liked, along with a very genuine sense of humor. He was unsuited to do anything in the movie business, but I had given him a salary, a desk, an office, a secretary and an opportunity to look busy and feel useful. Then one day, without telling me about it, he fired one of my friends. When I heard about it, I went to his office and told him that my friend was not going to be fired, and from somewhere inside me a tidal wave rose, crested and flooded, and I reduced him to a heap of shambling, stuttering, fast-blinking confusion.

I said he should consider himself fortunate to have a job, since anybody else with his qualifications would be in a poorhouse. I went over the history of our family and told him that he had ruined my mother's life and had used every opportunity to belittle me and make me feel inadequate. I took him apart with pliers, bit by bit, hunk by hunk, and distributed his psyche all over the floor. I was cold, correct and logical—no screaming or yelling—just stone frozen cold, and when he tried to make excuses, I slammed down an iron gate and reminded him what a shambles he had made of our lives. I told him that he was directly responsible for making my sisters alcoholics and that he was cold, unloving, selfish, infantile, terminally despicable and self-absorbed. I made him feel useless, helpless, hopeless and weak. I assaulted him for almost three hours and when he tried to end the conversation I said, "Sit down if you expect to be paid any money from this day forward. You will listen to what your employer is telling you. I am your employer and you are something of an employee—at least you bear that name—and you will do what I tell you."

In three hours I did what in thirty-three years I had never been able to, yet the whole time I was scared. I was frightened of what *he* would do to *me*. I had always been overwhelmed and intimidated by him, but the more I talked, the more strength and conviction I gained of my rightness and justification. It was like Joe Louis with Max Schmeling in their second fight: I hit him everyplace. He was naked and I was all over him like a cheap suit. Then, when I'd finished saying what I wanted to get off my chest, I dismissed him.

Afterward, I called everybody in the family and told them what I had done and they congratulated me. "Well, it's about time," my sisters said. But inside I felt tremendous aftershocks from what I had done. I thought the sky was going to fall on me because of what I had said.

A few days later I got a call from a psychiatrist who said that my father was seeing him and that he needed my cooperation because his patient was in a serious depression and "on the edge of a precipice."

"Well, Doctor," I said, "I appreciate your calling. When my father has gone over the edge of that depression and smashed himself on the rocks below—when he's hit bottom—please call me and I'll see if I can arrange something. . . ."

After that, I always kept my father on a tight leash so that he could never come near me and never get too far away. I had him under control and never let him go.

In the spring of 1965 I visited the Navajo Indian reservation in Arizona and met an old medicine woman. She was charming, with intelligent dark eyes, and I asked her if she could tell anything about me simply by looking at me. Through an interpreter, she said yes, she could, and she dipped her hand into a box of flowers beside her and sprinkled yellow cornflowers over my head and shoulders, letting them fall around me. She said alcohol had played a very important part in my life, and that I was about to be struck by lightning. As she said it, I felt a strange sensation streak through my nervous system.

"Both your parents are dead," she went on.

"No," I said, "one of them is dead—my mother—but not my father."

Within minutes, I was informed that there was a telephone call for me at the tribal office. It was one of my sisters calling, to tell me my father had just died. We both laughed, and I said, "And not a moment too soon."

I got in my car and drove all the way home. It took almost twelve hours. I was with a woman named Honey, who was from Holland, and when we got home and were in bed I told her about my father and how I felt about him. Then, as I began to drift off to sleep, I had a vision of him walking down a sidewalk away from me, then turning around to look at me, a slump-shouldered Willy Loman with a faint smile on his face. When he got to the edge of eternity, he stopped and looked back again, turned halfway toward me and, with his eyes downcast, said: *I did the best I could, kid.* He turned away again, and I knew he was looking for my mother.

Then, like her, he became a bird and started rising in the sky, soaring higher and higher until he found her beside a cliff, where she had been waiting for him.

My father was so secretive about money that we never found out how much he had when he died. He left his second wife their home and about $3,000 from an insurance policy, but he had hidden the rest—who knows how much—in bank accounts under false names. It's probably there to this day. Curiously, years before, he had done something accidentally that almost made him a success. After he died, the price of gold shot up and for the first time it became profitable to refine the tailings from the old gold mines on which he'd lost so much of my money. But by then we had long since disposed of them.

If my father were alive today, I don't know what I would do. After he died, I used to think, "God, just give him to me alive for eight seconds; that's all I want, just eight seconds because I want to break his jaw." I wanted to smash his face and watch him spit out his teeth. I wanted to kick his balls into his throat. I wanted to rip his ears off and eat them in front of him. I wanted to separate his larynx from his body and shove it into his stomach. But with time I began to realize that as long as I felt this way I would never be free until I eradicated these feelings in myself. With time, I also may have seen a little of him in me. Maybe it was in my genes all the time. He was a very angry man, as I was for most of my life. His mother had deserted him when he was four years old, and he must have experienced some of the same feelings I had. As children, my sisters and I never had much emotional security, and perhaps he didn't either. Physically and emotionally, each generation is linked, like the strands in an endless rope, to the generations before it and those that follow it, and families' emotional disorders can be transmitted from one to the next as surely as a genetic disorder. Like us, he had been left as a child to fend for himself emotionally as best he could. As I've said before, I don't believe any of us is born evil. We are all products of our childhoods and genetic and environmental forces over which we have little control.

My sisters have tried to help me understand my father more. As Fran reminded me in a letter, our father's father "was a mean-spirited, rigid, terrifying martinet of a person who had made life so unbearable for our grandmother that she ran off when Poppa was just four years old. Left him abandoned. . . . Left to a miserable, loveless and terrified childhood with a self-righteous, loveless disciplinarian instead of a father. That was our father's wound and terror from which he never recovered. He grew up to be six feet tall . . . and inside his strong masculine presence was a very complicated, troubled and isolated person . . . at odds with himself and often with the world."

Ultimately I realized that I would have to forgive my father if I was ever going to be able to get on with my life.

39

THE HAPPIEST MOMENTS of my life have been in Tahiti. If I've ever come close to finding genuine peace, it was on my island among the Tahitians. When I first went there, I foolishly thought I'd use my money to help them; instead, I learned I had nothing to give them and that they had everything to give me.

Tahiti has exerted a force over me since I was a teenager. It began in the library at Shattuck, when I used to thumb through the *National Geographic,* and it continued after I went to New York and searched libraries for any book that mentioned Tahiti and combed the film archives at the Museum of Modern Art looking for images of Polynesia. In the early 1960s MGM asked me to play Fletcher Christian in a remake of *Mutiny on the Bounty* and said it would be filmed in Tahiti. Previously David Lean had asked me to play T. E. Lawrence in *Lawrence of Arabia*; I had gone to Paris to meet with him and Sam Spiegel, and they had announced I was going to be in the picture. But when *Mutiny on the Bounty* came up and David said he expected to take six months filming *Lawrence of Arabia,* most of it in the desert, I decided I'd rather go to Tahiti. Lean was a very good director, but he took so long to make a movie that I would have dried up in the desert like a puddle of water.

From the moment I saw it, reality surpassed even my fantasies about Tahiti, and I had some of the best times of my life making *Mutiny on the Bounty*. The filming was done largely on a replica of H.M.S. *Bounty* anchored offshore, and every day as soon as the director said, "Cut" for the last time, I ripped off my British naval officer's uniform and dove off the ship into the bay to swim with the Tahitian extras working on the movie. Often we only did two or three shots a day, which left me hours to enjoy their company, and I grew to love them for their love of life.

While we were filming, reports began circulating that it was months behind schedule and millions of dollars over budget because of *me*. Initially I didn't realize this, but MGM was blaming me for budget overruns that it was responsible for, just as Twentieth Century–Fox had used Elizabeth Taylor as a scapegoat for its miscalculations and production excesses on *Cleopatra*. When I arrived in Tahiti, MGM still didn't have a usable script, the H.M.S. *Bounty* wasn't finished, and the ordinary preproduction preparations were several weeks behind schedule. Once filming started, the studio realized it had underestimated the cost of shooting a picture on location in French Polynesia, and then it fired the director, Carol Reed, causing further delays and extra expense. Dishonestly, MGM portrayed me as the source of the delays. It wasn't true, but reporters in the entertainment press, who didn't like me for refusing to give interviews, and who seldom did any independent digging on their own unless it involved titillation, accepted what MGM's press agents said; it fit their preconceived notion of an eccentric, cantankerous Brando, and quickly the distortions were carved in granite. For the first and only time in my life, I asked a press agent to present my side of the story, but then discovered too late that he was an MGM plant. Though he was supposedly working for me, he was on the MGM payroll and had been instructed secretly to keep placing the blame on me. I didn't learn about this until many years later. At the time, I was still of a mind to ignore what people wrote or thought about me, so I hadn't paid much attention to what was going on until the stories of my alleged profligacy had been woven into the tapestry containing all the other myths about me.

The first director on the picture, Carol Reed, was a talented Englishman whom I admired. When MGM replaced him with Lewis Milestone, we were told that Carol had had an argument with the studio and quit. Later I learned that he'd been sacked because he wanted to make Captain Bligh a hero. In reality, Bligh *was* a hero, but Charles Laughton hadn't played him that way. Since Laughton was the definitive Bligh, the studio didn't want to revise history in the new version, which wasn't a remake of the original but a kind of sequel that picked up where the other one left off. I had seen the 1935 version of *Mutiny on the Bounty* and was impressed with the performance of Charles Laughton but not with that of Clark Gable as Fletcher Christian. He hadn't even bothered to speak with an English accent; nor had Franchot Tone, the costar. They made no concessions whatsoever to the fact that they were portraying British seamen, and it seemed absurd. As always, Clark Gable played Clark Gable.

If I had been Trevor Howard, I would never have accepted the responsibility of playing Bligh in the remake because there was only one Bligh, right or wrong, historically correct or not. Laughton's characterization renders anybody else's useless. Carol Reed wanted to be historically accurate and to depict the mutineers as pathetic as they were in life. But the studio didn't want it that way, and I've never met a studio that had the integrity to stick to the truth if it was able to make more money by distorting it, and so Reed was dumped.

During a break in the filming, I climbed one of the tallest mountains on the island of Tahiti along with a Tahitian friend.

At the top, he pointed to the north and said, "Can you see that island out there?"

I couldn't see anything.

"Don't you see that little island out there? It's called Teti'aroa." Finally, I discerned a slender pencil of land lying on the horizon about thirty miles away, and before long, it was exerting as mystical a pull on me as Tahiti itself. I asked other Tahitian friends about it and was told it was owned by an elderly American woman named Madame Duran, who was blind. It had been given to her father, a doctor named Williams, by the last king of Tahiti, Pomerae V, and Williams had lived there for years, established a coconut plantation and was buried there. After he died, Madame Duran took it over, and she too had lived there for many years.

After the movie was finished, I continued to think about Teti'aroa and reread my books on Tahiti to see if it was mentioned. Somerset Maugham had written about it, and I discovered that a leper had spent most of his life there. A friend, Nick Rutgers, told me he had once visited the island, knew Madame Duran, offered to take me there and introduce me to her, so I returned to Tahiti. Since there wasn't an airstrip on the island, I had to hire a fisherman to take us to Teti'aroa. As we approached the island, I realized that the thin sliver of land I'd seen from afar was larger than I thought and more gorgeous than anything I had anticipated.

Teti'aroa was actually several islands: a coral atoll a few feet above sea level encompassing about 1,500 acres on over a dozen islands. By far the largest encircled a wide, crescent-shaped, breathtaking lagoon. A dozen varieties of birds watched as we waded ashore; ahead of us, thick stands of coconut trees stood in the sand like brigades of sentries adorned with feathery crowns; everywhere broad sandy beaches stretched in front of us. The lagoon was about five miles across at its broadest point and infused with more shades of blue than

My happy island of Teti'aroa. (Personal collection of Marlon Brando)

I thought possible: turquoise, deep blue, light blue, indigo blue, cobalt blue, royal blue, robin's egg blue, aquamarine. As I admired this astonishing palette, several flawless, white, flat-bottomed clouds rolled past me at about two thousand feet, as if they were on parade and I were on a reviewing stand. A shadow fell across the island briefly, then moved on, and the sun shone again like satin on the riotous colors of the lagoon. It was magical.

Madame Duran, who lived alone on the island except for a friend and helper named Annie, gave me a gracious welcome. We talked for seven hours without stopping. As isolated as she was, she knew that I was an actor. She rarely left the island, but she had a radio that was her only link to the world, and once she had heard me give an interview. She seemed lonely, but she was full of energy, curiosity, vitality and wisdom. She had been blind for almost twenty-five years, but could distinguish light from dark. She lived comfortably, she said, in a small house built of coral and cement, and got around by using a technique she had invented; she had strung wire from tree to tree and used it to guide herself around the island, holding on with a rag wrapped around her hand. When she came to a tree, she felt her way around to the other side, then grabbed the next wire and walked on.

Madame Duran was anxious to hear any news about America and told me stories about the island—about her father, shipwrecks and old Tahitian friends—and to this day I regret I didn't write them down. For company she had Annie, an old woman who was part Chinese, and at least forty dogs and cats, most of whom lounged in the shade around us as we talked. Her biggest nemesis was the dogcatchers from Tahiti. Whenever they tried to set foot on the island, she went after them with her umbrella.

It was a pleasant visit, and a few months later I returned to the island and brought her an apple pie. She had taken a shine to me and I to her, and I asked her to tell me more about the history and magic of Tahiti. Once again we talked for hours. I sensed that she might be growing concerned about her health because she was getting older, and I asked if she had ever thought about selling the island. "No," she answered, "I don't think so." But two or three years later I got a note from her in which she said she was thinking about selling Teti'aroa because she had hurt herself in a fall and might have to move back to the city where she had grown up, Vallejo, California, for medical care. When I asked how much she wanted for the island, she said $200,000. After we struck a deal, I called the governor of Tahiti, a Frenchman, and told him I planned to buy the island if it was acceptable to the Tahitian and French governments. After meeting with his cabinet, he assured me enthusiastically that I was welcome in the community, but that it would take a while to process the papers and he would let me know when they were ready. Puzzled by the delay, I asked, "Can you think of any reason why I would not be granted a permit to buy the island?"

"Oh, no," he said, "we're delighted to have you among us. We're *proud* to have you."

A year later, the paperwork still had not been completed and the governor left office. On his last day at work I received a telegram declaring: YOUR PERMIT TO BUY THE ISLAND OF TETI'AROA HAS BEEN REFUSED.

I thought that was the end of it, but the next time I was in Tahiti, I went to Teti'aroa to see how Madame Duran was getting along. The first thing she said was that she was disappointed that I'd changed my mind about buying the island, but now she had another offer, from an American businessman I knew; it had been approved by the government and she was going to accept it.

I was shocked, and said: "Madame Duran, I wanted to buy the island and still do, but I was denied permission to do so."

"How could permission have been refused?"

"I don't know."

She said, "The politicians here are as crooked as pigs' tails. You just keep trying."

Shortly thercafter I was in Paris and decided to look up the man who had been appointed the next governor of Tahiti, a suave, charming Corsican. After a couple of hours of trying to assure him that I would be a good neighbor, he said the government wouldn't stand in my way if I wanted to buy the island and Madame Duran still wanted to sell it to me. I contacted her, but she told me she was about to sign a contract to sell Teti'aroa to the businessman for $300,000. I told her what I'd been told in Paris, but said I couldn't afford that much.

"Well," she said, "I asked you to pay two hundred thousand and you agreed to it, so that will be my price."

I said, "I can't do that. It's unfair. If you can get three hundred thousand for it, please take it."

"No," she insisted. "It's yours if you want it. The only thing I ask of you is that you not cut down any of the Tow trees."

I made not only that promise, but also another to preserve the island in its natural state as much as possible. I have kept those promises. No one, incidentally, ever asked me for a bribe. I wouldn't have paid one if they had, though I suppose bribery begins with a smile that you don't mean, and I used as much charm as I could to persuade the government.

I urged Madame Duran to keep her house and live there for as long as she lived, but she said, "No, it's yours now. I'm going back to Vallejo."

Shortly after she returned to California, Madame Duran died.

40

ONCE I BECAME the lawful owner of Teti'aroa in 1966, I arranged to be taken there by a government boat from Papeete and to make the final landing in smaller craft filled with some of the things I expected to need on the island. Setting sail for Teti'aroa was as exhilarating a moment as I've ever had. There were about ten of us in two boats, Tahitian friends and me. When the government boat left us outside the reef, the surf was too high to attempt a landing through the channel I'd used on previous trips; however, one of the Tahitians said he knew of a pass on the opposite side of the main island, so we went around and the first boat made it to shore quickly. I was in the second boat, a big rowboat crammed with a lawn mower, a keg of beer, an electric generator, rakes, shovels and other tools, all packed in boxes that the five of us were using as seats. As we glided toward the reef following the route of the first boat, I felt the current begin to pull us toward the island, and in front of us saw row after row of eight- and ten-foot-high waves. They rose up and seemed to pause in a moment of uncertainty, then suddenly collapse on the reef with explosive force. Later I learned that when a big Tahitian wave hits a coral atoll like Teti'aroa, the pocket of air beneath the curl of the wave is densely compacted by the weight of the water, and when the wave breaks on the reef, the compressed air that is released erupts with ferocious energy, sending a huge tower of water into the air. We watched this spectacular show from outside the reef as we waited for the right moment to make our landing. A Tahitian at the front of the boat kept a watch on the waves, then said in Tahitian, "Let's go!" The five of us began paddling as hard as we could, and I'd never had more fun in my life. But suddenly I noticed we weren't going anywhere; then I realized that we were going *backward*. We were paddling as hard as possible, but we were going into reverse. I looked around and saw a wave that must have been thirty feet high coming from behind us with my name written on it. It said *Welcome to Tahiti, Marlon.* I looked fleetingly at the coral reef in front of us and couldn't believe what I saw; suddenly the reef had become a vast, dry meadow of stone tinted a pretty shade of pink. Like a gargantuan pump, the wave behind us had sucked almost all the water from the reef and assembled it into a giant fist that was about to smash us. It hit like Joe Louis, and when the pocket of compressed air detonated, we were launched toward heaven. We bounced two or three times in the sky on the top of the wave, then began rocketing toward the hard, pink reef at what seemed like eighty miles an hour at a ninety-degree angle. The Tahitians jumped out of the boat, but I didn't move fast enough. It crashed into the reef bow first and cracked in half, with me clinging to one half like a rodeo rider trying to stay on a crazed bronco. As the boat slammed into the reef, I heard another wave coming from behind and looked around: it seemed even bigger than the first one. I could either ride it out in my broken half of the boat or try to escape to the reef. I jumped onto the reef. If the wave smashed into the boat with me still in it, I figured, it might turn upside down. As soon as I jumped, the second wave exploded and dragged me several hundred yards across the coral, which was as sharp as razor wire, slashing my body from head to foot. Had I known what I learned later, I would have grabbed a piece of coral, held on to it and let the wave pass over me, then come up for air before grabbing another piece. But I didn't know that then, and I was a mess when I limped to shore. I could walk but was bloodied all over, and the Tahitians warned me that I was in for a bad infection from the coral.

There were no antibiotics on the island, so it meant I had to return to Papeete to see a doctor. We radioed for help, but it took four days for the government boat to return. This time it carried a special craft with a shallow draft that Tahitians call a reef jumper. They wait for a wave to pass, then attempt to skim across the reef before the next one.

From the island I watched the government boat arrive and lower the reef jumper into the ocean. A tall, distinguished-looking man with gray hair got in, followed by eight younger Tahitians. He must be their leader, I thought; he was a proud, patrician-looking figure. While the younger men waited for his orders with their long oars extended, he stood up and surveyed the reef like an ancient mariner, waiting for a pause in the waves and the right moment, reminding me of the legendary heroes of ancient Polynesia. You could see that he'd obviously had a lot of experience. He waited about twenty minutes, surveying the waves, gauging the speed of the wind, studying the patterns of the swells and breakers. The waves looked as big and powerful as they had four days earlier, but the gray-haired man seemed supremely self-possessed and confident. Finally he looked around and gave the signal. The eight men started stroking and pulling on their oars and the boat rocketed toward shore as if propelled by a two-hundred-horsepower motor. I was very impressed; it was beautiful to watch. But then a wave came up behind them and knocked the boat thirty feet into the air. Everybody went flying, half of them outside the reef, half inside, and their oars went everywhere. The boat turned over

On Teti'aroa. There were more fraught moments . . . (Personal collection of
Marlon Brando)

on its side, then rolled bottom up like a soggy doughnut. Suddenly I felt I had to rethink all those legends about Tahitians' knowledge of the sea.

Subsequently I learned that Polynesians who live on high islands seldom know much about low-island living and vice versa. The men I'd come ashore with the first time and those that came to help us the second time weren't used to landing on an atoll like Teti'aroa, which is only eight feet above sea level. A few feet offshore, it plunges straight down at seventy degrees to a depth of about three thousand feet. When a huge wave comes along, the reef pulls the footing out from under it, and then the wave crashes down and flings any boat in the wrong place into the coral like a battering ram. The reef around Teti'aroa can rip out the bottom of a boat with the efficiency of a carbide saw, as the wreckage of at least ten vessels strewn along it attests. Once, several years after I bought Teti'aroa, a family from California, sailing home from Australia, smashed their sailboat on the reef and swam ashore to one of the islands. Exhausted, with no food and suffering badly from shock and exposure, they were there for a week, thinking of themselves as shipwrecked survivors like the Swiss Family Robinson, until they saw a passing boat and the fisherman told them that they were only a couple of miles from the hotel I had built on the island.

On my next trip to the island a few months later, I left Papeete aboard a three-masted, square-rigged sailing ship, the *Carthaginian*, which dropped anchor off the reef, and we rode to shore in a small boat across a placid sea. We passed through the surf without any difficulty, and I jumped out of the boat and swam over the reef. There were so many fish everywhere, beautiful fish of all colors and hues, that I could have closed my eyes and hit one with a spear anywhere I threw it. On the beach I walked to the end of one of the islands. Extending from it was a long, narrow sandspit stretching five hundred yards into the sea, and at one end, near the water's edge, was a small palm tree only a few feet high. It was dark by then, and I decided to lie down under the tree. Coconuts were scattered near its base, and I noticed that they were triangular-shaped. I picked one up and realized that by working it into the sand, I could make a wonderful pillow. I lay back with my head on the coconut, my feet in the water, and looked up into the sky while a sensuous breeze blew across me. The temperature of the water was almost exactly the same as the air around me. Then, for a moment, I remembered the great, worn face of Mr. Underbrink scowling at me from behind the principal's desk at Libertyville High School as he lectured me about how I would never amount to anything.

If you're so smart, Mr. Underbrink, I thought, why don't you have an island?

I slept under the coconut tree until dawn but before dozing off, I looked up into the stars and thought, Here I am on a tiny speck of land in the middle of a massive ocean on a planet in the middle of an inconceivably large area we call space, and I am sleeping on the skeletons of dead animals (which is what coral reefs are made of). After that night, I have never considered myself as the owner of the island, only that I have paid for the privilege of visiting it. I think of all the Tahitians who have been there before me, lain on that same beach and looked at the same stars five hundred or a thousand years ago, and I feel the spirits of those people whenever I go to Teti'aroa.

41

A DOZEN OR SO buildings built from native coral, cement and plaster were on Teti'aroa when I bought it, and most were badly in need of repair. I've always loved projects and began restoring the buildings while keeping my promise to change the island as little as possible. One of the first things we did was to rebuild the leper's house, plant flowers around it and dedicate it to his memory. Later I began what became a twenty-year endeavor to make the island financially self-supporting. We started work on a modest hotel built in the Tahitian style, a school, homes for the Tahitians who worked on the island and, after our cook pulled a can of DDT off a shelf and mistakenly used it instead of flour to bread some fried fish, a rudimentary airstrip. Until then a mishap on the island could have been fatal. With no doctors or nurses, medical help was thirty miles away, and the only way to get it was to hail a passing fishing boat or wait for a chartered boat from Papeete.

Even before the incident with the DDT, I was reminded of the precariousness of life on Teti'aroa while I was diving in the pass between two of the islands. I'm a pretty good swimmer, and I decided to see if I could free-dive—without using an air tank— all the way to the bottom, forty feet down. On the way I passed several reef sharks six or seven feet long, enough shark to make me worry, but I didn't seem to bother them, so I kept going. Holding my breath, I touched bottom, but there, waiting for me, was a solitary shark that was a lot bigger than the others. It turned its head, gave me a look and then began swimming in my direction. I didn't like the way he looked, and he obviously didn't like the way I looked. Unfortunately I was in his back-yard. He started swimming faster, moving his body back and forth to gain purchase in the water, and when he was a few feet away I thought I could see him sizing up my calf for his lunch. I'd read somewhere that in situations like this divers are sup-posed to look the shark squarely in the face and smack it on the nose. Instead, I started clawing my way to the surface like a scalded cat. Whether the shark followed or not, I don't know; I don't even remember getting to the surface.

This incident reinforced my sense of isolation. If the shark had taken a bite out of me, I probably couldn't have gotten off the island for treatment until it was too late. I wasn't on Teti'aroa when the cook mistook DDT for flour, but those who ate the fish became very sick. Fortunately two people missed the meal and were able to look after the victims until a boat came by and took them to Papeete. Still, I decided we needed an airstrip.

In the mid-seventies, after I'd owned the island a few years, the hotel was operating in a bare-bones fashion and the airstrip was in, an elderly Tahitian called Grandpère went fishing and returned with a fat red fish about three feet long. He said it was a red snapper, but to me it resembled a picture I'd seen of a red poison fish that appeared occasionally off the lagoon. I told Grandpère so, but he assured me that this wasn't a poison fish. "It looks like one," he said, "but it isn't."

"Okay," I said, figuring that if you have gray hair in Tahiti you must know what fish are safe to eat.

At two o'clock the next morning, I woke up with no sensation in my lips; they were completely numb. My feet were tingling, the palms of my hands were itching, and I had a headache as big as a Buick. I knew it was the fish, though I hadn't eaten very much of it. I had read stories about fish poisoning in the South Seas and didn't want to die that way: depending on the toxicity of the species, some kill you within hours and some take three or four days to send you screaming into the arms of death. I had heard stories of people ripping the flesh off their bodies because they itched so much. I got up and went around the island and learned that everybody who had eaten the fish was sick. Being captain of the ship, I had to give what medicine we had to them, and then radioed Papeete to send a charter plane to take them off the island.

Sickest of all were Grandpère and four of his friends. They had eaten the poison fish with *fafaru*, a Tahitian version of Limburger cheese to the ninth power: scraps of fish (usually intestines and innards) are left out in the sun to rot in a coconut shell filled with seawater until the mess stinks and worms flock to it. Then the shell is emptied and fresh seawater is mixed with the bacteria left by the rotting process to create a bacterial soup that is then used to marinate fresh fish. After four or five hours the fafaru is ready to eat and it smells like the foot of a dead alligator left out in the sun for two months. It is putrid beyond description, the only thing I've ever seen buzzards refuse to eat. In fact, I've heard that buzzards have fainted from the odor.

Not all Tahitians eat fafaru, but some, like Grandpère, adore it. At meals they usually sit downwind of everyone else at the table, but you can still smell people who have eaten fafaru a mile away. Unfortunately, Grandpère and his friends had put pieces of the poison fish in their fafaru the night before, and they were in terrible shape. The plane took them to Papeete, where their stomachs were pumped and they spent two or three weeks in the hospital enjoying a vacation.

Although we established an air link between Papeete and the

island, it was never first-class service, or anything approaching it. It was usually provided by an ambitious pilot on Papeete who decided he was going to establish an airline with one and a half planes, though because of breakdowns it was more often like half a plane. Before takeoff, one of the passengers had to get out and crank the propeller.

Once, after spending a few weeks on the island, I had to go to Los Angeles for a movie and the pilot arrived from Papeete in what for him must have been a sleek, fancy, upscale airplane, a *two-engine* crackerbox that Wiley Post would have discarded. There were five of us leaving Teti'aroa that morning, but a few minutes after we took off one of the propellers stopped turning. "Mayday, Mayday," the pilot said into his radio, "my starboard motor has quit. . . ." Then he turned around and told us casually, "Don't worry, this thing can fly on one engine."

I knew enough about flying to know that when one motor conks out, the pilot has to use a hard right or left rudder to compensate for the loss of power on one side and keep the plane from flying in circles. The pilot did what he was supposed to do quickly, and since we were only about five minutes out of Teti'aroa, he turned around and headed back to the island. But now the other motor started choking and missing.

"All right, everybody," I said, "we're going to have a contest. Everybody put your palms up. We're going to have a sweat contest. The person who sweats least . . ."

As we descended over the reef and the pilot took aim on the landing strip, the second motor kept kicking in and out, then the motor that had failed originally suddenly came to life. But when it kicked in, it started pulling us toward a grove of coconut trees at the edge of the airstrip; then the pilot applied the opposite rudder, and we veered away in the other direction. The motor quit again. With the second engine still fluttering in and out, once more we veered toward the coconut trees. The trees, I recalled, had once stood up to a 110-mile-an-hour hurricane, and I wondered what would happen when an airplane ran into them. While I was pondering this, the warning bell indicating that the plane was in a stall went off. As I listened to its bleating and the sound of the engines alternately dying and coming to life, I had the thought, What a funny way to go it would be, to die on this gorgeous island.

By now we were flying straight toward the coconut trees; they were only two or three hundred yards away and I admired how pretty they were up close. Suddenly the original motor that had failed came to life with a roar and the plane veered away from the trees after cutting off several fronds with one wing.

After the pilot had slammed the plane down on the runway, I sat in my seat and thought, Well, Marlon, I guess not today.

After I got out of the plane, I kissed the pilot on both cheeks as French custom dictated, looked up at the coconut trees and remembered that I had to be in Los Angeles the following day. I went back to my room, threw myself on my bed, looked out through the shell curtains at the lagoon and said to myself, To hell with it. Though they sent another plane to pick us up later in the day, I stayed on Teti'aroa for another two weeks. I simply didn't feel like going back to Los Angeles yet.

42

SO MANY THINGS happened during the sixties and seventies that now a lot of those years are a blur. I was still trying to
give my life some meaning and enlisted in almost any campaign
I thought would help end poverty, racial discrimination and
social injustice. But that wasn't all I did in those years; there
was a lot of partying, getting drunk, having fun, jumping into
swimming pools, smoking grass, lying on beaches and watching
the sun go down. During the sixties in Hollywood, everybody
was sleeping with everybody. It was part of the game to screw
the other guy's wife or girlfriend and vice versa, and I did my
share of it. As always, making movies was a means to an end:
earning enough money to feed myself and my family, make my
alimony payments, pay for my projects on Teti'aroa and help
people in need. I did as much playing as I did worrying about
the state of the world, but I still felt that films ought to address
issues like hypocrisy, injustice and the corruptness of government policies. Sometimes I would decide to stop making movies
altogether and I told my secretary to send back all scripts
unread because I didn't want to make any more money.
California is a community-property state, which meant that my
wife of record was entitled to half of everything I made, and
sometimes I refused to work.

I still couldn't help being concerned for people who were less fortunate than me, who were up against it or were treated wrongly by others. Above all, I detested those who abused authority, whether they were parents or presidents, and trampled on other people. Injustice, prejudice, poverty, unfairness and racial discrimination offended me, whether it involved groups not fortunate enough to be favored by our political system or individuals like Caryl Chessman, whose execution I opposed because I thought he had been unjustly condemned to die.

The movie about the United Nations that I had intended to make when we organized Pennebaker in 1955 evolved six years later into *The Ugly American,* which was based on the book by William J. Lederer and Eugene Burdick. I played a U.S. ambassador, Harrison Carter McWhite, a vain and seemingly well-intentioned man who was sent to a fictional country in Southeast Asia and brought with him all the misconceptions and self-interest of the American ruling class. I regarded him as a metaphor of the ways the United States condescendingly and selfishly treated poorer nations in the so-called Third World. In hindsight I now realize that the movie was also a metaphor for all the policies that led to Vietnam and the loss of 58,000 American lives, largely because of myths about the "Communist conspiracy" and the "domino theory" that sprang out of the heads of the Dulles brothers.

As I've already mentioned, when I first heard about the UN's technical-assistance program and America's foreign aid, I had thought of them as wonderful examples of the haves helping the have-nots with compassion and charity. But when I visited Third World countries for UNICEF, I had realized that the policies of the industrialized nations were not only selfish, self-serving and misguided, but also weren't working. In the name of all that was decent, the United States and companies like the United Fruit Company claimed the right to run the world;

throughout Latin America and Asia the United States bank-rolled any government, no matter how corrupt, that agreed to oppose communism and to favor American interests. But the populations of these countries were being alienated by us. The leaders of the so-called free world created dictatorships and propped up tyrants whose only indigenous support was among the wealthy elite, resisting ordinary citizens' democratic dreams. Tolerating murder and corruption, the United States rational-ized that it was better for a nation like the Philippines to have a tyrannical dictator like Ferdinand Marcos, who opposed com-munism, than a leader who would be responsive to peasants' wanting a share of the prosperity that was concentrated in the hands of only 2 percent of the population. The CIA destabilized elected governments and intervened in other countries' internal affairs. Our government created dictators who robbed, cheated and murdered their people with impunity, but as long as they were against communism, it let them get away with any-thing, including murder. Further, if we sent any aid to these countries, there were strings attached. It wasn't because we wanted to fight starvation, ignorance, disease and poverty; it was because of self-interest, greed and the myths about com-munism.

When *The Ugly American* opened in Bangkok, Kukrit Pra-moj, a former government minister of Thailand who in the movie played the prime minister of our fictional country, threw a party and invited Thailand's entire diplomatic corps. I flew over for it and, as one of the guests of honor, was seated in a prominent position where everybody could see me. The princi-pal entertainment was a formal Thai opera, which consisted of dancers in bare feet moving very slowly. It seemed to take them years to move their eyes from one side to the other and cen-turies to move their hands or feet. Before long, I couldn't stay awake, and someone beside me had to keep poking me to keep me conscious. It would have been a terrible insult to fall asleep, because I was the guest of honor. Between acts, the music stopped and I had to get up and walk over to the players and, with appropriate gestures and greetings in Thai, tell them through a translator how wonderful they were. It was hard to make a sensible commentary about the wonders of the Thai opera, but I was told that in the next act the Monkey King would attack and there would be a fierce battle. At last, I thought, some action and excitement are coming up. It is difficult to credit, but this part of the opera was even slower than the others; the high point was some finger-wagging and eye movements that each took about a minute to complete. Fighting the two stevedores who were pulling my eyelids down, I overcompensated and must have looked like a zombie with my eyes frozen open.

I don't know how I made it through the performance. Afterward I met all the diplomats and dignitaries at the event; there were handshakes all around and much conversation in French, Thai, English and broken English. I was nearly dead asleep, but for some reason I enjoyed it all very much. Back at my hotel, I collapsed on the floor because the air conditioning was coolest there. My feet itched terribly but I didn't know why. Before I finally fell asleep, I remember thinking that if only the hog gnawing on my heels would stop chewing on me for half a minute everything would be wonderful.

Strange as it may seem, it was nights like these that made being in the movies worthwhile. They gave me a chance to meet people like Justice William O. Douglas, Martin Luther King, Jr., Dag Hammarskjöld, Sukarno, Jawaharlal Nehru, Indira Gandhi and Robert and John Kennedy.

When JFK ran for president, I believed he was a new kind of politician whom I could admire, so I supported him, even though I have rarely voted in my life. He was not only charming but bright, and he had a sense of history and curiosity and an apparent sincerity about wanting to right some of the wrongs in our country.

At a fund-raising dinner I attended, Kennedy began working the room, table-hopping and shaking hands with everyone. "You must be pretty bored by all this," I said when he got to me.

"As a matter of fact," he said, a little startled and perhaps offended, "I'm not bored at all. I'm interested in what people have to say, what their opinions are and—"

"C'mon," I said. "You mean you're thrilled to death to sit here and make cracker-crumb conversation with a lot of purple-haired ladies?"

"I like those ladies," Kennedy said.

"Oh, c'mon."

Kennedy looked at me with undisguised hostility and suspicion until I smiled at him and said, "You really can't be all that serious."

He smiled back, and it was a lovely smile, when he realized that I was not being critical, that I was simply saying, in effect, that just once I'd like to hear a politician tell the truth.

After dinner a Secret Service agent came over and told me the president wanted to see me.

This will be interesting, I thought, and followed the man upstairs to Kennedy's hotel room. He hadn't eaten at the fund-raiser because he was so busy shaking hands, so he was going to have dinner now and invited me to join him. But before that we proceeded to get drunk.

Kennedy was unbridled, spirited and full of zest and curiosity about the women I knew in Hollywood. Then he changed the subject, looked at me suspiciously and said, "We know what you've been doing with the American Indians," wagging a finger at me.

"Well," I said, "I know what you've *not* been doing with the American Indians."

Changing the subject again, he said, "You're getting too fat for the part."

"What part?" I asked.

"That's not important. It's the fat that's important. . . ."

"Are you kidding?" I said. "Have you looked in the mirror lately? Your jowls won't even fit in the frame of the television screen. When they have to go in for a close-up, they lose half your face. You look like the moon on television. I can hardly see your face, it's so fat."

Kennedy said he weighed a lot less than I did, and I said, "No, you don't." So we headed for the bathroom, both of us weaving, and I got on the scale. I can't remember what my weight was, but when he got on it I put my toe on the corner and made him about twenty-five pounds heavier, so that he weighed more than I did. "Let's go, Fatso, you lost," I said.

A few years later, while the Vietnam War was beginning to blossom into the tragedy it became, I went back to Asia for a UNICEF emergency-food program in the northeastern Indian state of Bihar, which had been struck by a devastating famine. The suffering moved me to make a forty-five-minute movie about it, which I filmed with a sixteen-millimeter camera. I traveled with UNICEF workers from village to village by Jeep over such rutted, muddy roads that it took longer to drive seventy-five miles on some of them than to fly between Los Angeles and New York. Most of the villages were laid out in a figure eight: on one side lived the Brahmans and the Indians of other upper castes; on the other side lived the untouchables. Usually the wells on the untouchables' side of town were dried up, and no one had the money to drill a new one, yet they were forbidden to take any water from the wells used by people of higher castes because according to their beliefs they were unclean and would pollute them. Even if an untouchable received water in an earthen jug from a Brahman well, it was believed that he would pollute the Brahman.

My mind became bent trying to follow the logic of all this and the ways in which the untouchables were treated. They had to sweep the streets and to gather up human dung with their hands. To the Hindus they were not only untouchable, but unhearable. In times gone by they couldn't play musical instruments in some villages because they would pollute the ears of any Brahmans who heard the music; they couldn't walk on some roads because they would be *seen* and thus pollute the vision of the Brahmans; they had to carry a bell when they walked to announce their presence so that Brahmans could avoid unintentional contact. In one village I saw an untouchable standing outside a store trying to be heard. The merchant came out on his porch and asked, "What do you want?" The untouchable answered, "I want some rice." The shopkeeper told him how much it cost, then backed off; the untouchable placed some rupees on a post outside the shop then backed away, the merchant came out, took the money, put the rice on the post, then disappeared, and the untouchable came forward slowly and took the rice. He had accepted his position in the hierarchy. Meanwhile the shopkeeper had to perform a religious ritual to purify himself because he had been polluted by the untouchable's money.

The Bihari children I filmed were emaciated and covered with smallpox lesions and scabs; many were dying. Usually there was no hospital for many miles; if there was one, it was understaffed and had little medicine or food. The hospital beds were gray with flies and the children were laid out on them according to caste; even there the untouchables were outcasts. In almost all the villages, children suffered from malnutrition and diarrhea. Mothers had no milk because they had had no food and little water. One little girl came up to a relief worker who was offering her food and she reached out with the folds of her sari to collect it, but the garment was so threadbare there wasn't a square inch of cloth strong enough to hold the food.

In many villages cows had chewed the thatch off the roofs

because they had nothing to eat, and people were so thin it seemed incredible that they could walk. If you touched the cheek of a child, a hollow spot remained in her flesh after you removed your hand; the skin had no resiliency and was like that of a cadaver.

In one village I was photographing a group of Indians when a woman came out of the crowd and offered her baby to the camera as if it possessed a magic that could save her child. As I photographed dying children, it seemed surreal that not far away people were killing each other in Vietnam. How I would have liked to take a tiny portion of the money being spent on bombs for that country to hire teams of hydrologists who could go from village to village digging new wells.

India's caste system is the most insidious social system man has ever devised, though in principle it is no different from caste systems in all societies. Similar hierarchies exist in all anthropoidal systems, among humans, baboons, chimpanzees and gorillas. In India the system is simply more complex and stratified, with some nineteen thousand subcastes in Hindu society. People born into inferior castes are presumed to have done evil in a previous life; at the top of the hierarchy, the Brahmans claim to be descendants of the holiest priestly class. Yet even some Brahmans won't marry other Brahmans because they are not in the same subcaste. Because of Gandhi, it has been illegal since 1949 to treat untouchables as inferior, but laws can't change how people think. Even with all his force and power, Gandhi barely made a dent. This appalling system, with variations, is common in all societies, including ours, as a result of the fundamental human drive to organize into groups and identify others as inferior. It is ironic that when the British, whose class system is as rigid, if not as complex, as the Indians', ruled the country, they treated the Brahmans as if they were a lowly caste.

In the United States we've always had our own untouchables—American Indians, blacks, homosexuals. Who knows who will be next?

On my last day of filming, after photographing a child who had died right in front of me, I put my camera down and cried. I couldn't take any more. I knew that I had to get the scenes I had filmed to the American people and thought if I did so, the whole country would be appalled and do whatever it took to ameliorate this misery. When I got home, I showed the film to Jack Valenti, who became president of the Motion Picture Association of America after serving as a presidential aide; he told me he had shown it to President Johnson, but that was the last I heard of it. I showed it to as many prominent people in Hollywood as I could, but nobody offered to help arrange to show it in movie theaters as a documentary, even though among those who saw the film there wasn't anybody with a dry eye later, except for the wife of one producer, who said, "You know, Marlon, we ought to take care of our own first"—one of our famous phrases. After striking out in Hollywood, I thought the picture might reach an even wider audience on television, so I showed it to an executive at CBS News, who said, "It's an effective film, but we can't use it."

"Why not?" I asked.

He said, "Because our news department produces all its own stuff; we don't requisition or use outside documentaries."

"Why not? I was there. What I'm showing you is the truth."

"Well, we have policies we have to follow, and we can't make exceptions."

NBC told me the same thing, so I never got the film on television and that was the end of it.

43

ONE FACT ABOUT MY LIFE I constantly find amazing: I was born only sixty-two years after one human being could still buy another human being in America. I remember first being amazed by this discovery when I was an adolescent, and wondered how it could be. I read the history of black people, began to empathize with them and tried as best I could to imagine what it would be like to be black—which, of course, is impossible, though it took me many years to learn that. I began thinking of African Americans as a heroic people because of their enormous resiliency acquired over almost four hundred years; despite slavery and torturous treatment by whites, they had never allowed their spirit to be broken. Through every adversity and hardship, they preserved something, even if it was only their music or religion. They were yanked out of their homes in Africa, forced to endure a long trek to a seaport in chains, then imprisoned at sea before being delivered somewhere to be sold. They survived not only these hardships but the uncertainty and shock of not knowing where they were headed or what would happen to them when they got there; then they were thrust into what must have been a terrifying world of a different language, customs and culture. Families were split up and sold to slave owners who forced them to work like animals on whatever diet their masters deigned to allow them. They had to live this way from generation to generation, beaten down and made to feel like animals. The ones who survived had to be very strong, which is why I've always thought of American blacks as being different from African ones; their ancestors had to endure so much that only the strongest could survive.

When Lincoln gave blacks their so-called freedom, it was transformed with the speed of summer lightning into the share-cropper system. Then came the KKK, the lynchings, the theft of their constitutional rights and all the modern kinds of slavery. Blacks were free, but discrimination was so complete and insid-ious that all it did was change the form of slavery. White people were in the majority, and blacks have been conditioned from birth into thinking of themselves as inferior. They sense it every day; they are denied hope, yet have survived adversities while enriching our culture enormously. Much American humor comes from blacks; so does our music. Blacks taught the world how to dance, from the jitterbug to rock 'n' roll, and I believe they were largely responsible for helping liberate Americans from the puritan attitudes toward sexuality that weighed down our culture for most of this century and the one before it. Along with their music, sex was among the few things granted slaves, because when they procreated it meant a new chattel. Their dancing and music were expropriated by whites, but through it they taught us, and others in much of the rest of the world, to be aware of our sexuality and be less inhibited by the impulses that are a natural part of all of us.

When the civil rights movement took shape in the late fifties and early sixties, I did whatever I could to support it and went down South with Paul Newman, Virgil Frye, Tony Franciosa and other friends to join the freedom marches and be with Dr. Martin Luther King, Jr. At the March on Washington, I stood a few steps behind Dr. King when he gave his "I Have a Dream" speech, and it still reverberates in my mind. He was a man I deeply admired. I've always thought that while a part of him regretted having to become so deeply involved in the cause of racial equality, another part of him drove him to it, though I'm convinced he knew he would have to sacrifice himself.

I have never been so moved by anything as the words King spoke the night before he was murdered in Memphis: "I just want to do God's will. And He's allowed me to go up to the mountain. And I've looked over, and I've seen the promised land. I may not get there with you . . ." but his people would reach the promised land. "I'm not fearing any man." He said he would like to live a long life, for longevity had its place, but, "Mine eyes have seen the glory of the coming of the Lord. . . ." It was almost as if he were announcing his death; somehow he knew it was near and inevitable. I believe he was ready to die. He had accomplished much, but I think he felt such anguish and pain that he was near the end of his tether. His mission in Memphis had simply been to get a small wage increase for the city's garbage collectors, a job that was among the best a black man could hope for. His bravery and courage in the face of imminent disaster still move me.

After King's murder and the assassinations of Bobby Kennedy and Medgar Evers, black people could rightly say that they no longer had any reason to have faith in nonviolence and passive resistance. Mayor John Lindsay asked me to walk with him through the streets of Harlem to cool things down after Dr. King's assassination, and I agreed, not realizing it was a political act meant to court black votes. The mayor's staff alerted the press, so as soon as we arrived we were surrounded by photographers. People from Harlem began pushing and shoving me; I thought they wanted to ask me for an autograph, but instead they were pleading for jobs.

After I returned to California, I read an article about the

At a civil rights rally in a crowded church in Gadsen, Alabama, in 1963.
(AP/Wide World Photos)

Taking a "goodwill" walk through Harlem in May 1968 with New York
mayor John Lindsay. (UPI/Bettmann)

Black Panther party, whose members the year before had invaded the state capitol in Sacramento. I didn't know anything about them or their agenda, but I was curious, and so I called their headquarters in Oakland and spoke to one of the leaders—either Bobby Seale or Eldridge Cleaver, I don't remember—who invited me to Oakland. I was met at the airport by a contingent of Panthers, who took me to Eldridge's apartment, where I stayed most of the night with him, his wife, Kathleen, a man named Crutch, Bobby Seale and a seventeen-year-old Black Panther named Bobby Hutton.

I was hungry for information about the Panthers and still trying to understand what it was like to be a black man in America. Other than my friendship with Jim Baldwin, I had no frame of reference and felt I had to know. Eldridge spoke with incisive and impressive intelligence about poverty, prejudice and white resistance to black equality. He was a sensitive man but, like a lot of Black Panthers whose masculinity had been threatened by racism, he spoke with bravado. He said that by being aggressive in pursuing their constitutional rights, the Panthers wanted to give younger black men more pride in themselves. At a fundamental level I believe that all they really wanted was respect as human beings; one of the realities of being young and black in America, Cleaver said, was not having any black heroes to worship or identify with. All the history books, all the movies and television shows, he said, were about white people. However, it wasn't this kind of prejudice that hurt blacks the most, he said; it was that in a white-dominated society, it was as if blacks didn't count.

We talked until almost four A.M., and I learned a great deal about a variety of subjects, but especially about the day-to-day experiences of being a black man in Oakland—of being stopped and searched by policemen simply because he was black, of being degraded, belittled and called "nigger" by cops, of applying for a job and seeing in the eyes of employers that as soon as he entered their doors the job no longer existed.

About two weeks later, Bobby Hutton and Eldridge Cleaver were trapped in a house and surrounded by the Oakland police. The house caught fire, and when Bobby Hutton walked outside, the police shot him, killing a beautiful boy. Eldridge, who was still inside, took his clothes off when he saw what had happened, then came outside with his hands up and his fingers spread, totally naked. It was an intelligent move because there were too many witnesses for the police to assassinate a man who plainly had no weapons. I'm sure this act saved his life.

The killing of Bobby Hutton confirmed everything I'd heard during that long night in Oakland. The next day I flew back to Oakland. Jim Farmer, the founder of the Congress of Racial Equality, was also there that day, and it was one of the few times in my life I have felt real danger. There was so much tension in Oakland that I sensed the police would use any excuse to kill someone sympathetic to the Black Panthers. The Cleaver house still reeked of tear gas and it made my eyes water, even though the doors and windows had been thrown open. Glancing around, I saw Farmer, whom I knew only slightly, looking at me with hatred in his eyes. They told me that he despised me because I was just another knee-jerk white liberal to him.

At Bobby Hutton's funeral, I began to sense why Jim Farmer had looked at me that way and to understand—as I have at other moments in my life in other places when I was among people I wanted to help—that I was an outsider. I sat in the second row at the church. Behind me women were sobbing, and in front of me, in the first two rows of pews, the Black Panthers sat silently and stoically. Bobby Seale spoke about Hutton and was fearless in denouncing the Oakland Police Department. The coffin lay open, and on its handle was a bouquet of yellow chrysanthemums; as Seale spoke, a few chrysanthemum petals dropped and fell on Bobby's face and chest. Then the Panthers lined up to pass by his coffin in their black uniforms, black berets, dark glasses and leather jackets. Most simply paused,

Bobby Hutton's funeral. A sense of being an outsider. (UPI/Bettmann)

I attracted some abuse in a civil rights march in Torrance, California, 1963. (AP/Wide World Photos)

looked down at him and raised their fists in a salute. Then one came forward, took a cartridge out of a carbine and placed it in Hutton's hands. Not one of them cried, though I couldn't contain myself. There was a coldness in the church that was palpable and formidable, rooted in a long history of suffering; they were beyond tears.

Those Panthers made me realize how protected my life had been as a white person, and how, despite a lifetime of searching, curiosity and empathy, I would never understand what it was to be black. There were limits to empathy; it was impossible for me to walk in their shoes. I had been determined to join them in their battle, but I was an outsider and always would be. Later this was brought home to me when several blacks told me they disliked me because I was a white man trying to fight a black man's war. Among them was Rap Brown, who lambasted me as a shallow liberal poking his nose into a world he didn't know and in which he didn't belong. Brown's point was well taken; white people would never be able to understand what it is like to be black in America, and to live the kind of life Toni Morrison writes about so eloquently in her books. They are books of genius, but for all the beauty of her prose, for all its anguish, pain, perception, humor and devotion to the black race, and no matter how touchingly and explosively she communicates, white people are never going to understand what it is like to be conditioned from childhood into believing that you are hated, unwelcome and inferior.

When Congress finally began to pass civil rights legislation, I wrote to Jimmy Baldwin that it wasn't because of "Kennedy, Johnson, Humphrey or any of the rest of them. It was Bessie Smith, Emmett Till, Medgar Evers, yourself, Rosa Parks, James Meredith . . . many who were, as you've often said, 'witnesses who managed to survive.' "

After the passage of the civil rights bill, the Black Panthers seemed to become less relevant, and there was a split in the party leadership. Huey Newton and Bobby Seale gave up violence to achieve the Panthers' goals, while Eldridge Cleaver went into exile. With the passage of the bill, everybody hoped that life would improve for blacks, and in some ways it has; they now have a little more opportunity than they once did. One thing hasn't changed, however: what is most crippling for a young black child to realize is that he has little chance of achieving his hopes because unconsciously he is still trained to believe that he has no chance. It is not the racism of the Ku Klux Klan, which everybody recognizes is a ship of fools, that debilitates blacks, but the subtle, insidious racism that robs black children of pride and self-esteem so that they never have a chance.

44

SOME OF THE PICTURES I made during the sixties were successful; some weren't. Some, like *The Night of the Following Day*, I made only for the money; others, like *Candy*, I did because a friend asked me to and I didn't want to turn him down. I was ridiculous in that picture, and everyone else in it was diminished by it. Some of the movies made a lot of money; some didn't. I was interested in other things, but I had to make a living and took what was available.

What I remember most about the pictures during those years was the fun of traveling to different places and making new friends. *Bedtime Story*, my first movie after *The Ugly American*, was the only one I ever made that made me happy to get up in the morning and go to work. I couldn't wait for the day's shooting to begin. I've never been a comic actor and am not very good at it, but this script about a couple of con men who happily preyed on women for money and sex on the French Riviera was hilarious, and working with David Niven was a treat. How he made me laugh. David was one of those British actors who, like Laurence Olivier, refused to play down—that is, use an accent beneath his station. He had a wonderful, understated, sophisticated wit that reduced me to a guffawing bowl of

Above: Clowning on
the set of *Bedtime Story*
with David Niven; Frances
Robinson is seated. (Univer-
sal Pictures/Courtesy of the
Academy of Motion Picture
Arts and Sciences) Left: A
love scene with Rita
Moreno, my partner in
crime in *The Night of the
Following Day*. (Universal
Pictures)

Jell-O. The first day on the set, I noticed that David seemed nervous; when he read his lines, his hands were trembling so much that the pages of his script were shaking. I asked him about it later, but instead of admitting that he was nervous he responded with a hilarious zinger that bowled me over. I think Niven was born with a curse, a voice in his head that constantly told him, "You'd better make everyone laugh today and charm them too, because if you don't, you're dead." He wanted to be thought of as an aristocrat, and he liked to hang out with the sort of gentry who owned chalets in Gstaad and berthed their yachts in Nice. In some funny way, I think he felt inadequate, and his ability to charm and make people laugh gave him confidence and strength. His humor was very English. I couldn't act well on that picture because I was always breaking up. Together we wasted a lot of film. After I blew six or seven takes in one scene, I tried looking over his shoulder so I couldn't see him, but I still couldn't deliver my lines. Out of frustration, the director went to a close-up of David and put me off camera; even then, I couldn't stop laughing, so he pleaded with me to go to my dressing room; I did, and put my face into a pillow to stifle the sound, but David told me later that on the set he could still hear me laughing.

These were the kinds of memories, along with travel and experiencing new cultures, that made making movies fun. I also enjoyed a picture called *The Saboteur: Code Name Morituri* because my pals Wally Cox and Billy Redfield were in it. I played a World War II saboteur sent on a secret mission aboard a ship commanded by Yul Brynner, who wasn't a great actor but who taught me a lesson about making movies. Yul was a nice man, but like David Niven, he liked to hang out at chic places and be seen with fashionable people, which didn't appeal to Wally, Billy or me. Someone, probably Wally, joked, "I wonder what Yul would look like if he ever put his legs together." This was because he was constantly striking the magisterial pose he used in *The King and I,* with his legs separated, planted firmly on the ground, and his hands on his hips. But Yul did something in that picture that impressed me. In one scene I thought his acting was very stagy and artificial, but when I saw the scene on film it succeeded because the lighting was effective, and I learned he had suggested to the lighting man how to light the scene. I had never paid much attention to lighting, and it made me realize that the man who sets it up can do a lot for your performance or break your neck if he wants to. With lights, he can add drama to your face, make it dull, or put you in darkness. From then on, I began checking with the lighting man before doing a scene, using a mirror to see what effect different lighting gave my appearance and performance.

Another picture I enjoyed making was *The Nightcomers,* a 1971 thriller based on Henry James's *The Turn of the Screw* that was directed by Michael Winner, an Englishman who, like David Niven, had an arch sense of humor as well as a stout, characteristically British sense of class. In a big country house near Cambridge that he used for the filming, he outfitted a beautiful dining room with expensive china, linen and cutlery, and said it was to be used only by me, Alice Marchak, Jay Kantor, my friends Philip and Marie Rhodes and himself. I said I didn't find that type of class distinction appropriate and wanted to eat with the other actors and members of the crew, but Michael said, "Marlon, I am sorry to say this, but the crew do not wish you to eat with them. They are much happier in the next-door canteen eating on their own and not worrying about the overpowering presence of their employers and a major star."

I left and went into the canteen room, sat down at the table, and when the other actors and crew members entered holding their lunch trays, I held up my hand urging them to sit near me, but they all walked on. "Marlon," Michael said, "it's no good waving your arms about; none of these people are going to sit with us. They'd all much rather gossip among themselves and they're all terrified of you." Apparently he was right, because no one would sit near me except him and my friends from the other room. The next day, when we had to shoot some scenes in a churchyard, Michael again arranged a special dining room for me and my friends—this time in a local vicarage. I invited two of the actresses in the picture, Stephanie Beacham and a famous old English character actress, Thora Hird, to join us. At first they didn't say much, but after I kept asking them questions and encouraging them to talk, Thora began speaking virtually nonstop in a thick northern English accent that I couldn't penetrate.

Afterward, I said to Michael, "I couldn't understand a word she said. Why didn't you help me?"

"Well, Marlon," he said, "you invited them, and since they're very nice people I thought you would deal with them splendidly." Thereafter, I ate in my dressing room or trailer while Michael used the dining room with the linen tablecloths. On the last day of filming, however, when he arrived for lunch I was seated there with all my friends. For a moment he looked pleased, but then we all got up at once and walked into the canteen to join the other actors and crew for lunch. He joined us.

Six years later, when I went to London for the filming of *Superman*, I invited Michael for dinner at a house that had been rented for me in Shepperton, a house that was colder than the ice cave in the picture; if the water heater was turned on, for some reason the furnace wouldn't function. When Michael noticed that I'd stuffed the inside of my clothes with newspaper he asked about it and I told him that it was a trick I'd learned long ago as a hobo.

During the evening I asked him, "How do you pronounce the word 'integral'?"

"In*te*gral," he answered.

"No, I think it's pronounced *in*tigral."

"That's not how it's pronounced in England," he said.

I responded that there must be only one proper pronunciation for the word, and repeated that I thought it was *in*tigral. He insisted he was right, so I said, "Let's have a bet."

"All right, Marlon—a hundred pounds," he said, and walked toward me offering his hand.

"No," I said, "let's think of something else . . . I know: the loser has to sell French ticklers in Piccadilly Circus for one hour."

"Come on, Marlon," he said, "you know you'll never do that. I think a bet is important and has to be honored, and I don't want to lose our friendship because you lose the bet, which you're definitely going to, and then won't go down to Piccadilly."

"I promise you I'll go, there's absolutely no question of it," I said, and we shook on it.

Late the next afternoon, which was the first day of filming on *Superman,* Michael telephoned. "Why didn't you call sooner?" I asked, and told him I'd already figured out how I was going to pay off the bet: by selling French ticklers in Piccadilly Circus disguised as a blind beggar.

"Unfortunately you don't have to," Michael said.

He had checked the Oxford English Dictionary and established that there was only one pronunciation of the word: *in*tigral. A few months later, after asking his chauffeur to buy a large number of French ticklers of various shapes and sizes from a chain of London sex shops for £2, he stood in Piccadilly for an hour offering them for £1. Despite the bargain price, he sold only a couple—and those to friends who happened by. Disposing of the rest of his inventory, he told me, was daunting. Too embarrassed to ask his staff—a religious lot—to destroy them, he spent an evening cutting and shredding them in a waste basket.

The Nightcomers: Michael Winner, with condoms, paying off his bet in Piccadilly Circus (Personal collection of Marlon Brando); with Jay Kantor and Winner on the set (Personal collection of Marlon Brando); a love scene with Stephanie Beacham (Avco Embassy/Courtesy Kobal Collection).

. . .

Besides traveling often to Tahiti, I spent a lot of time during the sixties exploring New Mexico, Arizona, South Dakota, remote parts of California and other places. I would get on a motorcycle and ride off by myself, or with a girl, in search of somewhere interesting. Once I bought a new bike, left the highway and rode across Death Valley, racing across the desert as fast as I could. The temperature was at least 115 degrees and the engine gave out; it hadn't been broken in properly and simply died from heat exhaustion. I couldn't restart it and had to walk out several miles. A park ranger told me I had been lucky to survive and pointed out a spot not far from the ranger station where two people not long before had expired from the depletion of fluids and electrolytes in their bodies.

While I was making a western called *The Appaloosa* near St. George, Utah, Lisa, the designer from New York who thought she had saved my life with sperm therapy, came to see me. I offered her a ride on my motorcycle. We were steaming across the desert when we came upon the shriveled cadavers of thirty or forty cows lying in the sagebrush. It was an eerie tableau. Later I realized they must have died from radiation blown north from a nuclear test in Nevada or by nerve gas from a military installation in Utah. This was in the same area where John Wayne had made a movie in which several members of the cast and crew were exposed to radiation and later died of cancer. I've always found it ironic that John Wayne, the gung-ho proponent of nuke 'em American militarism, may have died as a result of radiation from atomic weaponry.

I drove Lisa a few more miles and decided that the desert was a perfect place to make love. The desert, and beyond it a backdrop of rose-colored mountains, were beautiful; except for a few birds, the two of us could have been alone on the moon. But as I started to climax, the earth began to shake; suddenly it seemed as if a million tons of TNT were being detonated

The Appaloosa: anxiously on location in Utah. (© Phil Stern Photo)

beneath us, and as the earth shook, an enormous, vibrating tremor swept through my entire body. What kind of an orgasm is this? My God, this is magical! I thought. This is the orgasm to end my life; I'm going to die of orgasm right here in the middle of the desert. Then there was a tremendously loud blast.

Lisa looked up at me and asked, "What was that?"

Then it occurred to me that the sound had probably been from some young air force pilot in a supersonic jet flying fifty feet off the ground. It happened so fast that I never saw the plane—if there was one. But if there had been, the shock waves and sonic boom washed over us at exactly the right moment. I've never had an orgasm like that before or since. For a moment I thought I was going to die. What a way to go!

45

YEARS AFTER OUR troubles over *The Egyptian,* I saw
Darryl Zanuck humiliate his son Richard unmercifully. He had
hired Richard to run Twentieth Century–Fox, then fired him
and announced his dismissal as if it were a personal triumph.
He said things no son should ever hear from his father. Later,
when I ran into Zanuck at the Stork Club in New York, I stood
beside his table and said in a voice that everyone could hear
that he should be ashamed of himself.

I saw this happen again when I worked with Charlie Chaplin
on *A Countess from Hong Kong.* Chaplin was an actor I had
always admired greatly. Some of his films, such as *City Lights,*
still move me to tears as well as laughter. In the beginning of
that movie, he introduces himself and establishes his character
in a hilarious scene by having the camera discover him asleep in
the arms of a statue. At the end of the film, after he has been
sent to jail for stealing money to pay for a blind girl's operation
to give her sight, he passes her flower shop. He recognizes her,
but of course she does not know him because previously she
was blind. He is now a tramp with holes in his shoes and the
ragged tail of his shirt sticking out of his trousers. He is stunned
when he sees her. As he starts to walk past, she runs out from

the shop and pins a rose in his buttonhole; then when she feels his suit and shoulders, her face brightens, and the audience realizes that she recognizes with her fingers the man who helped give her sight and whom she loves. The viewer experiences not only her love but his shame as she realizes that he is a tramp. The moment is magical, one that reaches into the audience's unconscious, which only the best acting can do. Chaplin knew exactly what the audience would experience. I don't know if it was conscious or instinctive, but he understood the myth he had created with the Little Tramp and attached himself to it tenaciously.

Comic genius or not, when I went to London to work with him late in his life, Chaplin was a fearsomely cruel man. He was almost seventy-seven when he offered me the part of a diplomat named Ogden Mears in *A Countess from Hong Kong*. In this comedy set aboard a luxury liner sailing between Hong Kong and San Francisco, Sophia Loren played an impoverished former dance-hall girl who stowed away in my room. Although I revered Chaplin, who had written the story based on a voyage he had taken from Shanghai in 1931, when he offered me the part in 1966, I told him I didn't believe I was right for it. I've always been leery of comedies, but he insisted that I could do it, and since I regarded him as a genius, I agreed to be a marionette in his hands. I figured he must know something I didn't, that he thought I could add something to the picture not apparent to me, and that I could help him achieve it.

But *A Countess from Hong Kong* was a disaster, and while we were making it I discovered that Chaplin was probably the most sadistic man I'd ever met. He was an egotistical tyrant and a penny-pincher. He harassed people when they were late, and scolded them unmercifully to work faster. Worst of all, he treated his son Sydney, who played my sidekick, cruelly. In front of everybody, he humiliated him constantly: "Sydney, you're so stupid! Don't you have enough brains to know how

With Charlie Chaplin, the director, who also played an elderly seasick steward in *A Countess from Hong Kong*. It was one of my disasters.

(Universal Pictures/Courtesy of the Academy of Motion Picture Arts and Sciences)

to place your hand on a doorknob? *You know what a door-knob is, don't you?* All you do is turn the knob, open the door and enter. *Isn't that easy, Sydney?"*

Chaplin spoke to his son this way again and again and reshot his scenes over and over for no reason, berating him and never speaking to him with anything except sarcasm. Oona O'Neill, Charlie's wife, was always there but never defended her stepson. It was painful to watch, especially after Sydney told me that Chaplin treated all his children this way. He said that one of Charlie's sons had gone to Paris over his objections, returned home at Christmas and knocked on the door. Charlie opened it and broke his nose with one punch, then slammed the door, leaving his son bleeding on the ground, and refused to let him in. He was a very rich man, but from what Sydney said, he never gave his children any money to speak of. For example, Sydney dreamed of opening a restaurant, but his father, who was worth millions, wouldn't lend him anything.

"Sydney, why do you take this?" I asked him one day. "Why don't you walk off the set? Why don't you tell him off? Why do you accept this kind of humiliation? There's no reason for it."

"He's getting old," Sydney said, and made excuses for his father: he was having problems with the picture, he had the flu, he was worried about this or that.

I said, "None of that's an excuse for being so sadistic, especially to your own son." But I could never persuade Sydney to stand up to his father, and he continued to take the abuse.

One day I arrived on the set about fifteen minutes late. I was in the wrong and I shouldn't have been late, but it happened. In front of the whole cast Chaplin berated me, embarrassing me, telling me that I had no sense of professional ethics and that I was a disgrace to my profession.

As he went on and on, I started to fume. Finally I said, "Mr. Chaplin, I'll be in my dressing room for twenty minutes. If you give me an apology within that time, I will consider not getting on a plane and returning to the United States. But I'll be there only twenty minutes."

I went to my dressing room, and after a few minutes, Chaplin knocked on the door and apologized. Thereafter he never got in my way, and we finished the picture without further incident.

Charlie wasn't born evil. Like all people, he was the sum of his genetic inheritance and the experiences of a lifetime. We are all shaped by our own miseries and misfortunes. He knew what was touching, funny, sad, pathetic and heroic; he knew how to tap the emotions of his audiences to arouse them, and he had an intuitive knowledge of the workings of the human personality. But he never learned enough to understand his own character.

I still look up to him as perhaps the greatest genius that the medium has ever produced. I don't think anyone has ever had the talent he did; he made everybody else look Lilliputian. But as a human being he was a mixed bag, just like all of us.

46

ASIDE FROM ELIA KAZAN and Bernardo Bertolucci, the
best director I worked with was Gillo Pontecorvo, even though
we nearly killed each other. He directed me in a 1968 film that
practically no one saw. Originally called *Queimada!*, it was
released as *Burn!* I played an English spy, Sir William Walker,
who symbolized all the evils perpetrated by the European powers on their colonies during the nineteenth century. There were
a lot of parallels to Vietnam, and the movie portrayed the universal theme of the strong exploiting the weak. I think I did the
best acting I've ever done in that picture, but few people came
to see it.

Gillo had made a film I liked, *The Battle of Algiers,* and
was one of the few great filmmakers I knew. He is an extraordinarily talented, gifted man, but during most of our time
together we were at each other's throats. We spent six months
in Colombia, mostly in Cartagena, a humid, tropical city about
11 degrees from the equator and not far, I thought, from the
gateway to Hades. Most days the temperature was over 105
degrees, and the humidity made the set a Turkish bath. Gillo's
first shot was from the window of a tiny cubicle, supposedly a
prison cell in an old fort, with the camera looking down on a

Burn!, directed by Gillo Pontecorvo, in which I played Sir William Walker, a British adventurer. (United Artists/Courtesy Kobal Collection)

courtyard where a prisoner was being garroted. When I saw that Gillo was wearing a long, heavy winter overcoat despite the heat, I couldn't believe it. With the movie lights blazing, it must have been over 130 degrees in the room. But he filmed take after take and never removed his overcoat.

"Gillo," I finally asked, "why are you wearing that heavy coat?" He was drenched in sweat. "Gillo, why don't you take it off?"

He shrugged, pulled his collar up, looked around and said in French, "I feel a little chilly, I don't know why. I'm afraid I might get a cold."

"That coat's not going to help you. If you're ill there's no sense in weakening yourself more by losing all that fluid."

"I'll be all right," he said and turned away.

I walked over to one of the members of the crew and said, "Unless he's getting the flu, he's doing something very strange. He'll exhaust himself and pass out from the loss of so much perspiration."

During the next break, Gillo came outside and I noticed that he was wearing a pair of brief blue trunks underneath the overcoat. An odd combination, I thought, swimming trunks and an overcoat in this heat? While I was watching him, he pulled a handful of small objects from one pocket of the coat and shifted them to the other. I went over and asked him, "What are those?"

"Do you believe in luck?" Gillo asked.

"You mean fate?"

"Luck, *fortuna.*"

"I don't know," I said. "I guess so. Some days you feel lucky, some days you don't."

He dug his hand into his pocket and pulled out a small piece of plastic that looked like a curly red chile pepper. "What is that?" I asked.

"A little something for good luck. Touch it," he said, adding that it would bring good luck to the picture.

I did, and asked where his good luck charm came from.

"Italia."

"What do charms like that cost?"

"Nothing." He reached into his pocket again, brought out dozens of little chile peppers and gave me one. He seemed happy that I'd accepted it, and said I'd helped assure that the picture would be a success.

I've since met other Italians who won't go anywhere without a charm in their pockets, but Gillo took superstition to cosmic heights. One of his friends told me that he always wore that overcoat whenever he directed the first shot of a new movie, and insisted that the same prop man be in the shot wearing the same pair of tennis shoes. He was the man who was strangled in the first scene, and the tennis shoes had been painted to look like boots. On Thursdays, I was told, you must never ask Gillo for anything because if he refused you it would bring him bad luck. He also never allowed the color purple to appear in his pictures, or for that matter anywhere in sight, because he considered it bad luck. His obsession over the color was limitless; if he could, he would have obliterated it from a summer sunset.

Gillo was a handsome man with dark hair and beautiful blue eyes who came from a family of diverse accomplishments; one brother, he told me, had won the Stalin Peace Prize, another was a Nobel laureate, and his sister was a missionary in Africa.

Despite his warehouse of superstitions, Gillo knew how to direct actors. Because I didn't speak Italian and he spoke little English, we communicated mostly in French, though a lot of it was nonverbal; when I was in a scene, he'd come over and with a small gesture signal "A little less," or "A little more." He was always right, though he wasn't always clever about knowing how to stimulate me to achieve the right pitch. He was a good filmmaker, but he was also a martinet who constantly tried to manipulate me into playing the part exactly as he saw it, and often I wouldn't go along with what he wanted. He approached everything from a Marxist point of view; most of the people who worked for him thought this dogma was the answer to all the world's problems, and some of them were sinister. They were helpful to Gillo, but I didn't much care for them. Some of the lines he wanted me to say were straight out of the Communist Manifesto, and I refused to utter them. He was full of tricks. If we disagreed, he sometimes gave in, then kept the camera running after saying "Cut," hoping to get me to do something I'd refused to do. In one scene I was supposed to toast Evaristo Marquez, the actor playing a revolutionary leader who was my foil and the hero of the picture, but Gillo didn't want me to sip from my drink after the toast; I was to spill my wine onto the ground as a snub while Evaristo sipped his. At that moment in the picture this gesture did not seem to me to be consistent with my character, and so I refused to do it; I wanted to really toast him. Gillo let me do it my way, then kept the camera turning after the take was over and got a shot of me throwing my drink on the ground because I thought we had finished the shot. When I saw the picture, this was the shot he used.

In another scene on a very hot day, when I was wearing only shorts and a jacket for a shot above the waist, Gillo wanted me to say something I didn't want to say and made me repeat the scene over and over, thinking that he would finally exhaust me and I'd do what he wanted. But after about the tenth take I realized what was going on and asked the makeup man to get me a stool. I strapped it to my rear end and continued doing the scene my way, then after each take lowered myself onto the seat and pretended to be reading *The Wall Street Journal,* which Gillo detested as the symbol of everything evil. After scores of takes, he finally gave up; I'd worn him out.

Most of our fights were over the interpretation of my character and the story, but we fought over other things, too. Gillo had hired a lot of black Colombian extras as slaves and revolutionaries, and I noticed that they were being served different food from the Europeans and Americans. It looked inedible to me and I mentioned this to him.

"That's what they like," Gillo said. "That's what they always eat."

But the real reason, a member of the crew told me, was that Gillo was trying to save money; the food he was giving the black extras cost less. Then I learned that he wasn't paying the black extras as much as the white extras, and when I confronted him about it, he said that if he did the white extras would rebel.

"Wait a minute, Gillo; this picture is about how whites exploited the blacks."

Gillo said that he agreed with me, but he couldn't back down; in his mind the end justified the means.

"Okay," I said, "then I'm going home. I won't be a part of this."

I went to the airport at Barranquilla and was about to get on a plane for Los Angeles when Gillo sent a messenger with a promise to equalize the pay and food.

Making that movie was wild. Everybody smoked a strong variety of marijuana called Colombian Red, and the crew was stoned most of the time. For some reason making a movie in Cartagena attracted a lot of women from Brazil. Dozens of them showed up, mostly upper-class women from good families, and they wanted to sleep with everybody. After they went home, some told me, they intended to see a doctor who would sew up their hymens so that when they got married their husbands would think they were virgins. The doctors in Rio must have made a lot of money from that movie.

My truce with Gillo didn't last long. Although he raised the pay for the black extras and briefly gave them better food, I discovered after a few days that they were still not being fed the same meals as Europeans working on the picture. We were shooting scenes in a poor black village; the houses had mud floors and stick walls, and the children had distended bellies. It was a good place to shoot because it was what the picture was about, but heartbreaking to be there.

"You can't feed these people that kind of crap," I told Gillo. This time he ignored me, so I got everybody on the crew to pile their lunches against the camera in a pyramid and refuse to work.

Gillo came up to me angrily with his team of thugs and said, "I understand you're dissatisfied with lunch."

"Yes."

"What would you like to have for lunch?"

"Champagne," I said, "and caviar. I'd like to have some decent food, and I'd like it served to me properly."

Somewhere Gillo found a restaurant that sent my meal to the set, along with four waiters in red jackets with dickeys on their chests and napkins over their arms. When they set up a table with linen and silver and candles, I said, "No, the candles shouldn't go there; they should go here, and the forks should go on the other side of the plates." Then I touched the bottle of champagne and said it wasn't chilled enough. "You'd better put it on ice a little longer."

I fussed with the table setting while the crew and people from the village gathered around to watch with their arms folded. In their eyes I must have been the epitome of the self-indulgent capitalist who wanted everything. Gillo sent a publicity photographer to take a picture of the event, and herded some black people into the background. After everything was arranged perfectly, I searched the crowd for the poorest, sickest, unhappiest-looking children I could find, invited them to sit at the table, and then served them the meal. The people cheered, but as far as my relationship with Gillo was concerned, the episode made the situation worse.

We continued to fight while other problems came up: a key member of the crew had a heart attack and died; the cameraman developed a sty and couldn't do any filming; the temperature got even hotter, with all of us working long hours and flirting with sunstroke. The few union rules in effect were much more lenient than they were in the United States and everybody's temper was short. I also found it increasingly amusing that a man so dedicated to Marxism found it so easy to exploit his workers. Meanwhile, Gillo's superstitions knew no bounds. If somebody spilled salt, Gillo had to run around the table and throw more salt on the ground in a certain pattern dictated by him; if wine was spilled, he made the guilty party dip a finger in the wine and daub it behind each ear of everyone at the table. It was sad but hilarious. I began doing things to irritate Gillo, asking him for favors on Thursdays, wearing purple and walking under ladders; once I opened the door of my caravan, shone a mirror on him and yelled, "Hey, Gillo, *buon giorno,*" and then smashed the mirror. In Gillo's eyes breaking a mirror was a direct invitation to the devil to enter your life. Once he raised his glass at lunch in a toast and said, *"Salute."* I raised my glass while everybody drank, then spilled my wine with a flourish on the ground, which to Gillo was the supreme insult. He got a gun and stuck it in his belt, and I started carrying a knife. Years before, I'd practiced knife-throwing and was fairly accurate at distances up to about eighteen feet, so sometimes I took out my knife and hurled it at a wall or post a few feet from him. He shuddered slightly, put his hand on his waist, rested it on the butt of his gun and then eyed me sternly, letting me know that he was ready for battle, too.

One day when we were having one of our arguments over how the movie should be played, I screamed at him at the top of my lungs, "You're eating me like ants . . . you're eating me like ants." I didn't even know it was coming out of me. It made him jump nine feet in the air. Another day, we came close to a fist-fight over a scene showing four half-naked black children pushing and pulling the headless body of their father—the man garroted in the first scene—home to be buried. Gillo shot part of the take in the morning, then adjourned for lunch. When I returned to the set afterward, he wasn't back yet and the wardrobe lady was holding one of the children in her lap.

"What's the matter with the boy?" I asked.

"He's sick."

"What is it?"

"He vomited a worm at lunch, and he has a very high temperature."

"What's he doing here then?" I said. "Where's the doctor?"

She said Gillo wanted the boy to finish the scene because if he didn't he would have to find another child to play the part and lose part of a day's shooting.

"Does he know he's sick?"

"Yes."

I called a doctor and told him to get to the set as fast as he could. When he arrived I said, "Take my car and get this kid to the hospital right now."

When Gillo returned from lunch, I was steaming and so was he because I had sent the boy away. We came within inches of mixing it up; only the fact that he was shorter than me kept me from punching him. Several days later I couldn't take Gillo or the heat anymore. I needed a vacation. People were dropping like flies from illness and exhaustion. I drove to Barranquilla and left for Los Angeles at four A.M. A day or two later, I got a stinging letter from the producers saying that I was in breach of my contract, and that unless I returned to Colombia immediately, they would sue me. I wrote back demanding an immediate apology for their preposterous accusations—all of which were true—and said I couldn't possibly think of returning after being so excoriated; my professional reputation was at stake. I knew the producers' threats were empty because I had learned long ago that once filming starts, the actor has the edge; too much money had been spent to abandon the project; and even if they could win a lawsuit it would take years to adjudicate, by which time all the money they'd invested on the project would be gone. If he knows what to do, the actor can get away with almost anything under these circumstances. Most of them are too intimidated to do anything, but I wasn't.

After a five-day vacation and a letter of apology, I told the producers I would finish the picture, but only in North Africa, where the climate was more pleasant and the terrain and settings similar. They agreed, if I would just return to Colombia for a few more shots. I didn't want to see the country again, but I agreed to go. They booked me on a Delta Airlines flight from Los Angeles to New Orleans and a connecting flight from there to Barranquilla. When I walked onto the plane at Los Angeles International Airport, I asked a flight attendant, "Are you sure this is the flight to Havana?"

She opened the cockpit door and told the captain, "We've got a guy out here who wants to know if we're going to Havana."

The captain said, "Get him off the plane, and if he doesn't leave tell him we'll have the FBI here in two minutes."

"Oh, please," I said, "I'm awfully tired."

The flight hostess, who didn't recognize me, said, "Get off the plane, buddy."

I was delighted because I was in no hurry to go back to Colombia, so I ran down the ramp at full speed to the concourse. As I sprinted past the check-in desk one of the agents said, "Is there anything wrong, Mr. Brando?"

"No," I said, out of breath, "they just seemed a little nervous, and I don't want to have any extra trouble and worry on the flight." Then I ran like a gazelle, expecting the agent to telephone the pilot and say, "You just kicked a movie star off the plane." Sure enough, an agent was waiting for me as I tried to sprint past the ticket counter.

"Mr. Brando, we're awfully sorry," he said. "We didn't know it was you; please accept our apologies and go back to the plane. They're holding it for you."

"No," I said. "Not now. I'm terribly upset. I'm usually nervous about flying anyway, and if that pilot is so nervous I don't think I'd feel safe flying with him . . ."

The story made the papers and the airline apologized, but it did give me a longer vacation because there wouldn't be another plane out of New Orleans for Barranquilla for three days. Unfortunately, they chartered a special plane to meet me in New Orleans and I had to return to Colombia after only two days.

All of the above to the contrary, however, Gillo was one of the most sensitive and meticulous directors I ever worked for. That's what kept me on that picture because, despite the grief and strife, I had the deepest respect for him. Later, when I wanted to make a movie about the Battle of Wounded Knee, he was the first director I thought of to do it.

47

I HAVE ALWAYS BEEN lucky with women. There have been many of them in my life, though I hardly ever spent more than a couple of minutes with any of them. I've had far too many affairs to think of myself as a normal, rational man. But somehow I always thought there must be something—someone—out there. There was something: huge alimony payments, and if not that, enough trouble for fifty men.

With women, I've had what you might call a Rolodex life. I enjoy identifying and pushing the right emotional buttons of women—which usually means making them feel that they are of value to me and offering them security for themselves and their children. The less likely I was to seduce a woman, the more I wanted to succeed. Doing rude things to nuns was always a fantasy. In a hospital once, I tried; her name was Sister Raphael and she was quite beautiful. She often came to my room to see how I was feeling, and because there was something unusually extroverted about her, I thought, Somewhere in her there's got to be a touch of the tart. So I tried—and failed. Whatever human responses may have been stirring beneath her habit, she was committed to God, and no force on earth is more powerful than a strong belief system, religious or otherwise.

When my timing was off and two women crossed paths, it often led to problems because of their presumption of exclusivity. Once when I fled my house after two women had discovered each other there at the same time, I remember thinking, Marlon, you're fifty-six years old and are cowering in a stand of bamboo; aren't you ridiculous?

In such situations honesty is not an effective remedy. One woman, an actress who had the notion that I was planning to spend the rest of my life with her, was naked in my bedroom when she asked, "Where were you last weekend?" As she walked toward me, I flinched and covered myself like a boxer. She smiled and said, "What are you afraid of? I'm not going to hit you!"

"Just a reflex," I said. Then it occurred to me that it was time to quit lying. This is absurd, I thought, why not tell her the truth? It's stupid to lie to her.

So I told her I had spent the weekend with a woman she knew, and she grabbed my hair and started pummeling me. She was screaming and I couldn't get away because of her grip on my hair. Finally I grabbed her with both arms, shoved her across the room, ran down the hall stark naked, grabbed my car keys and scampered out the door, cutting my feet on the walkway. It was December and very cold; I was naked, my lips were blue and my feet were bleeding. After I started the car, I suddenly worried that the woman might be hurt, so I skulked back to the house, peeked in the bedroom window and saw her sitting on the bed speaking on the telephone. I went to a neighbor's house, borrowed a blanket, put it around me and, still freezing, started driving without a destination in mind. Then I thought of my friend Sam Gilman, who didn't live far away, and decided to seek sanctuary with him for the night. On my way to his house, I remember asking myself, Is this the way you want to live, Marlon? Driving down Ventura Boulevard in the middle of the night without any clothes on?

I banged on Sam's door, and when he saw me standing there holding a blanket over my private parts, he roared with laughter. I said, "Sam, have you got any Valium?"

At this he howled.

"Sam, have you got any clothes?" He gave me a pair of Jockey shorts and an army shirt and socks, and when his wife got up and saw me, she started laughing, too. I said, "Sam, it's not funny." At this he almost had a stroke.

Several hours later I went home and the woman was gone, though I kept seeing her for another five years.

One afternoon I was home in bed with a girl when we looked up and saw an airline hostess in her uniform staring down at us. I suddenly remembered I'd made an appointment with her but had forgotten about it. Since I had allowed the girl I was in bed with to think that we would be together forever, the stewardess had arrived at an awkward moment, though to her credit she handled it well: she dropped her overnight case on the floor and said, "I see you're busy now, so I'll go into the kitchen and get something to eat. I'm starving."

I apologized to the girl in bed for embarrassing her, made up some lies about the stewardess and renewed my pledge of undying love. But she got up, dressed and went home, and I can't say I blame her.

Another time, another woman found a piece of lingerie in my bedroom that didn't belong to her. When she challenged me about it, I laughed, thinking that joking would pacify her. Instead, she slammed me on the head with her keys, which were strapped to an eight-inch piece of oak. Blood streamed down my forehead, across my eyes and dribbled on the floor, creating a crimson pool on the carpet. I have a high threshold of pain and it didn't really hurt me, but I didn't tell her that. I pretended to lose consciousness and dropped slowly to the floor, smearing the blood across my face with my hands to make it look worse.

By then she was reduced to tears, and in a panic ran around the house looking for bandages and medicine and telling me she was going to take me to the doctor.

"No, no, I'll be all right," I said. "But I can't see. I don't know what's wrong. *I can't see.*"

I turned the situation into an advantage and defused her rage, though she never did forget about that lingerie.

Though I generally have a good memory, I've had affairs with women whom I met later and didn't remember. Once, at a party in Los Angeles, I eyed a fetching woman across a room, a svelte, sloe-eyed woman with a fine face and dazzling figure, and said to myself, Damn it, Marlon, there goes the afternoon. Putting on my best Charm Boy act, I went over to her, stared into her eyes and said, "Excuse me, I think I've fallen in love. May I sit down?"

She looked at me with an inscrutable Mona Lisa smile but said nothing, so I asked her why she was smiling.

"Am I smiling?"

"If you have to ask me whether or not you're smiling, you're in trouble," I said.

"Well, perhaps I am."

Switching to automatic pilot, I went ahead with my act and she became very engaging, with both of us playing out our roles in the mating dance preordained in every anthropoid culture, all leading toward sexual coupling and its intended purpose, procreation. I followed her down the alleyways of our flirtation and thought we were headed toward my intended destination when she said suddenly, "You know, we've met before."

"Really? It couldn't be. I'd never have forgotten your face. Never."

"Well, we have."

"Where?"

"You really don't remember, do you?" she asked.

"You're kidding me," I said. "You must be joking."

"We met in Tahiti."

"Where in Tahiti?"

She named a hotel in Papeete.

"We met there?"

"Indeed we did."

"Where did we meet there?"

"In your room."

"How do you remember it so well?" I asked.

"Because my room was two doors away from yours."

It turned out that one night in Tahiti I had made love to this fascinating lady, and then she had gone out of my life. Recognizing my blunder and trying to recover from it, I said, "Do you think for one minute I could ever have forgotten that night? It is embossed on my brain. I never expected to see you again. Of course I remember you; it was one of the great nights of my life!"

While I doubt that she ever truly believed me, the flirtation led to its predictable conclusion. She was a Brazilian archaeologist, a remarkable woman and a wonderful dancer; the way she set her foot down was like nothing else I've ever seen. She was beautiful and exotic, but she wanted a monogamous relationship, and when she realized my instincts led elsewhere, she sometimes expressed her displeasure in a volatile way. After we resumed our affair, I was in a swimming pool at a big Hollywood party with an old friend from New York, Jeff Brown, a quiet, staid fellow who I think was amazed by the bacchanalian atmosphere, and we were talking while in the pool when suddenly she came over and hit my head with the heel of her shoe. She was drunk and hit me so hard that I grabbed her and pushed her across the pool as far as I could. But my head still hurt, so I ducked underwater to make it feel better. When I came back to the surface, Jeff was looking at me. He had a broken nose. His face looked like a crushed strawberry—a huge, flattened, bloody, crushed strawberry. His mouth was wide open and he was looking at me in astonishment. "What the hell's the matter with you?" he asked the woman, who said, "Oh, my God, who are you?"

She had recovered quickly after I pushed her, and just as I had ducked underwater, she had hauled off and tried to hit me again, but this time Jeff got it in the nose.

48

IN SOME WAYS I think of my middle age as the Fuck You Years. If I met a man who had a certain kind of overt masculinity, he became my enemy. I would find his weakness, then exploit it. I adopted his manner until I made a fool of him, which often took the form of sleeping with his wife. I used to be very vengeful. I agreed with something that George Santayana said: "To knock a thing down, especially if it is cocked at an arrogant angle, is a deep delight to the blood."

I have a different attitude now, but during those years I loved the thrill of taking certain risks: it was like rock climbing, scaling the vertical wall of a granite cliff without a safety rope, or jumping out of a plane and waiting until the last moment before pulling the ripcord, unsure that my parachute would open.

As I've observed, there was a lot of extracurricular fucking in Hollywood and Beverly Hills during the early sixties. At parties one of the popular pastimes was a variation of the kids' game of "It." The hostess turned off the lights and in pairs everybody went into hiding inside the house—and they were usually big houses. If the guests designated as "it" found you in the dark and could identify you by touch, they were no longer "it." One night I went off with the wife of a songwriter who had a little too much testosterone in his personality for my taste. While hiding with her in the darkness, I started to do what comes naturally, but she said, "No, not here, not here."

"Why not?" I asked.

"They might turn on the lights."

"So what?"

She answered, "But I'm married."

A few days later, she called and told me her husband had gone for a few days to their home in Palm Springs. We were upstairs in bed when we heard a car come up the driveway and then the garage door open and close. We knew it was him, so there wasn't anything for me to do except climb out the window. I lowered myself over the edge, grabbed some ivy hanging from the wall and tried to descend cat-burglar style to the ground, but I lost my grip and fell about seven feet into a huge bush that broke my fall and stabbed my legs with branches as sharp as spears.

For thirteen years I had an affair with a very attractive Beverly Hills woman. She is still alive, so I'll call her Lenore. Our kids grew up together, and I knew her and her husband very well. He was a physicist with a medical degree, as well as five or six others, and he owned a lot of patents that made him extremely wealthy. I used to park my car a few blocks from their house in the middle of the night and in my tennis shoes stroll leisurely down the street, vault over their back fence and open the back door, which she left unlatched for me. Her husband was usually asleep upstairs in his room, and I would walk up the back stairs, where she'd be waiting for me, sometimes in the shower. For some reason we conducted a lot of our sex in the bathroom, where she was both athletic and imaginative. Then we'd either go to bed or I'd leave. Being upstairs with her husband so close by added excitement to the adventure. Before dawn I usually got up and hid under her bed in case he came in, and sometimes I would fall asleep, which was taking a chance because sometimes I snored. Lenore's children occasionally came in, and after a while they knew what was going on, but they were good soldiers about it. Since our kids used to play together, we had almost a familial relationship.

Lenore's husband, Arthur, was very intelligent but affected an aw-shucks persona. He pretended to be unsophisticated and said things like "Gosh!" "Gee whiz!" "Golly!" and "For heaven's sake!" On the other hand, he kept a loaded Saturday night special in his room.

One summer night, I climbed over the fence and found the door unlatched as usual. After opening it, I turned to tighten the latch; I was supposed to lock the door after entering. While I was doing so, Arthur walked out of the kitchen and was standing two or three feet away from me in the dark when I turned around. I jumped about four feet, and he beat me by at least two feet. "Oh my gosh!" he said. "You scared me."

I was paralyzed and couldn't think of anything to say. My brain simply stopped working, though it functioned enough to remember Arthur's gun. A headline flashed through my mind: ACTOR KILLED—MIDNIGHT INTRUDER SHOT, MISTAKEN FOR BURGLAR. It had happened to more than one playboy. After a few seconds I said the first thing that came out of my mouth: "Boy, am I glad to see you."

Then I tried to find the right face to go along with the words, whatever they meant, but there wasn't an expression I could come within a mile of, so more words came out of me like bubbles: "God, Arthur. I'm really glad to see you. I've got to talk to *somebody* about this . . ."

These words flew out of my mouth as if they were coming from someone else, and I thought to myself, What are you talking about, you maniac?

Finally I said, "Arthur, can we talk?" I put my hand on his shoulder. "I've got a problem." I went on. "Can we talk?"

"Why, sure," Arthur said.

"Let's go out to the sunporch," I said. I knew the house well and that a walk to the sunporch would give me about forty-three feet and thirty seconds to come up with something to explain why I was in his house at 2:50 A.M., to say nothing about the door being unlatched.

When we got there, I slumped down in a chair, looked over at him and said gravely that one of my sons was missing from home. "Have you seen him?"

"My gosh, no."

"You haven't seen him at all today?"

"No."

Now I had a toenail grip on a theme, but only a toenail; if I made a slip, it was a straight drop about nine hundred feet down. But I gained a little more ground by saying, "You know, he's not home. I don't know where he is. He hasn't been home all day. I've been worried sick."

My son was home asleep, of course.

"Well, we sure haven't seen him around here," Arthur said sympathetically.

"I don't know whether to call the police or what," I said. "Maybe he's just out joyriding with some friends, or maybe he's in trouble, but I'm worried. The only thing I could think of was that he might be here—you know, the kids are always staying overnight with each other. I thought of telephoning, but I didn't want to wake everybody up."

Then I realized I had taken the wrong road; instead of telephoning, I had merely jumped over his fence, climbed up his driveway and opened his back door with the apparent intention of waking up the whole household. I wanted to escape from this cul-de-sac as fast as I could, but before I could say anything, Arthur said, "Well, maybe Lenore might know where he is."

"Lenore? She's probably dead asleep."

But Arthur said, "Well, gee, let me wake her up. I think she'd want to know about this . . ."

At that moment, Lenore came down the stairs in a sexy peignoir, looking radiant, with her hair beautifully combed, ready to receive the paramour who had climbed over her fence. As she descended the stairs, she looked at Arthur and me sitting in the sunporch and burst out laughing, howling one of those laughs that go on and on and knock you to your knees. The sight of me looking up at her with my worried, second-hand Hertz-Rent-a-Face and Arthur trying to look compassionate, with his chin arched and his eyebrows pointed to the ceiling, made her explode, and she couldn't control herself. She grabbed a potted palm near the foot of the stairs, desperately trying to remain erect, choking on the sad news conveyed by my face, and still couldn't stop laughing.

My heart was pounding like a jackhammer and my blood pressure must have been 200 over 6. Why was she laughing? Was she hysterical? She couldn't possibly think the situation was amusing. There she was in her lovely nightgown, with her hair combed, at three A.M. howling with laughter. How could she be behaving this way? Ignoring her laughter, I asked with a straight face if she had seen my son recently.

At this, the potted palm Lenore was clinging to fell over; she couldn't hang on to it. I was so frozen with terror that I didn't see what Arthur was doing as this was going on. I didn't dare take my eyes off the doorknob in the hall. That's where I was looking. He was on my right. She came from the left into the sunporch, and I was staring past her at the doorknob, thinking that I was going to be attacked by the same hysterics if I looked at her, so finally I said, "I don't think there's anything funny to laugh at."

Somehow, in her mind it was uproarious to see two men sitting in her sunporch in the middle of the night, especially one who was as guilty as a safecracker caught in the act, looking desperately for a reason to be in her house, and whose only excuse was, "Have you seen my son?" Eventually she stopped laughing, threw herself in a chair and said, "No, I haven't seen him." And with that Lenore, a very nimble-minded woman, launched into a performance that would have delighted Stella Adler. What temerity she demonstrated: if I had been a daredevil for jumping over her fence, imagine what she became, a collaborator and partner in bringing the escapade to a conclusion. Once she stopped laughing, she quickly grasped the picture. She could read it in our faces, and what she couldn't read, she imagined, and joined Arthur in expressing her support for me and for my fatherly concern.

Finally I said, "I'd rather not call the police. You know what I think I'll do? I'll just go home and wait. He'll come home. I'll just be patient instead of panicking. What do you think, Arthur?"

Arthur agreed that this was probably the best thing to do, so I got up and thanked them profusely while my chin quivered a little and Lenore nearly went into spasms while trying to keep from laughing.

"Where did you park your car?" Arthur asked.

"It's down around the corner," I said, and thought to myself that if I had to run into another patch of stupidity and make up another unbelievable story, I wasn't going to make it.

I said good night, and tried to reach the door as fast as I could while Arthur was saying, "Well, gosh now, you be sure to let us know . . ."

I walked out the door a free man, and maybe even did a little jig at the corner.

In hindsight I'm sure Arthur knew what was going on all along. Like Lenore and me, he was very good at playing a part. Eventually he killed himself, not because of Lenore or me, but because of a long illness that wasted him.

49

AT HOME ONE NIGHT, before leaving to visit a woman in Beverly Hills whose husband was spending the night in the hospital for some tests, I ate a quart of ice cream. That wasn't unusual, but at the time I was getting ready to start a new movie and was on a strict diet, so after I ate it, I stuck my finger down my throat and threw up. (No, I am not a bulimic, but occasionally I do things like that.) The vomit was pink, but it didn't alarm me, and I drove down Benedict Canyon to my friend's house. After Sylvia and I did the usual wrestling around, we watched television until she got sleepy and went upstairs to bed. I finished watching the program, then got up to go home, but suddenly felt as if I were standing on the edge of a trembling precipice, inches from falling into the void. Through the fragile mists of overwhelming dizziness, I remembered the pink vomit and thought, Uh, oh, I must be bleeding internally.

I knew I needed help, so I crawled up the stairs on all fours to Sylvia's bedroom; it was a narrow spiral staircase that was almost vertical, and I can still see the fuzzy carpeting looking up at me a few millimeters from my nose. All the while I kept thinking, If I die here, her husband's going to know what she's been doing. Then the same voice in my head said, Finally, Marlon, somebody's going to make you pay for your sins.

I struggled up the spiral staircase one step at a time, then crawled down the hall to the side of Sylvia's bed and said, "You've got to get me to a doctor, I'm sick."

We both understood the situation: if I passed out there, she'd have to call the paramedics and her husband would discover I had been in the house at three A.M. If she took me to the hospital, people would see her with me. If I died, it would be even worse. Sylvia did something rather brave that I'll always be grateful for; without a beat, she said she was taking me to the hospital. Maybe she didn't have much choice, but she saved my life and it was courageous of her. She drove me to the UCLA Hospital, where emergency-room nurses sat me on a gurney and started asking me questions. A doctor came in, asked more questions, shook his head and said he didn't think anything was seriously wrong with me.

"Doctor," I said, "I'll tell you what's wrong with me. I'm bleeding internally. Stick a tube down my throat into my stomach, and you'll see that there's blood in there."

"Well, we're not certain of that."

"You'll never know until you try it," I answered.

They did what I suggested and pulled out a lot of black fluid from my stomach. I suspected I had split my esophagus doing my imitation of a bulimic, so by then I must have been bleeding internally for at least four hours.

"What happens if you can't stop the bleeding?" I asked.

"We'll take you upstairs and operate on you."

"How can you operate on me if I'm already going into shock?"

"Well, we don't know how much blood you've lost, so we're going to pump your stomach." They pumped the blood out, then pumped ice water down my esophagus, which stopped the bleeding. The next day they ran a tube with a camera lens down my throat and confirmed what I had thought: there was a tear in my esophagus. They put me on soft foods for ten days, and I was fine, but the experience left me with a herniated esophagus, which in later years I've tried to control with biofeedback and meditation.

I've gone on and off diets for years, usually before starting a new movie. When I have to lose weight, I can do it. It wasn't unusual to drop thirty-five or forty pounds before a picture. I ate less, exercised more and it came off. The hard part was putting myself in the right psychological mode, so that eating stopped serving as an avenue of pleasure. I'm not fat by nature. I got fat mostly because I loved brownies, ice cream and everything else that makes you fat. One reason for this, I suspect, is that when I was a kid, I'd come home from school to find my mother gone and the dishes in the sink. I'd feel low and open the icebox, and there would be an apple pie, along with some cheese, and the pie would say: "C'mon, Marlon, take me out. I'm freezing in here. Be a pal and take me out, and bring out Charlie Cheese, too." Then I'd feel less lonely.

Food has always been my friend. When I wanted to feel better or had a crisis in my life, I opened the icebox. Most of my life, I weighed about 170 pounds, though when I had my nervous breakdown in New York, I dropped to 157. After forty, my metabolism shifted gears, but I kept eating as much as ever while spending more and more time in a sedentary relationship with a good book.

There probably isn't a diet I haven't tried. During the seventies, one of them limited me to a quart of lemon juice and a few ounces of feta cheese daily. After spending the night at a woman's house in Santa Monica while on this diet, I woke up after she'd gone out to do some errands and had a terrible pain deep in my stomach. I drove home, swallowed some antacid pills and fell asleep even though I was almost doubled up with pain. When I woke up an hour or so later, I had a bad case of diarrhea and threw up. My vomit was black, so was my stool, and I felt dizzy. I didn't know what was wrong, but I had the presence of mind to know I should do something before I passed out. I went to the bedroom to call for help and distinctly remember asking myself, after I fell face first on it, What is the telephone doing down here? Falling down must have provided my brain with enough blood to keep me going because I managed to tell the telephone operator that I was afraid I might pass out while we were speaking, gave her my name, address and telephone number in case I did, then asked her to call my psychiatrist and tell him I needed help. He drove over, and as he walked me to his car all I could think of was that he wasn't strong enough to pick me up if I lost consciousness. Finally, as we were driving to the hospital, I realized I must have a bad case of internal bleeding again; I hadn't eaten anything except lemon juice and feta cheese for three weeks, and the acidic citrus juice must have cut a hole in my stomach.

By the time the doctor got me to the hospital, I'd lost half my blood. My blood type is O-positive, and for some reason the nurses couldn't find any supplies of it; if I remember correctly, all the O-positive blood was frozen. They sat me up on a bed-pan and took my blood pressure every two or three minutes. I suspected I was in shock and dying from a loss of blood. From the way the nurses acted, I also suspected they were worried that I could go any second. They were overly polite, talked a little too loud and moved a little too rapidly while assuring me that everything was going to be all right. When Alice, my secretary, arrived at the hospital, I saw fear in her eyes. A doctor gave me several injections, and after what seemed like an hour or more, they came up with the blood needed for my transfusion. Once they did, I was okay. Later Alice said the doctors had told her I came within inches of dying. She also swears she saw me praying in the emergency room, but I've never believed her.

50

NONE OF US EVER fully understands the psychological forces that motivate us, nor can we—not yet, at least—understand all the biochemical reactions that occur in our brains and direct us to make one choice rather than another, to follow one path and spurn others. But I think one thing is certain: everything we do is a product of these biochemical reactions. As Francis Crick, the codiscoverer of the structure of DNA, wrote recently, " 'You,' your joys and your sorrows, your memories and your ambitions, your sense of personal identity and free will, are in fact no more than the behavior of a vast assembly of nerve cells and their associated molecules."

It is risky, even foolhardy, to ascribe adult behavior to a single event or even a series of events in childhood; there are more grays in the palette of human behavior than blacks and whites, and I know this. But as I grew older and pursued one exotic, dark-skinned woman after another, I couldn't help but wonder if I wasn't always trying to replace Ermi, my governess, whose soft, dusky skin has seldom been far from my mind since I was seven. She was the ideal embedded in the emotional concrete of my soul. Once I lost her, I suppose I spent most of the rest of my life trying to find her. Along with my mother, Ermi may also

have had a lot to do with my refusal—or was it my inability?—
to trust women after I grew up. If you've never had warmth,
love or affection, it is hard to give it, or if you've had it and it
has been stolen from you, if you think you've been rejected and
abandoned, you fear being hurt again. My mother abandoned
me for a bottle when I was little more than an infant; then Ermi
deserted me. True, she was simply leaving to live her own life
and to get married, but to my seven-year-old mind, after having
lived with her so intimately, after devoting my young life to her,
after being abandoned by the only other woman in my world,
her disappearance was desertion, and my world collapsed.

After that, I always wanted several women in my life at the
same time as an emotional insurance policy to protect myself
from being hurt again. Because I didn't want to be hurt again, I
found it difficult to love and to trust. So, like a vaudeville jug-
gler spinning a half-dozen plates at once, I always tried to keep
several romances going at the same time; that way, if one
woman left me there would still be four or five others.

I enjoyed the women's company, but a someone named
Harvey was always standing in the corner, an invisible rabbit
called a relationship. All but a few women wanted me to
promise that their love would be returned in equal measure,
and that it would be forever and undying. Sometimes I told
them what they wanted to hear, but I have always thought that
the concepts of monogamy, fidelity and everlasting love were
contrary to man's fundamental nature. Sure, adolescent, childish myths tell us what love ought to be, and so do the songs we
sing; they all proclaim one way or another: I love you . . . you
love me . . . we're going to love each other forever . . . I'm going
to love you till I die and after I die I'm still going to love you,
until you die and we're together again in heaven. The songs are
part of our cultural mythology, promulgating values that collide
with our fundamental nature, which is the product of billions of
years of evolution.

My Stage and Film Life

With Sophia Loren in *A Countess from Hong Kong*. The script called for me to chase her around the sofa, yelling, "Take off those pajamas or I'll tear them off! You heard me! Take them off!" The director was Charlie Chaplin, probably the most sadistic man I've ever met. (Universal/Courtesy of the Academy of Motion Picture Arts and Sciences)

My first film, *The Men*, with Teresa Wright. I was cast as an army lieutenant whose spine had been smashed. I had no idea what it was like to be confined to a wheelchair, so I asked to be admitted to the Birmingham Veterans Hospital in southern California as a paralyzed veteran. (Stanley Kramer/ Courtesy of the Academy of Motion Picture Arts and Sciences)

The stage version of *A Streetcar Named Desire*, 1947: I wasn't Stanley Kowalski; I was the antithesis of him. Onstage: Peg Hillias, Kim Hunter, Karl Malden, Richard Garrick, Jessica Tandy, Rudy Bond, Nick Dennis, me and Ann Dere. (©Eileen Darby)

I thought the motion picture of *Streetcar* was better than the play. In many ways, Vivien Leigh *was* Blanche. Some years later I learned that Tennessee Williams (inset top) had been eager to have me, rather than a Hollywood star, in the play. He wrote his agent: "It will remove the Hollywood stigma." (© 1951 Charles Feldman Group Productions)

With Mary Murphy in the Fox commissary during the making of *The Wild One*. We were still in character at lunch. None of us in this film, my fifth, ever imagined it would encourage youthful rebellion. (©Phil Stern Photo)

On the Waterfront. On the day Kazan showed me the completed picture I was so depressed by my performance that I got up and left the screening room. Inset: With Lee J. Cobb and Rod Steiger, my "brother"; we improvised the film's famous taxicab scene.
(Courtesy of Columbia Pictures/Academy of Motion Picture Arts and Sciences; insets: The Kobal Collection)

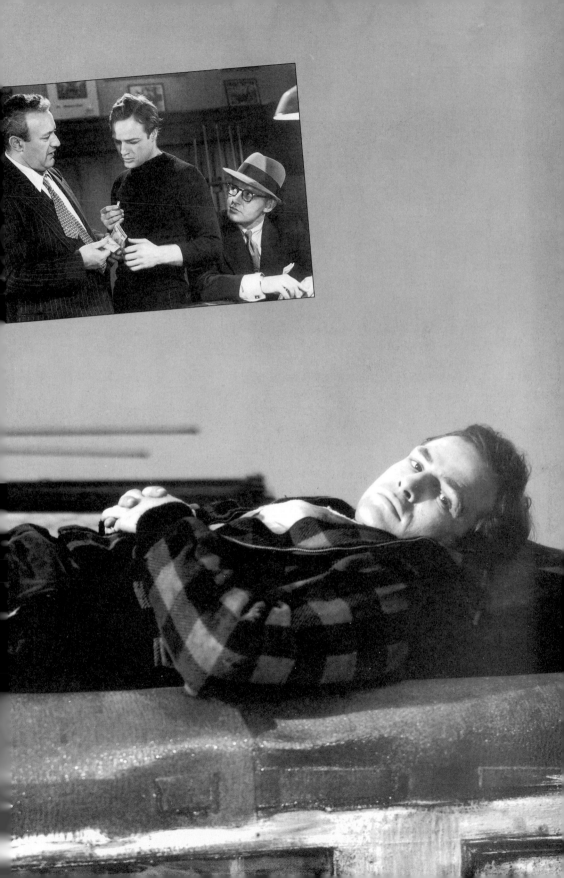

Guys and Dolls, 1955. I seem to have carried the antics of gambler Sky Masterson into Vivian Blaine's dressing room. She took my fooling around in good spirit. I posed reading the Yiddish daily *The Jewish Daily Forward* for a friend of photographer Phil Stern. (©Phil Stern Photo)

Off-camera in *Guys and Dolls* with grimace, two-step and trombone. Jean Simmons (above, and right, in a dressing-room rehearsal) was an indulgent costar. (©Phil Stern Photo) The sound engineers sewed my words together on one song so tightly that when I mouthed it in front of the camera, I nearly asphyxiated while trying to synchronize my lips. In *The Freshman* (facing page), Matthew Broderick must have had the same feeling. (Tri-Star) Near right: Portrait of the artist as a young gambler. (©Phil Stern Photo) Far right: Chess during *The Chase* (Courtesy Columbia Pictures), and, below, wigging out in *Candy* (Marlon Brando).

At a party with James Dean. We were both midwestern farm boys who were recast as rebels. He mimicked not only my acting but also what he believed was my lifestyle.
(Personal collection of Marlon Brando)

As Napoleon in *Desirée,* 1954: I thought it superficial and dismal. (Twentieth Century –Fox/Courtesy Kobal Collection)

I did some of my finest acting in *Burn!,* 1970. (United Artists)

In *The Ugly American,* 1963. (Universal/Courtesy Kobal Collection)

In *The Young Lions,* 1958: I wanted to show positive aspects. (Courtesy of the Academy of Motion Picture Arts and Sciences)

As Johnny in *The Wild One*, 1954:
I related to him.
(Courtesy of Columbia Pictures)

As Don Corleone in *The Godfather*,
1972: an encounter with the Mob.
(Courtesy of Paramount Pictures)

A Dry White Season, 1989.
(Personal collection of Marlon Brando)

As Mark Antony in *Julius Caesar*, 1953:
a lack of experience.
(MGM/Courtesy Kobal Collection)

Making *Mutiny on the Bounty*
in Tahiti led to the happiest
moments of my life. I climbed
one of the tallest mountains
and saw Teti'aroa; I became its
lawful owner in 1966. Trevor
Howard (above, left) was
Captain Bligh. Right: A stroll
among the palms with Tarita.
I grew to love the Tahitians for
their joy in life. (Above and left:
© 1962 Turner Entertainment Co./
Courtesy of the Academy of Motion
Picture Arts and Sciences; right: Personal
collection of Marlon Brando)

With Liz Taylor between takes in *Reflections in a Golden Eye*, John Huston's 1967 picture based on Carson McCullers's sultry Southern novella. It was condemned by the National Catholic Office for Motion Pictures. (© 1967 Warner Bros.—Seven Arts International Ltd./Courtesy of the Academy of Motion Picture Arts and Sciences) Right: As Matt in *The Appaloosa*, 1966. I worried about radiation from the nuclear tests. (©Phil Stern Photo)

I had one of the more embarrassing experiences of my professional career with Maria Schneider in *Last Tango in Paris*, when my penis shrank to the size of a peanut. (United Artists/Courtesy Kobal Collection)

When we made *The Formula*, 1980, George Scott asked me: "Are you ever going to say a line the same way twice?" I am credited by MGM with replying: "It doesn't make any difference, George, because I know you know a cue when you hear one." (MGM/Courtesy Kobal Collection)

As the Godfather, 1972.
(Courtesy of Paramount Pictures)

As Jor-El, Superman's father, 1978.
(© 1978 Film Export A.G.)

In *Apocalypse Now*, 1979, as the mad
Colonel Kurtz. Facing page: Off-camera
moments with children. Below: With Francis
Ford Coppola. I shaved my head without
informing him. I was good at bullshitting
Francis and he bought it. It was probably
the closest I have come to getting lost in a
part. (Bottom photo: Omni/Zoetrope/Courtesy of
the Academy of Motion Picture Arts and Sciences;
all others: Stephanie Kong/SYGMA)

I bumped into Marilyn Monroe
at a party. While other people
drank and danced, she sat by herself in a corner almost unnoticed,
playing the piano. We had an affair.
The last time we spoke was two or
three days before she died.
(The Kobal Collection)

I don't think I was constructed to be monogamous. I don't think it's the nature of *any* man to be monogamous. Chimps, our closest relatives, are not monogamous; neither are gorillas or baboons. Human nature is no more monogamous than theirs. In every human culture men are propelled by genetically ordained impulses over which they have no control to distribute their seed into as many females as possible. Sex is the primal force of our and every other species. Our strongest urge of all is to replicate our genes and perpetuate our species. We are helpless against it, and are programmed to do as we do. There may be variations from culture to culture, but whether it is in Margaret Mead's Samoa or modern Manhattan, our genetic composition makes our sexual behavior irresistible.

Although I let some women believe I loved them—and in some cases I may have meant it at the time—there was one woman I loved more than any other.

I was in my early forties when I met Weonna in Rome. She had a part in *Candy* and was with a friend of mine. He and I had the same rivalry I'd had with Carlo Fiore; we both tried to seduce each other's girl. After he introduced me to Weonna in a hotel lobby, he went off and I put it to her succinctly.

"Why don't we go upstairs and fuck?" She answered, "Why not? Let's go!"

That was the beginning and the end of the seduction.

Weonna was born only about a hundred miles from my birthplace. She had written a little, done some acting, modeled for a while, made some money in real estate. She was an extraordinary piece of construction, with white skin, soft, natural blond hair, freckles, a lot of moles, green eyes, and a voice with the slightest hint of an Irish accent, a hand-me-down from her mother, who was from Ireland. She made me laugh harder than any woman I've ever known. She was quick to understand and laughed at me a lot, too. Like my mother and grandmother, she had a sense of the absurd, thought the outrageous and imposed no limits on her imagination. She was amusing, witty, intelligent, eccentric. But she was also troubled. She distrusted people, drank too much and occasionally used drugs—not hard drugs, but pills. It was spasmodic; she would use them awhile, then swear off them, be clean for a while, then start again, and I'd have to take her to a hospital because it was the only place where she could stop. Still, we had a lot of fun together, and even now I often laugh at what we laughed at then.

One night I took Weonna on a mission to steal a stack of pipe, and before the night was over, she nearly had a heart attack. Not far from where I lived in California, a large parcel of land owned by the Teamsters' Union had remained undeveloped for years while contractors erected houses all around it; and if I didn't feel like going to sleep yet, sometimes I'd drive over there in my Jeep and cruise around the property with my lights out for the fun of it. One day construction crews arrived, set up equipment on the property and started work on what looked like a big development. But after a while, everything stopped abruptly and the workers left, leaving behind stacks of building materials, including a pile of three-inch irrigation pipe. I was doing some work on my house and needed some pipe, so I took Weonna to the site at about two A.M., hooked up my Jeep's winch to several pieces of pipe and began reeling it in. Within a few minutes, a helicopter was overhead sweeping a bright spotlight back and forth across the construction site. I dropped my pipe wrench, and when the wavering cone of light settled on the Jeep, I waved frantically to it, as if to say, "Please come down here, I need help."

I had no idea what I was going to say to the cops, but it was the first thing I could think of. Then an amplified voice boomed out of the sky: "Stay where you are. Do not move. You are under police surveillance."

I kept waving and smiling like a stranded sailor who has been spotted by a passing ship after spending half his life on a desert island. A minute or two later, a police car with flashing lights skidded to a stop about fifty feet from us.

Among the problems I had to deal with was the fact that the cable from the winch on my Jeep was still attached to the stack of pipe. I whispered to Weonna, "Whatever I say, agree with me. Agree with me when I tell them what happened. We're going to have to tell a few lies."

"I'm not lying," she said. "*You're* the one who got us into this, and I'm not going to be part of it."

I thought her disloyalty unbecoming, but I didn't get a chance to argue with her, for just as I was about to say something, the police car hit us with a spotlight and neither of us could see anything. I tried to put a look of happy relief on my face and hollered, "Thank God you found us! I thought we'd be here all night."

When they saw that a woman was with me it apparently eased the cops' sense of alarm, and one of them approached the Jeep. I thanked him profusely and said, "I took a wrong turn on Mulholland and ended up out here in the boondocks and got stuck in the sand. I tried to use the winch by tying up to that stack of pipe to see if I could bootstrap myself out, but the wheels kept spinning. Would you call a tow truck to get us out of here? I'd be very grateful."

All the while, I was hoping he wouldn't look at the ground, because if had he would have realized that no one could get stuck in a quarter inch of sand. He started walking back to the police car to call a tow truck, but before he'd taken four steps, I said, "Wait a minute, Officer. Before you call, maybe I should try it one more time."

I started the Jeep, pressed the throttle all the way to the floor until the engine roared like a threshing machine at harvest time, then put it in gear and let out the clutch very slowly with one foot still firmly on the brake. The Jeep shook, shuddered, rocked and slowly started to move as I let out the clutch. After I'd driven a few feet, I got out and told the officer, "I think I made it. Boy, that was lucky. Thanks a lot, I really appreciate your help. I don't know what I would have done if you hadn't come."

He accepted my thanks and drove away. I followed him back to the road and we went in opposite directions on Mulholland Drive while Weonna's cold silence let me know what she thought of me. I was feeling really pleased with myself until in my mirror I saw the police car do a U-turn and start coming after us. Oh, shit, I thought, he's figured it out.

The car raced up behind us with its flashing lights and I stopped. By now Weonna was bug-eyed, almost shaking. One of the policemen came over to my window with a flashlight and said, "You know, Mr. Brando, my wife would never forgive me for not getting your autograph."

"Why, sure, Officer," I said, wanting to kiss him, "do you have a pen and a piece of paper?"

51

MOST OF MY LIFE, I was a very jealous person, but I tried hard to hide it. I was afraid that if someone knew I was jealous, he or she would use it against me. I'm different now; I've realized that jealousy is a pointless, wasteful emotion I can't afford, but it wasn't easy for me to give up the emotions of a lifetime.

Weonna was as jealous and mistrustful as I was, and the other women in my life made her angry—sometimes, though not always, with justification. Late one night, before I installed barbed wire and an electrified security fence around my house, we were awakened by a noise and saw a woman standing at the foot of the bed.

"Who are you? What do you want?" I asked, holding the covers up around my neck like ZaSu Pitts in an old movie.

"Who am *I*?" she responded. "Who is *she*?"

She pointed her finger at Weonna, who was as startled as I was. I couldn't collect my thoughts and kept saying, "Who are you? What do you want? Who are you?"

"What do you mean, who am I? I suppose you're just saying that because you don't want her to know who I am."

Weonna was starting to look at me suspiciously.

"Look," I said, "I don't know who you are or what you're doing here."

"I suppose you didn't see me at the bus stop this afternoon."

"What bus stop?"

"*What* bus stop?" She laughed sarcastically.

"Look, you're going to have to get out of my house right now."

"I'm not going anyplace," she said. "You're getting rid of *her*, that's what's going to happen."

"Okay, I'm calling the police."

Weonna got out of bed shaking her head in disgust; she thought that I knew the woman. I grabbed her and said, "Wait a minute, Weonna . . . *wait one minute*. I don't know this woman. I've never seen her before in my life."

Then the bed jiggled and I turned back and saw that the woman had stripped off her clothes and slipped naked into bed beside me.

"Would you get out of here?" I said. "*Now*. How dare you?"

I was mustering the most theatrical show of vocal force and righteous indignation that I could manage at that hour of the night, but Weonna said wearily, "Never mind, I'll go. There's no sense getting excited, I understand. I'll go."

"Weonna, Weonna . . . I do not . . . I . . ." I was as tongue-tied as if I'd been hit over the head with a skillet by a linebacker. Finally I managed to pick up the phone beside the bed, wave it at Weonna to show her I was serious, and said, "I'm going to call the police, who will come here and remove this woman. You have to believe me."

I reached over and pushed the naked body out of my bed. She fell halfway to the floor as I said, "Get out of here," then dialed the police station, told the desk officer that someone had broken into my house and wouldn't leave, and asked him to send a policeman to take her away.

In five minutes, a patrol car arrived with two policemen. "Do you want to press charges?" one asked as they escorted the woman out of the bedroom after she'd put her clothes on.

"No," I said, "just take her away."

I spent the next fifteen minutes insisting to Weonna that I didn't know the woman. Her response was an ever-so-slight curl of her lips denoting suspicion and disbelief, as if the incident confirmed her conviction that I was unfaithful and a masterful liar and manipulator. I couldn't blame her because in those days that's exactly what I was. Still, I finally managed to calm her down and we drifted back to sleep. We were snuggled together an hour later when we heard another noise and woke up simultaneously to find that the woman was back in the room, her face ablaze with anger. She glared at Weonna and said, "Haven't you gotten rid of her yet?"

I said, "Look, we're not going through this again. I'm going to call the police, and this time you're going to go to jail; this time I'm going to press charges. Do you understand?"

I dialed the police department and talked to the same sergeant I'd spoken to the first time. "Excuse me, Officer, this is Marlon Brando calling again. The woman you took off the property is back and she's annoying me, so please come and get her." I was stuttering and stammering like Edward Everett Horton.

Very slowly and with deliberation, the policeman said, "Mr. Brando, we have a lot of things to do tonight; we're having a pretty busy night. A lot of things that we have to deal with are really serious, and coming and getting women out of your house is not one of them."

I put a stern look on my face, glanced at the woman and said, "All right, Officer, thank you very much. Thank you," and hung up the phone.

"They'll be here in twelve minutes," I said. "Now this time you're going to jail. I will press charges, you should know that, and you'll go to jail for at least a year."

At that the woman ran out of the room and I never saw her again.

Another time, Weonna and I were in bed when she woke me with a hard poke in the ribs. Startled, I was about to complain when she mouthed, *"There's someone in the house."*

"How do you know?"

Weonna had extraordinary hearing. She shook her head to indicate that she knew she was right. I got out of bed and went to a closet to get a shotgun I used to keep in the house; then, naked, I walked into the hall, unclear what I was looking for or what I would do if I found it. I remember thinking, You're naked, Marlon, and what's going to happen if they see you like this? They're not going to take you very seriously. I certainly wouldn't take a naked guy seriously if I was a burglar.

I walked down the hall into the living room, still gripped by this thought, but couldn't find anybody, so I returned to the bedroom with my shotgun and told Weonna that the coast seemed clear. She looked at me with a frightened expression and mouthed, *"They're in the bathroom . . ."*

In the bathroom I found an attractive young woman hiding behind the door. The sliding glass door to the deck was open, and she had come through it. I pointed the gun at her and said, "As quietly and quickly as you can, lie down and put your face in the rug—*now.*" She started to say something, but I said, "Do as I tell you." She followed orders and went down on the floor and pressed her face into the carpet. Her purse was in her hand and I said, "Push your purse toward me very gently," which she did. I opened it and looked through her wallet, which was very neat. I found a Screen Actors Guild card and said, "Are you an actress?"

The woman, whose nose and mouth were buried in the carpet, mumbled a muffled, "Yes."

"What are you doing in my bathroom at three A.M.?"

Still mumbling, she answered "I thought you might have some work for me."

"This is probably the least likely place to find work," I said. "What you've chosen to do is highly inefficient and very unprofessional. Stand up. Here's your purse and there's the door. Don't ever come back here again and don't ever, for your own welfare, do this to anybody else because it's dangerous."

I don't know if she ever found a job in the movies.

Those two weren't the only women who have shown up at my doorstep. The lure of celebrity does strange things to people. One woman camped outside my house in the rain for three days while a young Tahitian boy named Alphonse was visiting me. Because of an accident at birth, one of Alphonse's feet had turned inward, and I had arranged for him to come with his grandmother to Los Angeles to have corrective surgery. Actually she was not his real grandmother, but an elderly woman who looked after him and whom he called grandmother. One day she told me a woman was waiting outside to see me. I told her I wasn't expecting anybody, and that I made it a rule never to talk to strangers who showed up at my door. But I looked out the window with my binoculars and, sure enough, there was a woman standing in the driveway. Deciding that she was another nut, I told Grandmother that I didn't want to see her. Three days later, despite a tremendous rainstorm, the woman hadn't moved, and by now Alphonse's grandmother was very upset. She didn't understand it; she had never seen anything like it and pleaded with me, "Please let her in, she must be very cold and wet. I want to give her some food."

Grandmother was so compassionate that I knew I had to do something, so I went outside and spoke to the woman. She was very striking-looking, a mulatto in her early thirties who spoke with a clipped British accent. Her clothes were wet and she was chilled, so I invited her into the den at one end of my bedroom where a fire was blazing. Grandmother gave her a blanket and a cup of coffee, and as she warmed herself, she told me her story. After seeing *One-Eyed Jacks,* she said she had gone to a cafe and ordered a cup of coffee. While she was sipping it, she said she saw the reflection of her eyes in the coffee, then a reflection of *my* eyes—her eyes changed to mine as she was looking into the coffee—and thereafter she saw my eyes every-where she went and believed that some kind of spirit had turned her into me. She told me all this in a very formal and dignified way.

I asked where she was from and she said, "I was born in New York City."

"Where?"

"Harlem."

"Then how is it that you speak with a British accent? Have you been living in England?"

"No, I've never been there."

"Have you been around English-speaking people?"

"My boyfriend is from England."

Apparently she was affecting his accent, and she did it so well that she could have probably gotten a job as an announcer with the BBC. She said that she had come to my house under orders from her psychiatrist. After she told him she was me, he advised her to see me in the flesh and then she would know she was wrong.

"It must have taken a lot of courage to do this," I said. "As you can plainly see, I am not you, I am somebody else; I'm a dif-ferent person. For some reason, you needed to imagine that I was you."

At first she was disbelieving and confused, but slowly she began to relax. She was quite attractive, and for a moment or two I had evil fantasies, since my bed was only a few steps away. But I'd grown up a smidgen by then and chased such thoughts out of my mind, and eventually she left. I gave her my phone number and she called several times afterward, usually frantically, when she'd had a relapse and again thought she was me, so her psychiatrist would advise her to call me to confirm that it wasn't true. She also called after she read that I was in the hospital, and I assured her that I was all right and that she didn't have anything to worry about.

These calls went on for years and years, then gradually tapered off. The last one was several years ago, and now she was speaking with a German accent. I asked her, "Have you got a new boyfriend?"

"Yes."

"Is he German?"

"Yes, how did you know?"

For several years I saw Weonna off and on and we loved a lot and fought a lot. She was a tough woman and gave as good as she got. She had an unerring sense of how to prick my insecurities and jealousies, and we had ferocious fights. I suppose neither of us was willing or able to change our ways. At our last meeting we stood toe-to-toe and really destroyed each other emotionally. It was a grisly collision: Weonna, to get back at me because she said I had hurt her, had seduced one of my sons. I didn't explode. I simply realized that it was over, and that there was no possibility of anything between us again. After what she did, it was impossible to patch it up. I reassured my boy that he should not feel guilty, that what happened had been a maneuver by her to stick a dagger in my heart, and that he had no reason to feel any remorse.

For about five years, I didn't see Weonna, though I thought about her often and from time to time heard news about her: she had moved to New Mexico, had given up acting, had done well in real estate and had entered law school. Then I heard that she had moved back to Los Angeles and that someone had seen her at a party. I suspected our paths would cross and I wondered with some excitement what would happen if they did. When I saw her at a party at a friend's home, my stomach jumped as if I'd been punched in the gut by a heavyweight. I screwed up my courage, went over, put my hands around her softly and said, "I'm very glad to see you, Weonna." She blushed, gave me her telephone number and we started talking on the phone again. She was as funny as ever, and to me there's nothing in this world as seductive, or that gives me such a sense of life, as laughing. It's medicinal.

Most of the women in my life have been women of color, like Ermi: Latin American, Caribbean, Indian, Pakistani, Chinese, Japanese. Weonna was the exception, an Irish potato, and unlike the others we had a lot in common because we grew up in the same part of the country, spoke the same cultural language, had similar histories, liked the same jokes—and fought the same way.

After that party, I saw Weonna two or three more times at others, and as always she killed me with her jokes. She was sensitive but had a lot of street smarts; she was also naïve and childlike. Finally, after we'd spoken several times on the phone and I'd bumped into her a few times, she said, "What's going to happen now . . . to us?"

"I don't know," I said. "I'm just as bewildered as you are." I hadn't touched her since that first party, and I too didn't know where we were headed.

Weonna told me she wanted to see a psychiatrist because there were problems she hadn't been able to work out, and I encouraged her. I also wrote her a letter saying that I forgave her for all the things she had done to me, and that I hoped she would forgive me for everything I had done to her. I said that I thought we had been cruel to each other out of ignorance and anguish, longing and fear, anxiety and stress, and that I realized it was important for me to forgive her. I didn't know then why I wrote that letter, but now I realize that in doing so, by forgiving her for having put a sword in my heart, I was gaining my free-dom.

Up to then I had spent my life searching for a woman who would love me unconditionally, a woman whom I could love and trust never to hurt or abandon me, a woman who would make amends for the pain inflicted on me by my mother and Ermi. But from that moment on, I started to accept all women without doubt. They were no longer my enemy, nor were they archangels whom I could count on to give me a perfect life. If I was ever going to be happy, I realized, it was up to me to achieve it and not to some woman who would enter my life with a holy grail filled with a magic elixir guaranteeing me a full and happy life.

I also realized that if I were ever to forgive myself for all the things that I had done, I had to forgive my mother. I didn't know it at the time, but when I forgave Weonna she symbolized my mother, and I was forgiving her at the same time. Ever since then, I have had good relationships with women.

After I sent that letter to Weonna, we saw each other again, and while not all the wounds were healed, I think we both knew that we would be getting back together. But as we waited for fate to deal us our hand, Weonna died. She was riding a horse she loved, which stumbled, fell and crushed her. She sus-tained grave head injuries and died within forty-eight hours.

At the funeral I looked down at Weonna in her coffin, put a bouquet of flowers in her hand, whispered to her that I loved her and then kissed her. I've missed her every day since. She gave me the gift of laughter.

Weonna had told me that when she died she wanted to be buried near her father in a Catholic cemetery in South Dakota. I told her mother about it, but she said that Weonna's uncle, a priest, said that she didn't deserve to be buried in a Catholic cemetery because she had left the Church. I wanted to strangle him, but her mother followed his wishes and Weonna was buried in a nondenominational cemetery in the San Fernando Valley, where she lies today. Sometimes I drive down the hill from my home and put flowers on her grave. Her mother is also dead now, and I've often thought of having Weonna's casket moved so that she can be with her father. I know that one day I'll do it.

52

STARTING WITH MY nervous breakdown in New York, I
went off and on to psychiatrists for many years, especially during recurring moments in my life when I felt depressed, anxious
and frightened but didn't know why. I wasted a lot of money on
them, but finally found one who could help me, Dr. G. L.
Harrington. But while he helped me in ways I'll never understand, in the end I had to solve my problems myself.

Besides suffering from depression, anxiety and fear, I had
another problem much of my life: until about twenty years ago,
I was a bomb waiting to go off. Once, while I was driving on
Santa Monica Boulevard in Hollywood, a bus driver began
honking at me from behind. I was driving at the speed limit and
didn't want to go faster, but he kept pounding on his horn and
finally raced around me and cut in sharply, nearly sideswiping
me. I stepped on the gas and chased him for five blocks until I
got a chance to swing in front of him, ram the bus and force
him to the side of the road. Then I jumped out of my car and
began smashing the glass door of the bus with both fists and
screamed at him to open it because I wanted to dismember him.
He cowered inside, and when I couldn't force the door open, I
drove off, convinced that I had made my point.

Another time, when I was in Cannes, I heard that Elizabeth Taylor, whom I liked, and Richard Burton, whom I didn't, were there. I wanted to ask them to be in a show I was producing for UNICEF, and arranged to have lunch with them on a yacht. It was only noon but Richard was already drunk. He was a mean drunk, and soon he started making racial slurs about my Tahitian children.

At first I overlooked them, but when he kept it up, I turned to him and said, "If you make one more comment of any kind about my children, I'm going to knock you off this boat."

Burton looked up at me foolishly and silently with swollen, bleary eyes while Elizabeth said, "Oh, Richard, stop that now . . ." He didn't accept the challenge, but if he had, I was ready to throw him into the harbor.

On another occasion I was in a nightclub in Hollywood listening to a singer who was not very good; her voice sounded a little like a goose with a sore throat, and she was overweight and considerably past her prime physically. She wasn't a pretty sight, but she was singing gamely. At the table next to mine, several people were ridiculing her with snide comments loud enough for her to hear them, and I thought, That poor woman is up there doing the best she can, at the age she is, trying to earn a living, and those men are humiliating her.

As they kept it up, I grew angrier and angrier. Finally, one of them recognized me and reached over and touched my arm, either to introduce himself or to ask for an autograph. In an instant I had overturned my table, then I went over to his and said, "If you want to live, don't ever touch me again."

He was frightened by my outburst, which even I hadn't seen coming. In those days there was a latent anger a few millimeters beneath the surface of my skin just waiting to explode, and it happened so fast on this occasion that I was nearly out of control.

Until five or six years ago, I had a temper that sometimes erupted unconsciously, though it was always against men and often directed against paparazzi, those pathetic predators with cameras who prowl the gutters of the world. I hated anyone who tried to invade my privacy, but them especially, particularly if it involved my children. Once after a party in Rome, I went to the front door to say good-bye to some of my guests, holding my son in my arms, when there was an explosion of flashbulbs. I went berserk. After taking my son back to the living room, I charged out of the apartment like Attila the Hun and threw a haymaker at one of the photographers, missed him by a yard and fell on the pavement, injuring my pride but nothing else because I was anesthetized by adrenaline. I went back to the apartment, got a champagne bottle and went after one rat-faced paparazzo. He ran down the street, jumped on the hood of a car, vaulted over its roof and climbed a wall. I chased him step-by-step for almost a block, holding the bottle like a cudgel. I'd almost caught him when he jumped onto a streetcar and escaped. If I'd caught him, I might have killed him with that champagne bottle. Later that night some of his friends, a gang of toughs, started banging on my door at about 2:30 A.M. I got a butcher knife in the kitchen and prepared for a bloody battle, but the woman I was with said she was afraid I was going to kill someone and started wrestling with me for it. She was the strongest woman I ever knew, and held on to my wrist with both hands. Finally I came to my senses and thought, This is crazy. I'm not going to go around killing people with a butcher knife. I called the U.S. Embassy and demanded to speak to the ambassador.

The night-duty officer said, "He's asleep."

I said, "Wake him up or he's going to read about himself in the morning." I was really furious.

When the ambassador came on the line, I said, "I demand that I get some kind of protection from the Italian government. I've been intimidated and assaulted, my family has been harassed and I want some action."

The next morning a couple of carabinieri were posted outside my door. When I opened the door, a flashbulb went off in a sneak attack by one of the paparazzi, but a policeman put a hand the size of a ham over the lens and took him away. At the police station they opened his camera, pulled out the film, and said, "We don't see anything wrong with this," and returned the spoiled, exposed film to him. No more paparazzi bothered me during that visit to Rome, but I nearly choked another photographer at the airport after he started taking pictures of my children.

Now I don't care, but in those years I was constantly in combat with the paparazzi. Once I hit a photographer, who was waiting outside a club in Hollywood with his face pressed against his camera, and knocked him out; when he came to, he looked around and saw the pieces of his camera on the sidewalk beside him. I felt sorry for what I'd done, bent over and collected the pieces for him. "Sorry," I said, and he said, "What happened?"

"I don't know," I replied. "Looks to me like your camera just exploded."

On my way to a restaurant in Chinatown in New York with Dick Cavett, I told one paparazzo who had been following us around most of the day, "Look, I'm here with a friend and you've been taking a lot of pictures all day long. I'd really appreciate it if you'd let us have a quiet dinner and leave us alone."

"Well," he answered, "if you'll take off your dark glasses and let me take a good picture, I'll think about it."

Faster than I imagined possible, I planted my feet, swung and broke his jaw. When he fell, I flexed my foot to kick him, when I suddenly thought, Marlon, stop this. Don't do it.

The next morning my hand was as big as a catcher's mitt. Figuring I'd broken it, I went to a doctor who X-rayed it, then said, "It's not broken."

"Well, thank God for that. Thanks a lot, Doc, I'll keep it bandaged and soak it in something."

"No," he said, "I'm afraid you're going to have to go to the hospital. See those little red lines running up your wrist? That's blood poisoning. If you don't take care of it, you could lose your arm."

The photographer's teeth had cut the sheath of a tendon, and the doctor told me there were more dangerous bacteria in the mouth of a human than in almost any other animal except a monkey. This didn't surprise me; I had assumed that the mouth of a paparazzo was a cesspool of bacteria. I spent several days in the hospital on my back with my arm soaking in hot compresses, but made sure that no one heard I'd put myself in the hospital by hitting a paparazzo.

Before finding one who could help me, I was a patient of five different psychiatrists. Based on my experience, most psychiatrists are people who feel comfortable trying to control other people because they can't handle themselves. Their experiences have overwhelmed them and they believe they will be able to cope only if they are in a controlling position over others. I've known a lot of them, and some have been among the nuttiest people I've ever met. My experience began with the Freudian analyst recommended by Elia Kazan, and continued with several therapists in California, including one in Beverly Hills whom I saw for many years. He was a neurotic, frightened man who wouldn't admit to having any fears, and who had read everything and knew nothing. He was spooked by anybody and anything, including his own hair; it was tight and curly, and he kept it cut short because he said he didn't want people to think he had any Negro blood. Once when we were discussing the Vietnam War, I asked, "What if we bomb Haiphong Harbor and China comes into the war on the side of the North Vietnamese?" to which he replied that there was nothing troublesome about the Chinese that couldn't be taken care of with three atomic bombs. He spent a lot of our sessions asking for money. If my business manager was a day late in paying his bill, the first thing he did was remind me. He made me see him five days a week, and he ended each session by saying, "We have to stop now; I have another customer." He pried into my brain and made me feel worse than I ever had, and when I needed him most he abandoned me.

This happened a few years ago when I thought I was in love with a Jamaican woman named Diana, who was vivacious and funny but at heart was vulgar and unrefined, a would-be actress with more ambition than talent. In the midst of an extended affair she told me that she had accepted an acting job in England, where she had once lived. When I told her I didn't want her to take the job, she said, "Oh, I'll be back."

"No, you won't," I said, "because if you go out that door, you'll never have a chance to come back through it."

Diana cried but said she was determined to be in the movie. I took her to the airport and kissed her good-bye, then went home and burned her picture and everything else she had ever given me. After Diana arrived in England, she sent me several telegrams, but I didn't answer them. I was devastated but couldn't let her know it.

My psychiatrist had been away on a long vacation when she left, and when he returned I walked into his office and sat down prepared to spill my guts and tell him how miserable I was. But he said, "You know, I don't think I can help you anymore." I had been his patient for ten or twelve years, and was desperately in need of assistance, but he rejected me. I had trusted him, but he was just one more analyst who got you hooked, then felt no accountability or responsibility for you. Even most auto mechanics guarantee their work, but not a psychiatrist. I had kept this man in groceries and cars for years, but now he rejected me.

"You can't turn me away," I said. "I have no place else to go." I didn't have enough sense to realize that I would have been better off never having met him. He got out of his chair, circled the room like an absentminded dog, and put his foot in his wastebasket while gazing out the window. The contents spilled all over the floor, but he was so preoccupied that he didn't place the basket right side up. It made me realize that he was as nervous and as frightened as I was, so I left in emotional pain.

Diana kept writing from England saying she missed me and wanted to see me, but I didn't reply. Then I went to London, where I was invited to a party and saw her there. I didn't look at her, but could see peripherally that she was watching me. I tried to get away before we bumped into each other, but when I got on the elevator, there she was. "We've got to stop meeting like this, don't we?" I said and tried to make jokes. In the lobby I went left and she went right, but feeling guilty, I turned, called to her and said, "Diana, I'm sorry things didn't go well this evening." She said something cordial and we each went our own way.

Several months later, when I was making *Last Tango in Paris*, Diana came to the set with a camera. She was now a photographer, trying on a new career. I said I was glad to see her and gave her a kiss. We were filming a scene at the time, so I suggested that we have dinner that night. We did, and had some laughs and talked about old times. Then we walked to the apartment where I was staying; she came upstairs and took off her clothes, but I went to sleep. I didn't feel anything for her. A few months later, Diana was back in California and called to say that she had a pain in her back and wanted a massage. She came over and took her clothes off, and I gave her a full massage, then fell asleep again. I didn't even think about making love to her. Once she had left me, I had no feelings left for her.

That Beverly Hills psychiatrist had no real insight about people, though it cost me a substantial amount of money to learn this. Back then, I was overly impressed with sheepskins. It took me a long time to realize that just because someone went to medical school and papered his walls with diplomas, it didn't mean he was a good analyst. It requires a rare and special talent to understand people, and it is hard to find.

A couple of years later I met G. L. Harrington, a wonderful and insightful man who, sadly, is now dead, a victim of liver cancer. It is a disease that usually kills within months but he battled it for five years before it took him. He was crippled in body but not in mind. His hip and one leg had been smashed in a car accident, and because he refused to let doctors amputate the leg, it was two or three inches shorter than the other one. It gave him a lot of pain, but he never complained. He was a handsome, rugged man with a low husky rumble for a voice and a lot of male hormones. In some ways he reminded me of my father. He was the kind of man I thought I would never like. I had always bridled in the presence of masculine men like him and frequently got into fights with them. I felt I had to be aggressive with men like him, that I had to defeat them. Harrington was such a man. He had been a pilot during the war, and to judge by the medals and decorations on his wall, a brave one. But while he had a masculine aura, he was also one of the funniest, wittiest, most creative, sensitive and insightful people I'd ever met. After spending years on couches, I was familiar with analysis when I first went to see him. Whenever I started therapy with a new doctor, I always tried to give him a list of my neurotic dysfunctions, which was what most of them wanted to hear. After a grace period, I decided it was time to give my list to Harrington. My wheelbarrow full of analytic misinformation, I wheeled it up to his door and said, "I want to get into some of the things that happened to me in the past."

"Oh, we'll get to them when the time comes," Harrington said, but we never did; he talked and laughed me out of it. We would discuss anything because he had great curiosity: electricity, airplanes, genetics, evolution, politics, botany and every other subject under the sun. I saw him once a week and always looked forward to it because he made me laugh at myself. Once I told him I had always been fascinated by writers like Kant and Rousseau, and that I gravitated to women with similar tastes, those with whom I had something in common.

With a straight face, Harrington said, "Tell me about this Japanese girl you've been seeing . . ." It was his way of telling me that what I had just said was idiotic: you've got a girlfriend who can't speak English, you have nothing in common with her, and yet you chose her.

Once I told Harrington, "I think I've got a lot of rage because of my father."

"What do you mean 'rage'? Because you're mad at your father?"

"Yes."

"Well, you're not mad now, are you?"

"Well, not right this minute."

He said, "Okay," and that was it, but for some reason it helped disarm my anger.

Another day I walked into his studio, a small room with a desk, table and two chairs, and sat down, and as usual he gave me a cup of coffee. Every morning his wife put a fresh rose on his desk, and on this day I noticed that it was magnificent. Two petals had fallen off and were lying next to it on the desk. I was entranced by it and said, "That's the most beautiful rose I've ever seen." Then I leaned over to smell it and said, "But it doesn't smell."

"I'd be alarmed if it did," he said.

"Why?"

"Because it's a fake."

He had put the two petals beside the artificial rose to convey the illusion of reality and to illustrate that everything in life was perception—that just because you assume something is true, it ain't necessarily so.

My sister Jocelyn also went to Harrington, and the two of us spent a lot of time on the phone comparing notes about our sessions with him. She loved him deeply because he was the father she never had. His wife was also very kind. She was a former concert pianist who sometimes played Rachmaninoff in an adjoining room during our sessions.

Once Dr. Harrington told me about a patient who came to see him; after ten or twelve minutes she stood up, said, "I've learned what I wanted to know, and I want to thank you very much," and then walked out the door. I always remembered this story, and once I asked him, "Why do we always have to talk for an hour? Sometimes I don't want to talk for more than twenty minutes." He agreed, and unless it was an important session that might go on for two hours, I'd get up and leave regardless of the time. One day after about three years I got up and said, "I don't know whether I have to come back here anymore. I'd like to come back and talk to you, but I don't think I *need* to."

And that was the end of my therapy. I never went back, but I was a different person for having known him. He was a wonderful friend who helped others in my family, too, and through humor he taught me a lot about myself. He simply had a talent for it. Most of all, G. L. Harrington taught me how to forgive—myself and others.

53

I SUSPECT SOME READERS who have reached this point in the book are asking themselves, "When's Brando going to talk about the Indians? Isn't he *obsessed* with the plight of the American Indian?" I bridle at this, more in exasperation than in anger, because I'm confronted with it over and over again from people who, perhaps to please me, mention "the plight of the American Indian" as if it were something that had happened on another planet in another era—like a drought in equatorial Africa or the Black Death in fourteenth-century Europe, as if the slaughter of hundreds of thousands of innocent people were some sort of a historical curiosity, even an act of God, that humankind had nothing to do with and bore no responsibility for. This grates on my soul.

What astonishes me is how ignorant most Americans are about the Indians and how little sympathy and understanding there is for them. It puzzles me that most people don't take seriously the fact that this country was stolen from the Native Americans, and that millions of them were killed in the process. It has been swept from the national consciousness as if it never occurred—or if it did, it was a noble act in the name of God, civilization and progress. The number of Indians who died because of what we called Manifest Destiny has always been a subject of debate among scholars, but I believe that the majority of informed historians and anthropologists now agree that between seven million and eighteen million indigenous people were living in what is today the continental United States when Columbus arrived in the New World. By 1924 there were fewer than 240,000 left; their ancestors had been victimized by centuries of disease, starvation and systematic slaughter.

If people acknowledged a similar ignorance about the Holocaust, they would be regarded with amazement. But that's how it is for most of us when it comes to Native Americans. To my mind the killing of Indians was an even larger crime against humanity than the Holocaust: not only did it take more lives, but it was a crime committed over centuries that continues in some ways to this day.

Ever since I helped raise funds for Israel as a young man and learned about the Holocaust, I've been interested in how different societies treat one another; it is one of the enduring interests of my life. In the early sixties I read a book by John Collier, a former U.S. Commissioner of Indian Affairs who was responsible for giving the Indians a token measure of self-government on their reservations during the 1930s, and I was shocked at how badly we had treated them. Then I read *The First Americans* by a Flathead Indian, anthropologist D'Arcy McNickle, and was moved. The book describes two hundred years of savage warfare by European settlers against the Indians, the massacres of native peoples from New England to California and how U.S. military leaders like Lieutenant General Phil Sheridan called for the outright annihilation of the race. Indians who escaped being cut down by such predators were killed by disease imported by European settlers, which was followed by forced marches, deliberate starvation and attempts to destroy their culture.

The book was an eye-opener, and I went to Santa Fe to visit

D'Arcy McNickle. After we had talked for several hours, I asked him where I could meet some Indians, and he suggested that I get in touch with the National Indian Youth Council. I went to a meeting of the organization and made many friends, a lot of whom I still know today, and thereafter I became absorbed with the world of the Native American.

In the early 1960s, several members of the Indian Youth Council from the Pacific Northwest told me that they had decided to challenge government limits on salmon fishing by Indians in western Washington and along the Columbia River. Century-old treaties guaranteed their tribes the right to fish at their accustomed places in perpetuity—"as long as the mountains stand, the grass grows and the sun shines." But sport and commercial salmon fishermen had persuaded state and federal agencies to limit their harvest, blaming the Indians for a drop in their own catch. This was after decades in which white people had built a string of dams on the rivers, often making it impossible for salmon to spawn, and after lumber companies had polluted streams and rivers with toxic chemicals and other garbage. The Indians wanted to challenge the restrictions because they clearly violated their legal rights to fish in the streams, and I offered to join them in doing so on the Puyallup Indian Reservation in Washington, with the expectation of being arrested and publicizing the "fish-in." I got in a boat with a Native American and a Catholic priest; someone gave us a big salmon we were supposed to have taken out of the river illegally and, sure enough, a game warden soon arrived and arrested us. He took us to a jail near Olympia, but I was released after an hour and half because, I was told, the governor didn't want a movie star's arrest to create more publicity for the Indians' campaign.

Even though I couldn't get arrested for long, my experiences with the Native Americans had given me a sense of brotherhood with them that has lasted to this day. I was introduced to

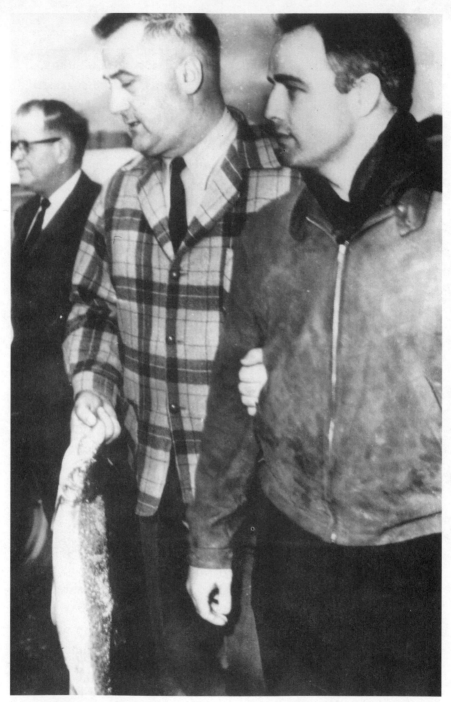

I am under arrest in Tacoma, Washington, in 1964 for catching a steelhead trout with a drift net at the mouth of the Puyallup River. I was participating in an Indian "fish-in" to dramatize that their treaty rights were being violated. (AP/Wide World Photos)

Indian food, Indian humor, Indian religion and the Sun Dance, an intense spiritual experience that the federal government had banned as part of its campaign to break the spirit and cohesiveness of Native Americans until they demanded and won the right to perform it again in the 1960s. One reason I liked being with the Indians was that they didn't give anyone movie-star treatment. They didn't give a damn about my movies. Everyone's the same; everyone shares and shares alike. Indians are usually depicted as grumpy people with monochrome moods, but I learned that they have a sardonic sense of humor and that they love to tease. They laugh at anything, especially themselves. If somebody stutters, everybody in the group stutters or pretends to go to sleep while the poor man tries to finish a sentence. But it's an honest humor, not cruel.

There is no doubt that alcohol is the bane of the American Indians; many of them have drinking problems, and a bottle was usually on the table whenever we sat down. I also learned that there's real time and Indian time: if a meeting is supposed to start at nine P.M. Indians start dribbling in about ten P.M.

After my first attempt at being arrested failed, we set out again, this time near a different reservation in Washington. We spent the night before in an unheated cabin with paper-thin walls, and I came down with a chest cold to end all chest colds. A damp wind blowing through cracks in the walls all night didn't help.

At dawn, when it was time to leave, I was coughing and hacking and had a high temperature. But the Indians looked at me expectantly, and I knew I had to go. I wrapped myself in a blanket and got in the boat while icy waves whipped up by the wind sprayed everyone, and as we left shore I thought, I'm not going to leave this boat alive. I suspected that I had pneumonia, that I was going to die and that my body would be dumped into the river. Hunched over, I told one of my Indian friends, Hank Adams, how awful I felt, and he said, "You know, my grandmother used to say, 'If you smile, you'll feel better.' "

I just looked at him and thought, What in this poor, pissed-on world are you talking about? I'm dying, and you're asking me to smile?

We traveled up and down the river for an hour waiting to be arrested, but no game wardens showed up. I don't mind dying, I thought, but to die so senselessly on a freezing river without even being arrested seems absurd. Only later did we learn that we'd been on the wrong river. Patrol boats were looking for us somewhere else; I'd faced death—or so my melodrama let me convince myself—for nothing. One of the Indians' lawyers got me to an airport, and I flew home and entered the hospital with pneumonia, where I swore that someday I would repay Hank Adams.

The fish-ins were important because in many ways they laid the foundation for subsequent Native American campaigns for civil rights. They were important for me as well because they acquainted me with what Indians were up against and how little support they had. I got to know extraordinary people, such as Clyde Warrior, a Ponca Indian with whom I often traveled around the country to Indian Youth Council meetings; he was a man with a sense of dignity I'll never forget, a wonderful sense of humor and great sense of pride in being Indian, and he taught me as much as anyone how much my own view of life was similar to that of the American Indian. There was Vince Deloria, Jr., a brilliant political scientist, writer and Indian historian, who had devoted his life to their support; and Dennis Banks, Russell Means and other young Indians who would later start AIM, the American Indian Movement. I also got involved with such groups as the Congress for the American Indian, Survival of the American Indian and the National Congress for American Indians, and traveled around the country trying to explain to state officials, congressmen and Attorney General Robert Kennedy that American Indians were being unlawfully mistreated.

I also met with Supreme Court Justice William O. Douglas. Not many people have intimidated me, but he had such presence and I had such respect for him that when I walked into his office with my briefcase filled with a portfolio of complaints about the treatment of Indians I couldn't say anything.

Douglas sat behind his desk looking kindly and attentive, and said, "Yes?"

I couldn't put three words together. After five minutes of my stuttering and stammering, he said, "Well, I have to go on the bench now. It's been a pleasure to meet you."

I rose and left, hardly able even to say good-bye to the great man.

54

AS THE NATIVE AMERICANS' civil rights movement spread and gathered momentum in the late 1960s and early 1970s, I supported it in every way I could—emotionally, spiritually and financially. I was outraged by the injustices they had endured; there is simply no other way I can put it. Our government signed almost four hundred treaties with the Indians and broke every one of them. These agreements almost always include this language: "As long as the river shall run, the sun shall shine and the grass shall grow, this land will be forever yours, and it will never be taken away from you or sold without your express permission." Yet all of them were broken with the blessing and sanction of our courts. Even when the federal government gave lip service to honoring the treaties, settlers, ranchers and miners ignored them and grabbed the richest valleys, lushest forests and lands with the most minerals. They squatted where they wanted, then persuaded Congress to legitimize the status quo and abandon the treaties that they were unlawfully ignoring. What would happen if Cuba abrogated its treaty granting America the use of Guantánamo Bay, one that can be lawfully annulled only with the consent of both nations? It would be considered an act of war, and smart bombs would rain on Havana. But if Indians even complain about a broken treaty, they are scorned, vilified or put into jail. I don't think anything equals the hypocrisy the United States has exhibited toward the Native American. Our leaders have called for their annihilation in the name of democracy; in the name of Christianity; in the name of the advancement of civilization; in the name of all the principles we have fought wars to uphold.

From Congress, the White House and human-rights groups, we constantly hear complaints about ill-treatment and genocide against this group or that. But no people has ever been treated worse than Native Americans. Our government intentionally starved the Plains Indians to death by slaughtering the buffalo because it was quicker and easier to kill buffalo than to kill Indians. It denied them food and forced them to sign treaties giving up their land and future. The Indians were rarely defeated militarily; they were starved into submission. In the Orient I once heard a phrase describing nineteenth-century Chinese peasants as "rice Christians." It was an allusion to the way in which Catholic missionaries converted them; if they attended Mass and religious instruction, they were given rice; if not, they starved. The same was done to subdue the Native Americans. Kit Carson applied a scorched-earth policy that burned the Navajo fruit trees and crops, then chased the Navajos until they were dead or starving. Those who went to reservations and showed any independence were denied food, blankets and medicine, or were given moldy flour and rancid meat that accelerated their annihilation. The government blamed the spoiled food on frontier traders, but while the Indians were being given tainted food and starved to death, the soldiers guarding them were well fed. Starvation was used as a national policy; it was an act of intentional genocide. It is no coincidence, I suspect, that when Hitler was plotting his Final Solution, he ordered a study of America's Indian-reservation system. He admired it and wanted to use it in Europe.

Starved, degraded and emotionally depleted, in the end the Indians had no choice but to submit. As Chief Seattle said when he surrendered his tribal lands to the governor of Washington Territory in 1855, "My people are few. They resemble the scattering trees of a storm-swept plain. There was a time when our people covered the land as the waves of a wind-ruffled sea covered its shell-paved floor, but that time long since passed away with the greatness of tribes that are now but a mournful memory. . . ."

Twenty years later, a great leader of the Nez Percé, Chief Joseph, made many accommodations to settlers while trying to preserve his people's culture. But as in so many cases, the government reneged on the treaties it signed with the Nez Percé: first it forced the tribe onto a wasteland that white men didn't want, and then, when gold and other minerals were found there, it ordered the Indians off it. The great warrior took his entire tribe—women, children, teepees and all—and, with another chief, Looking Glass, led it on a desperate flight of over 1,500 miles toward Canada, pursued by thousands of cavalrymen. En route, there were fourteen major engagements with the cavalry, and Chief Looking Glass proved himself a brilliant tactician. When they were finally stopped by the army, less than fifty miles from the Canadian border and freedom, Chief Joseph surrendered in a speech that summarized poignantly how a great and proud people had been devastated by the United States:

I am tired of fighting. Our chiefs are killed. Looking Glass is dead. Toohoolhoolzote is dead. The old men are all dead. It is the young men who say yes or no. He who led on the young men [Joseph's brother] is dead. It is cold and we have no blankets. The little children are freezing to death. My people, some of them, have run away to the hills and have no blankets, no food. No one knows where they are—perhaps freezing to death. I want to have time to look for my children and see how many of them I can find. Maybe I shall find them among the dead. Hear me, my chiefs! I am tired; my heart is sick and sad. From where the sun now stands I will fight no more forever.

After their lands were stolen from them, and the ragged survivors of what the writer Helen Jackson called *A Century of Dishonor* were herded onto reservations, the government sent out missionaries from seven or eight religious denominations who tried to force the Indians to become Christians. It was a clear assault on their religious beliefs and a culture that had thrived for millennia, as well as a blatant denial of the constitutional guarantee of freedom of religion. Missionaries divided up reservations as if they were a pie. They stole Indian children and sent them to religious academies or to the government school in Carlisle, Pennsylvania, where the children were beaten if they spoke their own languages. If they ran away, they were subject to severe punishment applied in military fashion. Yet these crimes are almost invisible in our national consciousness. If they give any thought to the Indians, most Americans project a montage of images from the movies; few conjure up anguish, suffering or murder when they think of Native Americans. Indians are simply a vague, colorful chapter in our country's past, deserving no more interest than might be devoted to the building of the Erie Canal or the transcontinental railroad.

After I became interested in American Indians, I discovered that many people, unconsciously at least, don't even regard them as human beings on the same level as themselves. It has been that way since the beginning; preaching to the Puritans, Cotton Mather compared them to Satan and called it God's work—and God's will—to slaughter the heathen savages who stood in the way of Christianity and progress. In the Declaration of Independence proclaiming that all men are created equal, the indigenous peoples of America were called "merciless Indian Savages, whose known Rule of Warfare is an undistinguished Destruction of all Ages, Sexes and Conditions." As he aimed his howitzers on an encampment of unarmed Indians at Sand Creek, Colorado, in 1864, an army colonel named John M. Chivington, who had once said he believed that the lives of Indian children should not be spared because "nits make lice!" told his officers: "I have come to kill Indians, and believe it is right and honorable to use any means under God's heaven to kill Indians." Hundreds of Indian women, children and old men were slaughtered in the Sand Creek Massacre. One officer who was present said later, "Women and children were killed and scalped, children shot at their mothers' breasts, and all the bodies mutilated in the most horrible manner . . . the dead bodies of females [were] profaned in such a manner that the recital is sickening. . . ." The troopers cut off the vulvas of Indian women, stretched them over their saddle horns, then decorated their hatbands with them; some used the skin of braves' scrotums and the breasts of Indian women as tobacco pouches, then showed off these trophies, together with the noses and ears of some of the Indians they had massacred, at the Denver Opera House.

The assault on American Indians continued into the twentieth century, but in different fashion. When I was going to school in the thirties, barely forty years after the army had butchered more than three hundred Oglala Sioux men, women and children at Wounded Knee, South Dakota, most textbooks dismissed the Indians in two or three paragraphs that depicted them as a race of faceless, ferocious, heathen savages. From dime novels to the movies, popular culture has reinforced our caricatures of American Indians, demonizing and dehumanizing them, and making folk heroes out of Indian killers like Daniel Boone, Andrew Jackson and Kit Carson. From its birth, Hollywood defamed Indians in pictures like *The Squaw Man*.

John Wayne probably did more damage than General Custer ever did to the Indians, projecting an idiotic image of a brave white man battling the godless savages of the frontier. Hollywood needed villains, and it made Indians the embodiment of evil.

But our treatment of Native Americans is only a single thread in the tapestry of human depravity. Side by side with man's extraordinary ability to think, there is an irrational aspect of his mind that makes him want to destroy on behalf of what he regards as his own breed. Darwin described an instinctive need of members of all species to protect and perpetuate their own group, but the human being is the only animal I know of that consciously inflicts pain on other members of its *own* species. When I was a young man helping to raise money for Israel, I was amazed by what was then a great mystery to me: how it was possible for seemingly ordinary Germans to machine-gun innocent children or herd people into gas chambers by the thousands. It seemed unfathomable that human beings could do such things to one another. But over a lifetime it has become apparent that we are capable of anything on behalf of our own group; the animus is an immutable product of billions of years of evolution.

People feel protected and secure in a tribe, as evidenced by the popularity of gangs in cities all over the world. Their members are responding to an atavistic impulse that has nothing to do with current social conditions; it is a part of every person and culture. The Holocaust wasn't unique: what made it different was its scale, which to a large degree was simply a product of technology and organization. From time immemorial people have responded to similar impulses to exterminate other groups; the Nazis were more efficient at it. Nothing has eradicated our fundamental instinct to kill one another, usually under the guise of what is inevitably called a just and noble cause, religious or secular.

There is a line in John Patrick's play *The Teahouse of the August Moon* in which the American officer assigned to bring democracy to Okinawa says, in effect, "We're going to create a democracy here even if we have to kill everyone to do so." *Julius Caesar* was a cynical play because it reflected how easily people can be manipulated for a supposedly honorable purpose. Brutus announces why he killed Caesar:

If there be any in this assembly, any dear friend of Caesar's, to him I say, that Brutus' love to Caesar was no less than his. If then that friend demand why Brutus rose against Caesar, this is my answer: Not that I lov'd Caesar less, but that I lov'd Rome more. Had you rather Caesar were living and die all slaves, than that Caesar were dead, to live all freemen? As Caesar lov'd me, I weep for him; as he was fortunate, I rejoice at it; as he was valiant, I honour him, but, as he was ambitious, I slew him. There is tears for his love, joy for his fortune; honour for his valour; and death for his ambition. . . .

Except for Mark Antony, his friends cheered Brutus.

Using slightly different but equally effective forms of manipulation, Goebbels's propaganda films bombarded Germans with photographs of Jews, then cut to a crowded warren of rats, the juxtaposition implying: *these are Jews.* We are all victimized by the incessant manipulation of our minds and emotions in church, at political rallies or while watching television commercials. The repetition of anything eventually affects us and becomes a part of us. The Nazis knew this, and employed it to convince Germans that it was perfectly proper to annihilate Jews.

Barely a century ago, American Indians were hunted for sport with Winchester rifles. Their hunters had been conditioned to regard them as less than human, like deer or quail. History is replete with similar crimes: under the cross of

Christianity, the Crusaders swept across the Middle East hacking people to death with swords that fittingly replicated the cross; white settlers slaughtered countless thousands of aborigines in Australia; the Turks slaughtered more than a million Armenians between 1915 and 1918; Stalin exterminated millions of peasants and intellectuals; the Khmer Rouge eradicated millions of Cambodians; during the so-called Cultural Revolution, millions of Chinese heeded appeals by their leaders to kill; and today the Serbs are practicing genocide on the Bosnians. The formula is simple and always the same: make the other group the embodiment of evil, dehumanize it, create an ideology that provides a noble rationale for purging the world of this evil, and seemingly civilized people become enthusiastic killers. Once another group is transformed into something less than human, it is astonishingly easy to arouse—as Hannah Arendt eloquently pointed out in *Eichmann in Jerusalem: A Report on the Banality of Evil*—the "will to follow," and to convince ordinary people that they are free to commit terrible acts in the name of what has been mythologized as a moral and high-minded cause. It is a reflection of the fortitude, tenacity and resiliency of the human belief system; a man is far more prone to kill you if you threaten his beliefs than if you rape his wife, because his belief system is the foundation of his sanity.

We are what we are taught. Get a child when he's seven, the Jesuits say, and you'll have him for life. Once these beliefs are planted solidly in our brains, we will do anything to protect them, no matter what they are. Virtually every religion preaches "Love thy neighbor as thyself," and that you should sacrifice yourself for the welfare of others. Yet many of the bloodiest wars on our planet have been fought over religion. I've always thought it was a form of child abuse to take an impressionable child and hammer into him convictions that, even if right, will torment him all his life. A child is too young to make rational judgments, but many religions do this because they want to gain control of the child's mind. It is all about power.

As observed previously, one of the unique characteristics of the human animal is suggestibility. Another is the urge to create and believe myths. The British author and philosopher C.E.M. Joad wrote that people have "an imperative need to believe," and that the "values of a belief are disproportionate, not to its truth, but to its definiteness. Incapable of either admitting the existence of contrary judgments or of suspending their own, they supply the place of knowledge by turning other men's conjectures into dogmas."

In one of the saddest chapters of American history in the twentieth century, the Vietnam War took the lives of 58,000 Americans, and I don't know why. Our country embraced a litany of myths about the threat of communism, the "domino theory" and the menace of a Sino-Soviet bloc that didn't exist. None of these threats ever existed. Intelligent people had at their fingertips enormous resources and information that were dead wrong. They weren't evil men, but until it was too late they could not see through the beliefs that imprisoned them. They were certain they were right, and millions of Americans unblinkingly accepted what they said. We could honestly believe that a people ten thousand miles from our shores were our dangerous enemies—so dangerous, in fact, that we had to lie that an American ship had been attacked in the Gulf of Tonkin by the North Vietnamese. It took ten or twelve years of a horrific war and tens of thousands of squandered lives to change this perception—though even now I sometimes hear people insist that we made a mistake by withdrawing from Vietnam when we did because we did so without "honor."

In short, we lose control of reality easily. We treated the American Indians in the same manner that Serbian people are treating the Muslims, that the Turks treated the Armenians and that Hitler treated the Jews. But we refuse to think of ourselves as a nation that committed genocide. Our paratroopers jump out of airplanes yelling "Geronimo," and the Pentagon names its helicopters "Navajo" and "Cherokee." In this perverse fashion, we glorify the American Indian, but the minute he makes justifiable demands, he is ignored by a nation that prides itself on being a champion of human rights, the right of self-determination, liberty and the pursuit of happiness. The cavalrymen and settlers who slaughtered the Indians weren't inherently evil; they were responding to a culture that demonized them. But this does not excuse our country's refusal to settle a debt that is long overdue. With the exception of the United States, virtually every colonial power that stole land from its indigenous peoples has at least started to give some of it back to its rightful owners—often kicking and screaming because the United States has goaded them into doing so. However, if you ask anybody in our government or a western rancher to give up even a square inch of land to Native Americans, he will look at you in bemusement. I've met a lot of these ranchers, and when the topic of the American Indians' ancestral ownership of the land comes up, they'll state: "I own this land because my grandfather established this ranch; my father lived here all his life; I've lived here all my life; and I intend for my children to live here on their own land." If I point out that Indians were living on "their" land long before their grandfathers, they always find a way to rationalize it: "Well, maybe, but *I* didn't take their land, so why blame me for it?" Or "You don't seriously expect me to get off my land, do you? Maybe it *was* taken from the Indians, but we were the ones who settled it, who built it into something, and who planted the crops. We've *earned* this land."

The rationalizations are unending. One of the strangest government policies is that largely because of the political influence of Jewish interests, our country has invested billions of dollars and many American lives to help Israel reclaim land that they say their ancestors occupied three thousand years ago. But if anyone tries to apply the same principle to the Native Americans, whose ancestors were here at least fifteen thousand years before the Europeans arrived, the reaction is that it is too late to turn the clock back now. It does no good to be logical about it; people do not respond to logic.

The history of the American Indian Movement—its successes and mistakes and the sordid story of how the FBI harassed and tried to suppress it—is too broad a topic for me to cover in this book, so I will only describe what I saw from the periphery. AIM comprised Indians from many different tribes who were generally more militant than those in other Indian groups seeking redress during the sixties and seventies for centuries of wrongs committed against their people. Many of the other groups had tried logic and conciliation, but got nowhere.

Dennis Banks, a Chippewa Indian, and Russell Means, a large, handsome Sioux who bears a stunning resemblance to Gall, one of the greatest Sioux warriors, are remarkable men. Both left their reservations, abandoning their roots and culture, to try to make a living on the outside; both got into trouble off the reservation and had to take humiliating jobs because it was all they could get. Like other American Indians who left their reservations, they faced a racism that perhaps is the most vicious of all: they encountered not only discrimination in jobs and housing but indifference. In mainstream American culture, they were considered nonentities, and people looked through them as if they didn't exist. Dennis and Russell met in Minneapolis and discovered that they shared a mutual problem; though they had left their reservations, they were unable to turn their backs on their culture. They did an about-face and decided to reenter it, and with others they started AIM, which soon had chapters all over the country, to press the government to live up to its treaties and promises. The FBI, other federal agencies, ranchers and white vigilantes, who in some cases allied themselves with corrupt tribal officials chosen in rigged

With Russell Means outside the St. Paul, Minnesota, courthouse where he and Dennis Banks were on trial in January 1974 for the 1973 armed takeover of Wounded Knee, South Dakota. (UPI/Bettmann)

elections, launched a war on AIM that was a blend of modern McCarthyism and the kind of armed campaign that had nearly exterminated the American Indian a century before. With SWAT teams, helicopter gunships, armored personnel carriers and an often-biased white judicial apparatus, the government poured all its resources into suppressing AIM. It spent millions to investigate the deaths of whites who were killed during the conflict, but when Native Americans were murdered, the U.S. Justice Department, Bureau of Indian Affairs and local authorities usually ignored it, once again treating the Indians as if they were less than human.

In early 1973, when about two hundred AIM members took over the village of Wounded Knee on the Pine Ridge Reservation in South Dakota, all they wanted the government to do was to allow free elections of tribal leaders, to investigate abuses within the Bureau of Indian Affairs and to review all Indian treaties. They occupied the village for seventy-one days before getting a conditional promise that their demands would be met—a promise that was only partly kept. If they had been any other group who held out that long—the Symbionese Liberation Army, black militants or an offbeat religious cult, for example—I believe they would have been attacked and killed. But Hollywood's fascination with American Indians has had one beneficial effect: thanks to films, they are internationally famous, and I'm sure the government held its fire because it was aware that the world would find one more massacre of Indians abhorrent.

Russell Means asked me to come to Wounded Knee, and I got as far as Denver, where an AIM member was supposed to meet me, but he was suddenly diverted to deal with an emergency elsewhere. So it was too late for me to get inside the reservation, which had already been surrounded by federal agents and other people with guns. I pledged all my resources to defend the Indians indicted at Wounded Knee and did what I could to publicize the unscrupulous ways in which the FBI and others in the Justice Department were persecuting Indians in a travesty of the legal principles our country supposedly held dear. The pattern was always the same: arrest the Native American leaders on the thinnest evidence (or none at all), take them out of circulation, put them on trial and keep the trial running as long as possible. When the Indians were acquitted, they felt exalted by their victory, but in the interim they had accomplished nothing. It happened over and over. When charges against Russell Means and Dennis Banks were finally dismissed, Judge Fred Nichol said the government had "polluted" the legal system by infiltrating their defense team with informants and had knowingly presented false evidence to the court because the FBI was "determined to get the AIM movement and completely destroy it." In the meantime, AIM had been deprived of two of its principal leaders for months.

In early 1975, Dennis Banks asked me to come to Gresham, Wisconsin, where a group of Menominee Indians had taken over an unused Alexian Brothers novitiate, claiming that it was on ground taken illegally from their tribe and demanding its return. When I arrived in Gresham, the novitiate was surrounded by helmeted National Guardsmen along with a ragtag army of local rednecks, rifles poking out the windows of their pickup trucks. Later I learned that some of the latter were in the Ku Klux Klan. I didn't know how I was going to get into the compound, but Dennis arranged it with the knowledge of the National Guard and the federal marshals. I'll never know why they let me in, though state officials said they hoped that I and Father James Groppi, a Catholic Maryknoll priest who was also admitted, might be able to end the dispute without bloodshed.

I was smuggled across the military perimeter late at night. Thirty or forty Menominees, two or three of whom had gunshot wounds, were holed up in the compound; they looked exhausted, but were determined not to surrender. Several wore a motto, "Deed or Death," on their shirts or tattooed on their arms. I had no doubt that they were willing to die if their demands weren't met. It was the dead of winter and very cold. The ground was covered with two to three feet of snow, and inside there were no lights, heat or water. The governor had ordered the electricity shut off, the heating system had failed, the pipes were frozen, the toilets wouldn't work and the stench was terrible. Every so often, there were gunshots—some fired by the rednecks, others by Indians. There was no place to sleep, so I curled up on a windowsill and dozed until someone woke me and led me to a room where there was a lighted fireplace and where an Indian boy who had been shot in the leg was being treated by a doctor who was part Indian. Throughout the night National Guard helicopters circled above us, panning searchlights back and forth in search of stray Indians and, incidentally, give the drunken, trigger-happy rednecks easy targets. Young Indians who called themselves Dog Soldiers—the name of elite groups of warriors among the Plains Indians in the nineteenth century—draped sheets over themselves and ran in and out of the snow, occasionally firing at the rednecks. One night they put the wounded boy on a stretcher, covered him with a sheet and ran out, intending to take him someplace where he could get better medical treatment, but about forty minutes later they returned with the boy still on the stretcher. By standing still and camouflaging themselves with the sheets against the snow, they had avoided being spotted by the helicopters, but while they were stumbling through the snow, the Indian on point looked to his right and saw two squads of armed guardsmen. They turned and ran back with the stretcher; when they were safe inside, one said, "Now I know why they call us AIM; it means 'Assholes In Movement.' " A few minutes later they took off again in another direction and eventually found medical help for the boy.

There were constant rumors that the governor had ordered the National Guard to retake the novitiate, which would certainly have meant bloodshed. But like all Indians I've ever met, those in the novitiate under attack joked no matter what the circumstances were, even when they were being fired on. We talked a great deal, and it was during such moments that I realized how much I related to their philosophy of life and how closely it paralleled my own. In terms of religion or philosophy, I suppose I am closer to what American Indians believe than to any conventional faith. Its essence is a sense of harmony and oneness, a belief that everything on earth—the environment, nature, people, trees, the land, the wind, animals—is interrelated, and that every manifestation of life has a purpose and place. Indians also believe that nothing is inherently bad; we are all in the same cycle of life, and there really is no death, only transformation. They follow what in many ways is a pure form of democracy: major decisions are made collectively by a consensus reached at councils, and chiefs are elected on merit; just because a young brave is the son of a chief, he doesn't succeed his father unless he has earned it.

The shooting continued sporadically day and night while the Dog Soldiers ran into the building to reload, then back into the snow to return the fire of the rednecks, whooping and yelling. It didn't seem real until a rifle bullet smashed into a chimney a few feet from my head on the afternoon of a sunny day. The temperature was up to about thirty-five degrees and I was tired of being penned inside, so I went up to the roof to enjoy a little sun. A second or two later, a brick exploded an arm's length from me. For an instant, I wondered what that was; then I heard the rifle shot, remembered that bullets travel faster than sound, and ran for cover. It was only another bullet, like millions before it, fired indiscriminately in the hope of killing an unimportant Indian.

The next day I was asked to represent the Indians in negotiations with the Alexian Brothers, the religious order that held title to the novitiate, in an attempt to end the standoff. I heard through the grapevine—I don't remember how—that the apostolic delegate, the Catholic Church's representative in Washington, had sent a message to the pope urging him to apply pressure on the Alexian Brothers to reach a settlement because the Church couldn't allow blood to be spilled in a dispute over real estate. I didn't let on during the negotiations that I knew this, but I told the officers of the Alexian order, who came from their headquarters in Chicago, that the Church had much to account for because of its virtual enslavement of Indians in its early California missions, that the Menominee Indians had originally owned the property which had been taken from them, and that the Church therefore had received stolen property. Our first meeting ended without an agreement, but was followed by others. Finally the Alexian Brothers offered a compromise: they would give the tribe the deed to the property, but the police wouldn't accept their request for amnesty in the takeover, which meant that some Indians would have to go to jail.

With the light of the afternoon sun fading fast, I joined the Indians in the main room of the novitiate to consider the offer. As always, I was impressed by their inherent sense of democracy and respect for the individual. In Indian fashion, they went around the room so that everyone could express his opinion about accepting the offer or fighting on. It was soon apparent that there was a deep division. One group said that they had won the battle and should give up and take their medicine, but some of the younger men wanted to shoot it out with the National Guard. One said, "Let's die as warriors. Our children will be proud of us and remember we were warriors."

They went around the room until one of them said, "Brando?"

I answered with something like this: "Many of you either have a patch on your shoulder or a tattoo on your arms. It does

Deed or death? I joined Dennis Banks, the leader of the American Indian Movement, in a January 1975 negotiation in Gresham, Wisconsin, for Menominee Indians who had seized an unused Alexian Brothers novitiate. (UPI/Bettmann)

not say, 'Deed *and* Death,' it says, 'Deed *or* Death.' You've gotten the deed; they made the accommodation. You won what you wanted and have all performed honorably. What you also have is an opportunity to continue fighting for your cause if you live. If you want to die, go outside and start shooting; the Guardsmen will take you at your word, and you'll be dead in a few minutes. But death is an easy way out. What you'll leave behind is a lot of trouble for your children. Who's going to earn money to pay for your family's needs? Besides, you haven't got enough ammunition to last very long. You can die, but you won't add anything to what's already been accomplished. This is a very small piece of land, and there's a lot of other work ahead. It will take a lifetime of dedication to right the wrongs you've suffered for hundreds of years, so I say, 'Take the deed and do the time.' " There were a few murmurs, but nobody responded, and then it was somebody else's turn to speak.

In the end they decided not to fight, and some of them told me afterward that my saying, "It says, 'Deed *or* Death,' not 'Deed *and* Death,' " had swayed them. They were arrested and we were all escorted into Gresham by National Guard troops. On the way I tried to talk to one of the guardsmen, but he looked at me as if I were a piece of rotten meat. I'd never seen such hatred in a man's face. I didn't have a ride to Milwaukee, where I wanted to catch a plane, so Father Groppi offered to take me. He also gave me a meal and a bed for the night, for which I was grateful because I hadn't slept or eaten much for several days. The next morning after breakfast, the priest said he was going to pray and asked if I wanted to join him. Sitting in a pew, I suddenly felt a great rush of emotion. I asked him if he would pray for me and give thanks that the standoff had ended without another massacre. As he did, I started crying. Tears flooded my face. I was overcome with feeling. I have no idea why.

It was all over except for one thing: in the end the Indians went to jail but never got the deed. Once again they had made a treaty with the white man, who had then violated it. The incident at Gresham was one more metaphor for the centuries-old relationship between the white man and the Indian.

Several months later two FBI agents were killed under circumstances that have always been in dispute, at a place called Jumping Bull on the Pine Ridge Reservation. The FBI called it an ambush; AIM said that the agents had provoked a clash. I don't know the truth. Two nights later seven or eight AIM members, some of whom I knew, showed up at my home in Los Angeles about one A.M. and said they were going underground because they were afraid of being hunted down and killed by the FBI in revenge for the deaths of the agents. After everybody was fed and rested, I let them take a motor home I used when I was on location and gave them radios so that they could talk back and forth on the road. Several months later I saw a television report that a motor home and a station wagon had been stopped by the police in Oregon. The FBI had the vehicles under surveillance and had asked the local police not to intercept them, but apparently a state trooper didn't get the word and tried to stop the Indians, so there was a shoot-out. Five in the station wagon, including Dennis Banks's pregnant wife, Kamook, were arrested, but he and another Indian evaded arrest, he told me later, by jumping out of the moving motor home. As it continued driverless along the highway, the police chased it, ran it into a ditch and opened fire on it while Dennis and his cohort disappeared into the darkness.

Dennis spent a month on my island in Tahiti before returning to California and serving a short jail term for a minor offense unconnected to the deaths of the FBI agents. Later I flew with him to a reservation in Minnesota in a plane flown by a young Indian who said he'd been a marine pilot in Vietnam and wanted to return to his roots. At the reservation we were invited to join a ceremony in the sweat lodge with several men from the tribe. Everyone took off his clothes and sat in a circle, shoulder to shoulder, while a medicine man poured water on a pile of hot stones, making the lodge as hot as a sauna. Then he began singing while we went around the circle and everyone expressed with frankness what was in his heart: worries and disappointments, bad experiences, resentments, hatreds—extraordinary revelations spoken by total strangers. When it was my turn, I said that I was grateful to the American Indians because they had taught me a great deal, and that I was inspired by their stoicism in the face of endless disappointment and shame. Only much later did somebody tell me that the pilot who took us to the reservation and shared our experiences in the sweat lodge was an FBI spy.

There was one more postscript to Dennis's trip in my motor home. The passengers in the station wagon included Anna Mae Aquash, a staunch member of AIM whom the FBI suspected of being involved in the deaths of its two agents. About a year after she was arrested and released, a badly decomposed body was found in a gully on a ranch in South Dakota. A Bureau of Indian Affairs pathologist did an autopsy on the corpse and said that it was an unidentified Indian woman who had died from exposure. The FBI cut off her hands, put them in a plastic bag and sent them to Washington for fingerprint identification—a barbaric act because they must have known that Indians believe that unless a body is whole, it cannot begin the next stage of its spiritual evolution. When the fingerprint check determined that the body was that of Anna Mae Aquash, her family became suspicious of the original pathology report and exhumed her for another autopsy. A second pathologist found a small-caliber bullet in her head, along with a lot of damage to her brain; she had been murdered, execution style.

When I heard about this, I called the original pathologist, told him who I was, and asked him how it was possible for him to have opened Anna Mae's skull, excised her brain and not noticed the bullet or the damaged brain tissue. "There seems to be a discrepancy between your findings and those of the other forensic expert," I said, "and I was wondering how you account for it. How could you not have seen a hole in the back of her skull?" The man replied that he had seen the second report and had no argument with it, but became indignant with me. "I don't have to answer these questions," he said. I replied, "Indeed you don't, but I'm going on television and people are going to ask me about what happened, so I called because I want to get the story correct." But the pathologist merely repeated exactly what he had said before.

I never got an answer to my questions. Anna Mae was assassinated, but to this day no one has ever been tried for her murder; to the federal government, she was just another dead Indian.

The American Indian Movement did much to inspire Native Americans and raise their cultural pride, though it never won many tangible victories in the struggle to redress centuries of wrongs. However, I don't think the story is over. Although Indians who ask for equity are still branded as rabble-rousers and dangerous militants, things are changing; maybe I'm overly optimistic, but history seems to be on the side of native peoples. In Canada the government has begun giving back tracts of land to its indigenous peoples; Australia is doing the same; even in the United States there have been small victories—court rulings that uphold some Indian fishing rights—and in Hawaii the return of some resources to native people. American Indians say that they realize that the descendants of the European settlers who took their land aren't going to get back on the ships that brought them here and return to Dublin, Minsk, Naples or wherever they came from; all they want is the return of *some* of the stolen native lands to shelter themselves and their children and to provide them with a future. They say that at least we should give them a small cut of the pie that we've stolen.

I believe it is inevitable that the Indians will succeed. A society cannot continue to claim that it favors expanding women's or gay rights, or spend its wealth helping a country like Israel reclaim its historical lands, and yet do nothing for its own native peoples.

55

I DON'T FAULT THOSE who think otherwise, but I've never thought much of giving prizes to actors; I consider it inappropriate. The Academy Awards and the hoopla surrounding them elevate acting to a level that I don't think it deserves. As I've mentioned, many people in Hollywood who I care about take the Academy Awards extremely seriously, and with a worldwide audience of a billion people, it's obvious that a lot of people elsewhere do, too. But that's the problem: they take it *too* seriously. When the world has so many serious problems, it's troubling that such an inconsequential event has taken on such importance. I know people who start planning what they're going to wear to the ceremonies six months in advance, and if there's any chance they'll be nominated, they begin memorizing their acceptance speech. If they win, they pretend their words are spontaneous, but they've lain awake for months mumbling to the ceiling what they will say.

The ceremony has its roots in Hollywood's obsession with self-promotion; people in the business have a passion for paying tribute to one another. I suspect it stems from the fact that so many of them are Jewish. It is a part of their faith to recognize and reward good works and be honored for them. This reassures them that they are worthy people, especially after having grown up in a culture where there is a great deal of guilt and pressure to excel. Jews who are recognized for good works even get a better seat in the synagogue, meaning that they are closer to God. Even the name of the organization, the Academy of Motion Picture Arts and Sciences, is an exaggeration. I laugh at people who call moviemaking an art and actors "artists." Rembrandt, Beethoven, Shakespeare and Rodin were artists; actors are worker ants in a *business* and they toil for money. That's why it's always been called "the movie business."

When I was nominated for *The Godfather*, it seemed absurd to go to the Awards ceremonies. Celebrating an industry that had systematically misrepresented and maligned American Indians for six decades, while at that moment two hundred Indians were under siege at Wounded Knee, was ludicrous. Still, if I did win an Oscar, I realized it could provide the first opportunity in history for an American Indian to speak to sixty million people—a little payback for years of defamation by Hollywood. So I asked a friend, Sacheen Little Feather, to attend the ceremony in my place and wrote a statement for her to deliver in my name denouncing the treatment of American Indians and racism in general. But Howard Koch, the producer of the show, intercepted her and, in his wisdom, refused to let her read my speech. Instead, under great pressure she had to ad-lib a few words on behalf of the American Indian, and it made me proud of her.

I don't know what happened to that Oscar. The Motion Picture Academy may have sent it to me, but if it did I don't know where it is now.

Mario Puzo sent me a copy of *The Godfather* shortly after it was published, along with a note saying that if a movie was ever made from the book, he thought I should play Don

The 1973 Academy Awards: I asked Sacheen Little Feather, an Apache, to decline the Best Actor Oscar for my performance in *The Godfather*. She is with Liv Ullmann and Roger Moore at right, and below with the letter I asked her to read denouncing the treatment of American Indians. (UPI/Bettmann)

Corleone, the head of the New York Mafia family he had written about. I read the note but wasn't interested. Alice Marchak remembers my throwing it away and saying, "I'm not a Mafia godfather." I had never played an Italian before, and I didn't think I could do it successfully. By then I had learned that one of the biggest mistakes an actor can make is to try to play a role for which he is miscast. You have to take a few risks now and then, but some parts you shouldn't play no matter how much they pay you, just as some roles are best left alone because they've already been done unforgettably by someone else. Only a foolish actor, for example, would try to succeed Jimmy Cagney as George M. Cohan, Robert Donat as Mr. Chips or Charles Laughton as the Hunchback of Notre Dame.

But Alice took the book home, read it and said she thought I should take the part if it was offered me. She didn't change my mind, though I did call Mario without having read the book and thanked him for his note. Mario, who had sold the film rights to Paramount, began writing a screenplay based on the book and called me from time to time and encouraged me to reconsider, without telling me that he was lobbying on my behalf at Paramount, where, he later informed me, executives were dead set against my playing the role. The principal resistance came from Charles Bluhdorn, head of Paramount's parent company, Gulf + Western, and Robert Evans, the chief of production. Bluhdorn believed some of the stories he'd read about my supposed excesses on *Mutiny on the Bounty,* and since Paramount had lost a lot of money recently, he didn't want to risk losing more on the *The Godfather.* To Evans I looked too young to play Don Corleone, who aged in the story from his late forties to his early seventies. I was then forty-seven.

When Mario sent me the finished screenplay, I read both it and his book and liked them. By then Francis Coppola had signed on as director and was beginning to rewrite portions of Mario's script. He also said that he wanted me to play the part, and suggested that I audition for it to convince the executives at Paramount. I told him I had my own doubts, but said I'd let him know.

I went home and did some rehearsing to satisfy my curiosity about whether I could play an Italian. I put on some makeup, stuffed Kleenex in my cheeks, and worked out the characterization first in front of a mirror, then on a television monitor. After working on it, I decided I could create a characterization that would support the story. The people at Paramount saw the footage and liked it, and that's how I became the Godfather.

A month or two before we were scheduled to start shooting, someone at Paramount—I think it was Evans—said that I looked too heavy to play the part, so I went on a diet. But I lost too much weight and had to put twenty pounds back on before the picture could start.

From the start, the real Mafia took a strong interest in our depiction of the fictional one, much of which was filmed on its turf in Little Italy in New York City. It sent a delegation to Bluhdorn and, I was told after the picture was finished, he agreed to meet certain conditions to obtain its cooperation, including a promise not to mention the word "Mafia" in the picture. I'm sure they let him know that it wouldn't be difficult for their friends in the New York labor unions to tie up shooting, and as partial payment I suspect that Paramount promised them some jobs on the picture. Several members of the crew were in the Mafia and four or five mafiosi had minor parts. When we were shooting on Mott Street in Little Italy, Joe Bufalino arrived on the set and sent two envoys to my trailer to say that he wanted to meet me. One was a rat-faced man with impeccably groomed hair and a camel's-hair coat, the other a less elegantly dressed man who was the size of an elephant and nearly tipped over the trailer when he stepped in and said, "Hi, Marlo, you're a great actor."

When Bufalino arrived, the first thing I noticed about him

was that one of his eyes looked to the left and the other to the right. I didn't know which one to look at, so, trying not to offend him, I alternated between them. As soon as he sat down, he started complaining about how badly the U.S. government was treating him. Wrapping himself in the American flag, he said he was a good American and a good family man, but the government was trying to deport him. Throwing up his arms, he said, "What do I do?"

I didn't have an answer, so I didn't say anything. Then he changed the subject and in a raspy whisper said, "The word's out you like calamari . . ."

This startled me. Somehow he'd learned that I often ordered a calamari lunch from one of the Italian restaurants on Mott Street.

Then, as if the two of us were involved in a conspiracy, he said, "You know, Marlo, I'd love to have you come over and meet the wife. One night the three of us could all go out for dinner. I'd like you to meet my family."

"Mr. Bufalino—"

He waved his hand and said, "Call me Joe."

"Well, Joe, see this script?" I showed it to him, riffling through the pages we were going to film that day. "Joe, this is just today; these are only the lines I have to learn for today, and it's really hard. I'm not running around chasing girls. I just sit in this trailer learning lines."

Bufalino seemed disappointed. "Well," he said, "maybe we can make it for lunch sometime."

I didn't know what to do next, so I said, "Have you ever seen a movie set?"

"No, I've never been on one before."

"Well, allow me," I said. "Let's go upstairs and I'll show you around."

I led him upstairs through a tangle of cables to the set of the office of the olive-oil company used in the picture. Standing close to me, he looked around and said, "I don't know how you keep from goin' nuts, with all these people and all these wires and everything . . ."

"I agree, Joe. The whole thing is really cockeyed, isn't it?" Then I looked into his cocked eyes and realized what I'd said. I spun around, trying to divert his attention to something on the set and to get a glimpse of his reaction peripherally. For a moment he blinked and I thought I saw a hurt look flash across his face, but the moment passed, and I babbled a mouthful of mush to fill the air with words, not knowing what in the world I was saying.

At last Joe smiled, thanked me for the tour and left me to get ready for the next shot. "See you, Marlo," he said. "Don't forget the wife and I would still like you to have dinner with us."

There were some terrific actors on *The Godfather,* especially Robert Duvall and Al Pacino. Bobby Duvall is one of those actors who never stop taking dares, which very few actors do. They work so hard at becoming successful that when they reach the top they become cautious and try to do the same thing over and over again because they're frightened of playing a part in which they might fall on their faces. Duvall takes chances and has fallen on his face, but far more times than not he has established a characterization that is not Duvall. He's a wonderful actor. The same can be said of Al Pacino. When I met him on *The Godfather,* he was quite troubled. Since then he's improved and, like Duvall, has shown that he is willing to take a chance and not be afraid where he's going to land.

At one point Charles Bluhdorn threatened to fire Francis Coppola—I don't remember why—but I said, "If you fire Francis, I'll walk off the picture." I strongly believe that directors are entitled to independence and freedom to realize their vision, though Francis left the characterizations in our hands and we had to figure out what to do. I threw out a lot of what

The Godfather: with Al Pacino,
James Caan and John Cazale
(top); Pacino (left); and
Robert Duvall (bottom).
(Courtesy of Paramount Pictures/
Academy of Motion Picture Arts
and Sciences)

was in the script and created the role as I thought it should be. When you do this, you never know whether it's going to work; sometimes it does, sometimes it doesn't. But after I had read the book, I decided that the part of Don Corleone lent itself perfectly to underplaying. Rather than portraying him as a big shot, I thought it would be more effective to play him as a modest, quiet man, the way he was in the book. Don Corleone was part of the wave of immigrants who came to this country around the turn of the century and had to swim upstream to survive as best they could. He had the same hopes and ambitions for his sons that Joseph P. Kennedy had for his. As a young man, he probably hadn't intended to become a criminal, and when he did, he hoped it would be transitional. As he said to his son Michael, played by Pacino, "I never wanted this for you. I wanted something else. I always thought that you'd be governor or senator or president—something—but there just wasn't enough time. . . . There just wasn't enough time."

I thought it would be interesting to play a gangster, maybe for the first time in the movies, who wasn't like those bad guys Edward G. Robinson played, but who was a kind of hero, a man to be respected. Also, because he had so much power and unquestioned authority, I thought it would be an interesting contrast to play him as a gentle man, unlike Al Capone, who beat up people with baseball bats. I had a great deal of respect for Don Corleone; I saw him as a man of substance, tradition, dignity, refinement, a man of unerring instinct who just happened to live in a violent world and who had to protect himself and his family in this environment. I saw him as a decent person regardless of what he had to do, as a man who believed in family values and was shaped by events just like the rest of us. The people who joined the Mafia in those days did so because they were set upon by people who wanted to take advantage of them. There was a war in Little Italy; members of a group called the Black Hand were extorting money from immigrants, who

A moment in *The Godfather*. (Courtesy of Paramount Pictures)

had to pay to safeguard their families and to make a living. Some knuckled under, but others like Don Corleone fought back, and this was the story of *The Godfather.* He would not surrender to the men who demanded a piece of everyone's action. He was forced to protect his family, and in the process he gravitated into crime.

At the time we made the film in the early seventies, there were not many things you could say about the Mafia that you couldn't say about other elements in the United States. Was there much difference between mob murders and Operation Phoenix, the CIA's assassination program in Vietnam? Like the Mafia, it was just business, nothing personal. Certainly there was immorality in the Mafia and a lot of violence, but at heart it was a business; in many ways it didn't operate much differently from certain multinational corporations that went around knowingly spilling chemical poisons in their wake. The Mafia may kill a lot of people in mob wars, but while we were making the movie, CIA representatives were dealing in drugs in the Golden Triangle, torturing people for information and assassinating them with far more efficiency than the Mob. I can't see much difference between the assassinations of gangsters like Joey Gallo and the Diem brothers in Vietnam, except that our country did it with greater hypocrisy. When Henry Cabot Lodge went on television and explained the deaths of the Diem brothers, you knew he was flat-out lying, but people didn't question him because we all believed the myth that the United States was a great country that would never do anything immoral. In many ways people in the Mafia live by a stricter code than do presidents and other politicians; I wonder what would happen if instead of having them swear on a Bible, we required politicians to promise to be honest at the price of having their feet encased in cement and dropped into the Potomac if they weren't. Political corruption would drop dramatically.

. . .

Thanks to a trick I stumbled on while I was making *The Young Lions,* I wasn't completely honest with Joe Bufalino when I told him I had to memorize my lines that morning he showed up on the set. When I first made movies, I memorized my lines from the script like other actors, or if the script was weak I'd improvise dialogue but still memorize it. As mentioned earlier, I learned on my first picture, *The Men,* how easy it was to spoil your effectiveness in a picture by overrehearsing and digging so deep into a part before filming began that you had nothing left to give when it counted. This had taught me how fragile a characterization can be on film and the importance of spontaneity. So after a while instead of memorizing my lines by rote, I started concentrating only on the meaning or thrust of a line during a scene, working from merely a suggestion of what it was about, and then improvising speeches as I went along so that they seemed spontaneous. The words might vary a little from those in the script, but audiences didn't know it.

On *The Young Lions,* I discovered an even better way to increase spontaneity. In that picture I had to rewrite a lot of the dialogue as we went along, and one day I didn't have time to memorize my new lines for one scene, so I wrote them on a piece of paper, pinned the paper to the uniform of one of the other actors and read the lines. The camera shot over my shoulder, showing my face in despair while I read. There was a practical advantage to what I had done because it saved a lot of time. You can easily spend three or four hours trying to memorize lines for a scene, and in order to prepare, some actors go around all day muttering them at the edge of the set. There are other things I would much rather use my time for than memorizing lines, so after *The Young Lions* I started reading dialogue from notes in every picture. Sometimes, with their permission, I wrote my lines on actors' faces or pinned cue cards on their costumes, or placed them offstage where I could see them.

On *The Godfather* I had signs and cue cards everywhere—on

my shirtsleeves, on a watermelon and glued to the scenery. If it was a long day and the director reshot a scene many times, I might know the lines by the end of the day, but I didn't have to memorize them in advance. I also discovered that not memorizing increased the illusion of reality and spontaneity, a step beyond the groping for words and so-called mumbling that some critics complained about in *A Streetcar Named Desire*. Everything about acting demands the illusion of spontaneity. When an actor knows what he's going to say, it's easy for the audience to sense that he's giving a writer's speech. But if he hasn't memorized the words, he not only doesn't know what he's going to say, he's not rehearsed *how* he's going to say it or how to move his body or nod his head when he does. Whereas when he *sees* the lines, his mind takes over and responds as if it were expressing a thought for the first time, so that his gestures are spontaneous.

Later, when I was making another picture, a stinker based on a novel by Steve Shagan called *The Formula,* I got rid of the notes and began using a better method to accomplish the same purpose: speaking my lines into a miniature tape recorder, then hiding it in the small of my back with a wire connected to tiny speakers that I stuck in my ears like hearing aids. When I was acting, I turned the tape recorder on and off with a remote hand switch, listened to my voice and repeated the lines simultaneously in the same way that speeches are translated into different languages at the UN. It took a little practice, but it wasn't hard, and because the earphones were small and hidden, audiences didn't know the difference. Subsequently I came up with a still better system: instead of a tape recorder, I hid a microphone under my clothes over my chest, put a two-way radio in the small of my back, and taped sending and receiving antennas on my legs. From about a hundred yards offstage, Caroline Barrett, who succeeded Alice as my assistant, now reads my lines to me into a microphone. As she speaks, I hear them in my earphones and repeat them. Since she also has a two-way radio, Caroline can hear my voice, as well as the voices of the other actors in the scene, and simply follows the script line by line. When I repeat the lines simultaneously, the effect is one of spontaneity.

People often say that an actor "plays" a character well, but that's an amateurish notion. Developing a characterization is not merely a matter of putting on makeup and a costume and stuffing Kleenex in your mouth. That's what actors used to do, and then called it a characterization. In acting everything comes out of *what* you are or some aspect of *who* you are. Everything is a part of your experience. We all have a spectrum of emotions in us. It is a broad one, and it's the actor's job to reach into this assortment of emotions and experience the ones that are appropriate for his character and the story. Through practice and experience, I learned how to put myself into different moods and states of mind by thinking about things that made me laugh or be angry, sad or outraged; I developed a mental technique that allowed me to address certain parts of myself, select an emotion and send something akin to an electrical impulse from my brain to my body that enabled me to experience the emotion. If I had to feel worried, I'd think about something that worried me; if I was supposed to laugh, I thought about something that was hilarious.

Sometimes, however, I had to experience an emotion I hadn't felt, like the reaction to dying; then I just had to imagine it. At the end of *The Young Lions,* I was shot fatally in the face. It was a wound, I decided, that would cause my blood to flow out of my brain, and that was how I would die. I imagined how I would be affected by blood suddenly draining out of my brain: I'd feel energy ebbing out of me, then for an instant realize that I was mortally wounded and that my life was over—all this within a few seconds. In the death scene in *Mutiny on the Bounty,* I wanted to appear to be in shock from having been fatally burned. I asked the crew to make a lot of ice; then I lay on top of it until my body was chilled and I was shivering and shaking and my teeth were chattering. While my body was responding physically to the cold, I also thought about how much I loved the Tahitian woman I had fallen for, what it was about her that I loved, and then about the pain, amazement and surprise of dying.

The bed scene in *The Men* also taught me to save my performance for the close-up, which usually comes at the end of the day. In a long shot you don't have to worry much about getting your emotions right; the physical action is what counts. The camera is so far away that it won't see the emotions you're supposed to experience, though I learned that it's always wise to check what's behind you; in a scene with a busy background, audiences can easily lose you, so you have to do something to help them focus on you.

In a medium shot, your body language and gesticulations become more important, though you have to turn up your emotions a little. But it's in the close-up that you really crank it up. The acting you do there is best conveyed by thinking, because if you're thinking right, it will show. If you're not thinking right, if you're busy *acting,* you're dead.

Correction: "think" is not the right word; you *experience* the emotion you want to convey. That's when you reach into your spectrum of emotions and send a signal from your brain to execute one of them. The close-up says everything. It's then that an actor's learned, rehearsed behavior becomes most obvious to an audience and chips away unconsciously at its experience of reality. The audience should share what you are feeling in a close-up. I have often reminded myself that I wasn't working in "motion words," but in "motion pictures." The close-up reveals your thoughts and feelings by the expression on your face, whether it's the raising of an eyebrow, chasing a piece of food around your mouth with your tongue, or making a tiny, fleeting statement by frowning. In a close-up the audience is only inches away, and your face becomes the stage. In a large theater it is the entire proscenium arch, so that no matter what you do, it becomes a theatrical event. When your image is so large and the audience has such an immediate perspective, the actor can enable the audience to experience his emotions in an intimate and personal way if he does his job right.

But as I've said, there are some parts where less is more, and underplaying is important, and never more so than in the close-up, when your entire face fills the screen. An example is the scene in *The Godfather* in which Don Corleone dies while playing with his grandchild in a garden. A few moments before he collapses, he surprises his grandson by stuffing a piece of orange peel into his mouth to simulate a set of teeth. I invented that business with the orange; I simply made it up on the spot. I used to do the same thing with my own kids; it's funny under almost any circumstances because it changes your personality hilariously, but in that scene it had a resonance that made the Godfather more human, and it was the kind of thing I thought the gentle character I had in mind would have done.

When I saw *The Godfather* the first time, it made me sick; all I could see were my mistakes and I hated it. But years later, when I saw it on television from a different perspective, I decided it was a pretty good film.

I had a lot of laughs making *The Godfather*. Mafiosi were always dropping in to watch us, and there were a lot of playful high jinks. In a scene in which the Godfather's family bring him home from the hospital after a failed assassination attempt, they must carry him up a flight of stairs on a stretcher, and before we did the shot, I told the cameraman to give me three hundred pounds of lead weights. Then I hid them under my blankets, which made the stretcher weigh over five hundred pounds, but nobody knew this except the cameraman and me. My family started carrying me up the stairs, but they couldn't make it; they were strong, but before long they were wringing with sweat, huffing and puffing and unable to get up the stairs. I said, "C'mon, you weaklings, I'm gonna fall off this thing if you don't get me up there. This is ridiculous!"

The camera operator nearly fell off his stool laughing, while Francis barked at the four men to hurry up. One of them kept muttering, "What the hell's going on? How can this guy weigh so much?"

After five or six takes, I raised the blanket and showed them the lead weights.

After we finished the picture, Sam Spiegel's secretary called me and said that an FBI agent wanted to interview me and would I be willing to talk to him? I said I would, and she told me that the agent would call me from San Diego. He did so, and we had a five- or six-hour conversation that covered a lot of ground. He wanted to know everything I knew about the Mafia, about making and financing *The Godfather*, whether I'd made any secret contributions to anybody, and so forth. He gave me lots of opportunities to rat on the Mob, but I smelled a different kind of rat.

"Listen," I said finally, "I have children and a good life, and I wouldn't want to see anybody hurt or threatened, so if I knew anything, which I don't"—this was not entirely true—"I wouldn't tell you." I'd decided that he was probably a member of the Mafia trying to find out whether or not I'd given the FBI any information that would hurt them. I'd gotten to know quite a few mafiosi, and all of them told me they loved the picture because I had played the Godfather with dignity. Even today I can't pay a check in Little Italy. If I go to a restaurant for a plate of spaghetti, the manager always says, "Come on in, Marlo, your money's no good here. . . . Look, everybody, here's the Godfather, the Godfather's here."

A few years after *The Godfather,* I went back to Little Italy for *The Freshman,* a comedy in which I played a benign gangster with a striking resemblance to Don Corleone. When I was dining one night with some of the crew, a man came over and said, "Mr. Gotti would like to see you and say hello. He's right across the street."

"That's nice," I said. I was curious, and with four or five other people from the picture, I went across the street to a shabby storefront or club house of some sort filled with mafiosi and decorated with a big sign that proclaimed THIS ROOM IS BUGGED.

With a silver pompadour as sleek as his silk suit, John Gotti was playing cards with several other men, and I went over to his table and said, "How do you do."

Gotti extended his hand but didn't get up. I think he didn't want to lose face in front of the others by appearing to be respectful, so he sat there with a smile and introduced me to his friends, an extraordinary group of characters straight out of the Mafia yearbook.

I've always liked to do magic tricks and often carry around a deck of cards with me, so I pulled one out of my pocket—it was a shaved deck used by magicians and card sharks—and said, "Take a card, John."

When he did so I told him to put the card back and then shuffle the cards. While he shuffled, I said I wanted to borrow a handkerchief, and instantly all of the mafiosi pulled out white handkerchiefs and waved them at me so that the place looked like a washline on Monday morning. I chose one, held the deck in my hand and told Gotti to pull away the handkerchief. When he did the only card left was the one he'd picked. As he looked

Filming *The Freshman* in Little Italy (AP/Wide World Photos), and with Matthew Broderick, the freshman himself, below (Tri-Star/Courtesy of the Academy of Motion Picture Arts and Sciences).

at it, I said something like "You know, you could make a living this way."

I didn't say anything more because suddenly the whole room had become as quiet as a tomb at midnight; the only noise was some shuffling of feet.

Suddenly I realized what everyone was thinking: had I tried to make a fool out of the boss in front of his crew? They didn't know what to believe. They looked back and forth at each other, trying to decide how to respond. I could feel the cerebral energy in the room as they mentally threw back their shoulders and asked themselves, Is this guy trying to show *disrespect* to John? Apparently no one thought it was funny.

"Thanks a lot, Mr. Gotti," I said after an awkward pause. "It was nice to talk to you," and I left without saying anything except good-bye.

Later one of the mafiosi called and said Gotti wanted to invite me to be his guest at a prizefight, but I told him I was too busy and couldn't make it.

Many articles about *The Godfather* called it my "comeback." I never understood what they meant except that it was a picture in which I played the title role and it made a lot of money, while several of my last pictures hadn't. Everything in Hollywood is measured in terms of money. If I had been in a stupid picture and it made millions of dollars, I would have been congratulated everywhere I went on my success. But because a good picture like *Burn!* didn't make money it was considered unsuccessful. In Hollywood they congratulate you on your ability to transfer currency from the pockets of the audience to theirs because that's their only measure of success. Any picture that makes money, no matter how stupid, vulgar, childish or inane, is embraced as a triumph.

It is different in other parts of the world, where making pictures of quality is as important as the box office. It has always been a mystery to me why countries like Italy, France and England, which have produced fine directors and fine actors, have never been able to capture much of the film market. The British have made many wonderful films, but have seldom had a financial blockbuster. British television is the best there is—a giant compared to our network dwarfs—yet Hollywood still rules the television and film market throughout the world. It is a tragedy.

56

IN *LAST TANGO IN PARIS*, my first picture after the *The Godfather*, I played a recently widowed American named Paul who has a quirky, anonymous affair with a French girl named Jeanne, played by Maria Schneider. The director was Bernardo Bertolucci, an extremely sensitive and talented man although, unlike Kazan, he wasn't trained as an actor and didn't address himself to the development of characters. This simply happens or it doesn't, though Bernardo did do something unusual on this picture. Usually actors have to conform to the writer's story and take on the characteristics he creates, but in *Last Tango* Bernardo tailored the story to his actors. He wanted me to play myself, to improvise completely and portray Paul as if he were an autobiographical mirror of me. Because he didn't speak much English and knew nothing about American slang, he had me write virtually all my scenes and dialogue, and we communicated in French and sign language.

Some of the lines I wrote for the picture may have a certain resonance to the readers of this book: "I can't remember very many good things about my childhood . . . my father was a drunk, a screwed-up bar fighter. My mother was also a drunk. My memories as a kid are of her being arrested. We lived in a small town, a farming community. . . . I used to have to milk a cow every morning and every night, and I liked that, but I remember the time I was all dressed up to take a girl to a basketball game, and my father said you have to milk the cow . . . and I didn't have time to change my shoes and I had cow shit all over my shoes when I went to the basketball game. . . ." I made up the dialogue from my memories of events, though not everything was accurate and they didn't necessarily happen in the sequence I told them. For example, my father didn't order me to milk a cow before a date, but as mentioned earlier I did take girls to games mortified that they might smell cow dung on my galoshes.

I had one of the more embarrassing experiences of my professional career when we were making this film in 1972. I was supposed to play a scene in the Paris apartment where Paul meets Jeanne and be photographed in the nude frontally, but it was such a cold day that my penis shrank to the size of a peanut. It simply withered. Because of the cold, my body went into full retreat, and the tension, embarrassment and stress made it recede even more. I realized I couldn't play the scene this way, so I paced back and forth around the apartment stark naked, hoping for magic. I've always had a strong belief in the power of mind over matter, so I concentrated on my private parts, trying to *will* my penis and testicles to grow; I even spoke to them. But my mind failed me. I was humiliated, but not ready to surrender yet. I asked Bernardo to be patient and told the crew that I wasn't giving up. But after an hour I could tell from their faces that they had given up on me. I simply couldn't play the scene that way, so it was cut.

This scene was one of several in which Bernardo wanted me to make love to Maria Schneider to give the picture more authenticity. But it would have completely changed the picture and made our sex organs the focus of the story, and I refused. Maria and I simulated a lot of things, including one scene of buggering in which I used butter, but it was all ersatz sex.

Last Tango in Paris received a lot of praise, though I always thought it was excessive. Pauline Kael in particular praised it highly, but I think her review revealed more about her than about the movie. She is the best reviewer I know, but I think she became too subjectively involved in the story and critiqued the film from her own unique set of values and biases. Her review was flattering, but I don't think the picture was as good as she said it was. To this day I can't say what *Last Tango in Paris* was about. While we were making it, I don't think Bernardo knew either, though after it was released, he was quoted as saying that it was meant to explore whether two people could have an anonymous relationship, and then sustain it after its anonymity was breached and affected by the outside world. But he didn't say this when we were making the picture. It was about many things, I suppose, and maybe someday I'll know what they are.

Last Tango in Paris required a lot of emotional arm wrestling with myself, and when it was finished, I decided that I wasn't ever again going to destroy myself emotionally to make a movie. I felt I had violated my innermost self and didn't want to suffer like that anymore. As noted earlier, when I've played parts that required me to suffer, I had to *experience* the suffering. You can't fake it. You have to find something within yourself that makes you feel pain, and you have to keep yourself in that mood throughout the day, saving the best for the close-up and not blowing it on the long shot, the medium shot or the over-the-shoulder shot. You have to whip yourself into this state, remain in it, repeat it in take after take, then be told an hour later that you have to crank it up once more because the director forget something. It takes an enormous toll. *Last Tango in Paris* left me feeling depleted and exhausted, perhaps in part because I'd done what Bernardo asked and some of the pain I was experiencing was my very own. Thereafter I decided to make my living in a way that was less devastating emotionally. In subsequent pictures I stopped trying to experience the emotions of my characters as I had always done before, and

Last Tango in Paris. Don't ask me what it was about. (United Artists)

simply to act the part in a technical way. It is less painful and the audience doesn't know the difference. If a story is well written and your technique is right, the effect is still the same: in a darkened room, the magic of the theater takes over and the audience does most of the acting for you.

When I arrived in the Philippines in the summer of 1976 for my scenes in *Apocalypse Now,* the film about the Vietnam War based on Joseph Conrad's novel *Heart of Darkness,* Francis Coppola was alternately depressed, nervous and frantic. Shooting was behind schedule, he was having trouble with the cameraman, he wasn't sure how he was going to end the movie and the script was awful. It bore little resemblance to *Heart of Darkness,* and most of it simply didn't make dramatic sense.

"Listen," I said, "you have me for a certain number of weeks and I'll do the best I can, but I think you're making an enormous error." I wanted him to return to the original plot of Conrad's novel, in which a man named Marlow describes his journey up the Congo in search of Walter Kurtz, a once idealistic young man who had been transformed by his experiences into a mysterious, remote figure involved in what Conrad called "unspeakable rites." In the original script Kurtz—my part—was a caricature of a reprobate; he was sloppy, fat, immoral, a drunk, a stereotypical character from a hundred movies. The part must have had thirty pages of dialogue; it went on and on while going no place theatrically. I thought it was an idiotic script, but I didn't say this to Francis. In such situations I've found it best to say, "This may be all right the way you're going to do it, but I think we're missing a bet by not changing it."

"In *Heart of Darkness,*" I told Francis, "Conrad uses this guy Kurtz almost as a mythological figure, a man who is much larger than life. Don't misuse him in the film. Make him mysterious, distant and invisible for most of the picture except in our minds. What makes Conrad's story so powerful is that people

A break in shooting *Apocalypse Now*. (Stephanie Kong/SYGMA)

talk about Kurtz for pages and pages, and readers wonder about him. They never see him, but he is part of the atmosphere. It's an odyssey, and he's the heart of the *Heart of Darkness*. The longer it goes on, the more he occupies the minds of readers as they imagine him." The same thing could be done in the movie, I said, "but you have to hint at it, make him such a mysterious person that the audience will wonder more and more about him until the end." When Willard, the army officer played by Martin Sheen, and the character based on Conrad's Marlow, heads up the river and people shoot at him, I said that neither he nor the audience will know whether Kurtz is going to appear, and as Willard keeps getting closer and closer, he becomes more frightened by the mystery of what may be ahead of him, and the audience will share these feelings. Willard doesn't know if he will survive the journey up the river, and as it continues he gradually loses confidence until he finally finds Kurtz, who *then* can represent the quintessence of evil.

If we locked ourselves into the portrayal of Kurtz in the original script, I said, it would be impossible to focus on the man's mystery, that which is truly ominous, because what is truly ominous must be unseen. I offered to rewrite the script based on the original structure of the book, and Francis agreed. I spent about ten days on a houseboat completely rewriting the movie and thinking about how my character should look. Conrad described Kurtz as "impressively bald. The wilderness had patted him on the head, and, behold, it was like a ball—an ivory ball. . . ." Without informing Francis, I shaved my head, found some black clothing and asked the cameraman and lighting crew to photograph me under eccentric lighting while I spoke half in darkness with a disembodied voice. After I showed him these tests, I told Francis I thought that the first time the audience hears Kurtz, his voice should come out of the darkness. After several long moments, he should make an entrance in which only his bald head is visible; then a small part of his face is lit before he returns to the shadows. In a sense the same process is going on in Kurtz's mind: he is in darkness and shadows, drifting back and forth in the netherworld he has created for himself in the jungle; he no longer has any moral frame of reference in this surreal world, which is a perfect parable of the insane Vietnam War.

I was good at bullshitting Francis and persuading him to think my way, and he bought it, but what I'd really wanted from the beginning was to find a way to make my part smaller so that I wouldn't have to work as hard.

I loved shaving my head. I'd never done it before, and putting witch hazel on my head and sticking it out the car window while we were driving to another location during those hot days in the Philippines was heaven.

Besides restructuring the plot, I wrote Kurtz's speeches, including a monologue at his death that must have been forty-five minutes long. It was probably the closest I've ever come to getting lost in a part, and one of the best scenes I've ever played because I really had to hold myself under control. I made it up extemporaneously, bringing up images like a snail crawling along the edge of a razor. I was hysterical; I cried and laughed, and it was a wonderful scene. Francis shot it twice—two 45-minute improvisations—but used hardly any of the footage in the picture. I thought it was effective, though it might have been out of place. I never saw the footage of the entire speech, so I wouldn't know.

57

IN THE MOVIE BUSINESS there is a crude but amusing saying: "The way to say 'fuck you' in Hollywood is *'trust me.'* " It's not always true. I've known wonderful, honest people there, but I've also run into a sizable number of whores, cheats and thieves. When this happens, you have to take charge of the situation; if you don't, they'll devour you. When I made *The Men*, I was one of the first movie actors to negotiate a one-picture deal instead of a long-term studio contract. Later, when the studio system, whose seven-year contracts had made indentured servants out of actors, collapsed, other actors began making similar deals. Like everything else, the price producers paid us was determined by the law of supply and demand and, like any other workers, our objective was to drive up the price as high as we could.

After the highest level that actors were able to negotiate reached 10 percent of the producers' gross receipts—against a minimum, generally $1 million or more—I said to myself, Marlon, you should ask for 11.3 percent of the gross. I had pulled the number out of a hat.

The producers asked, "Why eleven point three?"

"Never mind," I said, "I have my reasons."

Usually they paid it, though sometimes they promised to pay and then reneged. When this happened it was necessary to be forceful.

My first picture after *Last Tango in Paris* was a western, *The Missouri Breaks.* At the time I was still giving money to the American Indians and spending heavily on Teti'aroa, so I needed the money. It wasn't a good movie, but I had fun making it. There was a lot of pot smoking and partying, my friend and neighbor Jack Nicholson was in it, and much of the picture was filmed on the Crow Reservation in Montana, where I discovered a beautiful river and a lovely way to relax by floating down the river on an inner tube. At night, when most of the other people went to town, I liked to stay by myself and read in my trailer under a grove of cottonwood trees. One evening I heard a storm approaching in the distance. The clouds overhead were butting heads and putting on a spectacular sound-and-light show. As the horizon darkened, the thunder got louder and the lightning flashes closer. I began counting the seconds between each flash of lightning and clap of thunder, and as the interval shortened, I knew the storm was marching rapidly in my direction. I was tempted to stand outside and watch, but went inside the trailer to avoid being hit by lightning. The intervals got so short that the sound of the thunder and the flash of lightning were almost simultaneous, and then I heard a tremendous explosion right above me. When I got up in the morning, a huge, charred cottonwood branch was lying on the ground near the trailer, looking as if it had been severed by a blowtorch. Another few feet and it would have crushed the trailer with me in it.

Arthur Penn was the director of *The Missouri Breaks* and he encouraged us to improvise. I rewrote my part and made up a lot of nonsense. I was supposed to play what the script called a "regulator," a hired gun who went around the West assassinating people, and it was so boring that I decided to make changes.

First I played the part as an Englishman, then changed his name and made him an Irishman. I also played him as a gunman disguised as a woman, and invented a wonderful weapon by sharpening the ends of a four-spoked tire-lug wrench: when I threw it, it sailed like a Frisbee and stuck in anything; if I missed with one prong, another would hit the target. In one scene I had to chase a rabbit on a cutting horse, and I kept thinking that if the horse went down I would probably fall on this weapon I was so proud of inventing.

The producers had agreed to pay me my usual fee, but several weeks into the filming, they still hadn't signed a formal contract. I complained, but they kept making excuses. I knew they were trying to wait me out; after they had enough footage, they'd say their financing had fallen through and that they couldn't pay me what they'd promised. In situations like this, you can't always simply walk off a movie. You might not be paid for the work you've already done, and a studio can tie you up in court for years while cranking out publicity blaming you for its larceny. But as noted earlier, once filming begins, actors gain an edge over producers, who don't want to stop because if they do they'll lose whatever money they've already spent and still have no picture. Producers also hate delays because it can cost over $100,000 a day to keep a crew on location. Actors can use these circumstances to their advantage when others try to cheat them, as my experience on *The Missouri Breaks* demonstrated. After the producers repeatedly broke promises to sign the contract, I started slurring my speech and blowing my lines. If your technique is effective, nobody can prove you're doing it on purpose.

"I don't know what's wrong," I told Arthur Penn. "I'm having a lot of problems with this part. Be patient with me. I know I'll get it right sooner or later."

After a week or so, one of the producers flew to Montana and we had a big scene in my trailer about the unsigned contract. I threw a can of Coke at him and it smashed against a wall a few inches from his head. I missed purposely, pretending to be outraged. He was a fastidious man who couldn't stand a mess, and he immediately started wiping up the Coke, but when he finished he assured me that there had been a misunderstanding and that the contract would be signed shortly. It was, and suddenly I started remembering my lines again.

In *The Freshman* a few years later, I played the character who resembled Don Corleone, and Matthew Broderick played a college freshman whom I hired to make some unusual deliveries. I thought it was a funny picture, though it could have been even more comic. When I read the script, I laughed and laughed and couldn't wait to do it. It was a wonderful satire by Andrew Bergman, who had written an extremely funny movie I liked called *The In-Laws,* but he decided to direct it, which I think was unfortunate because his inexperience was evident in the way *The Freshman* was edited; a lot of potential was lost in the cutting room.

About the time we were finishing the picture and I was getting tired after weeks of working long hours, I spoke to a reporter in Toronto, where most of the filming was done, and happened to mention that this might be my last picture and that I was disappointed with it. As it happened, TriStar Pictures at the time owed me about $100,000 for some extra work on the picture. As soon as the story appeared, the studio apologized and paid the money I was owed, and I then issued a press release saying I hadn't meant what I'd said because I was exhausted after working so hard on the film.

I didn't always win, however. When Paula Weinstein, a producer, asked me in 1988 to play a lawyer who defends a wrongly accused black man in South Africa in *A Dry White Season,* I hadn't made a picture in nine years. Jay Kantor told her that my fee was $3.3 million, plus 11.3 percent of the gross, but she said she had to make the picture on a low budget because studio executives were leery about movies with political themes. The script by Robert Bolt, usually a first-rate screenwriter, wasn't special, but Paula promised to revise it to satisfy me, and so I volunteered to be in the picture for nothing. I thought the story was effective not only because it demonstrated how blacks were treated under apartheid, but because it gave a white audience an opportunity to experience through the eyes of a white South African how inhumane the policy was.

After I offered to work for nothing, MGM gave the go-ahead and the script was reworked, but never satisfactorily, in my opinion, and I had to rewrite my own scenes. When I went to London for filming, I discovered that the director, Euzhan Palcy, was a headstrong neophyte who was out of her depth, an amateur trying to play hardball. I felt that she offered nothing in the way of direction—no scene conception, no plan of execution—but I did everything I could to get it right.

A couple of months before the film was released, MGM showed me a rough cut of the picture and invited me to propose changes. Donald Sutherland was very good as the South African who discovers the corruption of his country's judicial system when it is applied to blacks. He is a man caught in a conflict between the traditions and values of his culture and his own sense of morality; he refuses to turn his back on the injustice directed against one of his employees, and becomes ensnared in tragic circumstances that culminate in his losing everything, including his life. But Euzhan Palcy had cut the picture so poorly, I thought, that the inherent drama of this conflict was vague at best. She had also made parts of the picture too transparently polemical; subtlety and sensitivity were needed, not preaching. The result was dramatic gridlock. Her approach was aggravated by the fact that several important scenes had inept and sometimes self-indulgent performances by amateur black actors she had hired in Africa, and one of the most powerful scenes in the picture, when I defy the judge in the

A Dry White Season: with Donald Sutherland (above); and with Michael
Gambon (below). (David James and MGM)

courtroom and say, "You are a pustule on the face of justice" and he has me dragged out of the courtroom, had disappeared. After I saw the rough cut, I implored Paula Weinstein and MGM to let me pay for recutting the picture to give it more tension and dramatic coherence.

These are a few excerpts from my letters:

If judicious cuts are made to avoid the pitfalls of summer stock performances and offensive rendering of scenes that interfere with the emotional build up of the sequences, you will have greatly advanced the forward thrust of the story. If not, every time a false note is hit, you weaken your grip on the nuts of your audience. You then will be obliged to pay a tidy sum trying to again crank up the viewers' emotional commitment to refocus their dwindling attention on the unfolding of our tale. The equation is simple: loss of dramatic tension is equal to the cube of the ingestion of popcorn. . . .

I have never put more of myself in a film, never suffered more while doing it, and never received so little recompense of any kind in . . . any motion picture over the last thirty-five years . . . let me honk my own horn. I have been in thirty-plus pictures, almost all of them financially successful. Some went through the roof. Some I directed. From early on I have directed my own stuff. I have, by any measure, been considered an accomplished professional . . . I believe this picture, properly supported and released, will win Academy Award nominations. . . . Let me briefly remind you that the picture "Shane" was cut four different times into practically four separate films. "Lawrence of Arabia" was in release when the prints were withdrawn and the picture was recut and went on to win Academy Awards. Pictures are made in the cutting room. Pictures are sold in executive offices. Please give me a chance to exercise over thirty-five years of my experience with films . . . we really want the same objectives. It is possible for MGM to wear this picture on its lapel with a measure of pride and with some change jingling in [its] pockets. You must understand that I have invested far too much energy, effort, passion and hope in this picture. I can't just sit here at ringside and watch somebody blow [it] with so much at stake for everybody . . . please try to understand that under the circumstances I am truly striving to be reasonable and cooperative. . . .

I offered MGM executives many specific suggestions on how to improve the picture without reshooting it, but they either didn't answer my letters, said that the director refused to make changes or claimed that it was too late to recut it. I resented having extended myself on behalf of the picture and a good cause, working hard at no charge, and not having been allowed to recut at least my part of the picture the way it should have been done.

Finally I called Connie Chung at CBS and told her I would give her an interview if I could speak about what had happened. I did, but MGM still refused to budge. Then Paula Weinstein called me from the Tokyo Film Festival, where the picture was being shown, and I pleaded with her again. "It's not too late," I said.

She said, "It *is* too late, we can't do it, if we had more time . . ."

"It's never too late. I'll still pay for the cutting," I said; "I'll pay whatever it takes."

Paula was making more excuses when she was interrupted by someone; then she said, "You've just won the best acting award."

"Did the picture win?" I asked, and she said, "No, the picture didn't, but you did."

She still didn't get the message and wouldn't change the ending. I felt betrayed, and the picture was a terrible flop.

I had only a small part in *Superman,* but since it was a popular movie and my contract gave me 11.3 percent of the gross, I made about $14 million for less than three weeks' work. When

Alexander and Ilya Salkind, the producers, asked if they could use footage from the picture in a sequel, *Superman II,* I asked for my usual percentage, but they refused, and so did I.

Several years later, the Salkinds asked me to be in *Christopher Columbus: The Discovery,* and I accepted because I wanted a chance to shape it into something close to historical truth. A picture about Columbus was sure to be made on the five hundredth anniversary of his voyage to the New World, but I didn't want him celebrated as a hero. Instead of a day for celebration, Columbus Day ought to be one of mourning. I wanted to tell the truth about how he and his minions exploited and killed the Indians who greeted them, but the script had wrapped him in all his myths as a great sailor and explorer.

I called Ilya Salkind and said, "Ilya, you can film this script the way it is if you like, but I think you're going to have a tragedy on your hands if you do; it's the most boring, poorly written, idiotically constructed story I've ever seen." I convinced him that he and his father were going to have a failure on their hands if they didn't stick to the facts, and persuaded him to turn the story around completely and portray Columbus as the cruel, ambitious man he was, a man who would stop at nothing, including exterminating the guileless Indians who offered him food and gold. I convinced the other actors, who were also unhappy, to agree with me, and Ilya asked me to put together the story the way I thought it should be told. I rewrote my part as Torquemada, the Grand Inquisitor in the court of Queen Isabella and, using false teeth, darkened eyes, and a huge hood I draped over my face to make me look like death, I designed an effective costume and makeup.

Everything was fine until Ilya's father, Alexander Salkind, arrived in Spain on the first day of filming. He didn't like to fly and had arrived late by train from someplace in Eastern Europe. When he read my script, he refused to use it and insisted on sticking with the original story, which was idiotic,

In *Superman,* with Terence Stamp, Jack O'Halloran and Sarah Douglas (above); bringing up Superman with Susannah York (left). (© 1978 Film Export A.G.)

An opportunity lost: *Christopher Columbus,* in which I was cast as Torquemada. Here I am with Rachel Ward as Queen Isabella. (© 1992 Peel Enterprises, Ltd.)

untruthful and uninteresting. It was a big mistake because the picture was a huge failure.

I was depressed and wanted to go home, but I knew Alexander would sue me if I backed out of my contract. There was nothing left for me to do except walk through my part. The other actors and I had nothing to work with. They tried hard, but I'm afraid I didn't. I mumbled my way through the part and gave an embarrassingly bad performance. The pay wasn't bad, though: $5 million for five days' work.

58

DURING THE TEN YEARS between *The Formula* in 1979 and *The Freshman* in 1989, I didn't make a movie except for my role in *A Dry White Season* because I didn't need the money. I was content doing other things: traveling, searching, exploring, seeking. I spent a lot of time on Teti'aroa, read a lot and became interested in many things, including meditation, one of many interests the luxury of time and money allowed me to examine during the eighties and early nineties.

Meditation was something I slipped into easily. I suppose it came out of acting. Because of the introspection that is a part of acting, I had developed a fairly strong sense of where my feelings were and how to gain access to them. I was fascinated by my ability to send an impulse from my brain to my body that enabled me to experience different emotions, and thought it would be interesting to know more about how the process worked. I consulted an expert on biofeedback, the discipline of controlling your physiological responses by monitoring your body's inner dynamics and learning to modulate them accordingly. I told him about the trick I had learned as an actor and asked him if he could measure any physical manifestation of it using instruments that measured galvanic skin response, the electrical resistance on your fingertips that varies according to activity in your central nervous system. He confirmed that the mental exercises I thought of as sending an electrical current from my brain to my body in order to experience a certain emotion did in fact have a physical signature; as I tried to control my emotions, the needle on the biofeedback instrument shifted back and forth, proof of a linkage between the directions from my brain and my body's response. In a distant and primitive way, it was a process similar to that which yogis and swamis, after years of training and practice, use through the meditative process to produce virtually any pattern of brain waves they choose. They reach into their minds, and with refined, introspective techniques achieve tremendous control over their bodies in pursuit of religious enlightenment.

I bought my own instrument to measure galvanic skin response and began experimenting with it at a time of considerable stress in my life. A doctor giving me an insurance physical for a new movie told me that my blood pressure was too high: 170 over 114. When I told him about the stress I was under, he said, "Well, no wonder you've got high blood pressure." He prescribed medicine to lower it, but I decided to see if I could do it on my own by meditation. With practice, I discovered that it was a very effective way to relax and reduce stress. I consulted a Hindu swami and others versed in the practice, read more about it and eventually began meditating daily. After a while, I was able to lower my blood pressure simply by thinking about it: now, when I'm in a stressful situation and feel my blood pressure start to rise, I can usually turn it down at will to as low as 90 over 60. I don't meditate every time I feel under stress because some stress is positive; if I'm playing chess, for example, my stress level goes up, but it's a pleasant experience. Stress is also heightened during sex, but it too is pleasurable. Negative stress occurs when you're stuck in a traffic jam on the way to the airport and realize you may miss your flight, or when you instinctively mistrust somebody who has just entered the room. When my stress increases in such circumstances, I now simply turn it off, as if it were a light switch.

During one of my first sessions with the biofeedback expert, I put on some headphones and he played a tape with sound waves recorded at the same frequency as my brain waves—though I didn't know this at the time. I lay back and relaxed, but before long I felt myself being pulled apart like a wad of chewing gum stretched until it was an invisible filament. That's what was happening to my mind: I was splitting in two, and it scared me. I felt panicked because I was losing control, and I started to resist it because I hate that feeling. When I was mentally back together, I asked myself, Why were you so frightened? Was it because you thought you were going to go mad? Was it going to make you die? Would it make you become a homicidal maniac? Or were you afraid you were going to slide into this state of mind and never return? None of these things was likely to happen, I decided, so I told myself to give in, surrender to it, experience the fear, let it take control of me, ride along with it and see what happens.

The next time I put on the headphones, I didn't resist and allowed myself to glide past the feelings that had made me so fearful the first time, and to travel along with them. After a few moments, I suddenly felt like a supersonic plane hurtling through the sound barrier. But once I was past the initial turbulence of that panic, everything became smooth and I was in a state of mind that can only be described as ecstasy. It lasted forty-five minutes, persisting even after the doctor returned and turned off the tape machine. I was in a dream talking to God. I felt peaceful, serene, utterly in repose, and I told the doctor, who seemed a thousand miles away, "I've never had such a sense of quietness or of beauty, tranquillity and peace in my entire life. I feel as if I had died and gone to nirvana."

The doctor said I had experienced *satori,* a state of consciousness that Zen masters consider one of sudden enlightenment. In diminishing intensity, the experience continued for three days before I was again in a normal state of mind.

Now I try to meditate twice a day for an hour or more. On only three occasions have I ever again achieved the sensation of satori, but it is always a pleasant, comforting experience. During the past few years, meditation has helped me enormously in dealing with a number of problems in my life. Through repetition, old emotional habits are replaced, and instead of getting excited, angry or anxious, I become calm. Repetition is as important to meditation as it is to many religious rituals. Catholic priests may order their parishioners to say ten Hail Mary's after confession; in Africa, Haiti and other places, religious masters put their followers into trances by exposing them to the repeated rhythms of drums so intense that the sounds go right through their bodies to become a part of them, and people surrender to the rhythm as they do during meditation. The mental processes are too subtle for me to understand or even to identify, and scientists haven't been very successful at deciphering them either. But in the theater I've seen how susceptible the human mind is to suggestion, and have wondered if there are related forces at play. As already observed, one of the strongest features of the human personality is how easily given it is to suggestion. If he's in a well-written play that is performed skillfully, a good actor can affect the body chemistry of an audience. He can increase the flow of adrenaline, make people feel sad, make them cry, make them angry or apprehensive. As an actor, you try to use the power of suggestion to manipulate people's moods, and that's not a lot different from what happens during a religious ritual.

It took the Vatican more than three hundred years to admit that Galileo was right, and some things about the world haven't changed. I am constantly amazed at the depth of intellectual prejudice in Western culture. Nothing is a fact unless it comes out of a petri dish. A certain type of political correctness discourages inquiry beyond certain limits; prejudice against responsible scientific research in certain fields—parapsychology, for example—is appalling. But nothing beats the apathy and skepticism regarding the mental disciplines of the Eastern religions. For at least two thousand years, yogis and swamis have been certain of the power of the mind over the body, as demonstrated by their ability to put their bodies in a kind of suspended animation that enables them to survive being buried underground for hours or even days. Their accomplishments cry out for more research, but to many Western scientists these powers and the insight that the swamis, yogis and other students of the mind have attained are merely tricks or scientific oddities.

This hasn't changed since the first British colonials landed in India and observed the extraordinary yogic disciplines; they all but ignored them because they considered Western culture the font of all wisdom and knowledge. Even now, if a scientist such as Linus Pauling acknowledges that Eastern religions have developed extraordinary mind-body relationships in pursuit of spiritual enlightenment, he is considered a flake. This isn't surprising because that's what usually happens when bright people with achievements in one field challenge the status quo accepted by specialists in others. Even Einstein, when he expressed opinions in fields other than his own, was thought of as an eccentric; Arnold Toynbee was told to stick to history and not venture into areas of science he knew nothing about because his ideas didn't conform to concepts that were in vogue at the time. Still, during the next century, as science shifts from its twentieth-century preoccupation with exploring the physical world to the far more interesting world of the mind and neurogenetics, this attitude will change. As Francis Crick has pointed out, brain chemistry is responsible for human thought, behavior and character—everything about us. I believe that we can control the mind, and that man will demonstrate a capacity to do things beyond his wildest imagination. I don't know yet what the limitations of my own mind are. I haven't reached them yet, but I won't stop searching for them until I die. It is territory different from anything I've ever explored before— uncharted waters—and I feel like an explorer. In many ways it is the most exciting expedition I've ever undertaken.

The more I have meditated, the more I have been able to control not only stress in my life, but pain. If I have a headache or stub my toe, I'm often able to locate the pain with my mind and will it away. So confident am I of this ability that when I decided a few years ago to be circumcised, I asked the doctor to do it without a pain-killer. I assured him that I could eliminate the pain using mind control during the operation. He was skeptical but said it would be an interesting medical experience, and he scheduled the operation. But when I arrived at the hospital, what seemed like its entire medical staff was waiting to witness the event. The prospect of seeing a movie star circumcised without anesthesia must have been a hot topic of discussion in the doctors' lounge. I didn't welcome the presence of uninvited guests, and since I go by instinct, I went home.

Later a different doctor agreed to do the operation without pain-killers, but he became frightened and an anesthetist was waiting for me when I kept my appointment. He said that because of medical ethics he couldn't circumcise me without using a pain-killer. Disappointed and angry but tired of the delays, I let the anesthetist give me a shot in my back. Nevertheless, I still wanted to show the doctors what I could do, and I told them to take my blood pressure. I had already meditated, brought my blood pressure down more than twenty points, and even put myself into one of those moments of satori that I rarely achieve. To this day, I'm sure that if they hadn't given me the shot, I would have felt no pain.

59

THE NINE YEARS during which I didn't make a movie afforded me the luxury of time to get to know my children better, as well as myself. I was beginning to come to terms with myself with the help of Dr. Harrington, and I spent much of that time under the thatch roof of my hut on Teti'aroa with my feet sticking out the door, looking through the shell curtains at the vivid colors of the lagoon; like the sunsets on Teti'aroa, they change constantly, depending on the sun and clouds. I sat like that for hours at a time contemplating my life, assessing my values, examining every little bird of thought that flitted through my mind.

My life on Teti'aroa is very simple—walking, swimming, fishing, playing with the children, laughing, talking. I feel a tremendous sense of freedom there. At night there isn't much to do except look at the stars, which I love to do, and most days I don't wake up until about eleven, when I hear the fluttering of wings over my hut and birds plummet out of the sky, hit the lagoon in a quick splash and with the grace of ballerinas grab a fish for breakfast.

There is fresh fruit off the trees for my breakfast, then a walk on the beach. Or I may spend an hour or two with my ham radio, talking to strangers around the world, telling them that my name is Jim Ferguson—the name of my childhood play-mate—and that I live alone in Tahiti. Nobody knows I'm a movie star, and I can be like anyone else.

Once when I was on Teti'aroa, for two or three weeks I would be drunk every day by lunchtime. I'd go down to the pool hall, shoot a few games and have a wonderful time. But it was a momentary lapse; I've never come close to becoming an alcoholic. It's never taken more than a drink or two to put me into a tailspin, and that's usually when I stop. There has been a lot of alcoholism in my family, but fortunately those family genes passed me by.

I've looked on Teti'aroa as a laboratory where I could experiment with solar power, aquaculture and innovative construction methods. I built one of the first sawmills in Polynesia that could turn coconut trees into lumber, and felt a great sense of accomplishment. I savor the smallest details on the island. Once I filled a hundred-foot-long piece of galvanized pipe with water, left it in the sun and produced steam through solar heating, which was very satisfying. Even the least achievement on Teti'aroa delights me. One of my most rewarding triumphs was to restore a rusted two-inch iron plug for a pipe. The salt air had corroded it so much that the threads seemed to be gone. I rubbed and rubbed it with a wire brush but couldn't dent the thick crust of oxidized metal. Then I remembered having read somewhere that lemon juice helped dissolve rust because of its high acid content. I picked a few limes off a tree, squeezed the juice, mixed it into a slurry with salt and rubbed it on the fitting. The acid ate through the rust and made the plug shine, revealing the lost threads. What a wonderful feeling! It was a small thing that gave me great happiness.

In its prime the hotel had twenty-eight bungalows, a kitchen, a couple of bars, a dining room and reception area. Over the years I have spent millions on it, though it has never been profitable. Some of the money was lost because of hurricanes, some to wishful thinking and unfulfilled dreams, some to projects started and never finished, some to thieves. A lot of people robbed me—a few who worked for me, others who were con men and came to the island promising to do things they never did, took my money and then disappeared. One operator promised to produce lobsters in the lagoon through aquaculture, and I invited about twenty scientists to the island with their wives. There was a lot of wonderful talk about harvesting lobsters that came to nothing. Storms frequently struck the island; every time we finished a new building, it seemed that another hurricane came along and damaged it. But I enjoyed all of it. Ever since I was a kid I've relished having projects, and I didn't want to spend all my time lying on the beach. We did a great deal on the island to protect the environment, including saving a lot of hawksbill turtles. They were depositing their eggs on the island, only to lose most of them to predators. We fenced the area, created a basin where the eggs could hatch safely, and fed the young turtles until they were large enough to have a chance of surviving at sea.

In that part of the world, I learned quickly, people fail at their peril to take hurricanes seriously. Shortly after the turn of the century, a glancing blow from one killed hundreds of Tahitians, and I was on my island in the early 1980s when meteorologists in Papeete sent a warning that a hurricane potentially as powerful as that earlier one was forming in a tropical depression near Bora Bora. Soon we were buffeted by stiff winds, the barometer fell, the surf outside the reef began to rise and the meteorologists predicted that the storm's main thrust would hit Teti'aroa within forty-eight hours. When the birds started to leave, we were told, it would be there soon. Then all of a sudden everything returned to normal; it became very peaceful, the winds died and the ocean was calm again. We thought the storm had passed us by, until a ham radio operator on Bora Bora warned me not to relax because the winds appeared to be loitering off Bora Bora and gaining more strength.

A week later the storm slammed into Teti'aroa with the fury

of an avenging angel, hitting us so suddenly that I didn't have time to call a plane from Papeete to evacuate people. Even the birds barely managed to escape in time. First there were high winds, then towering waves that smashed the reef with such force that it felt as if a thousand cannons were bombarding it from an armada of ships just offshore. But it was the *sound* of the hurricane that made it most frightening. It was a Wagnerian opera, the thunderous roar of the waves pounding the reef and winds screaming through the trees like ten thousand Mongol warriors on horseback wailing a war cry behind Genghis Khan.

The wind quickly knocked down the radio tower and made so much noise that we couldn't hear one another speak; we shouted, but the wind defeated us, and walking into it was like stumbling into the exhaust of a jet engine. I put on a sou'wester and told everybody they had nothing to worry about, but I had visions of a wave washing over us and taking us all with it. I'd read a lot about hurricanes and cyclones in Tahiti and knew that they sometimes generated waves eighteen to twenty feet high, and we were in the middle of such a storm. As the waves got larger, rain started to fall in torrents and the lagoon began to wash over the beaches while the current in the channel became swifter and swifter until it must have been racing past us at twenty knots. On the main island the water level was soon up to our shins, and furniture began floating past. I kept telling everyone to relax, that this was just an unusually powerful storm and wasn't it marvelous to be here and experience nature unleashed? I couldn't admit that I was terrified waiting for that one wave that would wash over us and take us out to sea.

At dawn the winds were still blowing hard when I left my hut to inspect the damage. Palm fronds strong enough to pull a truck were strewn all over the island. In places the water was still rising, but the worst seemed to be over. For another two days the storm continued to batter the island, and everybody huddled together, singing and praying. I slept in my sou'wester and tried to keep everyone calm, including a woman who was staying with me, a New Yorker whose most serious bout with inclement weather until then had been being snowed in at a country house in Connecticut. When the winds finally subsided, everybody, including her, pitched in and began the cleanup. A few hours later the weathermen in Papeete radioed that another hurricane was on the way. I called for a plane from Papeete to evacuate the island, but when it arrived, four or five of the Tahitians refused to leave; they said they trusted in God and if they left, it would insult him and risk his wrath.

I thought the Tahitians who wanted to be evacuated were leaving because they were frightened, but when they boarded the plane, I heard them joke about the fun they were going to have in Papeete, and realized that all they were thinking about was getting to town, having a day off, drinking beer, chasing girls and having fun. I had intended to leave on the plane, but when some people said they wouldn't leave, I couldn't either. I was captain of the ship and it wouldn't be right to let them fend for themselves.

The second storm was less severe than the first, but powerful nevertheless, and after it passed, I sat down in the lagoon in shallow water up to my waist with my friend from New York, a bright lady with whom I had shared much from the time I was nineteen or twenty. It was about five o'clock in the afternoon and the sky was spectacular. Every cloud appeared to have been torn in half, but the sky no longer seemed ominous and there was no wind. I had never seen a sky like it, nor have I since. Then suddenly it was sunset. Tahitian sunsets defy any ability to describe them, but if you have never believed in God, you are tempted to think otherwise when you see one there. They are celestial symphonies, a concerto of colors that shift in mood, tempo and color by the second: greens, grays, every shade of pink you can imagine, oranges, fiery reds and angel blues, while everything on the horizon changes constantly.

Once the sun sets, darkness arrives abruptly; you had better get home fast or you'll be groping around in the dark. There is no twilight in the tropics, though Tahitians tell me that if you are lucky, every once in a while you may see a sudden green flash in the sky just as the sun disappears. It's magic, they say. One of my favorite pastimes on Teti'aroa is to lie down on the grass at the end of the airstrip, wait for the sun to set and hope for a glimpse of that green flash. I never have, but many people I know have been luckier. A bright green light explodes in the sky, hangs there for an instant like a sudden, brief explosion of fireworks, then vanishes. Every time I go to Teti'aroa I wait for that magic, and someday I'll see it.

For half an hour after the sun goes down, the horizon continues to change color as the clouds reflect the unseen light. The tops of the clouds are always illuminated because they are the last to reflect the sun, sometimes at sixty or seventy thousand feet high. Once it's dark, you lie on the sand and wait for the first star. If you're with friends, there's a game to see who will spot it first. When it's completely dark, a celestial panorama begins unfolding above you: single lights turn on, then a string of them, then galaxies. I've never seen the heavens look so vast as they do from an atoll. The first light is usually a planet, Venus or Mars; then, very slowly, subtle, distant needle pricks appear in space, and as the last glow of the sunset ebbs away and it grows darker, the stars shine more brightly. Finally the sky opens and the Milky Way and other constellations explode in a panoramic umbrella of lights that reaches from horizon to horizon.

As I sat up to my waist in shallow water with my friend from New York that afternoon following the second hurricane and watched the night come on, she asked me if I had ever seen a shooting star. I told her yes, that you usually see them "over there" and I pointed up to the sky. Just as I said this, we saw the flash of a shooting star exactly where I was pointing. It was as if somebody were striking a match across the sky, but there was no sound, just a streak of light.

As I've said, small things mean a lot on Teti'aroa.

There have been several important influences on my life. Philosophically I've felt closest to the American Indians; I sympathize with them, admire their culture, and have learned a great deal from them. Jews opened my mind and taught me to value knowledge and learning, and blacks also taught me a lot. But I think Polynesians have had the greatest influence because of how they live.

In Tahiti I learned how to live, though I discovered I could never be a Tahitian. When I first went there, I had illusions of becoming Polynesian. I wanted to fuse myself into the culture. However, eventually I realized that not only were my genes different, but the emotional algebra of my life was unsuited to becoming anything but who I am, so I gave up trying and instead simply learned to appreciate what they have. I suppose I was learning the same lessons that I did from Jews, blacks and American Indians: you can admire and love a culture, you can even attach yourself to the edges of it, but you can't ever become part of it. You have to be who you are.

When I discovered Tahiti in the pages of the *National Geographic* in the library at Shattuck, what impressed me most was the serene expressions on the faces of its natives. They were happy faces, open maps of contentment. Living there has confirmed to me that Tahitians are the happiest people I've ever known. The differences between Polynesian and Western culture are deceptive. In the United States we think we have at our disposal virtually everything—and I emphasize the word "think." We have big houses and cars, good medical treatment, jets, trains and monorails; we have computers, good communications, many comforts and conveniences. But where have they gotten us? We have an abundance of material things, but a successful society produces happy people, and I think we produce more miserable people than almost anyplace on earth. I've traveled all over the world, and I've never seen people who are quite as unhappy as they are in the United States. We have plenty, but we have nothing, and we always want more. In the pursuit of material success as our culture measures it, we have given up everything. We have lost the capacity to produce people who are joyful. The pursuit of the material has become our reason for living, not enjoyment of living itself.

In Tahiti there are more laughing faces per acre than in any place I've ever been, whereas we've put a man on the moon but produce frustrated, angry people.

I can hear some readers say, "Why do you want to run America down, Marlon? You've had it pretty good!"

Well, America *has* been good to me, but it wasn't a gift; rather, I've earned it by the sweat of my brow and my capacity to invent and sustain myself. If I hadn't been in the right circumstances and had a lot of luck, I don't know what I would have become. I might have been a con man and gone to jail, or if I'd been lucky enough to get a job without a high-school education, I might have spent my life on an assembly line, had three children, and then at fifty or fifty-five been cast off like yesterday's garbage, the way a lot of Americans have been recently. This doesn't happen in Tahiti because it is a classless society, and this is probably the main reason I've gone there whenever I could during the past thirty years. In Tahiti I can always be myself. There's no fawning or kowtowing to people who consider themselves famous or more important than others. Tahitians have a quality I've never observed in any other large group: they have no envy. Of course, there are pretentious Tahitians who want to appear knowledgeable about the world and put on airs, but I've run into very few of them. What I admire about the people of Tahiti is that they are able to live in the moment, to enjoy what is going on *now*. There are no celebrities, movie stars, rich men or poor men; they laugh, dance, drink and make love, and they know how to relax. When we were making *Mutiny on the Bounty*, a Tahitian girl in the cast missed her boyfriend and decided to go home. The producer said, "You can't quit; you signed a contract. If you do, we'll sue you." The girl said, "Well, I've got a dog and a couple of goats, and you can have them."

The producer said, "Then we'll have you arrested," and she said, "All right." Then she left and they had to rewrite the movie. Hollywood meant nothing to her.

When I wake up in Tahiti, my pulse is sometimes as low as 48; in America, it's nearer 60. Living in our so-called civilized society makes the difference. There are no homeless people in Tahiti because somebody will always take you in. If there's a shortage of anything, it's of children; they love kids. It's not perfect. There's crime, fighting, disorder and family conflicts, but by and large it is a society where people are internally quiet and outwardly full of laughter, gaiety and optimism, and they live each day as it comes. Unfortunately, life is changing there as outside forces try to improve, as well as exploit, what they regard as a primitive culture. In all of Polynesia, there are only about 200,000 people, and they are constantly under assault, from patronizing and condescending religious missionaries to fast-buck promoters who consider them simple and primitive. They are neither primitive nor simple, but sophisticated in their own way of experiencing life to the fullest. Outsiders who call them backward do so out of racial snobbery and a prejudice rooted in the foolish notion that equates technological advancement with civilization. Westerners seldom acknowledge the extraordinary feats of early Polynesian seafarers who, without compass, radar or navigational satellites, but only by dead reckoning and a knowledge of the winds, traversed thousands of miles of uncharted waters in open ships. Along with the Micronesians, the Polynesians settled the Pacific, and their descendants enjoy life more than any people I know. Tahitian women are the toughest I've ever met. They are independent and have no inhibitions, about sex or anything else. After falling in love and having children, they usually stay with the same man, but not always; sometimes two or three women move in with the same man. They feel jealousy, have fights and feuds like everyone else, and when a Tahitian woman takes against a man, she's likely to tell everything about him to everyone. No secrets are left untold.

Most of all, Tahitians love parties. Once, when Charles de Gaulle was scheduled to visit Tahiti while I was there, the word was passed from village to village. Most people ignored his arrival until someone said there would be a party when he came. Then they flocked aboard buses, brought their drums and skirts and celebrated the joy of life, not De Gaulle; they didn't give a damn about him and didn't even know who he was. But when he sailed into the harbor, people stood in the water up to their necks, there were thousands of them, with food, flowers, tears and singing. It was then that I fell in love with the Tahitian soul.

I still have many dreams for my island. My greatest hope is to return it to what Polynesia used to be. Considering the many incursions from the outside world that it has had to endure to sustain itself, it's remarkable how resilient Polynesian culture has been. It has been invaded repeatedly by alien cultures: the Spanish, English and French; missionaries, whalers, tourists, hucksters, human sharks; and now television, perhaps the most insidious influence of all. The pressures are enormous, and the Polynesians must face the reality that they are living in a technological age and that it will be impossible to go backward. Now there are television, satellite dishes, jet airplanes, insurance policies, bank accounts, cutthroat real estate promoters and assorted other highwaymen who want to exploit Tahitians down to their last buck.

If I have my way, Teti'aroa will remain forever a place that reminds Tahitians of who they are and what they were centuries ago—and what, I'm convinced, they still are today despite the missionaries and fast-buck artists, a place where they can recreate and procreate and find enjoyment without being exploited by outsiders. I would like the island to become a marine park with technological systems that can help provide its inhabitants with more food. Because the population is growing rapidly, they will have to find ways to increase the yield of their land and lagoons. If I can do this, it will give me more pleasure and satisfaction than any acting I have ever done.

60

I CAN DRAW no conclusions about my life because it is a continually evolving and unfolding process. I don't know what is next. I am more surprised at how I turned out than I am about anything else. I don't ever remember trying to be successful. It just happened. I was only trying to survive. Much like a newly fertilized egg, I look now at some of the things I have done in life with astonishment. Fifty years ago, at a party at my home, I climbed out the window of my apartment in New York and clung to a balustrade eleven stories above Seventy-second Street as a joke. I can't imagine myself ever having done that. I have difficulty reconciling the boy I was then with the man I am now.

I suppose the story of my life is a search for love, but more than that, I have been looking for a way to repair myself from the damages I suffered early on and to define my obligations, if I had any, to myself and my species. Who am I? What should I do with my life? Though I haven't found answers, it's been a painful odyssey, dappled with moments of joy and laughter. In one of my letters from Shattuck, I told my parents, "In a play written by Sophocles . . . the Antigone, there are lines that say:

'Let be the future: mind the present need and leave the rest to whom the rest concerns . . . present tasks claim our care: the ordering of the future rests where it should rest.' These words written two thousand years ago are just as applicable today as they were then. It seems incomprehensible that through the fifteen thousand years since our species came into being, we have not evolved."

At fifteen, I was already aware that we have learned little from our experiences, and that our proclivity is to leave the correction of wrongs and injustice to a future we are not accountable for. Yet I spent most of the next fifty-five years trying to do the opposite. Frustrated in my attempts to take care of my mother, I suppose that instead I tried to help Indians, blacks and Jews. I thought love, good intentions and positive action could alter injustice, prejudice, aggression and genocide. I was convinced that if I presented the facts—for example, show people a film that I made about starvation in India—they would be aroused and help me to alleviate that suffering. I felt a responsibility to create a better world, propelled by the certainty that compassion and love could solve its problems. I am no longer persuaded that any significant change through a course of behavior will make any difference of lasting importance. Late in life I learned something that sustains me: my suffering for other people doesn't help them. I still do what I can to be helpful, but I don't have to suffer for it. Previously I had empathized with people who were less fortunate. My sense of empathy remains undiminished, but I apply it in a different manner. Through meditation and self-examination I feel that I am coming closer to discovering what it means to be human, and that the things I feel are the same that everybody else feels. We are all capable of hatred and of love.

Curiosity about why people believe as they do is one of the most consistent features of my life. Still, I don't think any of us ever knows with certainty why we do some things or how our behavior is a product of our genes or our environment or a blend of each; it is impossible to answer the question with precision. I have not achieved the wisdom of why I am alive, and I take large comfort in the knowledge that I never will. The mist of misperception defeats all of us.

Still, I no longer feel that I have a mission to save the world. It can't be done, I've learned. I didn't realize it then, but I think my attitude started to change when I made that film about the famine in India. On my way home, I stopped in Calcutta to visit Satyajit Ray, the Indian movie director, and we went out to lunch. When we left the restaurant, a sea of children in tattered clothing, broken, blinded, twisted and sick, engulfed us to ask for baksheesh. I was aware as we drifted through this swarm of broken kids that Satyajit was completely unconcerned, even unaware, and gently swept them aside absentmindedly. It was as though he were brushing his way gently through a wheat field. I asked him how he was able to do it, and he replied, "If you live in India, you see this every day of your life. If I sold everything I had to help these children, it wouldn't amount to a billionth of one rupee for any one of them, and they would all be back tomorrow. There is nothing I can do to solve this problem; some problems are unsolvable."

All my life, I had been a do-gooder, but I finally learned that what Satyajit said about the children of Calcutta was true: there are some problems that I can't do anything about.

I've also changed some of my views about the nature of human behavior. When I was young, I embraced the Judeo-Christian concept of good and evil, and its corollary, that all of us were responsible for our deeds because of the choices we made. I don't believe this anymore. Philosophers like Plato, Socrates, Kant and Spinoza have argued for millennia over the nature of free will, and of good and evil. Epicurus said that God was either uncaring and chose to ignore evil, or he was unable to prevent it and therefore not omnipotent. But Saint

Augustine, trying to resolve the paradox that Christians face about how a supposedly benevolent God could allow evil to exist, rationalized it by arguing that evil was not a product of God but was the absence of good, and that what at first appeared to be evil might turn out to be good in the context of eternity. This is how events like the Holocaust and the slaughter of the Native Americans are explained. But I believe that the roots of the behavior we call "evil" are genetic. I've never found any system—religious, social, philosophical, ethical, political or economic—that was able to suppress man's innate animus and predilection to gather into groups dedicated to exterminating other groups for their beliefs, profit, hatred or frolic. More people have been killed in the name of religion and the defense of dogma than any other single cause. Genetically determined behavior affected by environmental features seems to be the final arbiter of human behavior. I believe our genetic impulses are so strong that we cannot overcome them. No matter how well equipped we are to cerebrate, our minds are in direct service to our emotions, and yet we cling to the outmoded myths of goodness and evil in the Bible and the Talmud. Neither money, religious zeal, political revolution or even knowledge can alter the basic nature of the human animal. Nothing has ever made people good. I may have given away millions of dollars, but I realize now that most of it didn't do any good for the people I intended it for.

For over fifty years, the Cold War dominated our lives like storm clouds, and communism was blamed for most of the evils of the world. Now that the Cold War is over, the world is fragmenting and ethnic warfare has erupted everywhere, including the streets of the United States, where poverty, murder, violence and injustice are endemic. Our preoccupation with communism camouflaged a rottenness within the political and economic system of which we were so proud. There has been an illusion throughout history that when man made "progress," advancing technology would help him to communicate better so that the barriers of conflict and misunderstanding between us would crumble. But now that we have satellite dishes, global coverage by CNN, interactive TV, instant telecommunications, the most sophisticated equipment and the forensic wisdom of the Rand Corporation, our situation is worse than ever.

Whatever grains of optimism survive in me about the evolution of mankind are centered in the belief that genetic alteration, however fraught with danger, is the only possible solution to what Hannah Arendt referred to as the banality of evil. I don't think anything in the range of human existence since Neanderthal man—not fire or the invention of weapons or the wheel—equals in importance Francis Crick and James Watson's discovery of the structure of DNA. It will have an incalculable effect on society, religion and our concept of ourselves. Within a few years, scientists will finish mapping the human genome based on Crick and Watson's discovery, and with it will come an opportunity to alter the nature of man. Already scientists are beginning to unravel the sources of the neural disorders that produce anger and frustration, the will to kill and the hostility that produces war. They have already linked some genetic defects to certain kinds of aggressive and violent behavior; they are starting to make extraordinary advances in biogenetics and neurogenetics, opening doors that will lead to a clearer understanding not only of how genes affect our behavior, but how to alter that behavior. In the science of behavioral genetics, we're on the cusp of enormous change. The time is approaching when the genes of a chimpanzee can be altered to give him the gift of speech. Genetic engineering of human behavior will advance on a parallel track. If the human race has a genetic fault that causes errant behavior or self-destruction, it will simply be removed.

A fantasy, you say? I think it is inevitable—and necessarily so if our species is ever to stop killing its own kind.

Of course there will be an uproar in the churches when scientists have the power to engineer human beings. It will be argued that the design of human beings is God's province alone. There may even be enough resistance to advancing the science of behavioral genetics to halt temporarily what is doable, but whenever something is possible, sooner or later it will be done. The world has always been in a state of revolution between the old and the new, and new discoveries are unstoppable. The twenty-first century will produce a far bigger revolution in the biological sciences than the twentieth century did in the physical sciences. It has taken me seventy years to refrain from doing certain things that were destructive to me and to other people, and to resolve emotional conflicts that produced errant social behavior. With genetic implants I probably would not have been burdened with the emotional disorders that caused me to spend most of my life in emotional disarray. In the future, specialists will recognize the kind of trouble I had as a child and be able to do something about it.

If I had been loved and cared for differently, I would have been a different person. I went through most of my life afraid of being rejected and ended up rejecting most of those who offered me love because I was unable to trust them. When the press made up lies about me, I used to try to maintain an image of indifference, but privately I sustained great injury. Now it truly doesn't matter to me what anyone says about me. I have achieved honest indifference to the opinions of others except for those I love and hold in high regard.

Clifford Odets once told me, "I never heard what Beethoven was saying until I was forty." You gain a great deal simply by living long enough. In some ways I haven't changed. I was always sensitive, always curious about myself and others, always had a good instinct for people, always loved a good book and any kind of joke, which I think I learned from my parents, because they were both good laughers. But in other ways I am a vastly different person from what I was like as a child. For most of my life I had to appear strong when I wasn't, and what I wanted most was control. If I was wronged or felt diminished, I wanted vengeance.

I don't anymore. I am still contemptuous of authority and of the kind of conformity that induces mediocrity, but I no longer feel a need to lash out at it. In my twenties I always wanted to be the best, but now I truly don't care. I've quit comparing myself with other people. I don't worry if somebody is more talented than I am or if people invent vicious stories about me; I understand that they're people not unlike myself who are just trying to pay the rent and who close their eyes to the vulgarity of their deeds. I realize they are doing it for their own reasons. Moreover, in telling the story of my life in this book, I must acknowledge that I am guilty of some of the sins for which I used to despise others.

I believe it is fortunate that my parents died when they did; otherwise, I would have probably wrecked what was left of their lives before I found a better way to live. Now I am happier than I've ever been. My sisters and I rode out the storm together with the help of one another. Both grew into wise, independent women who beat alcoholism and created new lives for themselves. Frannie died this year, leaving a void in my life that can never be filled. But before she died, she found happiness, too; in her late forties she went back to college and became a successful teacher. Tiddy, after one career as an actress and another in business, became a wonderful therapist and applied her extraordinary insight to helping others.

"It's a long climb up Fool's Hill," my grandmother used to say about life, but Tiddy, Frannie and I made it to the top.

This book, an outpouring of what was long contained, has been my declaration of liberty. I finally feel free and don't give a damn anymore what people think about me. At seventy,

I'm also having more fun than ever before. The smallest details bring me joy—building or inventing something, being with my children or playing with my dog, Tim, laughing with my friends or watching an ant crawl on his way in my bathroom. Thanks to Dr. Harrington, my own efforts and the simple passage of time, I can finally be the child I never had a chance to be.

Recently I saw Kevin Costner's *Dances with Wolves,* and midway through it I started crying. I didn't know why. Then the image of the young Indian boy on the screen gave me the answer: it was like a homecoming, because I realized that in the past few years I have rediscovered a part of me that was clean, pure and straight and had been hidden since I was a child. Somehow I had come full circle, and I felt free.

I also finally realized that I had to forgive my father or I would be entrapped by my hatred and anguish for the rest of my life. If I didn't forgive him for the things he had done to all of us, I would never be able to forgive myself for the things I have done and felt guilty about and responsible for. Now I have forgiven him and myself, though I realize that to forgive with your mind is not always to forgive in your heart.

There isn't any end to this story. I'd be happy to tell it to you if I knew it. Just as I cannot imagine where I was before I sat under that elm tree at the end of Thirty-second Street with my hand stretched wide for those magical pods, so I continue to be an enigma to myself in a world that still bewilders me. While life itself remains incomprehensible, there is no point in wondering where I will be in the "never-to-be-known after-time," but I am certain that when my breathing comes to an end, the change will find me no more astonished than I was back on Thirty-second Street.

My mind is always soothed when I imagine myself sitting on my South Sea island at night in a gentle chiffon wind, with

my mouth open and my head way back, watching those twin-
kling points of light, waiting for that eerie, silent streak to
spread across the black sky and stun me again. I don't stretch
my hand out anymore, but I never get tired of waiting for the
next magic.

ABOUT THE COAUTHOR

ROBERT LINDSEY, former chief West Coast correspondent for *The New York Times,* is the author of *The Falcon and the Snowman, A Gathering of Saints* and other books, and also collaborated with Ronald Reagan on his autobiography, *An American Life.*

ABOUT THE TYPE

This book was set in Sabon, a typeface designed by the
well-known German typographer Jan Tschichold
(1902–74). Sabon's design is based upon the original
letter forms of Claude Garamond and was created
specifically to be used for three sources: foundry type
for hand composition, Linotype and Monotype. Tschichold named his typeface for the famous Frankfurt
typefounder Jacques Sabon, who died in 1580.